P9-BZZ-840

Peter Lehmann Publishing

Peter Stastny and Peter Lehmann (Eds.)

Alternatives Beyond Psychiatry

Preface by Robert Whitaker

Contributions by Volkmar Aderhold, Laurie Ahern, Birgitta Alakare, Karyn Baker, Ulrich Bartmann, Agnes Beier, Regina Bellion, Wilma Boevink, Pat Bracken, Stefan Bräunling, Ludger Bruckmann, Giuseppe Bucalo, Dorothea S. Buck-Zerchin, Sarah Carr, Tina Coldham, Bhargavi Davar, Anne Marie DiGiacomo, Constance Dollwet, Jeanne Dumont, Merinda Epstein, Sandra Escher, James B. Gottstein, Chris Hansen, Geoff Hardy, Petra Hartmann, Alfred Hausotter, Michael Herrick, Guy Holmes, Andrew Hughes, Theodor Itten, Maths Jesperson, Kristine Jones, Hannelore Klafki, Miriam Krücke, Peter Lehmann, Bruce E. Levine, Harold A. Maio, Rufus May, Shery Mead, Kate Millett, Maryse Mitchell-Brody, David W. Oaks, Peter Rippmann, Marius Romme, Marc Rufer, Gisela Sartori, Erich Schützendorf, Jaakko Seikkula, Andy Smith, Zoran Solomun, Peter Stastny, Chris Stevenson, Dan Taylor, Philip Thomas, Jan Wallcraft, David Webb, Uta Wehde, Scott Welsch, Salma Yasmeen, Laura Ziegler and Ursula Zingler

Translations by Christine Holzhausen, Katy E. McNally and Mary Murphy

Peter Lehmann Publishing · Berlin · Eugene · Shrewsbury · 2007

4

This book is simultaneously published in German by Peter Lehmann Publishing under the title *Statt Psychiatrie 2* (ISBN 978-3-925931-38-3, ed. by P. Lehmann and P. Stastny). Please find information on the internet at www.peter-lehmann-publishing.com/books/without/german.htm The italic explanations in the brackets are written by the editors.

Published by Peter Lehmann Publishing

Cover design by Reinhard Wojke, Berlin · Printed by Interpress, Budapest

Peter Lehmann Publishing, Zabel-Krüger-Damm 183, 13469 Berlin, Germany, Tel. +49 30 85963706 · Branch offices: Eugene, Oregon (USA) / Shrewsbury, Shropshire (U.K.). Please send all postal mail direct to our Berlin switchboard. info@peter-lehmann-publishing.com · www.peter-lehmann-publishing.com

British edition
ISBN 978-0-9545428-1-8
British Library Cataloguing in Publication Data.
A catalogue record for this book is available from the British Library.

American edition
Library of Congress Cataloging-in-Publication Data

Alternatives beyond psychiatry / Peter Stastny and Peter Lehmann, eds. ; preface by Robert Whitaker ; contributions by Volkmar Aderhold ... [et al.] ; translations by Christine Holzhausen, Katy E. McNally and Mary Murphy.
    p. ; cm.
    Published also in German under the title: Statt Psychiatrie 2.
    Includes bibliographical references and index.
    Summary: "61 therapists, psychiatrists, social scientists, lawyers, relatives and psychiatric (ex-)patients from all continents report about their alternative work, their objectives and successes, their individual and collective experiences. The book highlights alternatives beyond psychiatry, possibilities of self-help for individuals experiencing madness, and strategies toward implementing humane treatment"—Provided by publisher.
    Includes English translations of the German contributions.
    ISBN-13: 978-0-9788399-1-8 (softcover)
    ISBN-13: 978-0-9545428-1-8 (softcover)
    1. Mental illness—Alternative treatment. 2. Psychotherapy patients—Abuse of. 3. Mentally ill—Abuse of. 4. Antipsychiatry.
    [DNLM: 1. Mental Disorders—therapy. 2. Dissent and Disputes. 3. Human Rights. 4. Psychiatry—methods. 5. Treatment Refusal. WM 100 A466 2007] I. Stastny, Peter. II. Lehmann, Peter, 1950- III. Aderhold, Volkmar, 1954- IV. Title: Statt Psychiatrie 2.
    RC480.5.A472 2007
    616.89'14—dc22

2007029028

Contents

Why Psychiatry Hurts More Than It Helps

Actual Alternatives

A. Individual Strategies with and without Professional Support

6

B. Organized Self-help

C. Models of Professional Support

General and Specific Beneficiaries of Alternative Approaches

Realizing Alternatives and Humane Treatment

Why We Need Alternatives to Psychiatry

Appendix

Preface

The first question raised by a book titled *Alternatives Beyond Psychiatry* is this: Why do we need alternatives? What is wrong with the "care" that mainstream psychiatry provides? While there are many answers to that question, first and foremost we can look at one startling statistic, and that is the rise in the number of people disabled by "mental illness" over the past 50 years.

The modern drug-based paradigm of psychiatric care dates back to 1954, when chlorpromazine was introduced as the first antipsychotic medication. This, or so psychiatry would like us to believe, kicked off a great leap forward in society's care of the "mentally ill." Psychiatric researchers are said to have made great strides in understanding the biological causes of mental disorders and that has led to the development of ever better drugs for treating them. Yet, here is what all this "progress" has wrought: in the United States, the rate of the "disabled mentally ill" has increased nearly six-fold in the past 50 years, from 3.38 people per 1,000 population in 1955 to 19.69 people per 1,000 population in 2003. Since the introduction of Prozac[1] in 1987—this was the first of the second-generation psychiatric drugs said to be so better than the first—the number of so-called disabled mentally ill in the United States has been increasing at the rate of 150,000 people per year, or 410 people newly disabled by "mental illness" every day.

Other countries that have adopted a drug-based paradigm of care, such as the U.K. and Australia, have also reported a great surge in the number of people disabled by mental disorders in the past 50 years. This interesting fact leads to only one conclusion: mainstream psychiatry's paradigm of care has failed. It has not proven to be an approach that helps people struggling with mental distress of some kind—depression, anxiety, mania, psychosis, etc.—

---

1 Antidepressant, active ingredient fluoxetine, marketed also as Auscap, Deprax, Eufor, Flexetor, Fluohexal, Fluox, Fluoxebell, Fluoxetine, FXT, Lovan, Movox, Oxactin, Plinzene, Psyquial, Sarafem, Veritina, Zactin, etc.; component of Cymbyax

recover and get on with their lives. Instead, it has proven to be an approach that increases the likelihood that such people will become chronically ill.

We desperately need to think of alternatives to that failed paradigm of care. That is a big challenge, and yet the contributions in this timely and much needed book all ultimately point to a common starting point: if we want to help those struggling with their minds, we can start by thinking of them—as the Quakers did when they rebelled against mainstream psychiatry in the late 1700s and early 1800s—as "brethren." Not as people with "broken brains," but simply as people who are suffering. From that conception, a whole world of "care" follows. What does everyone need to stay well? Shelter, food, friendship, and something meaningful to do with his or her time. Any society that provides such care and support, along with a message of hope—that people can recover from whatever mental distress they may be suffering—makes a good start at providing an effective alternative to psychiatry.

There are chapters in this book that tell of such programs. There are proven alternatives to psychiatry, programs that have a track record of helping people get better. And there are reports of ways of coping with madness on an individual level. This book hopefully will encourage many, many other such efforts to take root and flourish.

Robert Whitaker
Cambridge, MA

Note about Liability

Psychiatric treatment is more dangerous than many (ex-)users and survivors of psychiatry and even physicians realize. Psychiatric drugs can cause serious adverse effects. Electroshock may cause permanent brain damage. Psychiatric drugs can also produce powerful physical dependence. For example, their withdrawal can cause sleeplessness, rebound and withdrawal psychoses, withdrawal-emergent tardive syndromes, return of base line psychological and emotional problems and even life-threatening withdrawal reactions (see Peter Lehmann, *Coming off Psychiatric Drugs*, Berlin 2004, pp. 25-38). Especially when psychiatric drugs have been taken for prolonged periods of time, experienced clinical supervision may be advisable or even necessary during the withdrawal process.

In referring to alternatives beyond psychiatry, we do not provide medical advice. Also this book is not intended as a substitute for professional help. Should you have any health care-related questions, please call or see your physician or other health care provider promptly. The publisher, editors, authors and suppliers are not responsible if you decide against this advice. Nor are they responsible for any damage you may experience from a medical and, in particular, psychiatric treatment.

If you are thinking about withdrawing from prescribed psychiatric drugs, it is important to realize that the problems which led to their administration may return when you stop taking them. Decisions to withdraw from psychotropic drugs should be made in a critical and responsible way. It is important to have a safe and supportive environment in which to undertake withdrawal (see ibid., pp. 311-321) and to consider the possibility that you may experience so-called relapse or worsening of your condition. Withdrawal may not work for everyone. Sometimes the difficulty of withdrawal or the base line psychological and emotional problems seem insurmountable, so people may decide to maintain on lower amounts of drugs or fewer drugs. Many psychiatrists do not support withdrawal and are convinced that people with psychiatric diagnoses like "schizophrenia," "psychosis," "manic depression" or "major depression" need psychiatric drugs or maintenance electroshock "therapy" for the rest of their lives.

If you choose to give weight to the various opinions expressed in this book, that is your choice, and is not based on any claims of special training or medical expertise by the publisher (for professions and experiences of the authors see pp. 417-430). No alternative medicine, holistic remedy, or self-help method referenced in this book is being recommended as a substitute for professional medical advice, diagnosis or treatment, and no comparisons are being made between such alternative methods and treatment with electroshock or psychiatric drugs. Neither the publisher, editors, authors nor suppliers make any claim that their information in this book will "cure" or heal disease.

All contributors and especially all (ex-)users and survivors of psychiatry in this book report about essentially positive experiences with alternatives beyond psychiatry. This is no coincidence because the editors only asked for positive experiences. Since many individual factors (physical and psychological condition, social circumstances, etc.) exert a remarkable influence on the way to cope with emotional problems, the authors' individual statements should not be interpreted as transferable advice for all other readers.

No responsibility is assumed by the publisher, editors, authors and suppliers for any injury and/or damage to persons or property from any use of any methods, products, instructions or ideas referenced in the material herein. Any therapy not initiated or completed as well as any use of a referral and/or subsequent treatment regimen sought as a result of buying and/or reading this book is the sole responsibility of the reader.

The publisher, editors, authors and suppliers undertake no responsibility for any consequences of unwanted effects either when receiving or when not receiving electroshock or taking psychiatric drugs or when withdrawing from them. They do not accept any liability for readers who choose to determine their own care and lives.

Peter Lehmann and Peter Stastny

Introduction

What helps me if I go mad? How can I find trustworthy help for a relative or a friend in need?

How can I protect myself from coercive treatment? Where can I talk to like-minded people about my own experiences with psychiatry and about my life? As a family member or friend, how can I help? What should I do if I can no longer bear to work in the mental health field? What are the alternatives to psychiatry? How can I get involved in creating alternatives?

Assuming psychiatry would be abolished, what do you propose instead? These are the main questions addressed by the 61 authors—(ex-)users and survivors of psychiatry, therapists, psychiatrists, lawyers, relatives, politicians and social scientists and relatives from all five continents.

Alternatives Beyond Psychiatry is a collection of reports and approaches from non-, anti- and post-psychiatric everyday life in different countries and provides an appraisal of individual and organized alternatives and measures that point to a need for structural change in the system. This is a book of practice and ideas, more personal than generalized. It offers suggestions, highlights contradictions and problems, and shows positive examples and models but does not provide easy answers.

Our alternatives beyond psychiatry are far removed from the academic remains of the '68 generation; nor are they a reform-oriented variant of Italian psychiatry, social psychiatry or community extensions of psychiatric institutions. Instead, alternatives beyond psychiatry are truly innovative, initiated and carried out by critical professionals and independent (ex-)users and survivors of psychiatry, the real experts in the psychiatric domain, dedicated to the right of self-determination, physical inviolability and social support.

Alternatives beyond psychiatry originate from an undogmatic and humanistic movement. Accordingly, the texts in this book are filled with a contrarian spirit and the fundamental conviction that (1) psychiatry, as a scientific discipline, cannot do justice to the expectation of solving mental problems that are largely of a social nature, (2) its propensity and practice to use force constitutes a threat, and (3) its diagnostic methods obstruct the view of the real problems of individuals.

Furthermore, the texts in this volume describe a commitment to (1) developing adequate and effective assistance for people in emotional difficulties, (2) safeguarding civil rights in treatment on a par with "normal" patients, (3) joining forces in cooperation with other human rights and self-help groups, (4) use of alternative and less toxic psychotropic substances and a ban of electroshock, (5) new ways of living with madness and being different—with as much independence from institutions as possible, and (6) tolerance, respect and appreciation of diversity at all levels of life.

This book has been published without any financial support from sponsors. We have no connection to the pharmaceutical industry and to organizations that are dependent on them, nor to Scientology or other sects and dogmatists of whatever color. Beyond health, nothing is more valuable than freedom and independence.

We would like to express our heartfelt thanks to the many supporters who have provided valuable ideas, translated, corrected, and illustrated, in particular Arno Hessling, Christine Holzhausen, Craig Newnes, Darby Penney, David W. Oaks, Katy E. McNally, Kerstin Kempker, Martin Urban, Mary Murphy, Paula Kempker, Pia Kempker, Reinhard Wojke and Tricia R. Owsley.

August 2007
Peter Stastny, Peter Lehmann

Translated from the German by Mary Murphy

Why Psychiatry Hurts More Than It Helps

Introduction

In 1995, when I (P.L.) was a member of the board of the German Association of Users and Survivors of Psychiatry (BPE), we were asked by the journal *Sozialpsychiatrische Informationen (Social Psychiatric Information)* whether we would be willing to participate in a survey on the subject of improving the quality of psychiatric treatment. We agreed to take part but changed the questions as the board members could not agree on whether any type of psychiatric treatment could be considered "quality." The following are some of the questions we put to 665 members of the association—(ex-)users and survivors of psychiatry who were more or less critical of psychiatry:

> Did the psychiatrists address the problems which led to your admission? Was your dignity respected at all times? Were you fully and comprehensibly informed of the risks and so-called side effects of treatment measures? Were you informed about alternative treatments? What was lacking to the detriment of qualitatively good psychiatric care?

Over 100 members of the association (BPE) responded to the survey. The result: only 10 percent of those who answered said that psychiatry had helped them find a solution to the problems that had led to their psychiatrization. Ninety percent said that their dignity had been violated. In response to the question of whether they had been informed about the risks and "side effects" of treatment measures, not one single person replied with "yes" (Peeck, *et al.*, 1995).

Later studies conducted wholly or in part by independent survivors, such as the European study *Harassment and Discrimination Faced by People with Psycho-Social Disability in Health Services* produced similar results. This transnational study was conducted at the behest of the European Commission. In it, the associations of (ex-)users and survivors of psychiatry and their families from the U.K., Austria, Germany, the Netherlands and France in conjunction with a Belgian research institute put the questions to families and (ex-)users and survivors of psychiatry. The result was the same: Psychiatric patients are systematically discriminated against in the medical and psychiatric sector.[1]

Conclusion: (ex-)users and survivors of psychiatry—and not only in Europe—are calling for changes in the psychosocial field, starting with a psychiatric system which respects human rights all the way to alternatives beyond psychiatry and a society free of psychiatry. Funding and rights, effective and appropriate help in emergencies, and the right to choose among alternatives—these are the solutions they propose and which accurately express their needs and wants.

Families of (ex-)users and survivors of psychiatry are also looking for alternatives, especially those families who are not linked to mainstream organizations of families of psychiatric patients such as NAMI (National Alliance for the Mentally Ill) or EUFAMI (European Federation of Associations of Families of People with Mental Illness), which are sponsored and influenced by the pharmaceutical industry. Whether this is the result of personal experiences such as in the case of Uta Wehde, a more theoretical analysis as with Kate Millett, or based on a historical review of psychiatry and its approaches to psychosis, as in Dorothea Buck-Zerchin's reflection of experiences over many years, the result is the same. They are demanding an alternative beyond psychiatry and the right to humane help for people in emotional distress.

Source

Peeck, G., von Seckendorff, C., & Heinecke, P. (1995). Ergebnis der Umfrage unter den Mitgliedern des Bundesverbandes Psychiatrie-Erfahrener zur Qualität der psychiatrischen Versorgung. *Sozialpsychiatrische Informationen, 25*(4), 30-34. Retrieved January 4, 2007, from www.bpe-online.de/infopool/recht/pb/umfrage.htm; for more details, see Lehmann, P. (1997). Variety instead of stupidity: About the different positions within the movement of (ex-)users and survivors of psychiatry. Retrieved January 4, 2007, from www.peter-lehmann-publishing.com/articles/variety.htm

Translated from the German by Mary Murphy

---

1   For further information see www.enusp.org/harassment

Dorothea S. Buck-Zerchin

Seventy Years of Coercion in Psychiatric Institutions, Experienced and Witnessed[1]

My name is Dorothea Buck, I am 90 years old, and a so-called historical witness. The theme of my presentation is: "Seventy Years of Coercion in the German Psychiatric System, Experienced and Witnessed." I will start with the forced treatment and forced sterilization that was inflicted upon me 71 years ago. In 1966, Alexander Mitscherlich wrote in his book *Krankheit als Konflikt – Studien zur psychosomatischen Medizin I (Illness as a Conflict: Studies on Psychosomatic Medicine, Vol. I)* in the chapter entitled "On the Complexity of Social Influences on the Origin and Treatment of Psychoses and Neuroses" about the treatment measures: "From the days of the primitive cultures, up to present times there have always been methods of torment. On closer examination, a terrible arsenal of tortures in themselves..."

This applies also to the present-day practices of restraints and forced medication, which continue despite the fact that much more effective and helpful treatments for schizophrenia, such as Soteria and Professor Yrjö Alanen's Need-adapted Treatment in Finland, have proven their worth for decades.

In 1936, 71 years ago, at the age of just 19, I went through the most inhumane experience of my life in a psychiatric institution. Even the experience of being buried alive during the 2nd World War was not as traumatic for me. I experienced the psychiatric system as being inhumane because nobody actually spoke with us. A person cannot be more devalued than to be considered unworthy or incapable of conversation. What made it even worse was the fact

---

1 Key-note speech from June 7, 2007, at the congress on "Coercive Treatment in Psychiatry: A Comprehensive Review," run by the World Psychiatric Association in Dresden, Germany, June 6-8, 2007 (corrections by the author, translation corrections by Peter Stastny)

that this happened at the *von Bodelschwinghsche Asylum Bethel* in Bielefeld, which considered itself a "Christian" institution. Bethel and its director, Pastor Fritz von Bodelschwingh, were held in high esteem and considered an embodiment of compassion in the parsonage, which was my parent's home, and by us children as well. But I got to experience a totally different Bethel, compared to the one I had heard about from the newsletter *Bote von Bethel (Messenger from Bethel)*.

On the light green wall opposite my bed one could read in large letters the words of Jesus: "Come unto me all you who are weary and tired and I will give you rest." How were we to be given rest? Rest was given with buckets of cold water poured over our heads, with lengthy baths in a tub covered with canvas that bore a stiff high collar in which my neck was fixed for 23 hours, from one doctor's rounds to the next. Rest was given with wet packs and with sedating injections of paraldehyde. A wet pack meant to be bound into cold, wet sheets so tightly that one could no longer move at all. From our body temperature, the sheets would become first warm and then hot. I would cry out in rage at this senseless restraint in these hot sheets. I just couldn't believe that the natural way of helping in the form of conversation and occupation was being replaced by these torturous "sedative measures." It was only natural that we got restless without occupation and diversion, without a single conversation, not even as part of the admission procedure, and from staying in bed all the time, despite being in good physical health. How were we to recognise this senseless kind of behaviour on the part of the doctors and nurses as "helpful" for us?

These methods of Emil Kraepelin, who had lived from 1856 till 1926, influenced our German psychiatry. The medical director of our *Hospital for Nervous and Mood Diseases* in Bethel, as it was then called, was one of his last students. Emil Kraepelin replaced the conversations that his predecessors, such as Wilhelm Griesinger, (1817-1868) and Carl Wilhelm Ideler (1795-1860), had kept going with their patients, with the silent observation of symptoms, the hallmark of clinical phenomenology or "nosological" psychiatry. As a result he was no longer capable of recognising his patients as fellow human beings, because that is only possible by speaking with them. The symptoms they observed took the place of the human being with his or her experiences. Kraepelin demanded "… a ruthless intervention against hereditary degeneracy, the elimination of the psychopathic degenerate, including the use of sterilization."

Thus the director of Bethel, Pastor Fritz von Bodelschwingh, demanded the sterilization two years ahead of the National Socialist Regime at the "Protestant Specialist Conference on Eugenics" held from May 18 to 20, 1931, in Treysa. He explained his position by saying that

> … the destruction of the Kingdom of God in any one of its members justifies the possibility or the responsibility for its eradication to take place. Therefore I would be concerned if sterilizations were only accepted as a response to an emergency. I would prefer to see these procedures as a responsibility that conforms to the will of Christ (From the conference minutes).

A truly monstrous "Kingdom of God" that granted us only a hopeless and idle custodial existence without the right to any communication, sanctioned by the words of the Bible.

On the other hand, Dr. Carl Schneider, the medical director of Bethel from 1930 to 1933, was opposed to the sterilization law:

> He considers it an error to assume that what is biologically valuable is also mentally valuable. For example, in patients with manic-depressive disorders "such a high level of social competence tends to be inherited," that it is impossible "to sterilize for purely medical reasons." Schneider's conclusion: "We know nothing about this issue, we are just drawing conclusions from experiments with animals and plants" (From the conference minutes).

Two years before the Nazis came to power, Protestant physicians and clergymen were calling for sterilization: "Those who are hereditary carriers of social(!) inferiority and need care should be prevented from procreating if possible" (From the conference minutes).

When I asked the charge nurse about the scars that my young female fellow-patients had in the middle of their lower abdomens, she explained that these were "appendectomy scars." Did they lie to us at home when they said that the appendix is located on the right side? Concealment of the fact that the operation I had been subjected to was in fact a sterilization seemed to be common practice here, even though the genetic-health law of 1933 required that those sterilized had to be informed by the physicians about the nature of the procedure.

Even after the operation, it was not a doctor or a nurse who told me what had been done to me, but a fellow female patient. I was distraught, because people who had been forcibly sterilized were not allowed to pursue a higher education nor could they marry a non-sterilized partner. I had to abandon my chosen profession as a kindergarten teacher for which I had prepared myself such a long time. Not to mention the lifelong stigmatization as being "inferior."

In the January 2007 edition of the *Deutsche Ärzteblatt* (a German medical journal), one finds an article about the absence of compensation for us "inferior individuals" up to the present day, which quoted a statement by Professor Werner Villinger, Bethel's medical director from the year 1934 on, made before a German Parliamentary Committee for Restitution on April 13, 1961:

... [Dr. Villinger] claimed that by paying compensation to people sterilized under coercion they would be damaged once again: "The question arises whether this might lead to the appearance of neurotic complaints and illnesses, which would not only diminish their previous subjective wellbeing and...their capacity to be happy, but also their productive capacity?"

On the 21st of January, 1965, Pastor Fritz von Bodelschwingh's nephew and successor, Pastor Friedrich von Bodelschwingh, argued as an expert before the Committee for Restitution in a similar manner, totally ignorant of our reality: "If one were to grant the sterilized people a right to compensation, this would cause them only unrest and considerable new suffering..."

Bethel kept on sterilizing patients long after 1945. Last year, in 2006, I received a call from someone telling me that Bethel had pressured her to be sterilized even in the 1970s. If only theologians and psychiatrists would doubt their own worth for our sake!

When some 60 asylum directors and psychiatry professors were informed for the first time about SS-Führer Viktor Brack's "euthanasia" program in Adolf Hitler's Berlin Chancellery in July 1939, all of them declared their willingness to cooperate in the killing of asylum patients, with the exception of Professor Gottfried Ewald from Göttingen. He explained his disapproval in detail. One single person sound in mind and soul amongst 60 professors of psychiatry and clinic directors! Where was their conscience, their courage and their compassion, the values that account for people becoming fellow human beings?

In Berlin, at Tiergartenstreet 4, regular and senior experts pronounced death sentences simply on the basis of questionnaires that had been filled out in the asylums. In six psychiatric killing centers, those who had been sentenced to death were gassed. When Hitler responded to the protest sermon of the Catholic Bishop Clemens August von Galen in Münster on August 3rd, 1941 by ordering a stop to the gassing on the 24th of August, 1941, the asylums took over and continued the killing by medication overdoses and starvation diets. According to the latest research results submitted by the historian Professor Hans-Walter Schmuhl nearly 300,000 asylum and nursing care home patients were gassed, poisoned and starved to death. 80,000 of these came from Polish, French and Soviet institutions. Considering that our politicians, psychiatrists and theologians have since nearly completely repressed this most drastic kind of compulsory treatment in the form of killing people whose lives were considered "devoid of value," it is mostly left up to us users and survivors of psychiatry to preserve the memory of those murdered in the name of psychiatry in our hearts.

After 1943, psychiatrists, who had turned out to be adversaries of their patients and in the period from 1939 to 1945 had proven themselves to be—in the literal sense of the term—their "mortal enemies," continued to convey to their students and to the public nothing other than an image of deficiency regarding their patients who had been classified as "incurable." Even on the 20th of April 1979—40 years after the beginning of the "euthanasia" program in 1939—the weekly paper *Die Zeit* ran the following headline on the front page, "A Society of Cold Hearts—In the Snake Pits of the German Psychiatric System." The article states that "… no minority is treated as disgracefully as the mentally ill."

The decades of backwardness of this kind of psychiatry have not been overcome despite considerable efforts in recent years. It remains devoid of conversation and uses medication even under coercion and restraint just to fight the symptoms, rather than aim for understanding.

Soteria and Professor Yrjö Alanen's Need-adapted Treatment in Finland have focused on the experiences and needs of patients for over 30 years by taking them seriously and giving immediate psychotherapy for those diagnosed with "schizophrenia" absolute priority over anti-psychotic medication. In contrast, the German Society for Psychiatry, Psychotherapy and Neurology assigns just 10 out of a total of 140 pages to the topic of psychotherapy in their draft version of *Treatment Guidelines for Schizophrenia*.

Cognitive behavioral therapy is the only form of psychotherapy they approve, but even this therapy they would only recommend when pharmacotherapy has failed. Today's German psychiatric system has fully adopted Emil Kraepelin's concept of a hereditary or genetically caused brain disease which is by definition devoid of meaning, just calling it a disorder of the brain metabolism instead.

Antipsychotic medication has existed since 1953. Since then, its immediate application has been the method of choice. A patient who is overwhelmed by his psychosis certainly wants to have his experiences taken seriously and wants to understand them. The immediate sedation with strong anti-psychotic medication cannot be taken as well-intentioned help from the patient's point of view. He or she will resist. To make the patients compliant with the medication, they will often be strapped to the bed by the waist and all four extremities restrained. At the first psychiatric world-congress in Germany after the 2nd World War, held in 1994 in Hamburg, jointly organized by Dr. Thomas Bock and our Federal Organization of (ex-)Users and Survivors of Psychiatry, the Federal Association of Relatives of the Mentally Ill, and the German Society for Social Psychiatry, the artist Jutta Jentges exhibited a large expressive painting of a person with arms and legs spread-eagled and tied to the bed with the question "Why?" She expresses the torment of being restrained even through the night. The restrained person has been furnished with a diaper, another kind of humiliating debasement. For many people who have had the agonizing experience of being restrained, it sometimes remains a life-long trauma.

During my five stays in psychiatric institutions between 1936 and 1959, this tormenting method of tying patients to bed by their hands, feet and waist, did not exist yet, and body-belts were used only rarely. Up to my 4th episode in 1946, it was common practice to wait a few weeks to see if the psychosis would recede on its own accord, before Metrazol (Cardiazol), insulin, or electroshock were applied. In 1936, these shock treatments were not yet available either. During my last psychotic episode in 1959, I experienced for the first time, along with all of the others on the ward, an immediate injection of high dosages of anti-psychotic drugs. I considered this to be a total dictatorship which prevented us from thinking and feeling and also caused extreme physical weakness; it was deeply repulsive. I was lucky to develop a skin rash after the first two days (of injections); when pills were shoved into my mouth instead, I was able to hide them under my tongue and dump them in the toilet. Nonetheless, it took me the same amount of time as my fellow patients to be rid of the psychosis. Today, liquids are used instead of pills, to prevent behavior like mine.

In contrast, how much more helpful, respectful and competent is the *Krisenpension* (Crisis Hostel) in Berlin, staffed in a "trialogue" manner by psychiatric survivors, family members/relatives, professionals and lay people, who work without using any kind of coercion. Here a person experiencing psychosis is taken seriously instead of being dismissed and reduced to a disturbed brain metabolism. Many people are looking for a way to understand themselves and their psychotic experiences. Whoever wants to understand their psychosis or did find a way to understand it, as I did, after five episodes at the age of 42 which enabled me to get rid of it 48 years ago, still has to find the necessary insights for this process all by themselves—even today.

For these reasons and as an attack against biological reductionist psychiatry, with its distaste for talking with patients, we started the "Psychosis Seminars" together with Dr. Thomas Bock at the Department of Psychiatry of the Hamburg University Clinic in the winter semester of 1989/90. We conceived them as an opportunity to exchange experiences between users of psychiatry, family members/relatives and professionals and called this a *Trialogue*. In this format, people who have gone through psychoses can talk freely about their deepest experiences, without having to take higher dosages of medication as would be the case in psychiatric institutions. This is way of exchanging experiences that gives equal rights for all and makes it possible to understand each other a lot better. In the 17 years of their existence, the "Psychosis

Seminars" were replicated in Switzerland and Austria, but far too few psychiatrists are taking part in them.

What is a psychosis? The problem of coercion and violence largely depends on this definition. The medical concept of a meaningless, genetically
caused disorder of brain metabolism devalues the patient, ignores him as a
person along with his experiences and virtually provokes his resistance.

What would happen if, instead of you—the psychiatrists—, *we* had the
power to define psychosis? We would define it as an emergence of something that is normally unconscious, in an attempt to resolve a preceding crisis
that we were not able to solve with our conscious capacities. We would also
say that this was the reason for the obvious similarities between the well
known schizophrenic symptoms and the stuff our night dreams are made of,
since they both originate from the same source—our unconscious. For example, the emergence of symbols, thinking and acting in symbolic terms are
considered symptoms of schizophrenia. Our dreams are full of symbols. Or
the fact that identifications with Jesus and other personalities can often be
found in schizophrenic episodes. In our dreams, we also identify ourselves
with the people who appear in them, which frequently signify ourselves. And
the same is true with the frequent occurrence of "ideas of reference and over-
valued ideas" in schizophrenia. These can only be understood within the context of an altered experience of the world in psychosis that reveals otherwise
hidden connections. The same applies to dreams. In *An Outline of Psychoanalysis*, Sigmund Freud mentioned, as regards to dreams, "… a remarkable
tendency to condense, to create new entities from elements that in our waking
hours we would surely have kept separate from each another."

Consequently, the illness is based on the fact that we consider our psychotic experiences real. If we recognized them as relating to a dream level
from the outset, we would not be ill. Therefore, we need to shift the contents
of our psychosis to the "dream level," which would enable us to hold on to
the *meaning* of our psychosis without maintaining its objective reality. Our
psychoses are often accompanied by emerging impulses and emotions,
which also come from our subconscious. I always live by these impulses or
by the inner, inaudible voice to prevent these impulses and feelings from getting bottled up. Some people do hear these voices. This definition of schizo-

phrenia is not debasing and invites people to deal with the contents of the psychosis and the preceding crisis, in order to understand oneself better and know how to handle oneself.

We experience and regard the emergence from the unconscious as "insertions" coming from outside ourselves. Therefore the British psychiatrist John K. Wing refers to the "experience of thought insertion" as a "central schizophrenic symptom." It is probably this experience of thoughts inserted from the outside that provides the basis for the term "schizophrenia." As soon as we realize that we are dealing with an emergence from our unconscious, which we experience as coming from outside ourselves because of a completely different way of thinking and imagining, which is like "being thought" rather than active thinking, then we can work towards an understanding of the psychosis and of the self. The fact that our psychoses are psychologically caused by preceding crises in our lives is known to nearly all who have had these experiences.

Many people are afraid of psychiatric institutions with their forced medication and absence of help in understanding either the psychosis or the self. From their very first contact with a patient, psychiatrists should prove themselves to be helpers and not opponents. My wish would be that the patients could—right from the start—present their disturbing experiences in group sessions, that they could talk about them, write about them, paint and draw them. I wish that they would be taken seriously with their experiences, without needing to fear unwanted psychiatric interventions. During this process, it would be very valuable to have the support of individuals who have experienced psychoses themselves and have overcome them, understood their meaning for their lives, and have been able to integrate these experiences into their regular lives.

Currently, there is a pilot project at the University Clinic Hamburg, Department of Psychiatry, called "Experienced Involvement" (EX-IN), sponsored by the European Leonardo da Vinci Program, where people who have experienced psychoses are being trained. Further details about this project can be found in the February 2007 edition of the journal *Eppendorfer* under the title *Vom Patienten zum Profi – Ein europäisches Projekt qualifiziert Psychiatrie-Erfahrene für die Hilfe anderer Betroffener (From Patient to Profes-*

sional: A European Project Qualifies (ex-)Users and Survivors of Psychiatry to Give Peer Support).

I experienced five different psychiatric hospitals from 1936 to 1959 with 23 professors of psychiatry, medical directors, senior physicians and their assistants. They all subscribed to a genetically caused, meaningless and incurable schizophrenia. As a result, I didn't experience a single conversation about the content of my psychoses or the life-crisis that led to them and certainly not about any meaningful connections. Psychiatric inpatients today still complain about this lack of dialogue.

I was encouraged by the publicist Hans Krieger who called for more considerate treatment of psychotic patients in several outspoken reviews of psychiatric and psychological literature in *Die Zeit* during the 1960s and 70s. He also had introduced us to foreign reform initiatives, such as Ronald Laing's Kingsley Hall and others. He is the one to be thanked for urging me to write about my experiences of psychosis and healing. In 1990, he edited my accounts in a book titled *Auf der Spur des Morgensterns – Psychose als Selbstfindung (On the Trail of the Morning Star: Psychosis as Self-Discovery*, currently published by Paranus [in the German language]). There you can see that I really had schizophrenia. Because according to Kraepelin a person who has recovered from schizophrenia never had schizophrenia.

How can we trust in a psychiatric system that rejects the concept of healing, because such healing would contradict the theory of a meaningless, incurable metabolic brain disorder? We older people, who have experienced psychoses have paid for this genetic-somatic dogma with forced sterilization and its consequences, and the "euthanasia" victims paid for it with their lives. Now is the time for the psychiatric system to become an empirical science based on the experiences of patients.

Kate Millett

The Illusion of Mental Illness[1]

How do we get to a point where a human being is bound to a table with locked leather cuffs and left to suffer this torment and indignity for hours at a time? What in law would condone that? What in our cherished system of civil rights and liberties would ever permit such an event? How do persons lose their every right through commitment hearings? How do they come to be drugged at trials where everything is at stake, even their liberty?

Somewhere the law has failed us deplorably; somehow lawyers are betraying their clients. Public defenders working for a pittance, not knowing their clients, ushering them through a kangaroo court where everything is staked against the victim. The law truckles before medicine in such hearings: everything the law stands for—in constitutional guarantees, in skepticism, in demanding proof and evidence—is prostituted before the claims of psychiatric medicine. The lawyer bows before the doctor, who says this person is "crazy." There is a complete abdication of the traditional legal responsibility to defend.

Consider how prolonged criminal trials are, how elaborate and concrete the presentation of evidence, the jury system, how many centuries have gone into the creation of the adversary process, how slow and incremental the gradual acquisition of constitutional guarantees and civil rights through the 18th and 19th centuries, their extension throughout the world in the twentieth. All whisked away in the unexamined moments of commitment hearings.

---

1 In 1992, Kate Millett gave the Cunningham Lecture in Law and Medicine at the Faculty of Law of Queen's University in Kingston, Ontario (Canada). This essay is a shortened and updated version of that lecture, published under the title "Legal Rights and the Mental Health System," in the *Queen's Law Journal*, Vol. 17 (1992), No. 1, pp. 215-223.

How does the state come to have such extraordinary powers over certain individuals? Where did the system of protection break down and why? It is said that these individuals are ill with a strange and terrible illness, for which they must be treated with force. Therefore, the law must become the hand-maiden of those who understand the disease. Legal measures must be obtained to exercise force, but the urgency to use them lies not with the law or its practitioners, but with another set of experts whom they must now serve. These practitioners must imprison and deprive their patients, this is the first step in their cure.

Let us examine the notion of treating someone by force. Treating them for what? For acting strangely, for talking too loud, for anger or stress or irrational behaviour, for conduct that offends? But surely we imply the law here, not medicine. Has such a person committed an offence against another, disturbed the peace, committed an assault? The remedy for that is in the law. How did medicine get involved? Then we are told there was no offence against the laws, but the neighbours are complaining, the family is up in arms. There might be a crime. Our laws do not permit persons to be arrested or incarcerated through preventative detention. There might be a crime, but in fact there isn't. Instead there is unacceptable behaviour, generally described but not observed. The person is not a criminal but the victim of a strange disease that can only be cured against his will.

What disease could ever be involved that the afflicted person would not wish for treatment? Physical medicine is not permitted to treat by force, the very notion of doctor and patient implies an agreement, a co-operation, a seeking out of aid and comfort. The essential nature of such treatment is voluntary. The idea of involuntary treatment is so improbable, so hard to defend on medical, legal, or moral grounds that it necessitates an appeal to mysterious circumstances.

But there are petitioners who want to force a regime of healing upon the offender. There are "interested parties" and relatives with a private desire to control who seek social consensus, support, and approval for their animosity toward an individual, the one singled out. Support for the use of social force against the individual is immediately at hand, as near as the phone. Society is prepared to arrest and incarcerate, victimize and deprive an individual of every right without any recourse. But it requires still a rationale, a label, a vehicle of belief, an accusation that carries weight. Madness fills this, so does heresy or political subversion. Crimes of the mind.

Psychiatry is the authority for this in our time and functions as an arm of social force, ultimately an arm of the state, with state powers, police powers, real locks and bars, drugs and torments. But it also embodies an idea, the idea that the individual carries an invisible disease, or taint, which no pathology can prove, but which experts can intuit and cure by force. This idea prevails by common consent, by publicity and propaganda, by the borrowing from the prestige of science itself and applying the force of the state and its overwhelming armory of physical power.

Psychiatry, calling itself medicine, must become an avenue of social control and state power outside the law, beyond it, with powers that surpass, abrogate and nullify, perhaps even contradict the law and its every guarantee to the individual. Centuries in development, these guarantees must in stipulated cases be abolished. The state permits the family to present its own choice of individuals to repress. The family, the state's chosen and appointed agent, operates through the medium of psychiatry, for the psychiatrist decides finally. You may want to incarcerate a relative, but you still have to find a doctor to oblige; the doctor decides ultimately. But the fact that families can present a victim is itself surprising, an informal kind of social control.

Now we all believe in the mysterious force, the illness, the mental disease. Your mind may just give in, collapse, succumb to some constitutional weakness. Invisible forces may strike you down. And belief is everything. It runs the show. It must only be extended, propagated, further institutionalized, funded, bureaucratized, turned into a thriving industry, the source of hundreds of thousands of jobs and "services," then millions.

The system would not work without force. It relies finally upon brute force, as does any system of social control. It also relies upon an ideology. Here the ideology is a perversion of reason and science, the medical model of mental illness. Many psychologists and psychoanalysts would agree that the medical model of mental illness is a misleading analogy, because psychologists believe that psychological suffering is the product of stress in environment, whether through one's personal history or through social circumstances. In other words life is very difficult: death is hard to endure, bereavement, the death of love, love's labour lost, hard economic times, lost employment, lost opportunities, the embittering frequency of every form of disappointment in life. This is a reality model, built upon reality.

The medical model, on the other hand, is not based upon any reality, nor is it medical, though it uses the prestige of physical medicine and the reality of physical disease to mystify us and to command a general social consent, lay or legal. Ultimately it is a communal mythology, which conveys enormous powers both to the state and to psychiatry through the commitment process.

Very few countries have not enlisted their complete faith—formally and informally, officially and privately—in the notion of mental illness and its corollary, mental health. Mental illness is a government commodity, a ministry, a department, a branch of every bureaucracy at the federal, municipal, provincial, state and local level.

Mental illness is thought to be as identifiable as pneumonia, as epidemic as AIDS, as potentially knowable and millennially curable as cancer. Our shared conviction of the existence of mental illness is miraculous, because at the beginning of the 21st century, after several centuries of scientific discovery and the triumph of scientific evidence, our communal faith in the existence of mental illness is completely religious and unscientific. We believe without any proof whatsoever. Without any evidence of what science means by illness. By this I mean pathology. In medicine, there is no disease or illness without pathology, and pathology is something one can see and prove. Physical medicine and science itself rest on proof—actual evidence of disease. Real microbes, real blood tests, real antibodies, real swelling and fluid, real edema, real cellular malformation. There are real diseases of the brain and nervous system which can be proven to exist in these ways: tumours, paresis, Alzheimer's, Huntington's chorea. These are true diseases with true pathological evidences.

When we speak of mental illness, however, we mean a number of so-called diseases for which there is not pathological evidence, even though we have believed in them for over a century. Schizophrenia is the leading mental disease, then manic depression. At the same time, their very existence is not always agreed upon within the psychiatric profession. Within classical psychology their existence as illnesses or pathologies or disorders is no easier to prove than in psychiatric medicine, since there are no pathological proofs, only behaviour.

To prove one is ill because one acts or behaves a certain way is very different from proving one is ill through reference to physiological evidence of such illness in the body. Evidence of illness through behaviour is not physically objective; there is no physical proof to refer to. Behaviour is a matter of observation and interpretation, and what is crazy to one set of eyes is perfectly explicable, even rational to another. What is outrageous to one observer is only bad manners to another, maybe even funny to a third. Possibly even justifiable. It depends on who is watching and even more upon the attitudes they bring to the observation of that behaviour: self interest, spite, coercion, rage, disapproval, the urge to control, punish, humiliate.

Pneumonia isn't like this: you have it or you don't, and if you have it, you want a cure. Accused of mental illness, you are on trial, the victim of aspersion, a figure on the defensive, and unable to defend yourself from a charge whose very existence is proof of guilt. Pneumonia is not like that; no one is hired to accuse you of it before the law or persuade a judge you are guilty because full of germs. You won't be isolated and dishonoured before your friends, fired from your job, lose custody of your kids. Pneumonia will never do this to you.

The idea of mental illness is simple: use human mental and emotional suffering as evidence of disease which only a highly specialized, highly trained, and highly paid class of healers—nearly a priesthood—can have any effect upon at all. And do not stop short of the most drastic treatments for this mysterious malady; use drugs and cruelty and fright, imprisonment and electrical currents to the brain. Psychoanalysis is ruled out as mere talk therapy and unscientific. Talk is too easy, like friendship or advice. One needs neither a prescription nor a licence to dispense it.

Human grief, uncertainty, life crisis, and the painful steps by which we divorce or grow or create or change: these are all moments of vulnerability when there is sure to be opposition from those around us and even from inside ourselves. We are as unsure to ourselves as always, unsure as men or women, lovers or siblings, children and parents. We can be mystified, overcome, shamed, cowed, reduced, and humiliated, especially if we are persuaded we do not know our own minds, feelings, responses, and motivations, and if we are taught to find our own mental processes and powers of reasoning unreliable and faulty. Then medicalize the entire human condition, define the mind as a series of mysterious imponderables, pretend it is a chemical construct of uncertain balance, an enigma we are at the mercy of and cannot control. Only biological psychiatry can tinker with this mercurial mix, adjusting it with drugs whose operation even the doctors cannot understand but which they claim do us no harm.

We are dealing with stigma and coercion, with state power and control over citizens, and with vast multinational drug cartels who stand to profit from the prescribed psychiatric drugs force-fed to victims of these mysterious illnesses, both when they are incarcerated against their will and upon their release, temporary and probational as it is. Liberty, life, food, shelter, and employment all depend upon submitting and consuming the drugs that brand and debilitate.

The drugs are referred to as "meds" or medication rather than medicine. The medication tranquilizes, dulls, slows down, speeds up, reduces or creates stress, distorts concentration and cognition, actually frustrating the rational powers of the mind. Meds are drugs; they do what drugs do—they distort. But they do not heal, since there is no pathology present, and mental and emotional stress and suffering are normal human conditions rather than sick or pathological ones.

Peter Breggin has made a general review of research studies on the damage caused by neuroleptic drugs (Haldol *[active ingredient haloperidol, marketed also as Dozic, Novo-Peridol, Peridol, Serenace, etc.]*, Thorazine *[active ingredient chlorpromazine, marketed also as Largactil, etc.]*, Mellaril *[active ingredient thioridazine, marketed also as Aldazine, Melleril, Ridazine, etc.]*, Prolixin *[active ingredient fluphenazine, marketed also as Anatensol, Modecate, Moditen, Permitil, etc.]*)—drugs patients are required to take even in freedom or lose their benefits (Breggin, 1990). Breggin looked at the effects of such drugs on the higher functions of the human brain, and he summarized studies from brain scans and animal research as well. He found that neuroleptic-induced brain damage is frequently masked by the drugs themselves, and therefore revealed only during withdrawal when the damage is irreversible.

This results in a tendency to lifetime drugging. Breggin also describes how psychiatric drugs quite literally "shrink" the brain, and, in addition to sedating the individual and frustrating intellectual process in the short run, they cause persistent cognitive deficits. He describes the neuroleptic-induced epidemic of tardive dyskinesia as an "iatrogenic (physician caused) tragedy" and calls on the medical Profession to take responsibility for the damage it has inflicted on millions of patients throughout the world. Beside metabolic and circulatory diseases like diabetes and hypertension, caused by more recently developed clozapine *(marketed as Clopine, CloSyn, Clozaril, Denzapine, FazaClo, Zaponex, Zopine, etc.)*-like ("atypical") neuroleptics like Zyprexa *(active ingredient olanzapine)* or Serdolect *(active ingredient sertindole)* you especially have to consider the risk of tardive psychoses: possibly developing a worsening or chronification of psychoses as a result of drug-related receptor-changes—emphasized by Robert Whitaker (2002, pp. 253-286) and Peter Lehmann (1996, pp. 99-104; 2003).

In contrast with the medical model, the humanistic psychological model has the value of respecting human rights with regard to commitment and forced treatment. But it is not the model in use in our society today.

Explained this way, the medical model sounds both wicked and foolish. It is. It is also a lay religion and a great threat both to our rights as citizens and human beings and to our ability to think logically and intelligently about difficult subjects like medicine and illness. The medical model is causal deterministic, it erases both freedom and responsibility, good and evil, choice and reason. All of this has enormous political ramifications. We are being managed and controlled. We are being brought into line, corrected and led along by social agencies, that vast governmental creation of state hospital, community health center, or private clinic.

Behind the ideas of "mental health" and "mental illness" are a vast industry and hundreds of thousands of jobs, salaries and positions, grants and expenditures, doctors, nurses, the entire system of guards in locked facilities, aids, security personnel and devices, the manufacturers of restraints and control devices, electroshock machinery, and finally the great pharmaceutical industry itself, the largest, together with munitions, and the most profitable manufacture in the world. Around it all are the thousands of procurer and support industries, the journals and educational facilities, the accreditation and certification bureaucracy, the records keepers and clerks, the convention facilities and training centers, the builders and maintenance forces, all the packages and providers, the institutional provisioners, even finally, the accountants and legal advisors.

There is a continual cry for more money, more research into mental disease, more facilities to house and sequester, broader latitude to commit and incarcerate. At the same time and with deplorable hypocrisy, a proliferation of oily pleas for greater tolerance and understanding, underpinning even wider expectations of illness, a more perfect understanding that we are all, to one degree or another, infected with mental illness and in need of ever expanding and invasive treatments.

There is so much money involved, so much power, so may jobs and careers that it has eclipsed organized religion as our most powerful way of controlling society and of setting and enforcing social standards. Moreover, its criteria are legal ones, legally enforceable: that is, they are literally and factually a matter of freedom and imprisonment through the process of commitment hearings, the mental health statutes, and the doctrine of substituted judgment whereby an individual is said to have no further capacity to make decisions. An individual convicted of mental illness has legally ceased to be—ceased to enjoy an autonomous condition and individual identity—for all purposes of one's own fate and selfhood.

This is a lot of faith to place in an imaginary disease, an illusory illness. The potential for social control, deliberate or incidental, is so overwhelming that one begins to see that this is a system in which abuse is not incidental but endemic, part and parcel of the concept. The result, indeed the purpose, is the creation of compelling social conformity. Even the Inquisition pales beside such a creation: it is hard to match the terror inherent in electroshock convulsions, four point restraint, and massive injections of mind stunning drugs. This system can apply absolute force over absolute helplessness.

But of course, social institutions do not operate this nakedly in general. In general, they are integrated into life, taken for granted, accepted as inevitable, useful, part of the general purpose of civilization or salvation. Consider the power and organization of state psychiatry: a system of international scope and size and complexity, pervasiveness and efficiency. Consider psychiatry's influence in the schools and universities, throughout our systems of employment and personnel, its influence on all aspects of the health system, the welfare system, public assistance, government subsidy, and private philanthropy. Most of all, consider the cultural acceptance and social appreciation of psychiatry, the elevated claims of the "helping professions," a social consensus of the highest dignity and greatest altruism. If not divine in its mandate, if not holy, then high and noble, the revealed truth of science, our contemporary and secular religion. Never mind that this is pseudo-science; the desire to believe has replaced proof or evidence. Assertion has been accepted as fact.

How does an illusion come to have the power of a fact? Though belief, through the assent of the governed. Since this system relies upon locks and bars and drugs and police powers, however, its force would be there whether you believed in it or not. Our belief gives it greater force, god-like force. It has had such force for those of us who have been its prisoners in body and in mind.

We are also the survivors of one of the meanest systems of oppression ever developed, and its victims and its critics. We are the ones to tell the truth, to say that mental illness is an illusion, intellectually and scientifically, but also a system of social control of unprecedented thoroughness and pervasiveness. It is our role to expose this illusion and to free us all—for we are all constrained, oppressed, limited, intimidated by this phantom of mental illness. We stand with reason against error and superstition, with imagination against conformity and oppression. What good fortune to be part of such a struggle for freedom and human rights.

Sources

Breggin, P. R. (1990). Brain damage, dementia and persistent cognitive dysfunction associated with neuroleptic drugs: Evidence, etiology, implications. *Journal of Mind and Behavior, 11,* 425-463.

Lehmann, P. (1996). *Schöne neue Psychiatrie. Vol. 1. Wie Chemie und Strom auf Geist und Psyche wirken.* Berlin: Antipsychiatrieverlag.

Lehmann, P. (2003). "Atypische" Neuroleptika, typische Unwahrheiten. *Pro Mente Sana Aktuell,* (1), 16-18. Retrieved January 3, 2007, from www.antipsychiatrieverlag.de/artikel/gesundheit/atypische.htm.

Whitaker, R. (2002). *Mad in America.* Cambridge: Perseus Publishing.

Uta Wehde

Antipsychiatric Work by Relatives

Unrestrained Anger and Commitment to Alternatives

Imagine you are very unwell, you are sad, you can't sleep nights, you are afraid, and past, present and future merge together in the darkest of images and colours. You haven't been feeling like this just for one day but for a long time and sometimes you think about ending your life.

My brother was in this situation in the summer of 1979. He went to a psychiatrist, not for the first time—more or less unwillingly at the behest of my parents who at the time could see no alternative. My brother was 22 and a student at the university.

That day, as he sat hopeless and silently in front of him, the psychiatrist said more or less the following to him: "You will never be able to complete your studies! You can't be cured and you should be in a mental asylum!"

The following day, my brother hung himself. The psychiatrist who had considered my brother as very suicidal later explained his "therapeutic" intervention as follows: "How can I make someone more depressed than he already is?" It was intended to stimulate resistance in a depressive patient and to provoke an opposite reaction to shake him out of his depression.

My brother certainly had many reasons to kill himself. He was standing over an abyss, ready to jump and this psychiatrist did nothing—on the contrary, he gave him the final push.

This experience is the basis for my antipsychiatric commitment. As a 16-year old, I learned in a very painful manner of the brutality and cynicism of the psychiatric system, whose treatment methods had already destroyed many identities. I didn't need to understand them, to analyse them—the logic of psychiatric thinking and actions—I had direct experience of their inhumanity!

Since then, I have carried a deep hatred within me, an unrestrained anger but at the same time feelings of powerlessness. When in 1987 I began to work in an antipsychiatric organization I was able to free myself of my hatred and to give it another form, transforming it constructively. Through this work, I learned something fundamental—about me and about the society in which we live, a society which has been deeply affected in its everyday thinking by psychiatric logic. During public events or personal discussions, I was made aware again and again just how unwilling people are to let go of this logic.

The group of so-called experts, which includes me as a psychologist, are especially at risk; socialized in their studies according to the biomedical paradigm, they quickly enter the one-way street of the diagnostic perspective and often fail to notice the walls they build up around others, but also around themselves. Equipped with the disease model, the diagnostic key and the appropriate terminology—life seems rather easy, doesn't it? I am healthy and the others are sick, I am "normal" and they are schizophrenic, I am the expert and they are the patients, I am clever and they are fools. It is just like the fairytale, *The Emperor's New Clothes*: the psychiatric system adorns itself with many terms and theories and prances through the world proudly calling itself a science. And when we look a little closer, examine its theories, terms and treatment methods?—then nothing but pitiful nakedness remains. But the system is as powerful as the emperor; empowered, courted and borne by the ruling normality. Antipsychiatry, at its heart, questions this normality, whose yardstick we all carry within us and which keeps us in line. In the final analysis, antipsychiatry concerns us all, just as much as the normality in which we live.

Against this background—as a committed relative—another normality, one of a science based on the experiences and knowledge of those affected is just as important as the creation of concrete alternatives for psychiatric survivors. It was, therefore, only logical in the course of my antipsychiatric work to become involved in the setting up of the Runaway House in Berlin; and since we succeeded, after fighting for 15 years, I have become active in *Für alle Fälle* (In Any Case), an association committed to further education and training from the perspective of independent survivors of psychiatry and to advancing user-controlled research.

Translated from the German by Katy E. McNally

Actual Alternatives

Introduction

When (ex-)users and survivors of psychiatry take their lives into their hands in order to advance their recovery[1]—assuming they were once labeled "ill"—should this be classified as non-compliance and "playing doctor" or as autonomous behavior? Doctors generally do not want patients to treat their cancers, stomach ulcers or infections on their own, nor do they want them hoarding an assortment of herbs and concoctions in their pantries to drive out their everyday madness and its particular variants. In spite of this, (ex-)users and survivors of psychiatry—alongside practicing professionals, who report about reasonable and effective help for people in emotional distress—are seizing the opportunity in the following chapters to report that they have indeed resorted to such "household remedies," partly out of despair in psychiatry and its often unsuccessful or harmful methods, and partly out of cautiousness, curiosity or self-initiative. Similar self-healing mechanisms were well known long before the so-called psychopharmacological revolution, even among psychiatrists.

Many rather simple and reasonable methods have been discovered and rediscovered over and over again by (ex-)users and survivors of psychiatry, especially when their efforts are supported by an attitude that supports such ex-

---

1 Recovery is a relatively new concept within the psychosocial arena and which is used by those critical of psychiatry as well as by psychiatry itself. "Recovery" can mean, among others things, re-discovery, healing, improvement, salvation or the regaining of independence. A positive connotation of hope is common to all uses of this term, but it has many different implications. For some, recovery means recovering from a mental illness, a reduction of symptoms or a cure. Others use it to signify an abatement of unwanted effects of psychiatric drugs after their discontinuation, or the regaining of freedom after leaving the mental health system, or "being rescued from the swamp of psychiatry."

perimentation in the psychosocial field. Psychiatrists are particularly keen on finding successful therapies, and are therefore prone to latch on to something that is yet unproven. When patients are encouraged to search for personal healing, they will take this up with considerable zeal. Unfortunately, many suffer needlessly for years, until they come to a realization similar to the one described by Bert Gölden of Germany after he discontinued the psychiatric drugs:

> Today, now that I no longer take any psychiatric drugs, my existence is once again overshadowed by anxiety. In other words, I sacrificed 21 valuable years of my life hoping pointlessly for an improvement or a cure. I find myself at the beginning once again and have to find a new form of treatment...Recognize your suffering and become your own therapist—help yourself, because no one else will (Gölden, 2004, pp. 100/102).

We hope that the specific and concrete alternatives described in the following chapters can be adopted much earlier by people who are confronted, perhaps for the first time, with psychological crises and their social consequences. Endless experiments with a wide range of psychiatric drugs and repeated psychiatric hospitalizations, for the most part result in nothing other than a lifelong career as a mental patient, with all of its unwanted psychological and physical "side effects." In such situations, an early discussion of individual strategies with and without professional help would be rather welcome, which might include the offerings of organized self-help as well as models of professional support. An intellectual and practical engagement with Soteria, Windhorse, or crisis centers, with Runaway Houses like the Villa Stöckle[1], with advance directives, supportive and possibly insight-oriented psychotherapy, as well as with general alternative views and approaches, could be especially useful to prevent those harmful long-term effects of psychiatry that are often seen as symptoms of an illness, or even its worsening and chronification. More important than the specifics of any particular type of intervention are fundamental issues such as the possibility of a trusting relationship with someone who genuinely cares and the generation

---

1 Named in honor of Tina Stöckle (1948-1992), a founding member of the Runaway House Project

of hope in the reality of recovery. Without these elements, even psychotherapy can be harmful.

Frequently people are still locked away, socially isolated or sidelined in psychiatric ghettos which limits their opportunities for contacts that might help develop different perspectives about their own suffering and about psychiatry. Although there are opportunities for day-to-day contact with one another within these ghettos, the lack of awareness and freedom prevents such constructive contacts. Relationships with other (ex-)users and survivors of psychiatry provide a chance for a mutually empowering exchange of stories and for the development of shared strategies to solve problems. A prime example is the International Hearing Voices Network, which has built solidarity among its participants primarily through the sharing of common experiences with others who hear voices, and thereby has irrevocably surpassed the boundary between "normal" and "crazy" in both directions. At the same time, these organizations of (ex-)users and survivors of psychiatry are used to develop coping strategies that can give each individual another chance at confronting extremely distressing experiences. The relevant necessary awareness and organizational know-how have been tested in many different varieties on an international level, so that today no psychosocial care system should exist without well-developed client-participation.

Source

Gölden, B. (2004). With patience. In P. Lehmann (Ed.), *Coming off psychiatric drugs: Successful withdrawal from neuroleptics, antidepressants, lithium, carbamazepine and tranquilizers* (pp. 98-105). Berlin / Eugene / Shrewsbury: Peter Lehmann Publishing.

Translated from the German by Mary Murphy

A. Individual Strategies with and without Professional Support

Peter Lehmann

What Helps Me if I Go Mad?

With contributions by Ludger Bruckmann, Chris Hansen, Andy Smith, Sarah Carr, Alfred Hausotter, Merinda Epstein, Harold A. Maio, Agnes Beier, Peter Lehmann, Zoran Solomun, Ursula Zingler, David Webb, Tina Coldham and Constance Dollwet

Watch out, you will find only positive reports here. Everyone here has come to terms with their madness, depression, mania, mental illness, crisis, suicidal tendencies—or whatever else the authors may call it—without getting caught up in the wheels of psychiatry. If we had asked for reports of catastrophic results, we would no doubt have received them in large numbers. People are always flipping out, going mad, and getting into the worst mental crises. Only some of them end up in the psychiatric system, duly classified and recorded, become chronic patients or even notorious in the public eye. It is no different in other areas of life. Many people commit heroic deeds that no one else knows about; or they commit crimes that don't come to light. There is more to the world than what can be found in files or newspapers—and as for psychiatry, there is more than what the average psychiatrist sees. Fortunately.

Situations that relatives often consider catastrophic and psychiatrists label as illnesses in need of treatment, are seen by the people going through them in a rather different light: as painful, distressing, or absolutely terrifying crises, but also as necessary experiences that can help them overcome certain life inhibiting situations that cause them misery.

The individual paths taken in order to deal with states of madness without landing in a psychiatrist's office are extremely varied. One could try to categorize them. But what use would that be in view of the unique story of every individual human being, their personal resources and their very unique ways of tackling their problems? May the patron saint of antipsychiatry protect us from a "theory of coping strategies in social therapy"—a new pigeonhole!

Read how people avoid psychiatry in times of crisis: by retreating to a quiet and safe place, through calming remedies, massage therapy, contact with animals, by approaching helpful people or through expressive artistic activity. Read how they deal with crises through reflection in self-help, therapy or writing, through disputing diagnoses, through political activism vis-à-vis psychiatry or self-critical observation. Read how they avoid further crises or make them unnecessary through consciously balanced lifestyles—starting with a proper diet and sufficient sleep, the choice of potential helpers in emergencies, to avoiding dangerous places or by thinking ahead and defusing crises though advance directives. And how others help—without psychiatry: through care, social support, attendance, staying close by, making inquiries, respecting personal space, and avoiding intrusion.

The following contributions are not patented recipes; this book is not trendy, how-to advice. The contributions are ideas or suggestions. It is possible to tackle emotional crises—beyond psychiatry.

Ludger Bruckmann:
Right from my early childhood, I have been absolutely terrified of going crazy. My mother, who looked after the mentally ill in a convent during the Third Reich, told me terrible stories about how they were tortured and transported away. To go crazy was the worst thing that could possibly happen to me. On top of that, mine was a very strict Catholic upbringing; sin and sexuality were synonymous. "Do not resist going down the road where the Lord leads you" was my motto.

I ended up in the madhouse in 1978 as a result of being such a dedicated Christian. I wanted to act in a Christian manner and sacrifice myself somehow or kill myself. I had been silenced by the contradictory behavior of people towards me. The faces of the people around had become contorted. They wanted to finish me off. I made mistakes at work. I withdrew into myself and became tied up in a calamitous maze of thoughts. I stayed outside of society, became suspicious, and ran off without any sense of direction. I wanted to die. I suffered severe physical pain and fled from other people. I ran to the entrance of the hospital and screamed that I was scared . Then I ran away again.

My older brother, who I trusted greatly, brought me to the psychiatric hospital. I was unbelievably terrified and thought he was in cahoots with the Mafia and that I would be horribly killed in the hospital. I thought I would never get out and had absolutely no trust in these people. I was afraid that under the influence of an injection, I would reveal something in my sleep that I was not supposed to speak about. I was given very strong psychiatric drugs that caused severe muscle tension. But after a few weeks I got better. My mother collected me and said that she did not have a crazy son.

A few weeks later, I was in the same state. My mother wanted to hide me and kept me locked up at home. I was no longer capable of undertaking anything of my own volition; I was in a situation I couldn't cope with and was badly in need of help. I was in a deeply melancholic and anxious state. In Essen, where I lived and worked, I was getting worse.

Then, my younger brother took me to Berlin and saved me from another hospital stay which would have lasted at least three months. This all took place in 1978. I undertook psychotherapy. For the first time, there was someone there who listened to me and asked me for my opinion. I started to laugh out loud and said that no one was interested in hearing about that. The therapist could see a person in me who had been damaged by the world. He immediately showed understanding for the way my life had gone wrong. He did not recommend any pills.

My episodes of madness came back time and again and frightened me. But I know that pills do not solve any problems. People who tell me "Ludger, there is no need to be afraid" are the ones who are helping me. My brother always answered the crazy things I came out with by asking me: "What happened then that was so terrible?" He was there. I could talk to him but he did not put me under any pressure. He let me be. When I felt like an ugly animal, Tina Stöckle, a member of the former Berlin self-help group *Irren-Offensive* (Lunatics' Offensive), held on to my shoulder and said: "I understand you." It was as if a stone inside of me had begun to cry and I sobbed bitterly about how terrible I had been to myself. Someone understood me and I realized I was a wonderful human being. Together with our lawyer Hubertus Rolshoven, she helped me get a place to train as an industrial mechanic. I now correspond with a critical survivor of psychiatry and we write to each other about our personal worries. Thank heavens I have people around me who protect me from psychiatry and its drugs and who give me tips on what to do when I run out of options. These are not always people who are against psychiatry; I am even grateful to my former personnel manager for not seeing me as mentally ill but instead giving me the chance to start a career in Berlin. Of course, I am also grateful to the man whose donation made the Runaway House possible.

I have not become a chronic patient, but instead have helped set up the Runaway House in Berlin. I am the only person who has worked there continuously since it was founded in 1996. I keep telling myself what it is important for me: I do what is good for me, for instance, getting up early, cycling, swimming. I do things that make me happy, I paint, I sew etc. It's all right for me to have unpleasant thoughts as long as I don't attach any great importance to them. I stay as grounded as possible with my thoughts in my own life. When things get very bad I turn to those people who would never put me into a madhouse. They let me be, they listen to me, and they put their arms around me. That is what helps me when I start to go crazy.

Chris Hansen:

In the panic of the moment, car skidding out of control towards a logging truck, my instinctual reaction was to slam my foot on the brake and turn my vehicle back in the direction I was driving. I was lucky—the road was wide, and the truck-driver swerved hard enough to miss me. Although hugely relieved, I thought nothing of it, and did the same thing next time I slid on ice, and ended up in a head-on collision. The outcome for me was minor damage to my car and my pride, and mandatory attendance at a driving safety course. There I learned that when skidding the best way to get back on track is to take my foot OFF the brake, and turn into the slide.

Like many before me, when a personal crisis struck, I ended up in mental health services. I survived, and as a result, thought that my "braking reaction" was the best option. It wasn't until I ended in a head-on collision with mental health services that the pain of the experience left me looking for better, more effective ways of dealing with and making meaning out of crisis.

I had become stuck in a patterned response to the world around me. My community encouraged me to see myself as the problem, as unacceptably "different," and in need of the superior help of "experts" to "treat" me. As a result, I became fixed in my identity as "broken," and therefore inferior, not good enough, and unworthy of being included as a valued and respected member of my community. Whenever there was a crisis, I became dependent upon mental health professionals to have the answers and fix me. They were the experts, not me.

This was, I now realize, a "fixed delusion." I was handicapped by having worked in the mental health sector myself, and had had a significant amount to personally gain from believing that those paid to provide mental health care were superior and more knowledgeable than those receiving. However, the cognitive dissonance set in for me whilst on the "sharp end of the needle" in a secure psychiatric ward. I realized that those who did most for me were not paid to be there. They were my fellow inpatients—many of whom had spent most of their lives in institutions. And the wounds inflicted by those who wore name-badges—many of whom had once been my colleagues—left indelible scars on my soul.

And so I came to reframe my experience of madness. I lost my job in mental health services as a result of a forced hospitalization. Seventeen diagnoses later, I now realize that this was, for me, a timely promotion. I surrounded myself with people with similar experiences, and we celebrated our difference together. I became angry at the injustice, exclusion and shaming of my community. I became a political (mental health) activist, and worked locally, nationally and internationally. I believe that I am the expert in my own wellbeing. In this age of evidence-based outcomes measures, I also am convinced that I am the evidence of what works for me.

Some of what has been called my madness I live with on a daily basis. I have difficulty planning, organizing, completing paperwork or sticking to deadlines. I can become paralyzed with disproportionate fear if I try to "pull it all together" at times. The biggest challenge is overcoming the shame and the messages from the rest of the world that this makes me a bad person. So I am learning to be honest about these difficulties and to ask people to support me in a non-judgmental fashion. It seems it is only possible to overcome this in the context of healthy relationships.

Some of what defined my times of crisis in the past were my habitual ways of relating to both myself and others when I became afraid. It is the fight or flight response that all of us develop in response to danger, conflict and chaos. We may take control, become aggressive or become passive victims. Knowing my habitual "braking response," I have planned to respond different-ly, in the context of reciprocal relationships in which I can maintain my sense of dignity and autonomy. I have decided who I want in my life at those times, and we have agreed upon and written down guidelines. I have a list of options that have worked in the past. Some of these are massage, rigorous ex-ercise and going to stay at a retreat. I have also included a growing list of things I would be willing to try, including a holiday in the Bahamas, a macro-biotic diet and learning to play the saxophone or a new foreign language. I know that I'm unlikely to remember these when the time comes, so it's useful to have a list to remind me. It is important to me that if people don't know how to respond to me, that they ask, and I am very clear that I want no deci-sions made about me without me.

Tangata motuhake is a New Zealand Maori term for people who celebrate their own uniqueness. It is also the name that some New Zealanders like my-self prefer to use to describe their identity as a mad person. I am honored to have the privilege of being a part of the community, which has enriched my life beyond my wildest dreams. A key to my survival has been *tangata motu-hake*: learning to celebrate, rather than despise my own uniqueness.

Andy Smith:

The treatments for my madness have caused neurological damage. Paradoxically, the services that assist with my physical disabilities have been most helpful for my madness.

Twenty-one years ago I removed myself from a mental hospital and have taken no so-called antipsychotic drugs since then. It took six years from my breakout to be able to assert myself about treatment. Keeping safe or away from psychiatrists, it comes to much the same thing, was vital in reaching that point.

In *The Divided Self,* Ronald D. Laing (1970) redefines the conditions referred to as "schizophrenia." His term "ontological insecurity," in essence a sense of unsafeness that reaches to the core of your being, is a more useful description than "dopamine-mediated psychosis." It allows for practical, non-chemical approaches, moving the question from containment to enablement. This concept enabled me to develop a sense of self, from which I was able to assert the right to self-definition.

Self-definition provides a clear understanding of the role of the external environment in provoking madness. Population density is a factor in reasonable people behaving badly. At times I look mad. I walk with a strange gait. People can stare and be confrontational. This is appropriated by my voices and visions, and the linkage of the internal and external oppression overwhelms me. The increasing frequency and effect of abusive encounters was one reason why my partner Eleanor and I moved to a small town on the coast. However, before leaving my flat I still do a risk assessment but of the risk I face *from* other people, rather than the risk I pose *to* others.

I have had an uncomfortable relationship with medicine. My mental health history has supplanted any manifest physical symptoms in importance in the mind of most medical practitioners. Whilst I had a "mental illness" label my physical health was a secondary consideration. To survive, I avoided contact with medicine. In effect, this denied me access to health care for many years. This is not unusual.

I have been fortunate to have Philip Thomas as my consultant psychiatrist. Philip not only accepted my right to self-definition but encouraged it. He kept the "caring professions" out of my life where I did not wish them to intrude. As a mad person with no primary health care, dealing with bureaucracies is more than usually complicated. All arms of the state presume you have primary health care and much relies on "a letter from your doctor." Philip provided those letters, but more importantly, his role as my consultant reassured those who might interfere without asking. Lastly, as I trusted Philip to act in my best interest, I was able to consult him when my madness became overwhelming, without needing to be guarded in what I said in order to preserve my liberty.

I now have an excellent GP, who supports my right to self definition. During our first consultation, he told me, "Psychiatry makes you ill."

Over the years my aim has changed. I no longer try to remain un-mad, but to structure my life to allow for the ebb and flow of my madness. The Herculean task of appearing "normal" had in the past been enough for me to go mad for that reason alone. I know that I am not a faulty normal person, either temporarily when outwardly mad or in the intervening periods when my madness is not apparent to others. Most treatments work on the supposition that we are faulty normal people. As a result treatments focus on irrelevant ends. In the past, I have been drugged until my madness wasn't manifest, but my madness was still there, just hidden by the psychiatric drugs. I also denied I was having the experiences labelled mad when I didn't want any further increase in psychiatric drugs. If an aim of psychiatric drugs is "to reduce the amount the patient voluntarily talks about their psychotic symptoms," then medicating me to this degree would work by that criterion. I did not manifest any of my internal distress, because I did not show any evidence of internal life at all. This is not the same as the absence of madness. Yet it was the gauge by which the success of treatment was measured.

Mental health services are not relevant or helpful in the way that I surf my waves of madness: less a life jacket, more a circling shark. However, knowing that mental health services won't help you doesn't mean that you're not still vulnerable to them.

In order for our wishes in treatment to be considered, Eleanor and I have developed our advance directives as a tool of assertion. I specifically preclude all the psychiatric interventions I find unhelpful, including most psychiatric drugs and all talking treatments. The "do not" list is balanced with clear guidance about what helps and should be done.

An advance directive represents a challenge to services and emphasizes the gap between the rhetoric and reality. Two years ago my social worker enquired at a local hospital with a "respite unit" about a respite admission for me. All went well until they saw my advance directive, where it explains that my propensity to harm myself increases in closed institutions (as is the case for many people living with self-harm). The hospital declined to offer me respite care for that reason alone, arguing that it would have an adverse effect on staffing levels. I was left gritting my teeth until the voices and visions became manageable, but this put an extra pressure on those who cared for and about me.

With the help of independent funding, I employ Gail as my Personal Assistant. Because I wanted someone to bring practical non-medical solutions to the challenges my madness poses, anyone who had trained or worked as a mental health professional was ruled out. Gail assists in dealing with my madness and its consequences. I become disorientated in any noisy or busy place. Gail accompanies me to meetings or attends as my proxy. Gail is a trusted external reference point for all social interactions. This really helps with taking risks in going to new places and meeting new people. My body doesn't remind me to eat; unfortunately I appear mad when my blood sugar drops. Gail keeps an eye on this and prompts me to eat. She prepares food for me to cook, as the less contact I have with knives, the better. Gail's role is tailored to meet my needs. It has transformed my life.

The clearest example of this transformation is that, for many years, the visions have been showing me my death. It is a terror they have used several times against me in different forms. Currently they show me my death whilst riding a horse. As a teenager I lived to ride, and only stopped in my 20s because the voices told me it was abusive to ride a horse. This was a dilemma: to take away the power of the vision of my death I would have to break a moral binding the visions had placed me under. With support from Gail and Eleanor, at the point that I felt the potential abuse of the horse was justified, I resolved to challenge the visions and voices by riding regularly. When the voices start berating me as we drive away from the riding school, Gail helps me stay safe and remain fixed in the here and now. Without this support, I couldn't move my battle with the voices and visions forward. One unexpected benefit of riding is that the non-verbal communications between the horse Velvet and I seem impervious to interference from my voices and visions. This communication helps dispel the feeling that I am abusing Velvet by riding her.

It might sound very expensive, employing Personal Assistants for people in distress. The savings dwarf the costs. When last living alone without support, I would typically be detained involuntarily for at least six months of the year and spend much of the remaining time as a day patient. A Personal Assistant would have saved approximately £ 600,000 on my lifetime care costs. It is possible I would have remained in employment, and be a net contributor to the state.

For the first time ever I have a degree of predictability in my life. I can make plans without the certainty that any plans I make will be thwarted by madness trapping me in my flat or hospitalising me. It's worth making plans now: they usually but not always come to fruition, just like for non-mad people!

When the voices and visions are overwhelming life goes on: I'm not trapped in my flat and my relationships don't collapse. Instead, as the nameless terror starts creeping around the edge of my life, Gail drives me into the countryside or to a remote part of the coast so that I can calm down in an environment that is not reflecting discord and chaos back at me. This allows me to stand aside from my madness. Together with riding and communicating with horses, this fulfils for me the role that meditation has for others. For the first time I can remember, I have joy in my life. It's a strange feeling, but it is there.

I insist on the right to assert my needs. This is only possible because I have freedom from mental health treatment. Services designed for the "mentally ill" are part of the problem, not the solution. Resources would be better spent on the meaningful enabling of individuals to assert their own definitions. Madness is a personal experience, unique to each individual. Its treatment must be too.

Sarah Carr:

> We view films in the context of darkness. We sit in darkness and
> watch an illuminated world, the world of the screen. This situation
> is a metaphor for the nature of our own vision. In the very process
> of seeing, our own skull is like a dark theatre, and the world we see
> in front of us is in a sense a screen. We watch the world from the
> dark theatre of our skull. The darker the room, the more luminous
> the screen (Dorsky, 2005, pp. 25-26).

I left my venlafaxine tablets *(antidepressant, marketed as Dobupal, Efexor,
Effexor, etc.)* in a bin in Amman, Jordan. I had been prescribed them following a serious episode of self-harm six months earlier and they replaced the
medication I had been taking previously. During my six months on venlafaxine, I had become unrecognizable to myself and to those around me. My
close friend and ex-partner, someone who had known me for 12 years, said
my emotional responses were completely alien, which upset her deeply. Trying to work was nearly impossible. It felt as though I was wearing a motorcy-
cle helmet, the visor of which was covered in blood. Each day I had to smear
away the blood to see where I was going. And even then I couldn't always see
where I was going. I was overwhelmed with thoughts of suicide and yet
knowing I could take my own life was, at times, my only comfort.

  Despite this, I managed to go to Jordan with friends to make a documentary
film about life in a Palestinian refugee camp there. The process of making the
film seemed to bring me back to life. The friend who was directing the film
also had experiences of mental distress and had once been prescribed venlafaxine. But she was off medication altogether, preferring to manage her mental health difficulties herself. She was a great inspiration and support to me
and through her I discovered that it was possible to live, even for a while,
without psychiatric treatment. Having a friend who shares both your experiences of mental distress and your love of something can change your life. In
this case, we both have a love of film—both making and watching films—
and this has been important in sustaining us through our own times of mental
torment. "We are peering over the edge of a cauldron in which fragments of
all shapes and savours seem to simmer; now and again some vast form heaves
itself up, and seems to haul itself out of the chaos" (Woolf, 1926).

When you make a film you are constructing something whole from fragments (frames or sequences). In editing, you are piecing together something that can become a unity of thought and feeling through word, sound and image. When you are experiencing internal chaos, the exercise of control and the act of creation in editing a piece, no matter the outcome, can be healing. The action and rhythm of assembling images and sounds so they work together (sometimes as if by magic) to make something unique can be calming when your thoughts are jumbled and rushing. When you are lost, you can rescue parts of yourself by this act of creation. You can make a mark to say you still exist. "And sometimes at the cinema, in the midst of its immense dexterity and enormous technical proficiency, the curtain parts and we behold, far off, some unknown and unexpected beauty" (ibid.).

When I am ill, cinema can be like a womb, a dark safe space where I can temporarily retreat into another reality while my own is too painful to bear. When I am disintegrating and feeling dependent it gives me a sense of autonomy and containment. When I am too agitated to read, it teaches me and tells me stories. When my mind is assailed by intrusive thoughts and voices, it gives me other images, other words, some familiar and some unfamiliar. When I am withdrawn and afraid of humankind, it keeps me in touch with humanity. For me it can be a light in the darkness.

This piece is dedicated to Captain Blackheart, Nataly Lebouleux and Werner Herzog.

Alfred Hausotter:
During my childhood and youth, I did not experience any significant psychological problems or illnesses other than pneumonia. I was proud that I missed school only once throughout my first 19 years due to a case of harmless edema.

When I became ill shortly before my final exam, I was therefore rather surprised. At first, I didn't recognize the illness for what it was: manic-depressive psychosis. To my detriment, I felt better than ever before, affected also by an increasing megalomania; I thought of myself as spiritually and physically superior to everyone.

After a few weeks of medical treatment in a psychiatric clinic, my initial elation turned into its exact opposite: listlessness and a strong inferiority complex, leading to thoughts of suicide. For three years I was given psychiatric drugs that held me in a rather subdued state. Occasionally, to feel a bit more "alive," I began to consume recreational drugs (hashish, LSD). Things went well until an overdose of Romilar tablets *(cough medicine; active ingredient dextromethorphan)* reawakened in me a psychosis that was even more intense than the first one: hearing voices, feelings of omnipotence undermined by powerful paranoid delusions—as well as a conspicuous lack of restraint in social situations. This time, my psychosis led to an involuntary commitment to a psychiatric clinic (diagnosis: schizophrenia).

The depression following my release from the clinic was so powerful that after a few weeks I attempted suicide, overdosing on the neuroleptics I had been prescribed (Leponex). Thankfully, I was only briefly unconscious and was released from the clinic 14 days later. Although I received other psychiatric drugs, my situation once again switched into mania and after three months, I was again admitted to the clinic for eight weeks. After repeated unsuccessful treatments, my confidence in traditional medicine, especially psychiatry, began to dwindle, and I decided to find my own way to recovery. Excited by the lectures of Sigmund Freud, Wilhelm Reich and others, I gave up my previous career and began to study psychology, believing that "Health isn't everything, but without it there is nothing!"

My initial confidence—founded on bio-energetic therapy (one year) as well as multiple months of talk therapy—was once again disrupted by a manic episode shortly before a difficult statistics examination. Although the symptoms of this psychosis turned out to be the worst and the most acute so far—the auditory hallucinations now became visual as well, and included visions that reflected a confused bodily awareness—I decided to get through this crisis totally without psychiatric drugs. Luckily, a semester break from my studies gave me adequate personal space to let my various delusional ideas come out relatively unfettered, without attracting excessive attention in public. My agitated phases, suppressed earlier with pills, were now expressed through artistic outlets like writing, drawing and music.

After six months, my psychotic agitation subsided gradually, and in the face of a new semester and its demands, turned into a more severe depression than I had ever experienced. An agonizing inferiority complex, difficulties breathing, as well as a general apathy sank in over a period of months, until I reached a point where I believed that I couldn't go on. I was considering suicide when I unexpectedly had the opportunity to travel to Amsterdam with some friends for a week. The hospitality, the relaxed social attitude, and the relatively carefree outlook on life shown by the people who live there gave me new courage to face life and I was able to get through this crisis without outside interference.

Influenced by the belief "a healthy spirit in a healthy body" I undertook my first fasting regime (5 days). Six months later, I undertook a longer fasting period of three weeks. The happiness I felt after completing this regimen was overwhelming. Not once before in my life had I experienced such physical and psychological well being!

During this time, I became acquainted with the raw food diet and adopted it enthusiastically. The relief from chronic suffering (meniscus pain, poor eyesight) that I experienced for brief periods during my fasting could now be achieved permanently by sticking to certain dietary adjustments. In order to keep my mental instability under control, I tried the most diverse methods: group therapy (8 months), bioenergetics (1 year), talk therapy (4 years), counseling-self-help group (1 year), yoga (consistently for 24 years), meditation (15 years), Tae-Kwon-Do and T'ai-Chi (20 years). Each of these helped me in unique ways to deal with my problems actively without relying on psychiatric drugs or relinquishing my responsibility to health experts.

Since my last psychotic break over 20 years ago, from which I, to emphasize once more, recovered without medication, I have had only two milder crises: the first lasted one month and I got through it without drawing attention to myself. The second crisis lasted one week and expressed itself only through the fact that I was somewhat overly excitable. For me, the fact that I survived is an acknowledgment of the central thesis of classical wellness-teachings (e.g., Konz 1995) and a steadfast trust in the self-healing powers of the body including all of its psychological peculiarities.

Merinda Epstein:

Since the 1970s, I have been involved in feminist politics. During this time, I have learned to name a truth about what medical science insists on calling "women's mental illness": male violence, child abuse, rape, assault, invisibility and powerlessness. In naming such truths, I have faced my own demons and won with the help of other women—not doctors. Naming things for what they are protects me from my madness turning back in on its self and encroaching on my personhood. Institutionalized societal silence on these vital community issues makes me mad. Feeling personally silenced makes me sick. Fighting back, finding my voice and refusing to shut-up are my remedy to despair. Through feminism I have learned about radical critique but also about dialogue and the power of story. These are personal tools in my "fighting madness" arsenal.

I am also a lesbian. Gay and lesbian politics has taught me about "coming out" and the importance of pride. It has also provided me with community. Uncontrived community is a sacred place when madness threatens to go feral. I now have two communities: the gay and lesbian community and the mad folks community. Both of these places provide solace when anger has gone past its useful date and when I feel powerless and anguished about the degree of discrimination and systemic oppression. The reciprocity created when mad folk care for each other works for me. These relationships are restorative because they largely remain untainted by the implicit patronism of professional "caring" ones.

Despite my own fight against patriarchy I still sometimes get caught up in it, dwelling on the many losses and failures madness (no matter how much I hype it up) has brought to my life. At these times, I sometimes get sad but hopefully no longer so despairing or ashamed. I cannot bring back my life losses, my career or my economic independence but now that I have given myself permission to be genuinely angry I can get through these very sad times and move on. It is at these moments of self-reflection that I turn to my garden and my animals. Neither my garden nor my dogs care very much about aspirational society. The garden is beautiful and makes me happy. The dogs just want an occasional walk and to be fed. We enjoy these things together.

Harold A. Maio:

What helps most when my disability threatens my ability is to realize that everyone has such experiences. My disability, labelled psychiatric, is no different in that respect. Once I accept the universality of my position, the next step follows logically: I have the power to re-establish balance in my thinking.

In a survey of individuals in California who had experienced the psychiatric system, the majority polled would, under no circumstances, return to seek help from that system. That is my second line of defense: realizing that the existing system of "help" is actually more damaging than therapeutic, I am again led to self-reliance.

Like anyone who experiences a crisis, it may take me a while to recognize that I am in crisis, that my reaction is counter-productive, or even destructive, and that I must re-establish control. Peoples' minds play games with them, even healthy minds, but one can re-establish balance.

For a while, I learned to make no decisions after 10 p.m. I usually panicked late in the evening and would make decisions I would later regret and change. Everything looked bleak late at night. Recognizing the negative aspect of late night decisions helped me postpone final answers until the next day. I still rely on this "delayed decision-making." First I address a problem, then I reach a solution-and then I postpone acting upon that solution for several hours. Sometimes the problems are simple, sometimes complex, but, whether addressing a totally personal issue or a complex political one, I do my best to delay action. I doubt that any worthwhile politician or businessperson acts any differently. Whereas I would once act upon suicidal ideation, the depression was so overwhelming, I now experience the depression without the need to act upon the ideation. I still want to, I just don't.

The depression itself is not so easy to address. I have not found the key to ending the thought patterns, and I am bothered by that, but I have learned to accept my disability and to live with it. That is another answer. If I had one leg, I could forever regret it, or accept it (what choice would I really have?) and get on with the rest of my life. If I were blind, I could forever regret it or get on with my life. Like anyone (with a labelled disability or not) there is really only one choice: Do the best you can with what you have, but realize that it is you who have the power within yourself. It cannot be found elsewhere, no matter how impressive the credentials of individuals who claim that power for you.

Many people have tried to define us as different, and have designed systems to accommodate that "difference." It is the systems that are wrong, we are no different. We, too, have accepted the idea that we are somehow different and have accepted their proffered "help," no matter how abusive. But the real answers lie within ourselves, within our own abilities. People who have been taught helplessness, experience helplessness; people who have been taught self-reliance, experience self-reliance.

One last word of caution: Simply because someone has experienced the same disability, does not mean that that person can relate empathetically. Nor is it true that, because someone has not experienced the same disability, that person cannot relate empathetically. I carefully choose the people to whom I turn for help when I decide I need support, and I choose not for their background, but for their ability to listen and relate. There are peers and professionals to whom I would never turn for help, and peers and, albeit a few, professionals on whom I rely. I am learning to make positive choices, even in the face of deep depression. I am learning.

Agnes Beier:

Over the last few days I was confronted with a situation such as I had not experienced in a long time. It was the sense of having no space at all for myself—I was ready to burst, explode with anger, a strange and new sensation for me—unbearably so! Not even as a child had I been faced with such a crucial inner test. Within me and all around, I felt like I was about to blow up.

I had handed over my apartment for two months to a close friend hiding out from her abusive husband. Convinced myself that I was capable of handling this too: to be without a place of refuge. Wouldn't I feel at home everywhere, if I'm at home within myself? But was I / am I still close to myself?

This was not easy, as I had already been without a place of my own for quite some time. In fact, I had been spending hardly any time in my own flat during the previous months. But now I had even given up my keys for a period of time. An unusual situation, quite disconcerting at first. How was I to find the way back to myself?

Back home to me?

Exhausted, I opened the door. But this time I didn't experience the immediate feeling of home-coming, which had always welcomed me in my apartment. What was I to do?

First, I decided not to cause myself any additional stress. I said to myself cautiously that I am not my apartment. It is perfectly acceptable to arrive here feeling knocked out, exhausted and sad. It is my oasis, I do recognize it! I rediscovered my apartment, thirsty for calm and exhausted from living in tight quarters with several people. The space had changed a bit but it was still s p a c e.

And then came a feeling of gratitude for this space that I may fill without being disturbed. Fill it with thoughts, with music, with sadness, with joy— with quiet. Gratitude has an almost magical effect, very quietly at first: thank you. Thank you again! Then joy. Over and over it comes to me that there is always something to be grateful for. Simply, I express my thanks for this place, for my space.

Over a number of years, I have introduced some personal rituals here, from listening to music in my spot by the stove, to incense ceremonies, needless to say not in my bed. I start out by making myself a cup of coffee and then I light a cigarette. Sometimes I might put a stick of incense in a dish and walk with it through the apartment. It is a joy to take the actual smoking incense into my hands, to put it into a bowl (filled with sand, charcoal and incense) and to enjoy the smell, the aroma. Not passively, like the spectator I was in church as a child. My apartment is just as holy to me as a church, because it is healing –every day can be a special holiday and I don't have to wait for Christmas, Easter or something like that. I decide which day becomes a holiday, usually I begin with music, then I sit down, sometimes with burning incense. Naturally, I put myself into a celebratory mood which means that my apartment has become a place of celebration as well. This is the first apartment to ever give me the sense of feeling safe. Now it is time for warmth. More smoke— this time from my stove with its viewing window, watching as the fire starts to burn on the grate, lying on the bed and just watching. I don't have to do anything. I can simply lie there, can do almost nothing else at the moment, because I'm too tired and have a severe headache to boot.

Why did I feel at home and safe again so quickly? From the repeated experience of recent years. In other words, a valued experience. Having practiced it for so long, I could resort to it fully wherever I lived. I just needed a refresher, a reminder once again, after spending much time without being alone.

I found it helpful that at least one corner of the apartment remained for me. It is a kind of altar, a temple and memorial-nook. It is not so important that everything remains exactly the same there. Just space, an area remained, as the room was getting more and more spare.

Constant, always ready, waiting for me, like a greeting that welcomes me when I return home from a long trip. Calming, when something stays the same in the outside world, even if only a tiny corner. Sometimes it is enough to just think about it; in other words, this feeling of security is so deeply rooted within me that I can carry it around wherever I go. Actually, I am quite familiar with all corners of my 240 square foot apartment, they are soft cornerstones of my inner security. My daughter and I had glued stars on the ceiling above my bed so there is either a canopy of stars or the whole wide world.

When I close my eyes, my apartment is not small at all but gigantic as the space around my heart opens up. This time I have come home to remember.

How did this apartment become a place of refuge for me?

Following several involuntary stays in psychiatric hospitals, I was no longer really able to trust anyone. I finally found the primal safety and homeland of my soul only in the years after my hospital experience in the quiet of my house. Or in nature, where I always feel safe and well taken care of.

Alone with no possible threat from the outside—in many quiet hours, practicing a form of meditation that I invented. It was like a question and answer game with myself, gleaning truths from my soul.

For me, who always wanted to discover and come to know things by myself, this is a very touching experience. Given my difficulties of "being able and wanting to trust," this is an opportunity of finding myself without others or any outside influence. I landed in a nonverbal world. My soul has no difficulty at all with silence, quite the opposite, as it is not afraid of a truth that does not need words at first. Words appear by themselves in silence and can be rediscovered again and again.

It is as if you are rediscovering a space which has, in fact, always been there, and which—I am fully convinced—is waiting patiently to be discovered by each of us. I too am allowed to discover this space, at my own pace, without any pressure. To stop myself from rushing, I try to breathe consciously. The word for soul in Sanskrit is *Atman*, just like the German word for *atmen* (breathe). Without any pressure, without changing pace, just to feel. The inner space of my soul doesn't need any particular apartment. But for someone lacking practice like myself, the outer protectiveness of my own space is apparently still quite indispensable.

Simply concentrating on my breathing, I become calmer, quieter.

Allow silence to take effect on me

When I really open myself up, I feel reluctant to call my inner and outer "getting quiet" a meditation because I don't know much about words or language. It is a new world which I experience again and again. I sit there quietly and breathe. At first thoughts come and go, I don't judge them, they are visitors going to and fro. Things settle down without applying any force, everything becomes still and wide. S p a c e.

New feelings and images well up in me. I am, I breathe, my heart beats, past and future are like a dream. Dream and space dissolve. Without expecting an answer, I sometimes ask where from, where to and why? Often, answers came to me like gifts, once I had taken advantage of the silence and space, because that is where my fear always disappeared.

Silence and space without fear.

In the safety of finding space and silence once again I can keep finding my inner world anew. Or perhaps it will find me too?

Peter Lehmann:

In 1977, I went crazy for the first time, as I tried to maneuver myself through an increasingly stressful situation. My marriage had just fallen apart; I was under pressure to finish my thesis which was an arduous labor. I struggled with anxiety over my exams, I argued with some of my roommates. I was in love with my new girlfriend and simultaneously having disagreements with her because she feared that she was pregnant and would need to get an abortion, leave the apartment or leave me altogether. Now all of this, which for 26 years, more or less out of my own free will, I had silently swallowed but apparently not digested, was breaking out of me.

The parties involved reacted all negatively, towards my—harmless—fantasies, my exuberant speaking, and my fear that I was being monitored, remotely controlled, persecuted, poisoned and brought to a madhouse to be de-brained and killed. The relatives to whom I went in order to type my thesis on their electric typewriter were extremely scared, and the doctor they called resented me for not wanting to play the customary patient role. The fellow students in Berlin and the girlfriend, who followed me to my relatives, reacted with silent shock. Unclenched by my crazy new perceptions, detached from all binds, I was finally profoundly unsettled.

To some extent my fantasies turned into bitter reality: I was carried off to the institution and locked up there for weeks on high doses of neuroleptics that more or less poisoned me and induced a coma-like state which temporarily brought me to near death. Eventually my liver was permanently damaged, I developed a tardive dyskinesia in the form of a rabbit syndrome (compulsive nibbling). Afterwards I became totally apathetic and finally had to be thrown out of the madhouse. To top it off, I was forced to submit to a community psychiatrist who dispensed depot neuroleptics.

Distraught over my misery and convinced that no positive readjustment of my life could ever happen, I decided to withdraw from treatment and to secretly discontinue my prescribed neuroleptics. After some time I recovered, and founded a self-help group in which I could gather together with other (ex-)users and survivors and also consider my diverse diagnoses. Quickly, I lost the belief in being a mentally ill schizophrenic. Through occupying myself intensely with my earlier crazy utterances and perceptions, I came to understand much of the content, shape and cause of my "endogenic psychosis;" I gained new self confidence, became more open and began to "expose" my feelings as well as I could.

After four years, however, I went crazy again. As I traveled to a television discussion in which I proudly expressed my criticism of psychiatry, my girlfriend, also a member of the self-help group, "betrayed" me with another group member—a man who I had felt consistently inferior to. Afterwards, he and my girlfriend were very nice to me and did everything to ease my suffering and to dissuade me of my jealousy. Should I have kept a grudge with them? Again, the state security services, CIA, KGB, Stasi and the neighbors were lurking behind every door.

I fled to my house and barricaded myself. Luckily now, unlike the first time, there was no one there threatening to call a doctor to give me a tranquilizer shot. Like the time before, I was confused: was I Peter Lehmann, living simply as a normal citizen and going crazy, or was I Peter Lehmann, all powerful instigator of world revolution, hunted by the united secret services?

I didn't call my current girlfriend, whose infidelity had burdened our relationship, rather, I picked up the telephone and called my childhood friend whom I had known since kindergarten. This time he was not on vacation. He listened to all of my anxieties and hopes for an hour without pressuring me to finish. Afterwards he didn't ask me why I felt the need to pursue emotional conflicts from a time when we were 11 years old, and he answered me clearly and earnestly, relieving me of my guilty feelings and even admitted some lapses of his own. Then I had a conversation with a long time friend, who didn't try to get rid of me nor disabuse me of my imaginings as signs of mental illness. Neither did she warn me of the danger of a "schizophrenic relapse" nor advise me to resume the neuroleptics I had discontinued long ago … and to a degree I was again Peter Lehmann, simply a normal citizen in Berlin, just rather excited at the moment and in danger of being inundated by the return of uncivilized, non-processed emotional conflicts.

I took a bottle of good Württemberg red wine, finished it almost in one gulp, lay down in bed and woke up the next morning as Peter Lehmann, a normal citizen, who had nearly lost it completely—nothing more but also nothing less: a person potentially becoming crazy who still had not realized how careless it is to push away his feelings during existential conflicts. That should never happen to me again.

Zoran Solomun:

How is it possible that my madness does not slip completely from my hands, if it once confronts the pointlessness of my life and the endless chain of violence in my own story? How is it possible to hold on to the positive in madness, which for me opens the door to autonomy? How can I attain this if it's associated with sorrow and desperation?

I recognize the loneliness, the absence of freedom and lose the floor under my feet, but I also abandon this numbing bittersweet loss. Ordinary people suffer it heavily when the floor underfoot is lost. Even one's own graveyard plot is purchased years in advance and shown to relatives with discreet and pacified mourning for one's own death.

Madness and the loss of the confident ego can also be the attainment of a new way of life; suddenly, the total sensibility turns around. My body is real. I consider the facade of the house in which I grew up, the individual grains of sand in the plaster. Or the pine tree in front of the house. I read a sad story and each word has the impact of a traffic accident. In the glint of inspiration, my madness is the premonition of another, stronger life, that I, as I am now, am terrified of—because of this I also suffer. How can I reduce the suffering, without the inspiration vanishing?

Entrance to the institution, diagnosis, psychiatric drugs, and "return to reality": how is it possible that we don't lose everything?

What should I do in a situation in which I can't do anything? If I don't know anymore who I am and how I stand? Apparently, I'm helpless. The only thing I can do is to find others with similar experiences to mine. If I'm afraid to look for them, if I fail to find them, then I will spiral into an ever-worsening self-denial. If we meet each other, I'll begin to doubt that violence and desperation are necessary but I will also begin to believe that they must remain a part of my past.

The pressure is strong and deep inside of me. Nevertheless, the process of turning to others and having others turn to me, would help to gradually free me from suffering. Solely the act of turning to others and others turning to me—the people that, facing the background of their own experiences, do not, out of fear, reach for tranquilizers (neither for themselves, nor to give to others).

We listen to one another, speak, and then listen again. We tell our truth, convinced of its existence, and we actually consider these perspectives to be truthful. And in this way we open the gateway to personal and encounter the warmth of others. This is the most normal thing that I expect from life.

Ursula Zingler:

In 1981, I had to have psychiatric treatment. The bullying behavior of my boss triggered a severe depressive phase. I had all the symptoms described by Hegerl and Niescken (2004). It was only after I had been unable to work for a year that I could muster the courage to confront my boss and tell him how unacceptable I found his behavior.

Realizations

I had lots of time to think during the nine-month period of outpatient treatment. I reflected on what I had been thinking about during my breakdown and realized that my approach to life had let me down. I didn't dare tell my husband what I had come to realize. Instead, I started to think of divorcing him and then committing suicide. A colleague advised me to go into the hospital for treatment. Another colleague offered to drive me to the hospital for a pre-admission consultation. Good advice and a useful offer. Because, in contrast to many other people, during my treatment I learned much about self-destructive behavior.

I was in an open ward of a university hospital for more than five weeks. Freed from the duties of a housewife, given the attention of an understanding ward physician and receiving the empathy of other patients, the hospital program (physiotherapy, sauna, sleep deprivation) offered me a great deal. I

- found myself tied up in contradictions when talking about my husband
- I found that my head and my heart were not in harmony.
- I recognized that I was better at taking the lead than at being submissive.
- I discovered how pointless it is to fight on several fronts at the same time.
- I learned that it was acceptable to ask for help.
- It was hinted that I had to learn to say no and that I had the right to put myself first.

Armed with this knowledge, without the support of a psychotherapist or a self-help group and without being recommended any more psycho-active drugs, I swore to myself: I would never again allow myself to end up in such a terrible state. I would never again be one of the living dead.

Implementation

I no longer thought of suicide. I am still in possession of this freedom. Whether I do well depends largely on myself. It is simply a question of how one thinks and how one deals with the unpleasant things in life. If I think positively, I feel well; if I think negatively, I feel bad. My decision was made—I was going to end my marriage rather than give up the aim of living a different life. To this day, my husband has shown understanding—although somewhat unwillingly—for my new way of life. I am very happy about this.

"Ms. Zingler, you need something just for you" a colleague once said to me. This comment fell like a seed on fertile soil. From that time on, for 12 years, I was an ombudsperson helping people with chronic psychiatric conditions. The discussions I had during this time opened up new ideas. However, the danger of being used was very great. One piece of advice was useful. "The saying goes: Love thy neighbor as thyself. It is not: love him more." I learned how to say no. Some time later I set up the local Initiative of (ex-) Users and Survivors of Psychiatry in Stuttgart and encouraged people who had been in psychiatric treatment to organize on a state and federal level. As a member of the Baden-Württemberg Board and of the Board of the German Organisation of (ex-)Users and Survivors of Psychiatry, I work with former and current psychiatric patients on reforming psychiatry for the benefit of those affected. Nowadays it is impossible for me to imagine a life not committed to social-political work.

Why I Could Not Say No

Why did I find it so difficult? After all it was for my own good, and protected me from being overtaxed. Fritz Riemann (1981) explained it in his book: "When the child misbehaved in the eyes of its mother—which usually simply meant that it didn't always obey immediately—she lay down on the sofa and 'died'…" (p. 80). It came to me when reading this that my mother didn't "die" but she said: "That makes Mummy sad." This was enough to stop me from doing what I wanted to do. Thus, not acting on my own desires became the guiding principle of how I lived.

Riemann speaks of "an unsuccessful 'turn-about' and a lack of development of the self." He explains that individuals with depressive tendencies have no strong impulses, desires or aims, nor are they able to reject excessive demands or even recognize them as such. Fear of loss and feelings of guilt prevent them from saying no. Therefore, all that is left to them is depression or an unconscious strike when the tolerance limit has been exceeded. It is no use trying to avoid the fear of ego development by reneging the existence of the self. Only the daring act of becoming a self-sufficient individual can help here (ibid., p. 85). All these statements described me. I dared. My conviction: To this day, because of this change of direction, I have avoided another mental breakdown.

According to Riemann (pp. 105-155), my husband could be classified as having an obsessive personality. He found it very difficult at the time to change a plan or a decision. In my opinion, he still criticizes too much. To avoid his "complaining" (ibid., p. 128) I carried out some tasks although I found them very annoying at the time and suppressed my own desires. Never again. There is no sense in permanently taking on other people's problems as your own.

I also found the behavior of my boss, which I referred to at the beginning, reflected there:

> These people are always afraid that everything will be uncertain, even chaotic if they loosen their control just a little, open up to something different and give a little slack…They always have to be mindful of applying more power, knowledge and practice to make sure that nothing unwanted or unexpected "happens"…One could generalize by claiming that the obsessive personality tends more towards avoidance rather than commission of sins (ibid., pp. 110/128).

I am no longer surprised about the lack of opportunities for further training, contradictory instructions and irresponsible actions. I used the knowledge I gained, took away his power over me and forced him to give clear instructions. This unnerved him and caused him to make mistakes so serious that our employer let him go.

Nip it in the Bud

Feelings of rage, of weariness, and pointlessness are still no strangers to me. I always search immediately for the trigger and the solution. My guide in doing this is: "Give me the serenity to accept the things I cannot change; the courage to change the things I can, and the wisdom to know the difference."

I don't ask for help from above, but I take the responsibility to work out the solution. The knowledge of personality structures taught me to accept my fellow human beings as they are. Calm and composure is required. Occasionally, I try to speak to those connected to my feelings of discomfort. Sometimes it is sufficient to give myself a break or a treat or to carry out tasks that are satisfying. In contrast to earlier times, I

- take note of my feelings, act according to them and talk about them
- am troublesome
- have stopped expecting that everyone has to like me
- protect myself from excessive demands
- make sure to live a life filled with variety.

David Webb:

Today I live without psychiatry for basically the same reason that I also live without heroin. I find that life is better without either of them.

Although I am now able to enjoy and celebrate my madness, it can still be a source of pain and difficulty. At these times, I no longer medicate myself with dangerous, potent drugs like heroin or the psycho-drugs I was taking when I was actively suicidal … though smoking tobacco is still a comfort for me, along with lots of tea, and I also enjoy a little too much wine in the evening sometimes.

What helps me most of all during difficult times these days is the lesson I learned back in 1999 that set me free of my suicidal madness. What I learned is that silence is my best friend. Silence is what I found at the heart of my being. Silence is where all my thoughts come from and where they all return to. This silence, not my sometimes crazy mind, is who I am. And in this silence, which was always and already forever inside me, I finally found peace after overlooking it for so many years. Now, whenever I need some peace, my silent friend is always there for me.

Through this silence, I learned that all I have to do is be true to myself—to be myself, nothing more and nothing less. This can be hard at times—my crazy mind plays lots of tricks on me. But at these times, my trusted silent friend is my guide. Be true, live truly, tell the truth (especially to myself) and the peace of silence is never far away.

Although silence is the bedrock of my wellbeing today, there are many other things that help me. My studies, my work in mad politics, the wonderful people I've met through this work with its many challenges but also so many joys. I try to be sensible and eat carefully and do some gentle exercise too, but I'm sometimes not very good at being sensible. I make sure I laugh a lot, which is pretty easy with so many mad friends, and try not to take myself too seriously, which is not so easy. Another trap I fall into is when I get too busy and ask too much of myself. But my mad friends—and silence—help me a lot at these times.

Tina Coldham:

When I first became unwell my whole world wasn't just shaken up, it was turned upside down, inside out, and thus changed forever. I have found ever since that I am always working on mental wellness, and adjusting my life to that aim. It is not a science. There is no science to remaining mentally well as opposed to the supposed science of being mentally ill. It is an art form.

Life is an ever continuing balancing act of activity, sleep, occupation, relaxation, sustenance and relationships. The vital part is to get the right amount of all these, at the right time, weighing up my needs against the demands of modern day living—a tricky business.

I came to this conclusion after some years of struggling to be what I was, do what I did before. It is pointless. That part of me is gone. The post-breakdown me is wiser and kinder to myself. However, daily living is always about compromising, and about considering my needs as paramount. I have to be aware that the amount of effort it takes to complete a task might just take the last of my reserves, and that takes me over the edge into depression and anxiety.

This is so despite the antidepressants. After so many years being on these drugs, my mind can find depression if it needs to. The drugs don't stop this. Indeed, after several failed attempts to be rid of them, I have come to realize I am addicted to them. And now, medical science is coming around to that idea too. I exist despite these chemicals washing around my system. In fact, because of this so-called medication, I am a depressive. If there are detoxification units for heroin addicts, why can't I book myself into a place that will unhook me from this chemical stronghold?

I measure my day carefully, and adjust my pace accordingly. I feel successful in living if I feel I have made a contribution during the week, while still having enough energy to enjoy small pleasures. Overall, I am making great strides forward. I did not envisage myself in the position I am in now, a few years ago. Realize your passions, channel your energy, and move forward gradually.

I need a good eight to nine hours sleep a night. I can function without that much, but I am not at my best. If I get into sleep deficit, I will need to catch up at a given opportunity. Sometimes after a busy week working, weekends are lost to sleep. I often have an afternoon nap if the mood takes me when I am at home. Sleep is also an escape from my depression and life's pressures.

I try to eat three healthy meals a day, which includes fruit snacks in-between. My lifestyle doesn't always accommodate this but I feel physically and mentally better for trying. And I don't beat myself up if I lapse, or go for a chocolate bar. The guilt is more destructive than the possible sugar rush.

I drink plenty of fluids; any tea and coffee decaffeinated to avoid triggering anxiety. I always have water with me for times when I'm thirsty and can't get a drink. I realize alcohol is an escape, a helpful relaxant, but overindulgence is a sign of pent up stress—so everything in moderation.

I need to make time to relax. Whether it is walking in the countryside, listening to music I love, or stroking the cat whilst admiring the flowers in the garden. I enjoy eating a meal out with my husband, and taking time to check in with him how his day or week has gone, maybe get some feedback on how he thinks I'm doing if I need it.

He often thinks I do too much. We have grown together in a partnership and made adjustments to both our lives to put our health and happiness foremost in our minds. He needs to do what he does, and we mix and match with my need to be busy and stimulated. I am always doing something to change the wider mental health establishment to be more user/survivor friendly. This is my main passion. The exercise of this often contradicts my personal mental health needs. This is the dichotomy. The unspoken understanding and emotional support from other users and survivors is invaluable. I draw strength from them as indeed I hope they do from me.

So I forge onwards. Living and learning, challenging and being prepared to be challenged. I cut my cloth to fit, so to speak. Perhaps the employment of an elastic waistband is more appropriate!

Constance Dollwet:

When I was 22, my life had hit rock bottom. I was stuck in a hole and didn't have the courage to climb out. At that point my soul pulled the emergency brake: I developed a persecution complex, panicked and went totally crazy. The results: confinement on a closed ward with the diagnosis "schizophrenia." Afterwards I was extremely fortunate to find a community of people in Wederath/Hunsrück in Western Germany who had experience with psychosis and who enabled me to work out my mental problems in a protected space—without any doctors or psychiatric drugs.

When I look back today after 20 years at the route I took, I can see very clearly what helped prevent me from going crazy again. The basic prerequisite for me was the fact that I was accepted by the members of the community with all my quirks, weaknesses and fears without any questions asked. In the acute phase after coming off Haldol, a method known as body-oriented intuitive trance experience helped me a great deal. This self-help method I learned in Wederath and might have been tailored-made for me. I had already begun to realize when I was young that bad experiences I could no longer recall had cast a shadow over my life. I assumed that I could dissolve this shadow on my own by discovering what these bad experiences were, and then bringing them to the surface and experiencing the associated emotions once again. The method I had learned allowed me to do just that. Thus, alongside my normal daily routine I was able, at my own pace and under my own direction, to gradually recall my emotional injuries, such as sexual abuse, in specific "primordial" scenes which had a strong effect on me. I was able to delve deeply into the associated emotions and, most importantly, I could express myself in appropriate ways: I cried, screamed, ranted, hit and kicked about. Such a turbulent process was of course only possible because my friends in the community afforded me with understanding and compassion and provided support, when necessary, around the clock.

In addition to the body-oriented intuitive trance experience, I also found it very helpful to learn to look over my shoulders and recognize the "patterns" I had used to weave my life. And, most importantly, I learned in the community to unravel the entangled patterns and thus to gain a reliable orientation. Another "tool" that helped me was intuitive self-therapeutic writing. In this way, I broke my silence and found words to express the unspeakable. Even today it is my chosen method when I need to quickly gain clarity, for instance about a difficult emotion. The foundation which reliably supported me through the long years was the structuring of daily life in our "living-learning-working community" which puts the human needs of the individual above all. In order to feel well, I have to take absolute care of what I need for myself: getting enough sleep, living according to my own rhythm, to be left in peace, physical activity, to be out of doors, a healthy diet, to keep myself warm, secure and snug like in a nest. I experience the joy of life when I can act like a child just as I feel like: to play, to mix everything up; to experiment, explore, discover; to be extremely cheeky, to shout, to stamp my foot; to be clingy and cuddle. And when the desires of my childish heart are fulfilled. Cheerfulness and laughter are part of me being a child. So I have found a way to express myself in cabaret which seems tailor-made for me. In particular, I experience great release in being able to laugh at myself.

As an adult I find it important to keep my attitude towards life in focus; to be able to look at myself from the necessary distance: to make sure that my self-assessment is accurate; that I am careful with myself and my fellow human beings and all living creatures; that I can distinguish between reality and illusion; that I recognize the motives for my actions and make the right decisions for myself. This is the only way to be sure that I can take responsibility for my life. What suits me is a simple everyday life in the countryside and a comfortable atmosphere with lots of "wiggle room." I love to do craftwork and to build things and I balance this out with writing. But most of all, everything is done according to my own timetable without any pressures of time or performance. What I absolutely must have is clear, unambiguous communication—honest, in other words, emotionally honest—with nothing suppressed and covered up. I have to be able to express difficult emotions directly whenever possible without being rejected for it. I have recognized that my emotional growth is furthered by me being there for my friends and housemates when they are going through crises and by supporting them in every way possible. Of special importance is taking the responsibility for my psychotically demented mother who I have been looking after for over seven years in our community. And finally, the personal contacts and exchanges with like-minded people during my work in self-help of (ex-)users and survivors of psychiatry.

Sources

Dorsky, N. (2005). *Devotional cinema.* Berkeley: Tuumba Press.

Hegerl, U., & Niescken, S. (2004). *Depressionen bewältigen – Die Lebensfreude wiederfinden.* Stuttgart: MVS Medizinverlage.

Konz, F. (1995). *Der große Gesundheits-Konz.* Revised edition. Munich: Universitas.

Laing, R. D. (1970). T*he divided self: An existential study in sanity and madness.* London: Random House.

Riemann, F. (1981). *Grundformen der Angst – Eine tiefenpsychologische Studie.* Munich / Basel: Ernst Reinhardt Verlag.

Woolf, V. (1926). The Cinema. *Arts* (June). Retrieved January 3, 2007, from www.film-philosophy.com/portal/writings/woolf.

Introduction, Bruckmann, Dollwet, Zingler:
Translated from the German by Mary Murphy
Beier, Hausotter, Lehmann, Solomun:
Translated from the German by Katy E. McNally

Regina Bellion

How We Discovered the Soteria Principle

I was not a human being. I was an illusion wandering through the centuries, invisible, immortal. I was the Fairy Margarine, infinitely lonely on this planet devoid of people. I had to do penance for guilt that was not mine—this was the only way to save the solar system from its ultimate destruction. My home was long gone. I ran through a stone desert with an icy wind blowing hard. I didn't feel the cold and there was neither night nor day.

Not being able to die depressed me. What use was it to me in my loneliness that I could recognize the invisible connections in the world and see the universal formula before my very eyes? It floated in green luminescent numbers above the telephone—the ultimate aim of science was apparent to me but I did not care.

I made telephone calls. I filled several answering machines. I wanted to know whether the few friends I had were still alive, whether they had so far been spared by the destruction of the world.

Shortly thereafter, everything changed. Someone made tea in my barren desert. I was put to bed, covered and told to stay there. I wasn't allowed to say another word. Later I would have time later to tell about the horrors of a world without people. Beings without bodies, mere spectres, forced me to drink and then to lie quietly again. Hands pressed rhythmically on my stomach until my breathing became regular. They wore the faces of my friends. The perfect disguise! These intruders were planning something evil. Only a sacrifice could appease them. Only my death could save the world from complete destruction. I had to hang myself—immediately. But I was not allowed to budge, they held me down. I thrashed about but they wrestled me to the ground. This desperate fight repeated itself, seemingly without end.

Later, a friend sat with me and told me that I had slept for an hour or so. It clearly pleased her. Still later I recognized a window, my window. I realized that it was daytime, and asked what day it was. The answer didn't mean anything to me. Much later, I discovered that I had spent the whole week in a psychotic state and that trusted friends had restrained me during the first few days so that I wouldn't go on a rampage and draw the attention of the neighbours. So the routine I knew so well was not set in motion: Neighbours, police, court, ambulance, psychiatry, neuroleptics, depression and all the difficulties associated with a stay in a psychiatric clinic. No officials had gotten wind of it—Thank God! Not so long ago, I had been threatened with the possibility of permanent hospitalization.

We were not a self-help group in the usual sense. We had met in a discotheque or through friends. It was not the idea of self-help that was important to us; but rather everything else we did together. We didn't even think of ourselves as a group. We cooked and ate together. We read to each other and cut our hair. Anyone with a stiff back would certainly get a massage. If someone played hooky from school they showed up early in the morning, climbed into my bed and we slept until lunchtime. We told each other about our desires, our dreams and our fears. We knew which of us might have a vision of a black panther in a moment of crisis or who would avoid their teacher because it felt as if thoughts were being transmitted into his head via eye contact. In the course of time, all seven of us had—at least to some extent—experienced hallucinations, depression or ideas of persecution. Five of us had experience with prescribed psychiatric drugs. Four of us had been committed to psychiatric institutions. This issue was not of particular importance to us. We were concerned with our everyday lives and the time we spent together. And for me it was important that I had friends—even though I had fallen through the net and was far away from official reality. With my schizophrenic tendencies, I had long been considered a candidate for permanent disability. Of course, there were also friends who had neither symptoms nor a diagnosis. But they soon understood that there can be a time when anyone may develop symptoms, for example hallucinations, and that these hallucinations are neither haphazard nor meaningless.

We all had bruises, not just me. My friends were exhausted, tired—and pleased because this time the crisis situation was brief, innocuous and handled discretely. They rejoiced at their success in doing something that no one had shown them and that they had improvised with trepidation. The ground under our feet was still very shaky. Each one of us needed some peace and quiet.

Afterwards, I kept away from the real world for a long time and avoided contacts. Finally, I started to wash up again and to approach some of the necessary chores in the house and garden. I was hungry, a good sign—I could feel my body. I felt a deep gratitude towards my friends and I was thankful to be alive.

This happened more than 10 years ago. Since then, none of us has been prescribed neuroleptics nor committed to a psychiatric hospital. At first we helped each other to prevent this from happening again. Now we take precautions—often in a way that outsiders cannot understand. We attend as best we can to our wellbeing, to make sure that things do not escalate to the point where reality disappears and we might find ourselves once again in the realm of psychosis.

We don't feel secure even though we have been doing this successfully for quite some time. But there is hope—for us and (this is the only reason I am writing this short report) for everyone who has to live with a diagnosis of "schizophreniform psychosis."

Maybe this story would have interested Loren Mosher if he had heard about it. Maybe it would have pleased him.

It didn't occur to us at the time that we could live through such a precarious situation again and that another one of us might turn into the patient. Our dangerous self-help enterprise had not been planned at all. We slipped into it because we didn't want to abandon each other in such precarious situations. One friend wanted to make sure that he could finish his training without too many gaps and conspicuous events. Another friend was trying to hold onto the custody of her child. For me, the prospect of permanent institutionalisation had been raised. It was all about our independence, our sphere of responsibility and our quality of life. These were the main reasons why we stuck together. It was also clear to us that everything had to be kept rather quietly.

In fact, we knew far too little about what we were in for. In the beginning, we didn't even know whether a psychosis could come to an end without psychiatric drugs. A few years later I heard about Soteria and asked myself just how similar their experiences were to ours. Learning of the existence of Soteria and similar initiatives where people like us are viewed favourably was extremely encouraging for us. I could hardly believe it.

Nobody is interested when a good discovery is repeated elsewhere in an amateurish fashion under catastrophic conditions. Nonetheless I would like to briefly describe the emergency service that we developed in the middle of nowhere, as our needs arose, and considering the fact that none of us had ever managed to ask for help in time:

The calls usually came after midnight, the caller spoke "schizophrenese" or could barely be understood. We went there right away, and if possible alerted others who might be available for later shifts.

The patient is usually restless and might do things that he would later regret. The greater the fear, the worse the aggression could become. To put in it plain language: damage to property and self-harm were the norm in our experience.

Of course, the patient wants to tell us what is happening from his perspective. In the previous hours or days, he has experienced important and strange things. For example he tells us about the machinations that are being planned against him and that he has finally come to understand their origins. Or he believes that he has to save the world. Or he has experienced something else that takes everyone's breath away. He could talk about such things for hours on end. We don't encourage him. Later, when the psychosis has passed he can talk about it as much as he wants. This is necessary so that everyone who has been involved can deal with what they have experienced later on. But for now, it is better that he not talk too much, calm is what he needs.

We answer his questions so that he can orient himself and at least have a dim awareness of reality. We tell him: you are experiencing a psychosis which will pass and I'll be staying here with you. We validate his experiences by saying things like: I trust that you are smelling poison, I just can't smell it myself.

The fear the patient is experiencing and everything that he does and says is always taken seriously. Subterfuges, lies or placations are completely unacceptable. Anyone who affirms the delusions of the sufferer out of their own insecurity is not a suitable helper. We found that out very quickly. When the delusions of the sufferer trigger the helper's own fears he must be quickly relieved and be given time to look after himself. This, too, was clearly brought home to us.

A suitable helper is someone whose presence is not generally felt to be disquieting, who is in good form at the time and can stay calm for a long time.

The most important task of the helper is to provide a pleasantly calm atmosphere, confidence and self-assuredness, while kindly standing by.

It is important that the sufferer begins to breath calmly and that he lies down. A psychosis, even if it lasts for eight or 10 days can pass while resting comfortably as long as there is always someone close by on whom the patient can rely in his instable situation.

The attendant helper is by no means simply a witness to unbounded madness. One can find out whether and when the sufferer experiences brief moments when he is in touch with reality. These are the moments when he hears and understands what we say to him quietly and soothingly. These are the very moments when the behaviour of the patient can be influenced. This is the point when he can be asked to lie down and breath calmly. Panic only begins to abate when breathing becomes regular.

These brief moments, when the surrounding reality is recognized, are islands of reality in a sea of psychosis. One can rely on these islands and make use of them. We experienced this every time with astonishment and gratitude. No matter how bad the psychosis is—the next island of reality will come. It is up to the helper how best to use these islands. The better and safer the sufferer feels on these islands of reality, the bigger they grow and the more numerous they become. Even someone who has rampaged for days and nights without sleep, someone who has demolished the apartment and has thrown dangerous objects, experiences islands of reality in between. It is good if he helped to become aware of these islands and set foot on them. Once he has landed there, the sufferer will attempt to get oriented and ask a question or recognize the person he is facing.

Even someone who speaks "schizophrenese" has islands of reality and moments of lucidity. This explains why it only takes a few moments until an acutely psychotic friend will let himself be held by someone and be helped to lie down.

In a psychotic state, I need quiet more than anything else, a reliable friendly environment and the security in the belief that my friends will keep our agreements, even if I recognize them only for brief moments. They appear to me as if they were emissaries from my mad world and are therefore planning terrible things against me. I have to defend myself against them. Bruises are the norm for everyone involved.

The constant switching between phases of unrest, which the patient creates, and phases of calm, created by the helpers, can last for days and nights. The attempt to bring about sleep with sleeping tablets is pointless. A psychosis that has reached the acute phase appears to have a dynamic of its own— like a night-time dream which can be influenced by outside factors but has to run its course. As long as the psychotic movie is running at full speed, a restorative deep sleep is out of the question. But someone who goes through the acute psychotic phase resting comfortably will have stretches of light dozing that give him some relief, if not actual sleep. Someone who understands that sleep becomes more or less normal after about a week at most will not be so unsettled by this issue. When the psychosis fades, sleep is light and disrupted. The psychosis is over when dreams return during sleep, at least according to our experience.

When the sufferer gets to a point where he/she experiences reality for more than just a few moments at a time, these windows should be used—even if he hasn't slept properly for days. Now is a good time to peel potatoes, sweep the kitchen floor etc. These kind of activities help re-establish a solid link to reality We have found this to be a very positive experience. I was able to get benefit from collecting firewood and digging up the garden.

Anyone who ever attends to a friend in a psychotic state is likely to experience rather frightening situations. This fear is all too justified. But once you have been through this a few times, a certain degree of composure is reached.

The fear that the helper experiences is eventually soothed by the patient. This feels like a gift every time. The patient suddenly wants to know what day of the week it is. Or he recognizes you and says: it is a good thing that you are here. Or he asks: how long did it take you back then? He is actually trying to find his way in the real world for a while.

When the psychotic movies gradually subside, when several hours pass without any significant hallucinations, when the patient can sleep for several hours at a time, then he finally notices what his friends are doing for him. He realizes that they need time for themselves and their own affairs. Intensive care is usually no longer necessary. But it takes weeks for the experience to shed its weight. When a psychosis abates—having experienced it without the damper of neuroleptics—I finally feel my own body. It is as if I return to myself after an extremely difficult and dangerous journey. I tire myself by working so I can sleep through the night; and this even becomes fun.

At this point, it is better that no demands are put on me and I am left in peace. Initially, I avoid the official world. I am better off in the garden and with the pets. The necessary day to day work moves very slowly. I need a lot of time for myself. During this phase I am quite happy—I feel my way back into the world and rejoice over being alive. A psychosis, experienced without hospitalization or neuroleptics has a completely different quality. I am sure that Loren Mosher was aware of this.

If I don't push away my psychotic experiences with psychiatric drugs then I am left with important material to help me rethink and reorder my life. I must deal with the images, scenes and films that I have experienced. I have to use them. They give me the key to the necessary changes in my life.

Back then, none of us believed that there was a place where patients with delusions, even if they became violent, could be treated with understanding and kindness. We didn't know that something like this was already being practiced in a few places by recognized specialists.

When I finally heard about Soteria, it became clear to me that Loren Mosher worked with his team according to principles similar to the ones that we naïve lay people had been using. Therefore, our way of helping each other could not have been too misguided. I hope that this effective type of treatment can succeed; I hope that Soteria succeeds widely.

Finally, I would like to emphasize one thing that we learned from the experiences into which we so naively stumbled: "It doesn't always have to result in full blown psychosis. If the beginning of psychosis is recognized early enough, it can be avoided." I was told this non-chalantly by an acquaintance whose patient career had begun in adolescent psychiatry. This was worth gold to us.

We try to recognize a psychosis early on, as soon as it appears as a speck on the horizon. We can have an impact against such a little speck, each in our own way. We have to be vigilant and pay attention to ourselves. In fact, we have to be constantly on the alert. During good periods it may be enough to take one critical look at myself per day. I have a whole catalogue of precautionary measures and I have to stick to them. Up to now we have been lucky. Since 1993 none of us has been hospitalised, there have been no suicide attempts, and none of us has been prescribed neuroleptics. Of course, we all sometimes hear voices or see something that really can't be there. We take that as a sign that things are getting to be too much and that we have to take better care of ourselves. And we are getting better at it all the time.

Loren Mosher would definitely pleased.

Translated from the German by Mary Murphy

Bhargavi Davar

Depression and the Use of Natural Healing Methods

Is depression a disease? This is a question that finds expression in general in the clinical literature. When I suffered severely disabling depression after the loss of a child under traumatic circumstances in 1996, there was talk about my "disease" status—recurring patterns of highly disabling thoughts, moods and behaviours, chronic relationship problems, etc. I was told about my "illness" by a psychologist, who however, did not tell me how this all affected my body, my spirit and my general world experiences.

I never believed in psychiatric cures, and carry a strong identity as a psychiatric survivor (That is another story). So I chose my own intuitive pathways of recovery, helped along the way by many, many useful sources of information and support systems on non-drug healing. I joined a rigorous physical exercise program. For several months, this was the only useful activity I could get myself to do every day, the depression was so disabling. The rest of the time was spent in the all consuming universe of NOTHINGNESS— sleeping, eating, destroying things in the house, and weeping, in addition to experiencing relentless, recurring thoughts of dying, nightmares and horrendous flashbacks. I experienced boundless anger against myself, others and the world. Luckily, I lived alone at the time, and the clinician was a friend, else, I would have been surely institutionalized as a person violent to self or others.

Two years passed by in this way, with slow internal changes. I accomplished little in the outside world, learnt a lot about myself, and about life and death. It took four years to kick "the depression" fully, without psychiatric drugs, much of it through developing body awareness and fitness. Other things which helped were extensive travel and new environments and friendships, compulsive readings on philosophy and psychology, introspection, dogged scheduling of every single day—often parts of a day—and political activity (being a part of the women's movement in India).

I cherish the learnings of these years, and am grateful to myself, for giving myself the chance to see what my mind / body / consciousness systems can do on its own, without the help of psychiatric drugs. Perhaps they would have reduced my suffering, perhaps even quickly, but it would not have brought *insight,* even less, spiritual growth. Insight is a longitudinal process, it has to be allowed to play out in time. There are no short cuts. Life has been good since, enriched by the insights of those four deafeningly sorrowful years, and the strengths accumulated later through food hygiene, meditation and other spiritual practices, study on the workings of the human mind, healing friendships, satisfying work, gardening (including growing vegetables), addressing a thyroid problem naturally, and rigorous physical workouts.

After many years of struggling with "the depression," and having been self-cured, I think of depression as multiply interacting states of mind, body and spirit trying to survive difficult existential circumstances. It is a manifestation of mind, body and spirit disharmony. I see the experience of depression as the first call towards bodily, mental and spiritual awareness, insight, recovery and rejuvenation. The experience of depression poses existential questions, including questions about life and / after death. The experience forces one to imagine oneself dead, and to deal, in mindfulness, with profound visual sensory experiences of dying. An acute awareness about time, temporality and momentariness develops, bringing much spiritual relief and relaxation. When I refer to bodily aspects, as described below, I include medical problems such as thyroidism as well as problems caused by our modern

life: pollution, environmental and food toxins, and allergies (see e.g., Daun-
derer, 2005). These aspects too are not covered in psychiatry very well. I,
therefore, do not think of depression as a disease and find the DSM *(Diagnostic and Statistical Manual of Mental Disorders)* highly unsuitable to describe that experience. Depression does involve internal *pain*, but a pain that
one is called to overcome. In the experience of depression, a self that is waiting to be reborn, is buried. (I believe in the right to choose death. Therefore,
this claim to rebirth must be treated as inclusive of this right, to allow destiny
to free one from what one is.)

I am not giving this out as a prescription! I understand and empathise with
others who see depression as a disease, and willingly choose psychiatric
drugs. For myself, I chose otherwise ... with happy results.

I present my understanding of depression, drawing from sources that I have
studied, and my intuitive knowledge. Multiple systems stress of mind, body
and spirit is manifested as major depression.

Psychiatry says that depression is a medical condition (a brain disorder)
and must be treated with antidepressants. But the picture is more complex.
The medical basis of depression is broader than just the psychiatric. If this
broad base is addressed, then perhaps, there is no need for psychiatry. There
is much evidence for an integrated medical picture about depression (see
www.alternativementalhealth.com and links herein). General health status
feeds into depression and *vice versa*. Health knowledge still needs to fill in
many gaps about the relationships between these systems, and an integrated
health discipline is yet to evolve. But mind and body medicine offers a number of useful insights (Moss, *et al.*, 2003; Shevrin, *et al.*, 1996). An integrated
explanation of depression, and well being, and an offering of a range of
choices, will be appreciated by users who seek help for depression.

It is well known now that structured "talk therapies" (evidence base reviewed in Davar & Wayal, 2004), particularly cognitive behavioural therapies, help vastly to deal with some aspects of depression. Traditional therapies address issues of relationships, the social world, and other psychological
aspects (thoughts, feelings and behaviours).

Talk therapies may work with some people, or in some cultures. The need
to express oneself, one's emotions and thoughts by talking is not a universal

phenomenon. Talk therapies will help those people who express themselves mainly by talking. Not everyone is comfortable talking. Healing systems must create choices for them also. In talking, only a small part of the brain is utilized, which brings up materials in our conscious mind. There are serious limits to talking, set by one's own unconscious, and the background of hidden traumas, deep seated in the primitive brain. Further, talking is not the only form of self expression for human beings. Our animal state allows us the freedom to experience and express ourselves through multiple senses and many inner faculties (poignantly referred to as the heart, the gut, etc.). Descartes fooled us into thinking that we are made up of only reason, language, thoughts and logic. He pushed the intuitive and the imaginative into the animal world. He wanted us to believe that we are above beasts, and above the realm of nature. Consciousness is however a larger vessel (Winkelman, 2000), and we are in good part, animals. We should not be deceived by Descartes' romantic philosophy of man.

Depression is commonly referred to as a "mood" disorder. In talk therapies, it is believed that mood is always accompanied by a thought, and if the thought is changed, the affect will automatically change. Here again, you see Descartes' romantic view of the ideal person, someone who is in control of their own thoughts and who can change their thoughts at will.

I want to approach depression from the other side, i.e., from the animal side. Let us for a moment forget that we are thinking beings. Or let it be so, that our thoughts are not in our control, or that they happen perchance. I want to propose that a "thought" or a "mood" always has some body effects. If those body effects are worked on, then the thought and the mood also changes. The implication of this is that, healing from depression importantly involves work on the body through body treatments.

When we talk about bodily dimensions, two points can be made. There is a physical side to "the depression" as well as the *embodied* side. The physical side refers to the biological / physiological / medical states. The *embodied* side refers to how the body is experienced by the person manifesting depression. There may be thoughts, affects and behaviours, conscious or otherwise, attached to one's image of and experience of the body. These topics must be addressed independently of the psychological dimensions in any healing intervention for depression. The evolution of mind-body therapies is an important recent development in the integrated sciences of well being (McGrady, 2003).

In pre-modern cultures, like India, Pakistan and Sri Lanka, for example, stress and depression are expressed primarily through the sensory and the extra-sensory body. The autonomic nervous system takes over, expressed as what has been described as bodily stress (Wickramasekara, 2003). A common form of expressing multiple systems stress is "pain," amorphous, ever present, wholesome, *pain*. Culturally accepted forms of body psychotherapies usually exist. In 90% of a worldwide sample of 488 societies studied, bodily catharsis of distress is commonly found, through trance and spirit (Chandrashekar, 1989). Traditional healing is a parallel health / mental health system for example spread all over India, where people approach to get rid of all kinds of mental, bodily and emotional distress.

Interventions for healing from depression must cover both these topics about the body: medical states as well as embodiment. It must focus on the body's medical conditions, its vegetative responses, body experience of stress, mindfulness about the body, and taking recovery measures through working primarily on the body. The integrated intervention for depression would extensively cover medical and metabolic history. Further it would address the autonomic nervous system responses through a range of body techniques such as relaxation, biofeedback, guided imagery, mindfulness training, breathing rhythms, trance, meditations, tai chi or yoga. These healing techniques build our sense of being centred in our bodies, heighten body awareness and build the necessary motivation for overall body discipline and having a satisfying human embodied experience. They tone up the cardiovascular system, regulate breathing, sleep, appetite, desire and other vegetative body responses, which are also at the core of a manifestation of depression.

Zindel Segal and colleagues have developed a promising model (mindfulness-based meditations) for healing from depression which mixes the traditional cognitive therapy with body therapy, to address the "deep soul needs of individuals" (Segal, *et al.*, 2002, p. IV). They describe a systematic study of this integration and report findings which—because of fewer relapses, promoting insight, lack of side-effects—are highly promising, including the fact that this approach builds better resilience than traditional interventions for depression.

Also, physiological / biological compromises form a large part of the explanation of depression. Prolonged environmental stress brings about hormonal crises. The central role played by the neuro-endocrine system in regulating mood is welcome news for a person manifesting depression. Ridha Arem, writing on the "thyroid solution" for depression, refers to the thyroid hormone as a "bonafide antidepressant." He notes the extensive overlap between depression and thyroid conditions. The psychopharmacologist Robert Hedaya also notes that 80% of his psychiatric patients had an adrenal dysfunction, and 30% had thyroid problems. Taking antidepressants can worsen the problem. Hedaya writes that "Hormones are the major links with mind-bodies connection" (2000, p. 174). Arem writes,

> … dealing with stress, maintaining a healthy and stable mood, and coping with life depend to a great extent on whether the thyroid functions properly and on whether the right amount of thyroid hormone is properly delivered and dispersed in the brain (2000, p. 4).

The role of food in mood swirls and swings has been written about. The glycemic index of a food (GI) has been measured, and we know that the higher the GI, the bigger the "sugar kick" in the body, leading to swift mood elevation and crash. Most of us are not mindful of subtle insulin / sugar related changes in their minds and bodies. However, these sugar surges, considered normal by most of us, and ignored, can be extremely uncomfortable to someone manifesting depression. For this reason we choose food which will not give us that mood kick, i.e., complex carbohydrates equalled by proteins, and avoid food which do, i.e. alcohol, caffeine, other psychoactive substances. Andrew Stoll (2002) wrote extensively on the benefits of Omega 3 in clearing up depressive symptoms. Omega 3 / Omega 6 imbalance can manifest in depression. Various nutritional deficiencies, common in India and in other low income countries, are also implicated in the manifestation of depression, notably vitamin B_{12}, folic acid and deficiency of zinc, and other micronutrients (see e.g., Randolph & Moss, 1980; Holford, 2004).

Some people argue that the neuro-chemicals found in the brain, are part of the whole body chemistry; and that it is better to supply the whole body with the essential nutrients, and help the body built its own neuro-chemicals, rath-

APPOINTMENT

MASSACHUSETTS GENERAL HOSPITAL
AMBULATORY CARE DIVISION

DATE	REQ. AREA

PATIENT IDENTIFICATION AREA

TO SEE FALK

OFFICE NAME

TELEPHONE #

REFERRED BY

TIME 3:30 AM/**PM**

DAY Tues

DATE 9 25 08
MONTH DAY YEAR

LOCATION

BLDG   **FLOOR / ROOM #**

PATIENT'S COPY

PATIENT APPOINTMENT

MASSACHUSETTS GENERAL HOSPITAL
AMBULATORY CARE DIVISION

INSTRUCTIONS FOR VISIT

1. TO CANCEL / CHANGE/CONFIRM APPOINTMENT: Call the telephone number on the front side of this slip. Call 24 hours in advance, if possible.

2. Blue MGH ID CARDS: You need a blue MGH card to get MGH Ambulatory Care. IF:

YOU DO NOT HAVE A BLUE MGH CARD

OR

YOUR INSURANCE IS DIFFERENT THAN YOUR BLUE CARD SAYS
GO TO A PATIENT REGISTRATION OFFICE IN THE WANG AMBULATORY CARE CENTER, THE COX BUILDING, OR YOUR HEALTH CENTER.

Allow one-half hour to get a card at these locations.
If only your Name or Address has changed, OR if the information on your card is correct but the date in the upper right hand corner has expired, the secretary who checks you in can make the changes and have a new card made for you.

3. HMO INFORMATION: If you are insured by a HMO, please call your primary care M.D. for a referral. Make sure the referral is sent in before your appointment or brought with you on the day of your appointment. If the visit is not authorized by your insurance plan, you will be responsible for payment.

4. FOLLOW-UP LOCATIONS:

✓	DESCRIPTION	BLDG.	FLOOR/ROOM
	BLOOD & URINE SPECIMENS		
	X-RAY (RADIOLOGY)		
	ECG (ELECTROCARDIOGRAM)		
	PATIENT REGISTRATION		
	PATIENT FINANCIAL SERVICES		
	OTHER		
	OTHER		

er than provide synthetic forms of neuro-chemicals. For example, only 5% of serotonin is found in the brain, and the rest is found in the vital organs of the body in different stages of production. Therefore, it is important to supply the whole body with the necessary building blocks, rather than supply the brain with the end products. Nutritional, particularly amino acid supplementation has been extensively used with success in the treatment of depression, due to the power of this argument.

In 2000, Hedaya referred to the US Surgeon General's Report on Physical Activity and Health of 1996 and concluded that "… physical activity may protect against the development of depression—inactive people have twice the risk of developing depression as active people" (p. 99).

Physical exercise results in the release of endorphins, a "feel good" hormone (Zehentbauer, 2001). Other benefits include making the metabolic and the cardio vascular system more efficient. Psychological benefits of being fit also need to be stressed (see the chapter by Bartmann in this book). Hedaya reviews literature which shows that physical exercise is as effective as psychotherapy in the treatment of depression.

How to integrate the needs of the "spirit" into this model of "treatment for depression" is yet to be thought about in more coherent terms. The faith-healing systems of care in India, found in every nook and corner, have useful insights and practices to offer, including ritual practices, possession, trancing, devotion and prayer. These practices have to be understood from the point of view of mental, bodily and spiritual discipline and creative transformation. Further study on this subject is required. However, for those who live out their existential / spiritual journeys, such study is merely academic, and does not touch life or nourish soul.

Sources

Arem, R. (2000). *The thyroid solution: A mind-body program for beating depression and regaining your emotional and physical health.* New York: Ballantine Books.

Chandrashekar, C. R. (1989). Possession syndrome in India. In C. A. Ward (Ed.), *Altered states of consciousness and mental health: A cross-cultural perspective* (pp. 79-95). Thousand Oaks: Sage Publications.

Davar, B. V., & Wayal, S. (2004). *Mental health, pregnancy and child birth: Evidence.* Pune: Bapu Trust.

Hedaya, R. J. (2000). *Antidepressant survival guide.* New York: Three Rivers Press.

Holford, P. (2004). *Optimum nutrition for the mind: Learn how to boost your IQ, improve your mood and emotional stability, sharpen your memory, and keep your mind young.* North Bergen, N. J.: Basic Health Publications.

McGrady, A. (2003). Psychophysiological foundations of the mind-body therapies. In D. Moss, A. McGrady, T. C. Davies, & I. Wickramasekara, *Handbook of mind body medicine for primary care* (pp. 43-55). Thousand Oaks: Sage Publications.

Moss, D., McGrady, A., Davies, T. C., & Wickramasekara, I. (2003). *Handbook of mind body medicine for primary care.* Thousand Oaks: Sage Publications.

Randolph, T., & Moss, R. (1980). *An alternative approach to allergies.* New York: Harper & Row Publishers.

Segal, Z. V., Williams, J., Mark G., & Teasdale, J. D. (2002). *Mindfulness based cognitive therapy for depression.* New York: Guilford Press.

Shevrin, H., Bond, J. A., Brakel, L. A. W. & Hertel, R. K. (1996). *Conscious and unconscious processes: Psychodynamic, cognitive, and neurophysiological convergences.* New York: Guilford Press.

Stoll, A. L. (2002). *Omega 3 connection: The groundbreaking antidepression diet and brain program.* New York: Free Press.

Wickramasekara, I. (2003). The high risk model of threat perception and the Trojan Horse role induction: Somatisation and psycho-physiological disease. In D. Moss, A. McGrady, T. C. Davies, & I. Wickramasekara, *Handbook of mind body medicine for primary care* (pp. 19-42). Thousand Oaks: Sage Publications.

Winkelman, M. (2000). *Shamanism: The neural ecology of consciousness and healing.* Westport: Bergin & Garvey.

Zehentbauer, J. (2001). *Körpereigene Drogen – Die ungenutzten Fähigkeiten unseres Gehirns.* 5. edition. Düsseldorf: Patmos Verlag.

Ulrich Bartmann

Running from the Crisis

Solving a crisis by jogging or walking? The first reaction to the idea that this is a serious option for addressing a problem is amazement. It is common to achieve physical fitness or to fight sickness caused by lack of exercise, like high blood pressure, high cholesterol and other similar maladies through slow endurance runs. Still not well known enough, though, is that exercise, and in this case slow endurance runs, commonly known as jogging—has extensive positive effects on the mind. This in spite of the fact that the therapeutic effectiveness of jogging has been well documented over time even compared to conventional medical treatments (cf. Bartmann, 2005; Sachs & Buffone, 1984). With this contribution, I would like to highlight some of these therapeutic possibilities as well as provide important suggestions for those that perhaps would like to undertake jogging as a form of self-help.

As a psychotherapist in a psychiatric hospital, I implemented jogging as a widely accessible form of therapy. Many of my colleagues laughed at this, others dismissed it completely. Only the patients themselves were enthusiastic whenever they managed to become actively involved in their own recovery (Bartmann, 1995).

At a time when new "therapeutic" modalities are constantly emerging, a critical viewpoint is necessary—Eichmann & Mayer listed over 2900 alleged or real psychotherapeutic treatments in 1985. In 1989, I proposed criteria that an intervention must fulfill in order to be claimed as a form of therapy. These criteria are listed in the following survey:

Criteria a therapy must fulfill:

1. One or more defined clinical entities to be treated
2. A specific application plan
3. Empirical evidence for the effectiveness of the treatment, whether it is alone or combined with other treatment
4. A scientific theory about the mechanism of action of the treatment
5. Criteria for qualification of therapists
6. The ability of the patients to help themselves over time
7. The specification of contraindications
8. The management of unwanted adverse effects

As an therapeutic intervention, jogging fulfills all of these conditions. We were able to demonstrate the effectiveness of running and walking in the area of depression (Reule & Bartmann, 2002) by reviewing 35 scientific studies. The studies show that jogging leads to a decidedly reduced depression.

Perhaps the personal accounts of individuals with psychiatric experiences would be even more convincing for the critical reader. The following was written to me by a woman in this regard:

> ...concerning me—years ago, out of long suffering with cyclothymia—I prescribed jogging for myself...I was familiar with the enormous urge to be active from my manic phases for which I was hospitalized and I would have considered myself lucky to jog regularly for at least one hour per day, instead of only being flooded with medications to no end.

And Lindner (2004) offers an impressive account of the way jogging helped him in overcoming his episodic manic and depressive crises, even when a lack of drive during depressive phases made running more difficult. He describes this as having "to practically beat myself out of bed every morning" and continues: "I told myself that it only depended on the next small step" (p. 149).

In the scientific literature on running, there is an abundance of empirical, well-confirmed evidence for the therapeutic effects of jogging concerning depression, psychosomatic complaints, fears and similar problems. There is still a lack of systematic studies regarding perceptual, cognitive and relational problems that are common in acute psychiatric services. Patients participating in my running groups with these type of disturbances were only individual cases. But they made it very clear to me that the well-documented therapeutic effects among other patient groups applied similarly to them.

Langwieser (2002) did a systematic study with this patient population in a community psychiatric service (SpDi) but their positive results only refer to eight clients. Nevertheless, a clear reduction of paranoid thinking through running was demonstrated. The most positive perceived effects by the participants of this group was an improvement of communication. This is also a very encouraging finding because it means that running could work against the social withdrawal of many patients.

The therapeutic effect of jogging is explained in various ways, with the psychological mechanisms, in my opinion, being best established at present (cf. Bartmann, 2005). Jogging plays a central role in strengthening self-esteem. A person who experiences a psychological crisis, regardless which kind, comes away with a shaken sense of self. In many cases, a person's belief in their own accomplishments and problem solving abilities is compromised to such an extent during an acute crisis, that the person comes to feel rather helpless. Therefore the reconstruction and strengthening of self-worth must be the most important task for an effective therapy that aims at patient self-determination. The slow endurance run can help immensely in this regard.

A recent analysis of 36 scientific studies concerning the strengthening of self-esteem and self-confidence Boettcher (2006) showed a consistently high impact of of jogging. The studies reviewed reflect an extremely varied group of clients all of whom showed evidence of raised self-esteem through jogging.

Anybody who runs, especially a beginner, immediately senses an increasing physical ability. From run to run, one sees very concretely how stamina and physical ability are strengthened. From this, a justified pride and an increasingly strong self-confidence develop. This confidence does not remain restricted to the physical sense of self, however. The beginning joggers, who didn't believe it possible to run these distances, experience a change in their personalities way beyond an improved athletic self-image. The experience of having achieved something, which they initially didn't think was possible, translates into other life situations. Courage to tackle problems that seemed insurmountable before is also increased. "I would have never thought that I could do it, but I got through it anyway," stated one of my running course participants after he managed to run for 45 minutes straight.

This is the deciding factor for the non (yet) runners to build up their confidence and thereby establish a basis to regain their emotional equilibrium: *The readiness to become engaged in this activity! To be proactive for one's own recovery.* With this, I would like to motivate to be proactive.

I know from personal experience that it takes some courage to begin running. I am not a "born" runner. As a high school student, I couldn't manage a 1000-meter run. A lung doctor diagnosed me with a funnel chest, which made me out of breath even on a minor ascent. In winter, I was only allowed to go outdoors with a scarf over my mouth—no wonder that, until age 35, I believed that I couldn't run. Three months after my first attempt, however, I was able to run for an hour non-stop! I remember very well that after 14 days, I could run five minutes (!) for the first time—I believed I had conquered the world. (Surely at that time I had conquered a *new* world.) Today, jogging is part of my regular routine, even in winter, without a scarf over my mouth! I hope that this self-portrayal can help reduce the anxiety about beginning to run.

The most important rule for the beginner is as follows: *run slowly!* This crucial rule is all too often ignored. The beginner's tempo cannot be faster than an speedy walk. Take a stopwatch with you or an easily readable wrist watch and run *slowly* for two minutes, afterwards walk for three minutes. Repeat this on the first day six or seven times. That's enough—even if you can do more. The amount and tempo of running must be planned in such a way that a successful experience is effectively predetermined. Whoever wants to run away from his problems, must avoid excessive demands that are likely to result in failure. A warning example is the letter by a reader of my running book (Bartmann, 2005), who suffered from depression. He wrote:

> I made the mistake at the beginning of running too fast, in order to get rid of my depression "fast." After every run I felt knocked out and rather diminished, until your book fell into my hands. Now I run at my own pace and after every time I feel as fit as a fiddle.

Plan your runs realistically. It's enough when you run two or three times per week at first. It should not be less than twice but no more than three times. The body must adjust to the new strain; give it enough time.

Repeat the above mentioned running chunks during the first week. In the second week, shorten the walking phase from three to two minutes and repeat the change from running to walking eight times. In the third week, run three minutes and walk two. In the following weeks, increase your running time—according to your own personal (!) progress. My book includes a detailed training plan for up to one hour of uninterrupted running. To reprint this plan here would exceed the scope. Record your running times, so that you are always able to see your progress. This will motivate you to keep running. Already after about eight weeks, in my experience, you will feel that you are doing *better* (This doesn't mean, however, that your problems are simply gone.).

Jogging is so excellently suited for coping with psychological problems because:
- it is possible to adapt the demands to each individual's needs,
- the task can be done alone or with a partner, according to one's personal preference,
- you don't have to join a club or pay membership for a gym,
- besides the purchase of good running shoes (get the best advice) there are no other costs,
- you can run at a time that fits *your* schedule—even at night,
- you may ultimately run wherever you like,
- and moreover you hardly have to consider side effects.

Naturally one notices at the beginning one or two muscles which had never been noticed before. But muscle aches go away quickly. Before beginning the running program you should consult your physician. There are a few contraindications for running like, for example, pronounced joint deterioration. Also the possibility of interaction with any medication should be clarified with a doctor. Psychiatric drugs may impact the movement flow in such a way that running becomes only possible in a very constrained fashion and should be substituted by the kind of exercises mentioned below. But do not allow yourself to be sidetracked into a potentially fatal protective position. If necessary, seek the advice of a sports-doctor if you have the impression that your primary physician or psychiatrist holds a negative opinion of your jogging.

And what do you do when you really cannot jog? Engage in different physical exercises. There are multiple opportunities to be active. Ride a bike or speed-walk. Speed-walking can be very helpful for very obese people as a way to get going, since it is easy on the joints. Speed-walking implies a rapid pace with active arm movements. Recently, "Nordic Walking" has been enthusiastically propagated, with its goal of intensify the arm movements with the aid of walking sticks. It should not be forgotten, though, that Nordic walking was a marketing idea of the Finnish company, Exel, to heat up the sales of the cross-country ski poles (Klawitter, 2006). It was clearly a success. I would suggest, however, to most of the Nordic walkers that I encounter when running, that they walk without these sticks since they seem to be rather a hindrance than anything else.

Whatever activities you might undertake, you should always have in mind that your activity should result in an experience of success, independent from the judgement of others. When this is the case, you have a good chance of running away from a crisis.

Sources

Bartmann, U. (1989). *Lauftherapie bei Krankenpflegepersonal.* Heidelberg: Asanger.

Bartmann, U. (1995). Wenn Patienten Laufen gehen: Laufen mit Psychiatriepatienten. In R. Lutz, & N. Mark (Eds.), *Wie gesund sind Kranke?* (pp. 211-215). Göttingen: Verlag für Angewandte Psychologie.

Bartmann, U. (2005). *Laufen und Joggen für die Psyche.* 4., revised and extended edition. Tübingen: dgvt.

Boettcher, C. (2006). *Laufen und Selbstbewusstsein.* Master's thesis. University of Applied Sciences Würzburg-Schweinfurt, Studies in Social Work.

Eichmann, K., & Mayer, I. (1985). *Kursbuch Psychotherapie.* Munich: Weixler Verlag

Klawitter, N. (2006). Ein Volk geht am Stock. *Spiegel Special,* (4), 45.

Langwieser, S. (2002). *Joggen als Methode zur Gesundheitsförderung von Menschen mit psychischen Störungen.* Master's thesis. University of Applied Sciences Würzburg-Schweinfurt, Studies in Social Work.

Lindner, U. (2004). I ran for my life. How I healed my depression. In: P Lehmann (Ed.), *Coming off psychiatric drugs: Successful withdrawal from neuroleptics, antidepressants, lithium, carbamazepine and tranquilizers* (pp. 142-151). Berlin: Peter Lehmann Publishing.

Reule, B., & Bartmann, U. (2002). Joggen zur Behandlung von Depressionen. *Forum Sozialarbeit & Gesundheit* (2), 54-58.

Sachs, M. L., & Buffone, G. W. (Eds.) (1984). *Running as therapy.* Lincoln: University Nebraska Press.

Translated from the German by Katy E. McNally

Miriam Krücke

Advance Directives—A Step towards Self-help

How do advance directives such as the psychiatric will, power of attorney or care dispositions, influence self-determined choices in crisis situations? Do psychiatric advance directives provide an opportunity to use the experience gained from previous crises, to mobilize resources, estimate risks and to decide how to act autonomously and with self-determination?

While writing my master's thesis *Advance directives and self-determined coping strategies from the point of view of (ex-)users and survivors of psychiatry*, in 2006, I conducted 10 interviews with people who had prepared an advance directive to be applied should they ever find themselves in the hands of psychiatrists. I got in contact with the interviewees via the German Association of (ex-)Users and Survivors of Psychiatry and similar networks. The following article is based on their contributions. At the request of some of the interviewees, I have used pseudonyms.

Advance directives are documents in which you can put down your wishes regarding future eventualities in a legally meaningful manner. They are used to assert and sustain self-determination in situations where people are no longer able to express their will, or are deemed to be lacking capacity to express their free will, as happens frequently during psychiatric interventions. In this sense, an advance directive is a step towards self-authorization. "It is completely normal for me to say as a person: this is what I have decided should happen to me in case of a recurring crisis or illness in the widest possible sense" (Thomas).

Many (ex-)users and survivors of psychiatry have hardly had any influence on what happens to them throughout their lives. Psychiatric power leads to powerlessness and apathy which in turn makes it very difficult to deal with life crises.

> To counter the hospital treatment in some way, to find any means
> of gaining influence was extremely important to me, because all
> you ever hear is that you can't do it, you have no chance. And for
> me this just became part of it: to realize that it wasn't true. And I it
> was very positive for me to have an opportunity to clarify and un-
> derstand this whole area in a structured way (Marlene).

Standing up for themselves and demanding something helps (ex-)users and
survivors of psychiatry regain responsibility for organizing their lives.

The concept of a psychiatric advance directive turns victims into experts in
their own affairs, (ex-)users and survivors of psychiatry become emancipated clients. Doctors and nursing staff are forced to adapt their traditional
view of their roles to new types of partnerships or service relationships as is
the norm in other areas of life. "Self-determination also means being viewed
as individuals and subjects instead of objects defined by diagnoses" (Rosa).

Advance directives in the area of psychiatry deal mostly with coercive
treatment and other possible repressive eventualities of psychiatric practice.
Furthermore, the prevention of psychiatric force can also influence the experience and course of crises.

> The actual crisis in my life is not addressed directly by a power of
> attorney—except by the fact that it enables me to avoid additional
> trouble, psychiatric treatment, being robbed of my freedom and its
> physical and mental consequences, in other words, avoid extra
> problems. Or to put it the other way round, if psychiatry does some-
> thing with me, it leads to a crisis. So I deal with the crisis by myself
> or avoiding it with the aid of the power of attorney (Anne).

Especially when a crisis—whether experienced as joyous or sorrowful—is
seen as meaningful and connected to living your actual life, psychiatric methods must appear paradox.

> Coercive psychiatric treatment is in itself a traumatic event that
> only reinforces the madness even more. With me, crises have to do
> with threatening experiences. If my crises have to do with a perse-
> cution complex and fears of being poisoned then it is logical that le-
> gal protection from such threats itself reduces the likelihood of fur-
> ther crises (Carlos).

Only when that which one fears has been averted, it becomes possible to realize positive elements of help and support in cases of crisis.

> Legal safeguards are one thing, personal precautions another. A psychiatric will is not an instrument for the unlimited realization of certain positive interests, in other words, I can't say: when I am in a crisis I want wine and chocolate ice cream. I can't force the psychiatrist to do that for me; I can, in fact, only reject something. Instead, I look for the opportunities and the help that I need. These two things are dependent on each other (Carlos).

At the same time the advance directive offers the opportunity to deal concretely with potential crises and their contingencies. You confront the fact that it may not be the last time that such a crisis occurs.

Devoting time to an advance directive raises questions and has consequences. For some people, this means specifying a framework for psychiatric treatment context and defining it anew. For others, it means trying to manage potential crisis situations in a completely different way, marshalling the support of key people and organizing everything to avoid being committed to a psychiatric hospital. "Yes, of course I have tackled the problem of how to deal with new crises. The declaration of intentions means that I have put down on paper the arrangements for my own personal crisis intervention plan" (Thomas).

Advance directives stimulate a more differentiated approach to the course of the crisis, including early warning signs, habitual responses and appropriate alternatives. In the same manner, the recourse to professional services can be organized before the event.

The current development of an informed opinion results from a systematic review of past experiences.

> The idea was also to find out at what point the course had been set, to what extent I myself was involved, basically the point when I—and I can do this now looking back—could have already recognized what kind of conflict situations I was getting into. I have learned to see clearly how my crises have developed and how I can behave and which people can help me. My psychiatric will specifies what kind of support I want instead of psychiatric drugs. I certainly consider the possibility of a relapse ahead of time. I have

given a great deal of thought to the causes of my madness and to alternative means of dealing with it (Carlos).

An advance directive demands of its author accurate and honest soul searching. It is likely that the seriousness of preparing a legally relevant disposition
demands a critical estimate of a potential crisis. The question "what helps me
when I go crazy?" and the presentation of one's own intervention strategies
and positive reflections can open up a broad spectrum of unsuspected resources while promoting the integration of helpful experiences in a comprehensive crisis strategy. Working out your very own ideas of what help is also
a way of averting new crises.

> By now I have searched for alternatives and possibilities and I must
> say—even if I do suffer another massive crisis—I will not end up in
> a psychiatric hospital…Basically, I have a great deal of leeway to
> allow something to happen and to know that I can try it out (Mar-
> lene).

Many (ex-)users and survivors of psychiatry know what is helpful or less
than helpful, even harmful, in times of crisis. Choices can be made with respect to the type of treatment and the environment that would be desirable.
What types of treatment do psychiatrists use? What can one expect upon entering a psychiatric service? What can I refuse? What treatment is acceptable
and under what circumstances? These are the types of questions that people
are considering and hope to find sensible answers for.

Many people want to be consciously aware when they emerge from a phase
of altered perception. The world has to be realigned during this process. Any
special experiences and behaviour can be connected to one's biography and
become integrated into everyday life. Psychiatric drugs which suppress or alter consciousness in other ways are often seen as an obstacle here, because
they limit the meaningfulness and understanding of extraordinary events.

> I ran around this dump for four weeks, day and night. We had al-
> most reached our limits and I was only getting homeopathic drugs
> which was actually a highlight of the experience. The psychosis
> just went away at that point. I could feel how things changed; I was
> capable to see other things again, to feel. That was something very
> special. Afterwards, there was no depression, there was nothing at

all like that. I went back to work six weeks later without any loss of capacity (Marlene).

Naming a representative who would have to implement the advance directive in case of an emergency, calls for a sensitive view of friendships and an accurate assessment of the social milieu. Since assigning power of attorney means handing over decision-making powers over such fundamental issues as consent to dangerous medical procedures, or refusing such, arranging for involuntary commitment, or even handling assets, this become a very delicate matter. It requires a sophisticated assessment of any potential recipients of such trust, and the reassurance that the person would understand and respect your own views on the issues. Trust in friendships and acquaintances is tested to the limit. It can be very painful if it turns out to be insufficient.

> I noticed that I never spoke about it to my current friends. They don't know me in crises situations. I have asked myself in my mind whether they would really grasp what I had written down and respect what I reject. I wonder whether they would really carry it out according to my wishes or whether they would be more influenced by the doctors. Perhaps they would be shocked if I reacted differently than usual and appeared to them as very confused. Maybe they will be horrified and ask what can be done about it, because it is so upsetting and maybe in the end they will listen to the doctors. I have spoken to some of my friends and have noticed that they have in fact quite contrary opinions (Sonja).

On the other hand it can be a great gain to know who might support you and to what extent, and whether they might even be prepared to get involved during a crisis. Such a process can turn acquaintances into allies.

Talking about the experience of being mad is very important for many people while psychiatry is often experienced as "speechless." Every person of trust listed in the advance directive must be included in all considerations that the directive is based so that they are in a position to act according to the intentions of its author during a crisis. Such a dialogue can put seemingly confusing actions into an understandable context and thus strengthen the loyalty of the others. It can also reduce the danger that people who show little understanding react in an injurious way during existential crises. Being able to free oneself from isolation is often felt by (ex-)users and survivors of psychiatry to be an effective protection against further crises. Precautionary provisions can stimulate outreach to others, and result in perhaps more meaningful and open connections to other (ex)users and survivors.

> Yes, responsibility consists of pushing through the treatment plan which you have drawn up yourself. You notice when things are helpful, like taking a walk, swimming or some kind of physical work. It is a question of self-observation. You learn a lot about self-help when you talk to people (Paolo).

Maybe this is the place to record some indications and wishes about support during the crisis. The ways that such support fits in with the individual needs can be specified in the directive. This means that you need to have a fairly clear idea of how you respond to other people during a crisis, or how people respond to you and the kind of reaction you would want.

When giving someone the power of attorney for certain domains, the author of the directive can achieve a sense of the kind of things they might still be able to do on their own and where they might need help and what can be arranged without their involvement. "So things like: does my employer get a sick note, stuff that I had never thought about, or who will look after my pets and my home, what happens if I go into the hospital…" (Marlene)

How binding an advance directive is depends, among other things, on its clarity and accuracy. Differentiated descriptions of the situations to which the disposition relates are the prerequisites for its usability. Therefore, the author has to make clear decisions. How important are decisions for handling a crisis? The intention of an advance directive is to avoid the repeat of certain negative experiences and to go down a new route.

> The connection between feeling certain that I could get out of the madhouse and that I was able to tell myself that I can handle this, even by myself, was very interesting to me. In fact, I did manage to get it together pretty quickly. I had this basic sense that I did not want that (the madhouse), which was backed up by my power of attorney (Anne).

A crisis is the height of an extreme experience but it is also a turning point, time-limited and followed by something new. A crisis questions what has been previously lived, and challenges certain habits. By interfering with our previous attitude to life, crises give us a chance to break out of cognitive prisons. Whether a crisis is a danger or an opportunity depends first and foremost on the perspectives and actions of the person going through it.

> The madness, before I came to psychiatry, was always interesting, due to its strong emotions and interesting thoughts. On the other hand, there were also terrible and frightening things that went through my mind. But still, I was very much alive with my feelings about life and that was very positive. I see a crisis, a life crisis, as a situation in which someone rearranges their life, when their life has become complicated and difficult and a solution may not be apparent. And in the course of this some people go mad and end up in psychiatry. But you can also see it positively. There is a new beginning after every crisis. It just depends what you do with it (Anne).

In psychiatric clinics, people learn that there is something not right with their thoughts and feelings, that it isn't real or has nothing to do with who they really are. They learn to doubt what they have lived through, to call it "sick" or "crazy." By stipulating an alternative to psychiatric treatment in an advance directive and by recognizing that alternatives actually exist, they have already distanced themselves from this image of illness in the biological sense. "The advance directive confirms that my problem is indeed not a medical one" (Karina).

At the same time, an advance directive opens up several ways of dealing with the situation. If you are not dissociated from what you are going through, you can do something.

> Get away from the idea that you are the victim of a disease and learn to take control. I can influence the crisis and regulate it. Maybe not everything but much of it. Use that influence and mobilize it. You can influence not only the illness but also your health. You can encourage health but you can also encourage illness. You have to be a bit careful, that is part of taking responsibility for yourself (Paolo).

Advance directives are not an absolute guarantee for self determination. They can be misused and ignored. Their effectiveness requires confident action on the part of its author as well as the person with the power of attorney and other trusted persons. Tackling your own wishes and desires, however, often leads to a change in personal convictions and to the motivation to assert oneself.

You have to think about a crisis before the crisis how you want to have it. Then you have already a plan for the future when it is most needed. And I know, even if they do not want to stick to what is on the paper they will have to contend with my sharp tongue. Because somehow I always manage to accomplish exactly what is written in the paper (Paolo).

Translated from the German by Mary Murphy

B. Organized Self-help

Wilma Boevink

Survival, the Art of Living and Knowledge to Pass on

Recovery, Empowerment and Experiential Expertise of Persons with Severe Mental Health Problems[1]

Recovery and empowerment are important topics in the WHO Mental Health Declaration and Action Plan for Europe and in the EU Green Paper on Mental Health (Bowis, 2006; Boevink, 2006a; Nettle & Boevink, 2005). The growing number of published first person narratives on recovery and empowerment shows that recovery from severe distress is possible.

This contribution aims at clarifying how individual experiences of mental distress, recovery and empowerment can be built upon to develop experiential knowledge and how a solid scientific basis could be worked out for this experiential knowledge.

The article is a combination of 1) personal experience with surviving distress, 2) experiential knowledge on the art of living with a psychiatric disability and 3) scientific research to learn about the effectiveness of strategies of recovery and empowerment.

---

1 In memory of Geert van Rossum (d. September 14, 2006), who suffered too much and died too young.

Overwhelming Experiences

In one of my psychotic episodes, I did not go outside the house. There was too much movement and there were too many sounds in the world outside. My brain could not put them in an order of importance. It could not set priorities anymore. I just had to deal with everything at the same time. So I stayed at home. There I started seeing weird things. I saw structures in the world which linked all kinds of different events together into one logical scheme. I thought the music on the radio was about me. I saw bad signs everywhere. There were for instance a lot of birds in my garden. I thought they came to get my soul. I was guilty. For all their baby birds that had not made it, they came to get my soul. And I saw my best friend, who committed suicide a few years before, sitting on a cloud, waving at me and laughing, waiting for a chance to take me with her (Boevink, 2006b).

Like many other psychiatric complaints, a psychosis is far-reaching and overwhelming. They involve a severe distortion of meaning. They render the world unfamiliar, unrecognisable, a threat. Psychiatric suffering can turn life into a living hell. Just "being" can no longer be taken for granted. Nothing can be taken for granted. Once you know that life will become unbearable beyond a certain boundary, once you know that you have such a boundary, very little can be taken for granted again. A psychiatric disorder is also accompanied by a sense of estrangement. What you *have* is often closely allied with who you *are*. The manifestations of the disorder sometimes dominate your entire personality. The distinction between the individual and the disorder is soon lost, and it is very difficult to regain.

When Psychiatry Takes Over

One of the consequences of serious psychiatric suffering is that you will find yourself as a patient in residential psychiatric care. This too is an overwhelming experience for many of us, especially the first time. It is difficult to cope with being a patient in a psychiatric hospital. This is a place where traumas are likely to be experienced, and where even abuse may be undergone or witnessed. My stay in the institution damaged me in several ways, however unintentional that may have been. When I look back at how undignified it was to be a psychiatric patient, the self-respect for which I fought through the years feels shaky. When I remember the humiliation inherent in being a patient, I feel so angry that I am liable to forget my resolution that such a humiliation will never happen again to me.

No matter how you look at it, psychiatric institutions are reservoirs of human suffering. Other people's misery that you see there is added to your own. This, to me, is one of the contradictions of psychiatry: we herd together people who are suffering and then expect them to feel better. Even someone who is relatively stable will be affected by the hectic and ever-changing tensions of an admission ward. So how can a person suffering from psychosis, at such a place with all these tensions, ever return from his or her psychosis?

An admission to a hospital means that you exchange your familiar, trusted surroundings for the hospital life and routine. You can no longer call upon the person you were. Your main role in life becomes that of a patient. This role should not be underestimated: it demands certain skills, such as the ability to adapt. As a patient, you have to fall into the rhythm and routine of the large hospital organization. You have to comply with the rules. Unfortunately, the dividing line between adaptability and submission is not always clear. And it can easily become less so over time. Once the sense of resignation has taken hold, you have absolutely nothing to help you regain your former life. A situation develops which could well endure until the end of your days.

The longer you remain a psychiatric patient, the more likely you are to forget the rules of normal life. You forget that life itself has its ups and downs, and you forget that you used to be a person with both good traits and bad. As a patient, you learn to blame all the negative aspects on your disorder. During my career as a patient, I learned to attribute every setback and every little disappointment to my disorder. I now know that everyone has the occasional bad day when nothing seems to go right and the entire world seems to be conspiring against you. But for a long time, that sort of day would set off alarm bells ringing for me because I thought that it was the precursor of a relapse. I had forgotten about life's everyday irritations.

For a long time I did not dare to take matters into my own hands, to lead my own life. I relied on the professionals: they were the experts. Other people knew how I should lead my life. I did not. When you are a psychiatric patient, it is extremely difficult to retain your self-esteem, your own values and opinions. And it is nearly impossible to explore or develop them.

The "Warm and Welcoming" Society

We (ex-)users and survivors of psychiatry wrestle with our mental condition and with the unpleasant side-effects of our care system. We also have to contend with the social consequences of our mental problems. We face prejudice and ever-decreasing tolerance in the community. That affects us in our social contacts, in the neighbourhood, in education and in finding a house or a job. Regularly, there are rants in the media denouncing our attempts to participate in society. Negative images are presented, based not on any facts but on emotions and the "rights" of whoever can shout the loudest. Those images present us as unpredictable, homicidal maniacs for whom the only answer is restraint and permanent confinement. There is no consideration for the social injustices, such as abuse and violence, which turned us with our sensitivity into persons in emotional distress to begin with (Janssen, *et al.*, 2004). In many European countries, there is a political climate in which the burden of the economic recession is shifted onto those people with the least money and the poorest health. It is not only our own individual problems which we have to contend with. We must also learn how to deal with the causes and consequences of those problems.

Survival and the Art of Living

I was not yet 20 when my first psychosis emerged. Twenty years have since passed. That first psychosis was not the last. I am still not rid of it. Am I expected to wait another 20 years until cure descends upon me? Well, to be honest, I am not willing to do so. I have decided that I will not wait for the doctor to give me a pill that will cure me. I have decided that my mental condition and I are two separate entities. I am *not* my disorder, I am more than this: a human with many abilities and facets.

My life—and that of many other users and survivors of psychiatry—is all about learning to cope with that which cannot be changed. We have not yet experienced the miracle of cure. For many of us, waiting for it to come along is a complete waste of time. The psychiatric system is not able to help nearly as often as it likes us to believe. Waiting for this to happen keeps us submissive and passive. It is better to ask: What are the obstacles in my life, and how should I deal with them? The question to be answered is: What do you want to do with your life and what care and support do you need to make that possible? We are not psychiatric disorders with care needs: we are *people* with lives to be led, some aspects of which may require professional care or assistance. It is relatively unimportant who provides such assistance or where we get it from. The prime aim of psychosocial care should be to enable us to lead our lives in the manner we wish. Care is a means to an end, not an end in itself.

To maintain an existence with a psychiatric disability is difficult enough. To build a life around that condition demands courage, perseverance and creativity. People with a psychiatric disability are true life artists. We tell each other about this art of living in our stories, and in doing so we face the things that overwhelm us—whether we speak about illness, disorder, disability, nonconformism, demoralisation or madness (Boevink, 2005; Buck, 2005; Chamberlin, 1979; Coleman, 1999; Deegan, 1988; 1996; Hausotter, 2006; Kempker, 2000; Klafki, 2006; Mehr, 1990; Stöckle, 2005). Through our stories, we are able to see the difference between who we are and the problems we have. We learn to formulate for ourselves what care we need. We develop stories in which we recognize ourselves. We search for the right words to do justice to our experiences and in doing so we regain our own identity. Through our stories we say, "this is my life, that is who I really am and this is how other people can help me."

User/survivor Movement Knowledge

We help ourselves with our stories. We do a lot to help ourselves. We have a wealth of experience in doing so. We learn to see the true value of our experiences and to see them in a meaningful way. We try to learn from them what we have in common and what the differences are. We attempt to identify what will help us and what will stand in our way (Jacobson, 2001; Ridgway, 2002). We develop knowledge: experiential knowledge. We pass that knowledge on to others: to the next generation of care service users, to give them strength and hope; to professionals in mental health care, as for them to learn to hear our voices; to people outside mental health care altogether, so that our human face can be seen and they can recognize, that we belong to the society.[1]

We help ourselves in many ways. User initiated projects are gaining in popularity and in substance. In countless areas, we have initiated activities on the basis of our own "helmsmanship" (guiding spirit vision, leadership). The underlying motivation is the conviction that our experiences will lead to renewed insights regarding psychiatric disabilities and their symptoms (Boevink & Escher, 2001; Coleman, 1998; Lehmann, 2004). We are also confident that we can contribute to more supportive and human mental health services than those currently in place.

Self-help and initiatives of users and survivors of psychiatry are a response to the fact that our individuality, our experience and our knowledge are not yet adequately represented within mainstream mental health care services (see also the chapter about INTAR by Ahern, Stastny and Stevenson in this book). For us, the emphasis is increasingly being placed on self-determination, our own responsibility and personal efforts, rather than devoting our strength to railing against the power of others and their agendas.

The psychiatric survivors' movement has a lot to offer. Perhaps more than we have realized thus far. We initiate new and creative projects which strengthen our position and offer a different perspective of living with a psychiatric disorder. We develop training courses for professionals and for fellow users and survivors of psychiatry, and we start new self-help groups. We educate and train our fellow users and survivors of psychiatry who want to integrate their experiences in professional roles. Yet, hitherto, there has been no general overview of the various European user and survivor initiatives[2].

---

1   See also http://akmhcweb.org/recovery

2   See for the American Consumer Operated Services Program Multisite Research Initiative (COSP): www.cstprogram.org; see for Europe to some extent: www.enusp.org/groups.htm

There is no comprehensive account of the specific strategies we use, the experiences gained have yet to be collated and no solid scientific basis for our methods has been established.

Facilitating Recovery and Empowerment

To contribute to the development of knowledge in the area of initiatives of users and survivors of psychiatry, in the Netherlands, long-term mental health care users in cooperation with Trimbos-institute, developed the TREE programme (Boevink, *et al.*, 2003).[1]

This programme combines the strategies and methods of initiatives of users and survivors of psychiatry which are thought to account for their success. It aims at enabling people with psychiatric disabilities to support each other towards recovery, empowerment and experiential expertise, thus enhancing their abilities to manage their own lives and to counter their marginalisation in society. To this end, the programme enables its participants to exchange experiences and offer mutual support. It also encourages them to develop knowledge and to use such knowledge by making it available to others. Last but not least, the programme promotes user/survivor led change within mental health care organisations in the direction of recovery-based services.

People with psychiatric disabilities can take part as a member of a self-help group, as a student of one of the courses, a volunteer or as a paid experiential expert. The programme offers the opportunity to:

- communicate with others about experiences that are overwhelming
- create some distance from these experiences and reflect upon them (develop your own narrative)
- make a we-story out of several I-stories (experiential story)

---

1 Research on recovery and empowerment has been made possible financially by the National Foundation for Mental Health (NFGV), in Utrecht. The TREE effectiveness study has been made possible by the Netherlands organisation for Health Research and Development (ZONMw) and by SBWU, the Foundation for Sheltered Housing accommodation in Utrecht, the Netherlands.

- make the experiential narrative useful for knowledge dissemination to fellow users and survivors of psychiatry, mental health care professionals and others
- participate as a (paid) trainer or lecturer in training programmes.

The underlying principle is that an important element in recovering from long-term mental distress is to develop and pass on narratives (Baart, 2002; Belgrad, 1992; Lohauâ, 1995). To make and to tell a narrative enables us to overcome whatever it is we are overwhelmed with, for instance a psychosis, because it enables us to recover our sense of self (Herman, 1992). Through story-telling we grow from being a disorder to becoming a person trying to deal with life (Mead, 1974). And it enables us to learn to formulate what it is we need to recover.

To develop your own narrative and compare it with the narratives of other users and survivors of psychiatry is the beginning of building experiential knowledge. A collective story is made out of several individual narratives. To this end we look for underlying principles, for what we have in common and for what distinguishes us from one another. And finally the experiential story is transformed and used for knowledge dissemination in training programmes and courses.

In the TREE programme, participants develop, transform and disseminate experiential knowledge. They perform these tasks themselves, as volunteers or in paid jobs in the mental health care organisations where the programme is implemented. If necessary they hire others, mental health care professionals perhaps, as prostheses to enable them to perform their tasks. The programme consists of:

- self-help groups and working groups
- one day training, courses and group discussions for fellow users and survivors of psychiatry
- training programmes for professionals
- consultancy and coaching of organisations that wish to implement the programme.

The programme is for and with persons with long-term mental problems and psychiatric disabilities. They often struggle with multiple and complex problems in several domains of life and most of them have impressive patient careers in psychiatry. As a consequence most of them face dependence from psychiatric care, lack of self-confidence and self-esteem, loss of identity and control over their lives as well as greater social vulnerability. There are no other criteria to enter the programme than to have (the courage to have) some interest in what it is about. We don't know what factors predict success. The programme is developed in order to create opportunities for recovery and empowerment and to facilitate whoever wants to make use of these opportunities. Inherent to this goal is that everybody can participate.

Practice will show for whom it is a successful opportunity and for whom it isn't. The programme is open to all users and survivors of long-term mental health care. There are no other criteria, no demands, no examination and one can use it as often and as long as one likes.

Toward Evidence for Our Wisdom

In the Netherlands, the TREE programme, or parts of it, is becoming more and more popular among people with psychiatric disabilities themselves as well as among care providers. Several mental health care organisations have started to facilitate their users to implement the programme. A nationwide operating team of experiential experts is now hired frequently to provide for kick-off meetings, support fellow users and survivors in their recovery and in making recovery narratives, coach persons with psychiatric disabilities to become experiential experts, train fellow users and survivors of psychiatry and professionals, give lectures, design new programme parts and guide the implementation of the programme.

Four implementation sites, throughout the country, with different models of the TREE programme are being evaluated. Two sites are organisations for sheltered housing. One site is an ACT (Assertive Community Treatment) network organisation and another site consists of two non-clinical, interdisciplinary teams of a large mental health care organisation. At the first two sites a quasi-experimental design is being followed. In the first year of the study, the TREE programme started in half the locations of the sheltered housing organisations. In the second year the other half follows. At the last two sites a randomised controlled trial design is followed. All respondents with an interest in the TREE programme are followed up to two years. Outcome indicators are identity (Kuhn & McPartland, 1954), confidence in mental health (Carpinello, *et al.*, 2000), empowerment (Rogers, *et al.*, 1997) and connectedness (Suurmeijer, 1995). A strong evidence for a positive effect of the programme will be found when:

1) the respondents starting in the first year show more progress than those starting in the second year;
2) those starting in the second year show as much progress in year two as those starting in the first year showed in year one.

The study started in 2004. Results will be available in 2008.

The Strength of Solidarity

I am convinced that from within the user and survivor movement we have set in motion a development which will prove irreversible. We put forward our own experiences and are able to reflect upon them. We listen to the stories of other people with psychiatric disabilities and we integrate those stories into our collective body of knowledge. We are coming to realize what themes and topics are of importance to us all, and we recognize the obstacles that face us. We are becoming aware of the (importance of the) history of our user and survivor movement. We are developing an understanding of power relationships and constrictive social structures. And against the dominant perspectives, we are demanding attention for the social aspects of individual psychiatric problems.

We are developing various initiatives and through them we transfer our knowledge to others. We train and advise users and survivors of psychiatry and professionals. We pass on the baton to those who follow us, supporting them in their recovery process. We are presenting examples of hope to those who consider their situation hopeless.

In doing so, we open up choices to people who did not realize they had any choice at all. And we help to find the resources which can bring those choices to fruition. That is the strength of our user and survivor movement. Sharing a sense of unity, passing on our knowledge to each other and feeling solidarity in difficult times.

Sources

Baart, I. (2002). *The shaping of identity in illness: A study on chronic illness and subjectivity.* Assen: Van Gorcum.

Belgrad, J. (1992). *Identität als Spiel. Eine Kritik des Identitätskonzepts von Jürgen Habermas.* Opladen: Westdeutscher Verlag.

Boevink, W. (2006a). *From alien to actor.* Lecture held during the public hearing on the Green Paper on Mental Health, European Parliament, Brussels, June 8. Retrieved January 3, 2007, from www.enusp.org/documents/boevink_alien.pdf.

Boevink, W. (2006b). From being a disorder to dealing with life: An experiential exploration of the association between trauma and psychosis. *Schizophrenia Bulletin 32*(1), 17-19.

Boevink, W., & Escher, S. (2001). *Making self-harm understandable.* Bemelen: Stichting Positieve Gezondheidszorg.

Boevink, W., Van Beuzekom, J., Gaal, E., Jadby, A., Jong, F., Klein Bramel, M., Kole, M., Te Loo, N., Scholtus, S., & Van der Wal, C. (2002). *Working together toward recovery.* Utrecht: Trimbos-instituut.

Buck-Zerchin, D. S. (2005). *Auf der Spur des Morgensterns. Psychose als Selbstfindung.* Norderstedt: Anne Fischer Verlag.

Carpinello, S. E., Knight, E. L., Markowitz, F. E., & Pease, E. A. (2000). The development of the Mental Health Confidence Scale: A measure of self-efficacy in individuals diagnosed with mental disorders. *Psychiatric Rehabilitation Journal, 23*(3), 236-243.

Chamberlin, J. (1979). *On our own: Patient-controlled alternatives to the mental health system.* New York: McGraw-Hill.

Coleman, R., & M. Smith (1998). *Workbook for voice hearers: From victim to victor.* Gloucester: Handsell Publishing.

Coleman, R. (1999). *Recovery: An alien concept.* Gloucester, U.K.: Handsell Publishing.

Deegan, P. (1988). Recovery: The lived experience of rehabilitation. *Psychosocial Rehabilitation Journal, 11*(4), 11-19.

Deegan, P. (1996). Recovery as a journey of the heart. *Psychiatric Rehabilitation Journal, 19*(3), 91-97.

Hausotter, A. (2006). *GottTeufel – Innenansicht einer Psychose.* Linz: Editon pro mente.

Jacobson, N. (2001). Experiencing recovery: a dimensional analysis of recovery narratives. *Psychiatric Rehabilitation Journal, 24*(3), 248-56.

Janssen, T., Krabbendam, L., Bak, M., Hanssen, M., Vollebergh, W., de Graaf, R., & Van Os, J. (2004). Childhood abuse as a risk factor for psychotic experiences. *Acta Psychiatrica Scandinavia, 109*(1), 38-45.

Kempker, K. (2000). *Mitgift – Notizen vom Verschwinden.* Berlin: Antipsychiatrieverlag.

Klafki, H. (2006). *Meine Stimmen – Quälgeister und Schutzengel. Texte einer engagierten Stimmenhörerin.* Berlin: Antipsychiatrieverlag.

Kuhn, M. H., & McPartland, T. S. (1954). An empirical investigation of self attitudes. *American Sociological Review, 19,* 68-76.

Lehmann, P. (2004). *Coming off psychiatric drugs: Successful withdrawal from neuroleptics, antidepressants, lithium, carbamazepine and tranquilizers.* Berlin: Peter Lehmann Publishing.

Lohauâ, P. (1995). *Moderne Identität und Gesellschaft. Theorien und Konzepte.* Opladen: Leske & Budrich.

Mead, G. H. (1974). *Mind, self and society.* Chicago / London: The University of Chicago Press.

Mehr, M. (1990). *Steinzeit.* 7. edition. Bern: Zytglogge.

Mosher, L. R. (2004). Non-hospital, non-drug intervention with first-episode psychosis. In J. Read, L. R. Mosher, & R. Bentall (Eds.), *Models of madness: Psychological, social and biological approaches to schizophrenia* (349-365). New York: Brunner-Routledge.

Nettle, M., & Boevink, W.: Response ENUSP to Draft EU Green Paper on Mental Health, May 26, 2005. Retrieved January 7, 2007, from the ENUSP web site: www.enusp.org/ documents/greenpaper- re-2005.pdf.

Bowis, J. (2006, July 18). Report on improving the mental health of the population: Towards a strategy on mental health for the European Union.

Ridgway, P. (2001). Restorying psychiatric disability: Learning from first person recovery narratives. *Psychiatric Rehabilitation Journal, 24*(4), 335-343

Rogers, E. S., Chamberlin, J., Ellison, M. L., & Crean, T. (1997). A consumer-constructed scale to measure empowerment among users of mental health services. *Psychiatric Services, 48*(8), 1042-1047.

Stöckle, T. (2005). *Die Irren-Offensive. Erfahrungen einer Selbsthilfe-Organisation von Psychiatrieüberlebenden.* Berlin: Antipsychiatrieverlag.

Suurmeijer T. P. B. M., Doeglas, D. M., Briancon, S., Krijnen, W. P., Krol, B., Sanderman, R., Moum, T., Bjelle, A., Van Den Heuvel, W. J. A. (1995). The measurement of social support in the "EUropean Research on Incapacitating DIseases and Social Support": The development of the social support questionnaire for transactions (SSQT). *Social Science and Medicine, 40*(9), 1221-1229.

Rufus May

Reclaiming Mad Experience

Establishing Unusual Belief Groups and Evolving Minds Public Meetings

I will describe my journey into working with self-help groups and then outline how we have established various self-help groups and public meetings that aim to empower people to reclaim their lives from dependence on traditional psychiatry.

Introduction

When I was 18 I witnessed first hand how society's approach to mental health wasn't working. I had been admitted to Hackney hospital, a psychiatric hospital in London, and was told I could not leave. Feeling lost after my girlfriend had left me and on the verge of adulthood, I had invested in a spiritual search for guidance. The messages I picked up from the Bible convinced me I had a mission. Seeking to discover what my mission was, I slowly deduced that I was quite possibly an apprentice spy for the British Secret service. I was eventually admitted to hospital when I became convinced that I had a gadget in my chest that was being used to control my actions.

The psychiatric hospital was like another world entirely. Queues for the medication trolley punctuated the boredom and general sense of hopelessness. Any resistance to the regime was quashed by forcible restraints and powerful injections. Many friends felt too scared to visit me. That experience, coupled with being given a diagnosis of schizophrenia, made me feel like a social outcast. When my parents were told it was probably genetically inherited, the die seemed irrevocably cast. Ward rounds felt like elaborate religious rituals conducted by the consultant psychiatrist, with an audience of

medical students and student nurses observing, while my insanity was confirmed and long term drug treatment prophesised.

I found the medication made me feel empty and soulless, I could not think
past considering my basic needs. The psychiatric drugs made me physically
weaker and affected my hormones so I became during this time impotent. I
was concerned about this. However, to the outside world because of the
mind-numbing effects of the drugs I was less focused on my spy and spiritual
beliefs. The doctors pronounced that I was responding well to the medication. I was determined to stop taking the tablets and injections as soon as I
could find other ways of staying calm and centred.

The majority of fellow patients were revolving door patients. I was told
"you'll be back." It was true, I was readmitted twice before I managed to escape the role of mentally ill regular customer. Luckier than most, as well as
my parents visiting me daily, a close friend came back from selling pots and
pans to US servicemen in Germany and began visiting me daily too. I started
to pick up on her belief that this breakdown or whatever I was having was
something I could get over. When I was 12 years old I had witnessed my
mother make a strong recovery from a disabling brain hemorrhage so, in-
stinctively, I knew that I could turn my life around with the right support. So I
decided not to believe in the doctor's wisdom and planned to get a job as soon
as I left hospital. While I was still in hospital I started going to churches and
community centres offering to do voluntary work. Although I must have
seemed a bit odd, I found many kind people who were willing to give me
tasks to do and slowly I started to rebuild some social skills.

When a friend and fellow patient, Celine, took her own life after being
heavily medicated it became a turning point in my life. It was a Caribbean fu-
neral and hundreds of people turned up for it. For me, it contrasted strongly
with the absence of support she had had when she had been alive and hearing
abusive voices from her past. I realised then that I had found a cause that I
could invest my energy into. We, as a society, were making people madder
and maybe I could do something about changing that. What if I could make a
different kind of come-back to the psychiatric ward as a mental health professional? Then perhaps in Trojan horse style, I could help dismantle the myths
of the psychiatric hierarchy. When a junior psychologist informally ques-

tioned my diagnosis of schizophrenia, suggesting a temporary psychotic episode instead, it made me think maybe psychology was a way of doing things
differently. So my mission was becoming clearer: I would train as a psychologist. I knew I needed to sort myself out to some extent before endeavouring
this journey.

My first job straight out of psychiatric hospital was working as a night security guard in Highgate Cemetery in London. I now think that patrolling the
heavily wooded grounds in the dark was a deeply therapeutic activity. With
no time to daydream, I had to stay aware and face my fears of the dark and the
unknown. I also think just walking in close proximity to nature was a very
healing process. It was during this time that I successfully came off my psychiatric drugs against doctors' advice.

I then spent several years doing a range of jobs and learning creative ways
to express myself using dance and drama. I shifted my focus from thinking
about myself to trying to help others while making sure I looked after my
mind and body. I used the outdoor gym on Parliament Hill for sports, and
breathing exercises as natural ways to manage my moods. I was careful to
avoid unreliable or abusive friends and stick with people who had stuck by
me. Studying sociology helped me understand the wider structures of society, demystifying such things as the class system and power relations between men and women.

I was reminded of the prejudice against the subject of mental illness when a
politically correct community centre refused to support me and a group of
amateur drama students putting on a play about a nervous breakdown. Nevertheless, through drama classes, I learned the art of re-inventing oneself
through improvisation. I will always remember how one of my drama teachers impressed upon us the message that "this life is not a rehearsal." My confidence in acting was useful over the next 10 years of care-work and psychology training where I chose to keep quiet about my former role as psychiatric
patient to avoid the possibility of discrimination. I had to act sane, and as if I
always had been!

For me, the dividing line between the mentally ill and the sane was more a
question of social boundaries than actuality. I had found some very mad people in hospital very helpful and some of the so-called well nurses quite bully-

ing and hostile. It suggested to me that, to some extent, madness was in the eyes of the beholder. I also knew that my own madness had been meaningful; for example, my fantasies about being a spy had given my life meaning and my search for a spying mission was a metaphoric search for a meaningful quest in my life. As I trained as a psychologist in the early nineties, it coincided with psychology as a profession beginning to get interested in trying to understand and work with madness, whereas previously it had been the domain of the more medical drug prescribing profession of psychiatry.

For the last 10 years, I have been working as a psychologist with people who have a broad range of mental health problems (see May, 2004). I know that to really help someone who is deeply suffering or confused we need to be very creative and offer a wide range of resources. Over the last eight years, I have shifted my focus from therapy to self-help.[1] This is because self-help networks appear to offer a genuinely more respectful and empowering environment for people to get on with their lives. I have also found holistic therapies and approaches to wellbeing very useful both for myself and others, including mindfulness and bodywork (e.g., Yoga and Tai Chi).[2]

Unusual Beliefs Movements

In England, we have taken the principles of the Hearing Voices movement (see the chapter by Romme and Escher in this book) into other areas of mental health. There has now been established a Beyond Belief Network that looks at supporting people with unusual beliefs. The Beyond Belief approach is rooted in the work of Tamasin Knight, a researcher and a mental health human rights campaigner, who has researched how people cope with unusual beliefs that may be termed delusions by mental health professionals (Knight, 2006). She found many people are able to live with unusual beliefs and get on with their lives. Examples of unusual beliefs that psychiatry might describe as "delusions" are beliefs about spiritual possession, alien abduction, telepathy, and global conspiracy.

---

1   Julie Downs (2000) wrote a good guide to setting up self-help groups.

2   If you would like to contact me, my email address is rufus@rufusmay.freeserve.co.uk

In her guide to living with unusual beliefs called *Beyond Belief: Alternative Ways of Working with Delusions, Obsessions and Unusual Experiences,* Knight observes:

> There are many people who have beliefs that meet the criteria for delusions yet who are living successful lives with no contact with psychiatry. This could include believing they are being persecuted by agencies such as the FBI, or that they have special knowledge that no-one else realises, or that they have cancer despite having several tests showing no evidence of this. The difference between them and those who receive mental health services is whether the individual can cope with their beliefs: whether they are distressed or preoccupied by their beliefs (2006, p. 3).

Knight highlights the fact that when people are treated by psychiatry they are generally only given treatments that aim to subdue their beliefs or persuade them they are not correct. However, Knight asks if the differences (between people with unusual beliefs who do and don't receive mental health services) are in coping, not in the "irrationality" of the belief; is it not more ethical to be targeting the *coping* rather than the actual beliefs themselves? Knight suggests that techniques that reduce fear and increase one's sense of control, using problem solving strategies and increasing ones repertoire of coping strategies are all helpful approaches to living with unusual beliefs.

This way of thinking about unusual beliefs follows from the ideas of the Hearing Voices movement that each person should be able to choose how best to understand their reality and that acceptance is an important stage in taking back power to manage one's experiences. It also fits with a social constructionist view that there is no one best way to view reality. As Knight illustrates the world views of a materialistic businessman and a devout religious practitioner would be very different but there are problems in stating that one is more realistic or evidence based than another. The concept of Mad Pride, which has a growing popularity in mental health system survivor movements, also demands that alternative realities and experiences be accepted and respected.

In a multicultural world, it follows that we should not be seeking to promote one allegedly superior (or insightful) world view but helping people live comfortably alongside each other's different understandings and perceptions. My experience in helping people who are thought to have psychotic be-lief systems over the last ten years suggests that accepting that people have a right to have unusual beliefs is an important approach to take. Traditional mental health services see this attitude as colluding with delusions and mak-ing them more real for the person. However, I have found that respecting that people's view of reality is of value and meaningful is often a useful way of joining with someone to look at how they see the world and what might be the best way forward for them. Sometimes I will challenge people's versions of reality but my aim is not to help them see the world more rationally, my aim is to help people get on with their lives and better negotiate their versions of reality with those around them.

Giving people choice about how to approach a distressing belief is impor-tant. For example if Jonathan thinks his neighbours are spying on him he can choose whether to investigate the evidence for this, or he can accept his belief as possibly accurate, and choose to focus on building his sense of self value and purpose (i.e., not let the "spies" get to him). This means that if Jonathan's neighbours are spying on him it won't affect him because his mind is focused on more meaningful activities and relationships. Most mental health profes-sionals are not trained to give people this choice. In the United Kingdom, many therapists trained in cognitive behavioural therapy, use guided discov-ery techniques to subtly guide people to shifting their beliefs without being open about this process or giving them a choice about how best to cope with their beliefs. I have found if people have had their beliefs for a number of years they may be quite attached to them, so ways that work respectful of their beliefs are likely to be much more helpful and less alienating than tradi-tional psychiatric and psychological approaches.

Tamasin Knight's research suggests that if someone is attached to an un-usual belief, rather than label and try to remove their belief, we should be helping people live with their unusual beliefs and get on in the world. The consequence of this thinking offers a real challenge to conventional mental health practice. When asked to intervene, psychiatry has tried to medicate away people's unusual thinking and therapies have sought to train people to think more rationally. The alternative approach is to educate society that there are many ways to perceive the world and *how* people relate to their beliefs and to the world around them is crucial to their quality of life, not the ability to think normally or rationally. Therefore self-help groups where different ways of thinking about the world are accepted and people can explore how to live with their beliefs are a crucial part of this approach.

In Exeter, there has been a self-help group called You Better Believe It! that has been going for three years. In Bradford, we have established a similar group called Believe It or Not! Our launch meeting was attended by 60 people and included presentations by Tamasin Knight and an African Shaman called Odi Oquosa. Odi talked about his own experience of using spirituality to overcome trauma and spiritual attack and the power of artistic expression and nature in the healing process. For Odi, madness is an initiation of a healing process; an awakening of the unconscious mind. For this healing to be enabled it is important not to suppress these experiences as western psychiatry has tended to do, rather we need to create artistic spaces where this unconscious state can be expressed symbolically, understood and lessons learned from it by the surrounding community.

The Believe It or Not! group has supported someone who believed they were possessed in seeking spiritual advice and guidance. Another group member who understands his intense experiences of powerful energy as Kundalini has been supported to access a Kundalini yoga class and related self-help literature. Joe was a group member who felt shy and wanted to improve his social confidence and relation-building skills. One meeting Joe presented this poem he had written about an experience he had that was very powerful for him.

> As I was walking late one night
> Out of the blue there came a light
> And the light said relax and don't take flight.
> Then all of a sudden, I didn't exist as one.
> I was the birds, I was the bees,
> I was the whistle in the breeze.
> I was the stars, I was the sky,
> I was the clouds floating by.
> I was the rivers I was the sea,
> I was the grass, I was the trees.

And I existed as everything but not as me.
But then I felt that this couldn't last
And there I was stood back on the path.
If that's enlightenment, without any shadow of a doubt
Please light shine on me whenever I am out.

There is a danger that traditional psychiatric services might dismiss this experience as a psychotic symptom. However at the Believe It or Not! group we felt there might be more meaningful interpretations of the experience. As a consequence of Joe's poem and interests we invited a Buddhist guest speaker to the self-help group to tell us about Buddhism. When Joe described his experience the Buddhist told Joe he had a special gift. Joe began attending Buddhist meditation classes taking up regular meditation practice. He also got involved in some voluntary work decorating the Buddhist's monastery. At the same time Joe kept up going to a Christian church and started going out more to Karaoke bars and night-clubs. With his increased powers of relaxation Joe became more socially confident and out-going. He then joined an on-line dating agency. This is an example of how the Believe It or Not! group has been helpful in developing someone's confidence and participation in different communities in Bradford. Within the Believe It or Not! group members tend to hold very different views about the world is but develop tolerance and acceptance of other's views. This is a very useful skill to have in the current climate we live in where different ideologies compete for supremacy; a more peaceful world will be one that accepts and values different versions of reality.

A druid (druids are traditional pagan priests/healers) has also regularly attended the Believe It or Not! group. When other group members talked about feeling under psychic attack he recommended reciting the phrase "I am the mirror of your soul, what you do to me you do to yourself," repeating this nine times while biting the end of one's thumb. A number of group members found this technique very helpful in thwarting spiritual attacks. We hope that the acceptance approach to unusual beliefs will follow the footsteps of the hearing voices movement and that the Beyond Belief Network will contribute to this development.

Evolving Minds Public Meetings

Evolving Minds public meetings[1] take place in two venues in the West York-shire region (Hebden Bridge and the city of Bradford). The aim is to create regular monthly public forums to discuss different approaches to mental health problems. This includes social, spiritual and personal approaches. We recognise that there is no one best way of understanding this subject. The meeting holds the belief that each person has wisdom and expertise about their own experiences and what is likely to be real and helpful for them, and that this wisdom needs to be valued and respected.

The aim of Evolving Minds is therefore to create a public space where dif-ferent understandings and initiatives that relate to mental and spiritual wellbeing can be shared. In this way, Evolving Minds hopes to generate an increased level of acceptance and understanding of experiences of distress and confusion (and creative ways to deal with this) in the wider communities we live in.

The name *Evolving Minds* comes from a film with the same title that looks at different ways of dealing with psychosis.[2] Evolving Minds Meetings came about after a public showing of this film in Hebden Bridge in November 2003. The film *Evolving Minds* directed by Mel Gunasena looked at alterna-tive approaches to dealing with psychosis. Over 70 people turned up to see the film and take part in the discussion, discussants included Mel Gunasena herself and there was a lot of interest in taking the issues the film raised fur-ther.

The Evolving Minds meetings have covered a range of topics including—Personal accounts of recovery; Forum theatre as a way of dealing with op-pression; Guided Meditation; Communicationz Promotin Recovery, a Man-chester based grass roots self-help and media group; How to survive living in a mad world; Binaural beat technology (a self-help strategy that uses stereo-phonic sound to change mood); Spiritual healing; Ways of reclaiming lan-

1 See www.evolving-minds.co.uk

2 To view see www.undercurrents.org/minds/index.htm

guage of self; Co-counseling; Discussion of the ideas of Ronald D. Laing; Creativity and mental health. Meetings have also looked at Self esteem; Eastern and Western perspectives; How to live with suicidal thoughts; Understanding paranoia; Using dance to process strong emotions; How does war affect us emotionally; Homeopathy and Herbal Medicine; Tree spirit healing. We also hosted a performance theatre piece which charted one person's psycho spiritual journey through madness. The numbers of people coming to Evolving Minds varies between 25 and 40.

Posters highlighting each meeting are put up around the local town helping to raise awareness both of the meeting and the issues it looks at. For example one poster read "How sane is it to be well-adapted to a sick society?" A series of drama work-shops have developed alongside the Evolving Minds meetings, using "Theatre of the Oppressed" techniques developed by Augustus Boal. The drama work-shops have looked at issues to do with identity and ways to challenge experiences of oppression.

The Bradford Evolving Minds organized a Mad Arts festival in Bradford which involved major shops and cafes in Bradford exhibiting Mad Art. It also featured a Mad Cabaret, an artist giving a lecture at the local University, a series of art workshops and a storytelling evening.

A Campaigning sub-group of Evolving Minds has also got involved in campaigning against the oppressive use of force in the mental health system. This has included two bed-pushes where we have symbolically escaped from psychiatric institutions.[1] The bed-pushes have achieved national and international media coverage, raising awareness about the human rights abuses that occur routinely in the psychiatric system and the need for social change regarding this issue. Finally, a weekly self-help group has been set up to support people to come off psychiatric medication. Group members have also developed a website (www.comingoff.com) that gives information on how

---

1   The Great Escape Bed Push is an annual protest action that happens each summer since 2005. Its aim is to raise awareness about the poor levels of choice of treatments and the widespread use of force used in the psychiatric hospitals. On British public traffic roads a pyjama dressed crew from sets off from a psychiatric hopsital pushing a psychiatric bed up to 60 miles to a place of safety and celebration, chased by an 8-foot syringe. For more information see www.bedpush.com

psychiatric drugs are thought to act on the brain; possible adverse effects and withdrawal problems; how to withdraw; what alternative strategies may be helpful in managing mood; plus personal stories of the coming off process.

Conclusion

The networks created by the self-help groups and public meetings in Bradford and Hebden Bridge (see the chapter by Thomas and Yasmeen in this book) over the last three years are starting to become an alternative resource to people who want to reduce or avoid dependence on conventional bio-medical psychiatry. People who were seen as quite disabled are recovering more active lives and starting to make valuable contributions into their communities.

Also family members, friends and other members of the community who have had contact with our activities are learning to be more accepting, creative and hopeful about distressing and confusing experiences and alternative realities. We are beginning to develop real alternatives to the established psychiatric tendency to medically label and suppress odd or distressing behaviour.

Sources

Downs, J. (2000). *How to set up and support hearing voices groups.* Manchester: Hearing Voices Network.

Knight, T. (2006). *Beyond belief: Alternative ways of working with delusions, obsessions and unusual experiences.* Lancaster: Self-publication; Berlin / Eugene / Shrewsbury: Peter Lehmann Publishing (2007, in preparation).

May, R. (2004). Making sense of psychotic experiences and working towards recovery. In J. Gleeson, & P. McGorry (Eds.), *Psychological interventions in early psychosis* (pp. 245-260). New York: John Wiley.

Romme, M., & Escher, S. (1993). *Accepting voices.* London: Mind Publications.

Hannelore Klafki

The Voices Accompany My Life[1]

People who hear voices do not want to be excluded from society and be solely treated with psychiatric drugs any more. Instead they want to learn the significance of their voices so that they can live in peace with them. They ask professionals and the public to reconsider their positions.

Three to five percent of the population hear voices or have heard voices at some time in their life. In psychiatry, hearing voices remains a symptom of a severe mental condition and even today treatment in most cases is solely by the use of psychiatric drugs. The hearing voices movement would like psychiatry to do some rethinking: those hearing voices need not automatically be ill. Many people who hear voices have never been involved with psychiatry and have no problems with the voices they are hearing.

Initial Strategies to Cope with Hearing Voices

It all began when I was 16 years old. I was very frightened and I couldn't explain what was happening to me. It took a long time until I was able to get along with the voices and it was a very difficult time in which I was often hospitalized. I didn't tell anyone about the voices but reacted physically to them. When they became unbearable, I collapsed and was brought to the hospital by ambulance. There, I was examined for epilepsy. At the end of the 60s epilepsy patients were still admitted to psychiatric units. Collapsing was the first strategy I developed for dealing with the voices. The next step was discovering that I could distract the voices from me. I managed this by giving them "mental nourishment." They became quieter while I read or listened to music.

---

1   Originally published in: Pro mente sana aktuell, 2002, No. 3, pp. 12-13

Also, when I was busy, they didn't talk as loudly nor did they try to persuade me as intensely. I made a deal with them that they should leave me alone during the day and in return, I would take time for them in the mornings. It took a while until this worked but then we had very animated conversations in which I learned to accept that they accompany my life. At the beginning I heard only negative voices. Later, positive voices came along, making suggestions and giving me tips. I lived a normal life in this way for 15 years without any great impairment by the voices.

Relapse, Psychiatry and Recovery

Great changes came into my life. A move, divorce and retraining brought on turmoil and stress. More and more often voices piped up that bothered and distressed me. They were like goblins who imitated me, made fun of my conversation partner or commented on my remarks. They disturbed my sleep, forbade me to eat and became very loud. In a very extreme situation, I had the feeling that the more wicked voices crawled into my head and in the form of an automated voice spoke the worst insults and commands which escalated to the point where they said that I was not worthy enough to live and that I should commit suicide. It was so unbearable that I left my body and had to be brought to a psychiatric center.

In 1990, I related the story of the voices for the first time in a psychiatric clinic. Since then I have been given six different psychiatric diagnoses; of these, schizophrenia has affected me most. Many neuroleptic drugs were tried on me but the voices were immune to all of them. My worst experience was when I had to take haloperidol, which was still psychiatry's first choice of drug. Rattled by the diagnoses of the psychiatrists and their solemn declaration that I was suffering from an incurable mental illness, I resigned to fate. As a result the voices became more and more aggressive. I fought a constant battle with them, turning me into a revolving door patient.

Observing the Voices as a Warning

In 1992, I found out about a psychosocial center where I met a social worker who supported me in the fight against the voices. She took me and my voices very seriously. Since then I have found my way back to my early relationship with the voices and I can take the louder voices as a warning signal that something is not alright with me. This can feel like great pressure coming from others or myself, or like a conflict situation which I had not experienced as such before. At other times the voices can be like unruly children which have to be dealt with strictly in an undisturbed place.

If I had only known how liberating it was to talk about my voices with other voice hearers! Only in our self-help group did I learn that I should see the voices in connection with my life-story. For this reason I suggest that other voice hearers should talk about their voices with like-minded people. Certain texts that address coping with voices have also helped me. Writing a voice-diary and sharing parts of it in the group was a further step to regain control over the voices.

Hearing Voices Network[1]: Demands on Psychiatry

The main reason I have not needed a hospital or psychiatric drugs since 1997 is surely due to the fact that I have become involved in the hearing voices movement. I always say "In helping others, I also help myself." I have progressed from a person who is afflicted to an expert for my own cause. The Hearing Voices Network in Germany (NeSt) has existed since May 1998. This network is composed of people who hear or once heard voices (experts through experience), their relatives and those working as mental health providers (experts through training). We relate on the same level and hope that our movement will continue to grow and that we can persuade psychiatry to change its approach. People who hear voices do not want to be excluded from society or solely be treated with psychiatric drugs any more. Instead, they

---

1 Addresses: Netzwerk Stimmenhören, Uthmannstr. 5, 12043 Berlin, Germany, Tel. & Fax +49 (0)30 78718068, stimmenhoeren@gmx.de, www.stimmenhoeren.de • Les Sans Voix, Case Postale 235, 1211 Genève, Switzerland, lessansvoix@gmail.com, www.chez.com/sansvoix • Verband Psychiatrie- und Psychose-Erfahrene der Schweiz (VPECH), Postfach 1957, 8040 Zurich, Switzerland, cell phone +41 (0)79 3517989, litschig-irrpeace@bluewin.ch, www.vpech-irrpeace.ch • Netzwerk Spinnen, Ottensheimerstr. 96/2, 4040 Linz, Austria, Tel. & Fax +43 (0)732 700924, office@nesp.cc, www.nesp.cc

want to learn the reasons for their voices so that they can live in peace with them. The Hearing Voices Network has posed the following demands:

- Do not automatically interpret hearing voices as a symptom for illness. Consider that 3-5% of all people hear voices or have at some point heard them. Many of them have never been in a psychiatric hospital and don't want to give up their voices.

- Accept our various and divergent explanations—each explanation that helps us to cope with the voices is better than none.

- Help us to translate what the voices are trying to say. For this reason, it is important to know what the voices are saying and wrong to want to silence them at all cost. Professor Marius Romme of the Netherlands said in 1991: "It is useless killing the messenger who delivers the message if the message stays the same."

- Help us to integrate the voices into our lives as an important part of us. Only then can we develop strategies for interaction with them.

- Hearing voices is not necessarily a problem in and of itself, often it is the inability of coping with the voices. Please give us courage by telling us that there are people who have learned to cope with the voices. The voices can even become an enrichment of life; learning how to influence them is quite possible, they can recede into the background, or even disappear completely.

Translated from the German by Christine Holzhausen

Marius Romme and Sandra Escher

INTERVOICE

Accepting and Making Sense of Hearing Voices

INTERVOICE stands for International Network, Training, Education and Research on Voices. Intervoice was founded by Marius Romme in 1996. The hearing voices movement took its first steps in 1987 when Patsy Hage challenged me (Marius Romme), her psychiatrist, with her critical comments about my clinical approach to her voices. She pointed out that rather than using voices only in order to make an illness diagnosis it would be more useful if I helped her learn to cope with the experience. The trouble was that, at the time I only knew people who could not cope with their voices. So how to get in touch with other voice hearers? In a popular Dutch talk show Patsy told about her experience and I told that psychiatry had not much to offer and we would like to get in contact with people who could cope with their voices. We invited people to react. Seven hundred people did react and Sandra Escher organised the first congress for voice hearers in 1987, attended by 350 voice hearers. At that congress the Dutch voice hearing organisation Resonance was founded. Through John Strauss, who attended the conference, we were able to get a publication in *Schizophrenia Bulletin* (Romme & Escher, 1989). This article was a starting point for sparking wider interest. Voices hearers, therapists and researchers developed a growing need to meet and to exchange information. In the beginning mostly people from Holland, England, Italy, Austria and Finland participated, who were soon followed by people from, Portugal, Germany, Sweden, Switzerland, Norway and Denmark. Some action was taken in America mainly through the work of Pat Deegan. Groups were formed in Malaysia as well as in Burma by Siri Blesvik, a professor of nursing who was originally from Norway.

In England, the concept received the most interest and was spread originally by Paul Baker, Terence McLaughlin, Mike Greerson, Ron Coleman, Mike Smith, Julie Downs and others like Mervyn Morris who promoted teaching this approach in Mental Health nursing and John Jenkins who spread the concept at the WHO level. It really got moving when the national network in England acquired a paid coordinator. In this role, Julie Downs was the motor that truly promulgated the concept, resulting in the formation of about 180 hearing voices groups. In England, the movement was from the beginning also strongly supported by Ron Coleman, a voice hearer and mental health activist, who some years ago started advancing it outside of Europe: in Palestine, New Zealand and Australia, and, most recently, a group in Iceland.

INTERVOICE is an international network in which individuals and organizations from 14 countries participate. Each year a congress is organised by one of the participating countries. In 2006, it was held in Dundee, Scotland, and in June 2007, in Lyngby, Denmark.

Paul Baker is the secretary, he deals with the membership and monitors the INTERVOICE online discussion forum, publishes newsletters and is now building the website www.intervoiceonline.org as international online community for INTERVOICE members and friends to encourage discussion and debate about the meaning of the voice hearing experience and to consider the latest work and research into this phenomenon.

The basic assumption of INTERVOICE is that accepting and making sense of voices is a more helpful alternative for recovering from the distress associated with voice hearing. This assumption is based on our research in Holland from 1989 onwards. In this research, we brought people who heard voices together in order to learn from their experiences. We also met people who heard voices but never became ill or psychiatric patients. We studied the similarities and differences between voice hearers who became psychiatric patients and those who did not. From these studies we learned that hearing voices in itself is not a sign of mental illness, but that it is quite possible to become ill and a psychiatric patient when a person cannot cope with them and with the problems that lay at their roots.

Persons who hear voices and have become ill and psychiatric patients show a different relationship with their voices than persons who hear voices and who do not become ill and psychiatric patients. They were able to connect their voices with problems they had encountered in their lives and could use their voices to their benefit, in other words, they were helped by them. In contrast, the psychiatric patients felt overwhelmed and threatened by their voices. The patient voice hearers, when they started hearing voices they generally do not see any relationship with what has happened to them. Also patient voice hearers often try to keep these voices powerless. This seems to make the experience of their consciousness more terrifying.

Accepting means realising that the experience of voice hearing is real, and making sense suggests that the voices are not something crazy, but have a purpose in learning to cope with problems in life. They are related to what has happened with a person. Some might remind the person of traumatic experiences; others are commenting on the person's reaction to their problems.

Some are commenting on the person's behaviour in a similar way as was done by the perpetrators who caused the traumatic experiences. Others are responding to a person's lifestyle; or holding up a mirror that reflects in a negative or positive sense the person's position in life and their feelings about it. Some voices are just helpful by giving sensible advice.

Voice hearers who can not cope with their voices mostly have tried to deny or get rid of what has happened to them, which is a problem solving strategy that does not work very well. Voice hearers who do not become ill, do recognize their problems and use their voices as helpers. To recover from the stressful aspects of voices, the voice hearer has to learn to talk about them, to try to understand them and change their relationship with them. That makes it possible to take ones life in ones own hands again and as Ron Coleman states "live your life not your voices." Hearing voices groups are a very adequate possibility to learn from.

From our research it became evident that most voice hearers start to hear voices after one or more traumata, in situations where they feel powerless and feel they cannot cope. By accepting the voices it becomes possible to make sense of them and relate them to actual problems in life.

Accepting voices and making sense of them is an approach in which voices are seen as signals of problems in life. Therefore it does not make much sense to treat them as a symptom of an illness, nor try to cure a disease that is supposed to produce these voices. Suppressing these voices is not the right learning experience for coping with them and the problems that lay at their roots. Suppressing the signal does not help solve these problems. The traditional line of thinking in psychiatry where voices are seen as a symptom of an illness and as resulting from a disease, is not only incorrect, but also harmful, because it alienates voice hearers from their experiences, makes them powerless and often turns voice hearing into a chronic problem.

Newer epidemiological research did confirm that hearing voices in itself is not a sign of mental illness. Research done by Tien (1991), Eaton and colleagues (1991) and van Os and colleagues (2001) shows evidence that hearing voices is a widespread phenomenon, not only with psychiatric patients, but in the whole population of people without a psychiatric diagnosis. There are more voice hearers who cope well with their voices, who experience them as helpful and use their voices to their benefit, than there are voice hearers who become ill and psychiatric patients because of the voices.

In cooperation with many, many others, we developed an approach that makes it possible for people to accept their voices, becoming the owners of this experience, make sense of these voices by understanding their relationship with what had happened to them in their lives, change their relationship with their voices and take their own life in their own hands again. "Take back the power that others have taken away from you." A nice example of the benefits of this approach comes from Hannelore Klafki, who disclosed in a radio programme that her voices had helped her become a powerful woman and guided her to finally stop being a victim (Klafki, 2006a, p. 58). Hannelore was one of the voice hearers who adopted the approach of accepting and making sense of voices after connecting with INTERVOICE and particularly listening to the experiences of Ron Coleman (Klafki, 2006b). Ron wrote a very stimulating book about recovering from the distress associated with hearing voices (Coleman, 1997). Other voice hearers, such as Peter Bullimore (2005), have also reported how they benefited from this approach.

We did six studies about hearing voices: bringing people who hear voices together (1989); exploring in depth the experience of hearing voices (1993a), comparing patient- with non-patient voice hearers (1996); developing a guide for professionals to help people cope with their voices and associated problems (1993b; 2000), studying children who hear voices (2005), the development from trauma to psychosis (2006). The seventh study develops evidence about the benefits of accepting voices (2007).

The most important results from these studies and that elements that promote recovery from the distress associated with voice hearing, as derived from experienced voice hearers, are as follows:

1) Hearing voices in itself is not a symptom of an illness, but a signal of problems.

2) Voice hearers can learn to cope with their voices, which is not simple but rewarding.

3) Voice hearing patients and non-patients have different kinds of relationships to their voices.

4) Accepting ones problems, working on self-esteem, and making choices support the recovery process.

5) Changing the relation to the voices is to become respectful to them, not fighting against them but talking to them slowly and with warmth, which has as a consequence that they also change their approach. It can also be testing out their power and experiencing that they are not almighty at all.

6) Recovering is also helped by understanding the metaphors of what voices say.

7) Interventions should at first be oriented towards anxiety reduction and only later phase on changing the relationship, taking back power and making choices.

8) Recovery is rooted in stimulating the capacities of the voice hearers by themselves and with others, and taking responsibility for themselves in a supportive and safe environment.

Recently some important studies appeared about the relationship between trauma and psychosis in general and hearing voices in particular (Read, *et al.*, 2004; Larkin & Morrison, 2006).

The approach of accepting and making sense of hearing voices is not only helpful with hearing voices but with other mental health problems as well like ideas of reference, paranoia and delusions by promoting different ways of thinking about ones problems in life (Bullimore, 2005; May, 2004).

Sources

Bullimore, P. (2005). From the experience: Paranoia and the life history. Lecture at the congress on "Emancipatie van psychotische ervaringen" in Maastricht, May 20.

Coleman, R. (1997). *Recovery: An alien concept.* Gloucester: Handsell Publishing.

Eaton, W. W., Romanonski, A., & Anthony, J. C. (1991). Screening for psychosis in the general population with a self-report interview. *Journal of Nervous and Mental Disease, 179,* 689-693.

Klafki, H. (2006a). *Meine Stimmen – Quälgeister und Schutzengel. Texte einer engagierten Stimmenhörerin.* Berlin: Antipsychiatrieverlag.

Klafki, H. (2006b). Making common sense of voices. *Journal of Critical Psychology, Counselling and Psychotherapy, 6*(1), 23-25.

Larkin, W., & A. Morrison, A. (Eds.) (2006). *Trauma and psychosis.* London: Brunner-Routledge.

May, R. (2004). Making sense of psychotic experiences and working towards recovery. In J. F. M. Gleeson, P. McGorry (Eds.), *Psychological interventions in early psychosis* (pp. 245-260). New York: John Wiley.

Read, J., Mosher, L. R., & Bentall, R. (Eds.) (2004). M*odels of madness: Psychological, social and biological approaches to schizophrenia.* Hove: Brunner-Routledge.

Romme, M., & Escher, S. (1989). Hearing voices. *Schizophrenia Bulletin, 25*(2), 209-216.

Romme, M., & Escher, S. (Eds.) (1993a). *Accepting voices.* London: Mind Publications.

Romme, M., Escher, S. (1993b). The new approach: A Dutch experiment. In M. Romme, & S. Escher (Eds.), *Accepting voices* (pp. 11-27). London: Mind Publications.

Romme, M., & Escher, S. (1996). Empowering people who hear voices. In G. Haddock, & P. D. Slade (Eds.), *Cognitive behavioural interventions with psychotic disorders* (pp. 137-150). London: Routledge.

Romme, M., & Escher, S. (2000). *Making sense of voices.* London: Mind Publications.

Romme, M., & Escher, S. (2005). Stimmenhören bei Kindern und Jugendlichen. In S. Escher, *Making sense of psychotic experiences.* Thesis at the University of Maastricht.

Romme, M., & Escher, S. (2006). Trauma and hearing voices. In W. Larkin, & T. Morrison (Eds.), *Understanding trauma and psychosis: New horizons for theory and therapy.* Hove: Brunner-Routledge.

Romme, M., & Escher, S. (2007). *Recovery from the distress with voices.* London: Mind Publications (in preparation).

Tien, A. Y. (1991). Distributions of hallucination in the population. *Social Psychiatry and Psychiatric Epidemiology, 26,* 287-292.

van Os, J., Hanssen, M., Bijl, R.V., & Vollebergh, W. (2001). Prevalence of psychotic disorder and community level of psychotic symptoms: An urban-rural comparison. *Archives of General Psychiatry, 58,* 663-668.

Maryse Mitchell-Brody

The Icarus Project
Dangerous Gifts, Iridescent Visions and Mad Community

The Icarus Project envisions a new culture and language that resonates with our actual experiences of "mental illness" rather than
trying to fit our lives into a conventional framework. We are a net-

work of people living with experiences that are commonly labeled as bipolar or related madness. We believe we have dangerous gifts to be cultivated and taken care of, rather than a disease or disorder to be "cured" or "eliminated." By joining together as individuals in communities, the intertwined threads of madness and creativity can inspire hope and transformation in a repressed and damaged world. Our participation in The Icarus Project helps us overcome alienation and tap into the true potential that lies between brilliance and madness (From our Vision Statement).

Psych Wards and Storytelling: The Early Years

When Sascha DuBrul, a founding member of the Icarus Project, experienced his first manic episode in 1993, at the age of 18, he was institutionalized and informed that he had a disease called "Bipolar I with Psychotic Features." This "illness," he was informed, would require that he remain on psychiatric drugs for the rest of his life or face the terrible consequences of his overactive and dysfunctional mind. In 2002, shortly after the suicide of a dear friend with a similar diagnosis, he wrote a piece on his own particular experience of madness. In the article, published in the *San Francisco Bay Guardian*, he asserted that he was "… part of a group of people that has been misunderstood and persecuted throughout history, but meanwhile has been responsible for some of the most brilliant of history's creations."

He emphasized the need to create a middle ground between the approaches of the psychiatric-pharmaceutical complex and those who would deny the existence of madness altogether.

Little did he know at the time that this article would jumpstart a project that would do exactly that. Among the dozens of heartfelt stories that he received in response was one from Ashley McNamara, who had experienced some of her most creative moments at her most "manic," and was struggling with many of the same issues. The two began corresponding and soon met in person. They realized that what was so powerful about the article in the *Bay Guardian* was that by telling the story of one man's experience of madness, so many others came forth to tell their own, surprised and empowered by the simple revelation that they were not alone. At the time, both Ashley and Sascha were full of the energy and creativity that is often pathologized as mania, and from these brilliant sparks, the Icarus Project was born.

Icarus Rising: The Myth and the Movement

Our organization's name comes from yet another story: the archetypal myth of the boy Icarus. His father, Daedalus was a master craftsman who along with his son, was imprisoned in a Labyrinth of his own creation. From wax and feathers, the loving father constructed a set of wings so that his child might escape their prison. He warned Icarus not to fly too low, lest the feathers get wet, and not to fly too high, lest the wax melt in the sun's rays. Icarus, with the impetuosity and ignorance of youth, paid no heed to his father's warning and approaches the sun, only to have his wings dissolve and tumble to his death in the Aegean Sea.

Icarus' wings were a dangerous gift. If used correctly, they could have borne him to freedom, but without proper care, they were his undoing. We at the Icarus Project believe that we too possess a dangerous gift: our madness. We recognize, having experienced both the emotional suffering of depression and suicidal thoughts and the uncertainty and burnout of mania, that our minds and indeed lives are sensitive and deserving of special care. However, we have also experienced the brilliance that is often a hallmark of our heightened sensitivity, and we are committed to learning how to navigate the space between the burning light and the tremulous depths, to find healing modalities that allow us to coast our way towards the liberation that our madness may also entail.

Sascha and Ashley took this story and turned it into the allegorical inspiration for the ideas that they would soon begin to make manifest. They decided to construct a website replete with articles, resources, artwork, and most importantly, forums where people from all over the world could meet to discuss their own experiences of madness, ones that didn't necessarily coalesce with the psychiatric mainstream. The website www.theicarusproject.net grew rapidly to include thousands of members, sharing their stories, offering support to each other, giving advice, and creating a community unlike any that had ever existed before.

In the fall of 2003, Sascha and Ashley received a grant to write a book based upon their experiences and those of site members. The volume, entitled *Navigating the Space Between Brilliance and Madness: A Reader and Roadmap of Bipolar Worlds* (published by The Icarus Project, 2004) is currently (August 2007) in its 5th printing and has been an invaluable resource for bringing our message into communities. Shortly after printing, with the help of connections, inspiration, and much hard work, the organization that started with a mission statement written by two manic people sitting in a tree suddenly found itself with substantially increased resources at its disposal. With the expansion of finances came the introduction of several others to form a national organizing collective, from which they began to develop and disseminate a radical community-based model of mental health peer support.

Dangerous Gifts and Wounded Healers: What We Think, What We Do and Why It Works

What is it about the approaches of the Icarus Project that's helped us to become so successful? Perhaps the most readily apparent answer is that we appeal to youth in ways that many other organizations don't, as evidenced by the fact that people under the age of 30 comprise the vast majority of our project. Many mainstream mental health establishments, with their drab institutional settings, heavily medicated members, and patronizing staff, have little that would appeal to some people, especially those who identify with countercultural movements. Indeed, who wants to be told that they have a brain disease? With our emphasis on creativity, inspiration, alternative healing modalities, radical egalitarianism, and a commitment to self-determination, we attract many who have been alienated by other approaches.

Our philosophy of autonomy, which stems from anarchist organizing principles, leads us to assert that individuals should be free to define their own standards of mental wellness. This belief facilitates the involvement of many diverse identifications and individuals within our movement, from those who use DSM *(Diagnostic and Statistical Manual of Mental Disorders)* labels to those who eschew them completely, from folks on psych meds to those who engage in alternative wellness practices, such as Reiki, yoga, meditation, movement therapies, and acupuncture. We also have room for those who wish to explore the long-acknowledged link between spirituality and madness with shamanic traditions or other sacred modes. For us, a key component of our work is reclaiming our right to self-definition, choosing how we each reckon and work with our madness. That said, many of us have found that when we cease to see our psychic pain and sensitivities as diseases, that labels like "madness" and "crazy" suddenly become imbued with new, more positive nuances. Instead of serving to further remind us of our difference and thus sickness, we can reclaim these words and make them terms of endearment or even of positive identification, much like the gay pride movement has adopted the word "queer."

So when we talk about madness as a word that we use as an indicator of pride, what are we proud of? Creativity, empathy, energy, sensitivity, revolutionary visions, compassion, and insight, to name just a few.

A common thread through all of our work is our emphasis on creativity and beauty. A widely acknowledged corollary of madness is inspiration and talent; however, this madness is often portrayed as a tragic illness that robbed the world of works of cultural value. We assert that this madness is an intrinsic part of the artistic spirit; indeed, many of us have noted that when we choose to go on psychiatric drugs, we often lose some of our creative fire. As a network of local communities, we help each other to create art, words, movements and minds that balance that creative fire with emotional well-being.

Creativity has long been at the fore of our work and is central to our understanding of dangerous gifts. Founding member AshleyMcNamara is a gifted visual artist; her paintings, drawings and graphic work are essential to our design sensibility. Ashley, like many others gifted with madness, has long asserted that her ability and inspiration often seem to be heightened when she experiences what some might label mania. Others among our membership are visionary writers, gifted poets, skilled web designers and soul-shaking musicians. We try to incorporate these gifts into the work that we do: as design elements on the web, articles in our publications, pieces in our art shows, performances at our events, and much more. However, our definition of creativity extends well beyond the traditional boundaries of the arts. We see the acts of organizing and support and facilitation and essentially all that we do as works of construction. When we take our radical mad visions and manifest them into our realities, we create a world worth living in. By working together on collective projects as individual artists, we not only have an added impetus to create but ideally a safety net to catch us if the fire burns too bright.

Those of us who experience madness might also describe ourselves as possessing "exquisite nervous systems."[1] That is to say that perhaps we are more sensitive than the general population, which allows us to take in more, to think more rapidly, and to perceive relationships, connections and details that others may not notice or consider to be of little consequence. Some would, and do, consider these heightened kinds of awareness to be indicators of mental illness. Labels like delusions, hallucinations, paranoia, hysteria, and anxiety are often put upon these sensitivities without regard for the additional harm that having one's functioning pathologized might inflict. People may find their minds creating scenarios or emotions that could be dangerous or unfavorable, but except in extreme crises when designated support people might intervene, it should be left up to the individual to determine when this is the case. In either case, it is precisely these sensitivities that allow us to be in tune with our inspirations and very often to act as pillars of support for others with similar experiences.

Having experienced extreme mental states and considerable emotional suffering, many participants in the Icarus Project have the opportunity to transform this trauma into a force for good. We call ourselves wounded healers, because we not only build upon past experiences and insights as we struggle for mental wellbeing, but may do the same for others who find themselves in need of guidance, support, or the simple affirmation that they are not alone. Of course, this is one of the foundational premises of peer support groups like Alcoholics Anonymous, from which we have drawn considerable inspiration. In our experience, those who are best equipped to do the work of supporting others in healing their psychic pain have been there themselves.

---

1   This phrase was coined by Gloria Mitchell, Ph.D., a practicing clinical psychologist and the author's tremendously perceptive and exceptionally supportive mother.

One of the ways in which the radical politics of the organizers of the Icarus Project come to bear on our philosophy is in our critique of monolithic culture and our emphasis on broad-based diversity. The dominant ethos of the cultural climate in the USA is an emphasis on sameness. Many of our "leaders" push programs and policies geared towards streamlining and homogenizing our world, from the way that we eat, to the way that we learn, to the very ways in which we think and feel about the lives that we lead. It is worth noting that American society does encourage a sort of superficial multiculturalism. However, this acceptance is contingent upon people's fulfillment of certain socioeconomic functions: as consumers or capitalists, and thereby preservers of the status quo. One need only look to the sprawling subdevelopments of suburbia or the vast fields of genetically engineered corn for easy examples of this burgeoning trend. Some would defend these developments as indicators of stability and safety. However, a crop sown in the same field year after year is much more susceptible to disease and destruction than if it were interspersed with other varieties or species. We believe that the psychological ecosystems of our culture work in much the same way. Diversity is essential to the wellness of a society. If we fail to think critically about the ways in which we live, and to continually explore alternatives, then we can only fall prey to the lethargy and xenophobia that are the corollaries of such an approach.

As such, we view a diverse psychological climate to be not only a tolerable but a necessary component of a healthy culture. Rather than simply medicating children who demonstrate an unwillingness to participate in a traditional classroom environment, perhaps we should see these children as sources of insight and inspiration into the development of new teaching modalities. Similarly, we see individuals who experience depression as a sort of indicator species for the health of our ecosystem as a whole; there is much in our world to be angry, anxious and sad about. Rather than simply learn how to cope with and function in a society that obviously needs changing, we also choose to explore means by which we might make the world we live in a place where we can truly be happy and fulfilled. We believe that community-based organizing around these issues can in fact itself be a means of addressing psychological suffering. What better way to cope with a world that is obviously insane than to work together to change that reality?

Activism as Healing Modality: The Organizing Philosophy of the Icarus Project

Over the past year and a half, the Icarus Project has expanded well beyond the radical media and web-based project that it was at its inception over four years ago.[1] Regular Icarus Project meetings currently occur in Minneapolis, New York City, Philadelphia and Portland, Oregon, and other allied groups include the Freedom Center of Northampton, MA, the Chicago Mad Tea Party, and the Bay Area Radical Mental Health Collective. Many of the meetings incorporate elements from both peer support and activist circles. One meeting format that some groups use allows an hour for inward support followed by an hour of outward action. In the first hour, members can share their experiences in a safe space, where we cultivate our powers as wounded healers, learn effective communication skills, and explore what it means to be mentally healthy outside of the mainstream. This process not only enables individuals to better equip themselves to address their mental health issues but also builds community through the identification of common ground and experiences. A foundational effort of our work is to connect people who previously had felt isolated from and alienated by traditional approaches to mental health, and inner support sessions are a key part of this endeavor.

From there, our meetings move into an hour or so of outward action. Many of us who come from an activist background found traditional meetings to be draining and disempowering; a common critique is that they emulate and reproduce the stress and trauma of the world that they intend to change. Icarus meetings attempt to dismantle this paradigm—we first build communal empathy via inward support before moving on to strategic organizing. Much of what we are working for is in fact this feeling of community. In a world that is so divisive and so encouraging of isolation, community itself is a revolution-

---

1   Address: The Icarus Project, c/o Fountain House, 425 W. 47th St., New York, NY 10036, USA, info@theicarusproject.net, www.theicarusproject.net

ary concept. Our organizing work consists primarily of extending this base of support. This includes outreach, the development of new materials, the expansion of our website, and the production of cultural and fundraising efforts such as art shows, concerts and other events. Our most recent publication is the first edition of our support manual, which provides ideas and suggestions for building workshops and groups, and is appropriately entitled *Friends Make the Best Medicine: A Guide to Creating Community Mental Health Support Networks*. Another important dimension to our organizing work is that we aim to develop relationships with groups that do complementary work. From other activist groups to alternative healers to academics involved in the post-psychiatry movement, we recognize that this diversity of approaches and skills can only strengthen our broad base of community-support into a multifaceted culture that truly offers an alternative to the psychiatric mainstream.

Icarus offers a place where people who locate themselves outside of this homogenous mainstream can come together and build a new culture of mutual support and iridescent psychological diversity. As Icarus Project organizer and performer extraordinaire Bonfire Madigan Shive says, "We are our own safety nets: we weave together" (2006). The Icarus Project's web-weaving work of cultural transformation gives us a newfound identity of proud mad ones, it allows us to find connections where previously there was isolation, and it creates the space for us to come together around our pain while building a world that reflects the gorgeous alternative visions that so many of us harbor in our dangerously gifted minds.

Sources

DuBrul, A. S. (2002). Bipolar World. *San Francisco Bay Guardian*, September.

Shive, M. B. (2006, January). Personal communication.

C. Models of Professional Support

Volkmar Aderhold, Peter Stastny and Peter Lehmann

Soteria

An Alternative Mental Health Reform Movement

In honor of Loren R. Mosher

The Soteria treatment model was introduced by the American psychiatrist Loren Mosher (1933-2004) in the early 1970s and named after the Greek goddess of safety and deliverance from harm. As director of the Schizophrenia branch at the National Institute of Mental Health, Mosher developed two federally funded research demonstration projects: Soteria (1971-1983) und Emanon (1974-1980). Their aims were to investigate the effects of a supportive milieu ("being with") for individuals diagnosed with "schizophrenia," who were experiencing acute psychotic episodes for the first or second time in their lives.

An Understanding of Psychosis

Mosher had a life-long skepticism vis-a-vis all models of "schizophrenia," primarily because they would stand in the way of an open phenomenological view. He saw the phenomenon, which is usually called "psychosis," as a coping mechanism and a response to years of various traumatic events that caused the person to retreat from conventional reality. The experiential and behavioral attributes of "psychosis"—including irrationality, terror, and mystical experiences—were seen as extremes of basic human attributes. Accordingly, the initial Soteria experiments were set up in an open, fairly unstructured fashion, creating opportunities for profound as well as everyday experiences and mutual learning and support.

Neuroleptics were considered as problematic due to their negative impact on long-term rehabilitation and therefore used only rarely. Specifically, during the first six weeks at Soteria these drugs were only given when the individual's life was in danger and when the viability of the entire project was at risk. However, benzodiazepines were permitted. If there was insufficient improvement after six weeks, the neuroleptic drug chlorpromazine was introduced in dosages of about 300 mg (Mosher & Menn, 1978).

Basically, any psychiatric drugs were supposed to remain under the control of each resident. Dosages were adjusted according to self-observation and staff reports. After a two week trial period, a joint decision was taken whether it made sense to continue the "medication" or not (Mosher, *et al.,* 1994, p. 17).

The Setting

Soteria offered a homelike environment in a 12-room house with a garden in a fairly poor neighborhood of San José, California and intensive milieu therapy for six to seven individuals. About seven full-time staff members plus volunteers worked there, selected for their personal rather than formal qualifications, and characterized as psychologically strong, independent, mature, warm, and empathic.

Soteria staff members did not espouse an orientation that emphasized psychopathology, deliberately avoided the use of psychiatric labels, and were significantly more intuitive, introverted, flexible, and tolerant of altered states of consciousness than the staff on general psychiatric inpatient units (Hirschfeld, *et al.*, 1977; Mosher, *et al.*, 1973). These personality traits seem to be highly relevant for success in this kind of work. Former residents became staff members on several occasions. Soteria employed a quarter-time psychiatrist, who visited the house once a week, and was available on call. Shifts up to 48 hours gave the opportunity of "being with" residents for extended periods of time and thereby going through complete biological/psychological cycles while avoiding disruptive separations due to staff rotations.

Procedures

Soteria was an open social system which allowed easy access, departure and return, if needed. The staff's primary duty was to "be with" disorganized clients without the expectation that they needed to be doing something specific. If frightened, they could call for help. The average length of stay was 4-5 months, and full or partial recovery was generally achieved within 6-8 weeks.

Everyone shared the day-to-day running of the house to the extent they could. Roles were only minimally differentiated to encourage flexibility, with little emphasis on hierarchy, which meant a relatively informal daily schedule. Integration into the local community was paramount.

Instead of traditionally defined, formal in-house therapy, Soteria residents appreciated the offerings of yoga, massage, art, music, dance, sports, outings, gardening, shopping, cooking, etc.

Special meetings were scheduled to deal with interpersonal problems as they arose, and family mediation was provided as needed. Continuity of relationships after moving out of the house was greatly encouraged.

General guidelines for behavior, interaction and expectation (adapted from Mosher & Hendrix, 2004):

- Do no harm.
- Treat everyone, and expect to be treated, with dignity and respect.
- Guarantee asylum, quiet, safety, support, protection, containment, interpersonal validation, food and shelter.
- Expect recovery from psychosis, which might include learning and growth through and from the experience.
- Provide positive explanations and optimism.
- Identify plausible explanations: emphasis on biography, life events, trigger factors instead of vulnerability; promoting experiences of success.
- Encourage residents to develop their own recovery plans; consider them the experts.
- Identify meaningful aspects of life beyond Soteria House.
- Do not assume responsibility for anything the clients might be capable of achieving—trust in self-help.
- Do not use the labels "schizophrenia" or "schizophrenic."

- Collaborate with residents, even if they do not take the prescribed psychiatric drugs.

Rules

Violence to self or others is forbidden, as are sexual relations among residents and between residents and team-members. Visitors are only allowed with prearrangement and agreement of the current residents of the house. Family members and friends are welcome, but it is preferred that they plan their visits ahead of time. No illegal drugs are allowed in the house. (In actuality, residents rarely used illegal drugs, certainly not in the house.)

Three Phases

1. Acute crisis: During this phase "being with" was employed as a practice of interpersonal phenomenology. The use of a special "soft" room was soon abandoned in favor of a fluid interpersonal way of "being with" in a variety of physical and social settings. As long as residents were not a threat to themselves or others, extremes of human behavior were tolerated.

2. Restitution: During this phase, the resident was expected to get involved in daily routines, which corresponded to a role change by the staff from parent-substitute to a more symmetrical peer relationship. In order to normalize the experience of "psychosis," it was related to the person's biographical context, framed in positive terms, and described in everyday language. Developing relationships was of great importance to facilitate a process of emulation and identification among clients, and to enable the staff to recognize any precipitating events and the painful emotions that stem from them.

3. Orientation to the world outside: This phase included role diversification, growing competence and the development of new relationships inside and outside the house: cooperation, planning, accommodation. It was common to reach a consensus among the entire group regarding the timing of a resident's departure. The naturally developing social network of peers remained available after discharge to support recovery and to facilitate community integration, which included direct help with housing, education, work and social life. If necessary, former residents were always welcome back, as long as space at the house was available. Mosher believed that this network was of crucial importance for the long-term outcome of the Soteria work. The "Soteria community" remained active for at least ten years after the program was closed.

Research Results

This remarkable programmatic innovation was evaluated with a fairly rigorous research design, funded by a grant from the U.S. National Institute of Mental Health (Mosher & Menn, 1978).

Due to the expectations of the research community in the 1970s, diagnostic categories like "schizophrenia" were used in the research design to assure comparability among participants. From a more critical and modern perspective, such diagnostic categorization is problematic and more than likely to include people whose experiences are absolutely not comparable. Nevertheless, a narrow focus on individuals who experienced a rather severe form of psychosis ("altered state") lasting for at least one month and with a great risk of being hospitalized involuntarily and subjected to high dosages of neuroleptics, contributes to the potency of the Soteria intervention, and provides a justification for taking it seriously.

Six-Week Outcomes: Both experimental (Soteria) and control groups (hospitalized) showed significant improvement. Since only 33% of the Soteria subjects received neuroleptics during the initial six weeks (but altogether only 12% continuously), Soteria proved to be equally effective for acute symptom reduction as hospital stays with routine neuroleptic use (100%).

Two-Year Outcomes: Both experimental groups (Soteria I & II) achieved equally favorable overall results in comparison with the control group, and significantly better results with regard to their independent living status. While the first experimental group showed a significantly lower rate of "relapse" as defined by recurrence of psychosis, and a significantly lower use of neuroleptics over two years (Mosher & Menn, 1978), the second group only showed a non-significant trend in this direction.

In their comprehensive re-analysis of both study groups, Bola & Mosher (2003) came to the following conclusions, still using the term "schizophrenia":

For all subjects, Soteria had a moderate effect-size advantage (+0.47 SD). For schizophrenia subjects, Soteria had a large effect-size advantage (+0.81 SD). 43% of subjects who went through the Soteria program did not receive antipsychotic drugs during follow-up, and had strikingly good outcomes (+0.82 SD). These findings demonstrate a striking advantage for early episode subjects treated at Soteria (Bola, Mosher & Cohen, 2005).

At the two year follow-up, the group free of psychiatric drugs (43% of all Soteria subjects) was performing well above the overall group mean on preventing rehospitalization, reduction of so-called psychopathology, independent living, social and occupational functioning.

It is clear that the 43% Soteria-subjects free from psychiatric drugs had a much better outcome than the entire control group treated with neuroleptics. There was also a moderate benefit for Soteria subjects who did not receive neuroleptics when compared to a sub-set of the control group who had a similar background profile that might have predicted a neuroleptic-free response (Bola & Mosher, 2002). This might either be due to the absence of psychiatric drugs or because of a greater benefit from the intense psychosocial treatment, or both.

Dissemination and Replicability of the Soteria-Approach

Similar programs have been developed in Europe and North America, mostly in proximity to psychiatric hospitals. Initiatives to promote such programs are currently active around the world. The Soteria model has been marginalized in psychiatric discourse and largely ignored in the psychiatric literature due to the expectation that neuroleptics should be used selectively, for example "if there was no sufficient improvement after six weeks" (Mosher & Menn, 1978). Thereby the program constitutes a challenge to the medical model, and the wide acceptance of hospital treatment as the standard of care for acute psychosocial crises (Mosher & Hendrix, 2004, p. 282).

Nevertheless, during the past 20 years, the Soteria approach has become quite influential within the debate about the reform of therapeutic methods. To this day, the Soteria model remains particularly encouraging for the movement of (ex-)users and survivors of psychiatry and for mental health workers who feel allied with it since it represents a concrete alternative to traditional treatment and is not dominated by neuroleptic use. By demonstrating the self-healing potential of individuals experiencing acute psychoses, it constitutes a major attempt to create a system of appropriate and effective support for people in psychosocial distress.

Since the founding of Soteria in 1971, there have been approximately 12 similar projects around the world, most of them in Europe.

Soteria Berne

In 1984, the Swiss psychiatrist Luc Ciompi founded Soteria Berne, having been "infected" during a stay at Soteria California seven years earlier. In distinction to Mosher, Ciompi (2001, p. 46) wanted to integrate Soteria Berne into the community-based mental health services network. In Berne, the phase-specific process is laid out essentially in a similar fashion as in California: Relaxation and protection from stimuli are emphasized in the acute phase, with a liberal use of the "soft room" where residents and supporters spend most of their time during the first days and weeks of their stay.

Compared to Soteria California, Berne uses considerably more neuroleptics during the reintegration phase and openly endorses its postulated benefits. The diagnosis of schizophrenia is used and openly discussed with patients and relatives. Individual and family psychotherapy are offered more frequently. While a fairly durable network of former residents did develop in Berne, it was not seen as an equally significant factor in achieving long-term psychosocial stability, as in the two California houses.

The results of this effort were not as impressive as in the original Soteria study, given that the outcomes in the areas of so-called psychopathology, social and vocational reintegration, and relapse rates were no better than at several other well-established control sites. However, only 9% of Soteria subjects returned to their parental homes, compared to 34% in the control group. The proportion of first-break subjects who were not treated with neuroleptics was only 30%, however, the average dosages for the entire experimental group were three to five times lower than among control-subjects (Ciompi, *et al.*, 1993). The four patients who remained free of neuroleptics for the entire two-year study period, showed the best overall results.

Soteria Berne did become firmly established within the local psychiatric system, serving as a model program. However, precisely this level of integration might have contributed to a watering-down of its radical nature and its effectiveness as a psychosocial intervention. Nevertheless, since its foundation, Soteria Berne has provided encouragement for service users and providers as a programmatic model and training site.

> Not unlike Loren Mosher I have come to the conclusion, after frequent and hardly innocuous dogmatic excesses, that the theoretical uncertainty and emotional immediacy of an engaged and empathic lay person—certainly within a steady dialogue with equally empathic experts—can come closer to the deeper truth of this enigmatic "disturbance" (or at least cause less harm) than any highfalutin theory (Ciompi, 2001, p. 179).

Currently, beside Soteria Berne there are projects in Zwiefalten and Munich-Haar (Germany), Stockholm North (Sweden), and several in Denmark.[1]

Additionally, the Soteria model has contributed to the occasional development of acute inpatient units that employ so-called Soteria elements, such as a live-in kitchen, availability of multiple relationships, involvement of relatives with the possibility of overnight stays, an open door secured by a reception area, a "soft room" and psychotherapeutic support. Initially, the main focus was the reduction of coercive measures and the promotion of an open-door policy. Support for patients in the midst of psychosis by "being with" is not routinely provided. Neuroleptics are generally given in low doses, but rarely avoided altogether.

As an answer to the risk of dilution and alteration of the Soteria concept, Mosher and Ciompi have developed the following catalogue of elements that must be in place before a program can call itself "Soteria" (Mosher & Ciompi, 2004). While there may be reasons to modify these elements, the question as to who might have the right to do so while still using the Soteria moniker is sensitive and remains unresolved.

---

1 The popularity of Soteria in German-speaking countries is probably a result of the dissemination of well-translated literature, the reports about Luc Ciompi's project and the positive reception of Mosher's work by German-speaking (ex-)users and survivors of psychiatry and critical professionals (see for example Wehde, 1991, pp. 46-50).

Soteria: Critical Ingredients

1. Facility: Small, community based, open, voluntary, home-like, living no more than 10 persons including two staff (one man and one woman) on duty, preferably in 24 to 48 hour shifts to allow prolonged intensive one-to-one contact as needed.

2. Social Environment: Respectful, consistent, clear, and predictable with the ability to provide asylum, safety, protection, containment, control of stimulation, support and socialization as determined by individual needs. Over time it will come to be experienced as a surrogate family.

3. Social Structure: Preservation of personal power to maintain autonomy, mute the hierarchy, prevent the development of dependency and encourage reciprocal relationships. Minimal role differentiation (between staff and clients) to encourage flexibility of roles, relationships and responses. Daily running of house shared to the extent possible. "Usual" activities carried out to maintain attachments to ordinary life—e.g, cooking, cleaning, shopping, music, art, excursions etc.

4. Staff: May be mental health trained and user/survivor-trained professionals, specially trained and selected non-professionals, former clients, especially those who were treated in the program, or a combination of the three types. On the job training via supervision of work with clients, including family interventions, should be available to all staff as needed.

5. Relationships: These are central to the program's work. They are facilitated by staff being ideologically uncommitted (i.e., to approach psychosis with an open mind), conveying positive expectations of recovery, validating the person's subjective experience of psychosis as real by developing an understanding of it by "being with" and "doing with" the clients. No psychiatric jargon is used in interactions with clients.

6. Therapy: All activities viewed as potentially "therapeutic" but without formal therapy sessions with the exception of working with the families of those in residence. In-house problems dealt with immediately by convening those involved in problem-solving sessions.

7. Psychiatric drugs: No or low dose neuroleptic drug use to avoid their acute "dumbing down" effects and their suppression of affective expression.

Also avoid risk of their long-term toxicities. Benzodiazepines may be used short term to restore sleep-wake cycles.[1]

8. Length of stay: Sufficient time spent in the program for relationships to develop that allow precipitating events to be acknowledged; usually disavowed painful emotions to be experienced and expressed and put into perspective by fitting them into the continuity of the person's life.

9. After-care: Post-discharge relationships encouraged (with staff and peers) to allow easy return (if necessary) and foster development of peer-based problem solving community based social networks. The availability of these networks is critical to long-term outcome as they promote community integration of former clients and the program itself.

Soteria as an "Ideological Movement" and a Guiding Idea

No definitive instructions or algorithms for the treatment of psychosis were formulated in either of the two original Soteria projects in California. It is not the psychosis—whatever this might be—that is being treated, but a human being in the midst of an altered experience who is being supported and accompanied, realizing that each individual is very different from the other, and consequently that there can be no "universal recipe" (Runte, 2001) and no universal diagnosis, or in the words of Mosher: "there is no cookbook." The uniqueness of each staff member is being recognized as well.

Referring to psychiatric drugs, Mosher and Hendrix summarized in 2004:

Today (2004) my position is that, since no real alternatives to antipsychotic drugs are currently available, to be totally against them is untenable. Thus, for seriously disturbed people, I occasionally recommend them—as part of collaborative planning with my client—but in the lowest dosage and in the shortest length of time possible. Instead of antipsychotics, however, I prefer to calm acute psychosis and restore sleep/wake cycles with an initial course of minor

---

1   We consider it self-evident that any prescription of psychopharmacological agents, especially in Soteria environments, should occur within an informed consent process—we do not overlook the general lack of information about risks and alternatives and the damages that can result even from low dosages and low potency neuroleptics—V.A., P.St. and P.L.

tranquilizers accompanied by in-home crisis intervention (Mosher & Hendrix, 2004, p. 303).

In sum, the Soteria idea has contributed to the fact that milieu- and interpersonal aspects of treatment, especially in German-speaking countries, are taken a bit more seriously.

In the past 15-20 years, we have been continually accompanied, overtly or not, by the Soteria model. It has become a measure of humane treatment methods, a humane approach towards patients, even a measure of the appropriate conduct of doctors (Marneros, 2001, p. 219).

Current Assessment and Outlook

The Soteria-model has provided a notable impulse for rethinking the therapeutic milieu within the acute care system, but has so far not been translated into actual services that would be available to a significant proportion of individuals who might benefit from them. In addition, several program models have emerged that have implemented some of the Soteria-elements within routine services. However, a continual "being with" that goes beyond a few hours can almost never be provided. Classical Soteria programs have not been established during recent years.

Presently, there is a risk that Soteria development might come to a complete halt, or even gradually recede, especially given the (quickly disproven) assertions that the new "atypical" neuroleptics could guarantee success thus obviating major changes in the delivery of clinical care. Under increasing financial constraints we are witnessing a further reduction of psychosocial treatments within services offered to individuals experiencing psychosis. No questions are raised within the psychiatric system about the absurdity that the use of overpriced "atypical" neuroleptics burdens the health system nor with the perpetual production of social and physical untoward effects due to these very same drugs.

In our view, the historical and therapeutic potential of the Soteria concept is far from exhausted. Quite possibly, the combination of Soteria-facilities with community-based psychosis treatment teams that work according to the Need-adapted Approach might offer the best chance to facilitate its survival

(Alanen, *et al.*, 1994, 2000; Alanen, 1997; Aderhold, *et al.*, 2003). Such an approach would significantly lower the average length of stay at Soteria and thereby its costs. Lehtinen, *et al.* (2000) and Seikkula, *et al.* (2003, 2006) have demonstrated that a community-based service system can offer treatment without neuroleptics for 40-70% of individuals experiencing a first psychotic episode. In three Finnish regions and two retrospective cohorts, these subgroups achieved the best results compared to their controls (see the chapter about Open Dialogues by Seikkula and Alakare in this book). This model was also successfully evaluated in Sweden (Cullberg, *et al.*, 2002).

It is also quite likely that an increasing awareness of the toxicity of the "atypical" neuroleptics—e.g., the drug-induced deficit syndrome, obesity, hypercholisterinaemia, diabetes, irreversible receptor-changes responsible for tardive psychoses and dyskinesias (Ungerstedt & Ljungberg, 1977; Chouinard & Jones, 1980; 1982; Lehmann, 1996, pp. 99-104), increased cell-death (apoptosis; e.g., Bonelli, *et al.*, 2005) and mortality, especially when prescribed in combination with other drugs (Henderson, *et al.*, 2005; Joukamaa, *et al.*, 2006)—will promote the reconsideration of psychosocial treatments and support their full potential. The aim would be to avoid neuroleptic drugs completely for as many patients as possible, or alternatively, to use the lowest possible dosage and thus contain the possible risks.

Neuroleptics are seen by psychiatrists as elements of a compromise formed in the absence of less damaging and effective interventions and not as a curative solution. Whenever possible, neuroleptics should be avoided. The open debate that was started at the membership assembly of the European Network of (ex-)Users and Survivors of Psychiatry (ENUSP) 1997 in Reading, England (Lehmann, 1997), concerning the ethics of the use and concerning especially the risks and dangers of psychiatric drugs, should continue with organisations of psychiatric professionals, relatives, legal professionals, politicians and users and survivors of psychiatry. Further Soteria services combined with community-based teams that use the Need-adapted Approach would enable multi-center studies with large sample sizes.

Such a treatment model could become a rallying point for service users, friends and relatives, especially in Europe. Professionals and family organizations still seem thwarted by the economic dependencies from the pharmaceutical industry that have invaded the entire medical system in an insidious fashion (Angell, 2004), as well as by one-sided beliefs determined by biological reductionism. Currently there is a notable effort, especially in England (House of Commons Health Committee, 2005), to contain the influence of the pharmaceutical industry on the medical system, the parents' organizations and also on a rising number of organizations of (ex-)users and survivors of psychiatry. There is a growing international movement to promote and disseminate Soteria (i.e., www.intar.org, www.soterianetwork.org) and similar alternative treatment programs, as exemplified by the most recent publication on this subject in *Schizophrenia Bulletin*, that came to the conclusion based on a metaanalysis of past Soteria-studies that "further research are urgently required to evaluate this approach more rigorously because it may offer an alternative treatment for people diagnosed with schizophrenia spectrum disorders" (Calton, *et al.*, 2007). Thus, there is hope that the pioneering work of Mosher (who proved that humane, non-medical support is the best way to help people undergoing severe emotional distress), will continue to provide fuel to an alternative mental health reform movement until alternatives to biological psychiatry are available.

Translated from the German by Peter Stastny

Sources

Aderhold, V., Alanen, Y., Hess, G., & Hohn, P. (eds.) (2003). *Psychotherapie der Psychosen. Integrative Behandlungsansätze aus Skandinavien. Gießen: Psychosozial-Verlag.*

Alanen, Y. O. (1997). *Schizophrenia: Its origins and need-adapted treatment.* London: Karnac.

Alanen, Y. O., Lehtinen, V., Lehtinen, K., Aaltonen, J., & Räkköläinen, V. (2000). The Finnish model for early treatment of schizophrenia and related psychoses. In: B. Martindale, A. Bateman, M. Crowe, & F. Margison (Eds.), *Psychosis: Psychological approaches and their effectiveness.* London: Gaskell.

Alanen, Y. O., Ugelstad, E., Armelius, B.-A., Lehtinen, K., Rosenbaum B., & Sjöström, R. (Eds.) (1994). *Early treatment for schizophrenic patients.* Oslo: Scandinavian University Press.

Angell, M. (2004). *The truth about the drug companies: How they deceive us and what to do about it.* New York: Random House.

Bola, J. R., & Mosher, L. R. (2003): Treatment of acute psychosis without neuroleptics: Two-year outcomes from Soteria Project. *Journal of Nervous and Mental Disease* *191*(4), 219-229.

Bola, J. R., & Mosher, L. R. (2002). Predicting drug-free treatment response in acute psychosis from the Soteria project. *Schizophrenia Bulletin 28*(4), 559-575.

Bola, J. R., Mosher, L. R., & Cohen, D. (2005). Treatment of newly diagnosed psychosis without antipsychotic drugs: The Soteria project. In: S. Kirk (Ed.), *Mental disorders in the social environment: Critical perspectives from social work* (pp. 368-384). New York: Columbia University Press.

Bonelli, R. M., Hofmann, P., Aschoff, A., Niederwieser, G., Heuberger, C., Jirikowski, G., & Kampfhammer, H.-P. (2005): The influence of psychotropic drugs on cerebral cell death: Female neurovulnerability to antipsychotics. *International Clinical Psychopharmacology, 20,* 145-149.

Calton, T., Ferriter, M., Huband, N., & Spandler, H. (2007, June 14). A systematic review of the Soteria paradigm for the treatment of people diagnosed with schizophrenia. *Schizophrenia Bulletin Advance Access,* doi:10.1093/schbul/sbm047.

Chouinard, G., & Jones, B. D. (1980). Neuroleptic-induced supersensitivity psychosis. *American Journal of Psychiatry, 137*(1), 16-21.

Chouinard, G., & Jones, B. D. (1982). Neuroleptic-induced supersensitivity psychosis, the "Hump Course," and tardive dyskinesia. *Journal of Clinical Psychopharmacology, 2*(2), 143-144.

Ciompi, L. (2001). Zum "Geist von Soteria." Eine persönliche Reflexion zu drei umstrittenen Fragenkreisen. In L. Ciompi, H. Hoffmann, & M. Broccard (Eds.), *Wie wirkt Soteria? Eine atypische Psychosenbehandlung kritisch durchleuchtet* (pp. 159-180). Berne: Huber.

Ciompi, L., Kupper, Z., Aebi, E., Dauwalder, H.-P., Hubschmid, T., Trütsch, K., & Rutishauer, C. (1993). Das Pilot-Projekt "Soteria Bern" zur Behandlung akut Schizophrener. II. Ergebnisse einer vergleichenden prospektiven Verlaufsstudie über 2 Jahre. *Nervenarzt, 64,* 440-450.

Cullberg, J., Levander, S., Holmquist, R., Mattsson, M., & Weiselgren, I.-M. (2002). One-year outcome in first episode psychosis patients in the Swedish Parachute project. *Acta Psychiatrica Scandinavica, 106*(4), 276-285.

Henderson, D. C., Nguyen D. D., Copeland, P. M., Hayden, D. L., Borba, C. P., Louie, P. M., Freudenreich, O., Evins, A. E., Cather, C., & Goff, D. C. (2005): Clozapine; diabetes mellitus, hyperlipidemia and cardiovascular risks and mortality: Results of a 10-year naturalistic study. *Journal of Clinical Psychiatry 66*(9), 1116-1121.

Hirschfeld, R. M., Matthews, S. M., Mosher, L. R., & Menn, A. Z. (1977). Being with madness: Personality characteristics of three treatment staffs. *Hospital and Community Psychiatry, 28,* 267-273.

House of Commons Health Committee (2005). The Influence of the pharmaceutical industry. Retrieved December 26, 2006, from United Kingdom Parliament web site: www.publications.parliament.uk/pa/cm200405/cmselect/cmhealth/42/42.pdf.

Joukamaa, M., Heliovaara, M., Knekt, P., Aromaa, A., Raitasalo, R., & Lehtinen, V. (2006). Schizophrenia, neuroleptic medication and mortality. *British Journal of Psychiatry, 188*(2), 122-127.

Lehmann, P. (1996). *Schöne neue Psychiatrie, Vol. 1. Wie Chemie und Strom auf Geist und Psyche wirken.* Berlin: Antipsychiatrieverlag.

Lehmann, P. (1997). For and against psychotropic drugs: Proposal as position-paper for the European Network of (ex-)Users and Survivors of Psychiatry. *European Newsletter of (ex-)Users and Survivors of Psychiatry,* (6), 4-5. Retrieved January 3, 2007, from www.peter-lehmann-publishing.com/articles/for_against.htm.

Lehtinen, V., Aaltonen, J., Koffert, T., Räkköläinen, V., & Syvälahti, E. (2000). Two-year outcome in first episode psychosis treated according to an integrated model: Is immediate neuroleptisation always needed? *European Psychiatry, 15,* 312-320.

Marneros, A. (2001). Stellungnahmen von unabhängigen Experten. In L. Ciompi, H. Hoffmann, & M. Broccard (Eds.). *Wie wirkt Soteria? Eine atypische Psychosenbehandlung kritisch durchleuchtet* (pp. 215-219). Berne: Huber.

Mosher, L. R., Hendrix, V., und die Beteiligten des Soteria-Projektes mit D. C. Fort (1994). *Dabeisein: Das Manual zur Praxis in der Soteria.* Bonn: Psychiatrie-Verlag.

Mosher, L. R., Hendrix, V. with D. C. Fort (2004). *Soteria: Through madness to deliverance.* Philadelphia: Xlibris Corporation.

Mosher, L. R., & Menn, A. Z. (1978). Community residential treatment for schizophrenia: Two-year follow-up. *Hospital and Community Psychiatry, 29*(11), 715-723.

Mosher, L. R., Reifman, A., & Menn, A. Z. (1973). Characteristics of nonprofessionals serving as primary therapists for acute schizophrenics. *Hospital and Community Psychiatry, 24*(6), 391-396.

Runte, I. (2001). *Begleitung höchst persönlich – Innovative milieu-therapeutische Projekte für akut psychotische Menschen.* Bonn: Psychiatrie-Verlag.

Seikkula, J., Alakare, B., Aaltonen, J., Holma, J., & Rasinkangas, A. (2003). Open Dialogue Approach: Treatment principles and preliminary results of a two-year follow-up on first episode schizophrenia. *Ethical and Human Sciences and Services, 5*(3), 163-182.

Seikkula, J., Aaltonen, J., Alakare, B., & Haarakangas, K. (2006). Five-year experience of first episode non-affective psychosis in open-dialogue approach: Treatment principles, follow-up outcomes and two case studies. *Psychotherapy Research 16*(2), 214-228.

Ungerstedt, U., & Ljungberg, T. (1977). Behavioral patterns related to dopamine neurotransmission. *Advances in Biochemical Psychopharmacology, 16,* 193-199.

Wehde, U. (1991). *Das Weglaufhaus – Zufluchtsort für Psychiatrie-Betroffene.* Berlin: Antipsychiatrieverlag.

Maths Jesperson

Hotel Magnus Stenbock

A User-controlled House in Helsingborg, Sweden

From 1995 to 2004 Hotel Magnus Stenbock was one of the most innovative user-controlled projects in the world and the only one of its kind in Europe. Numerous articles in various languages were written about it (for example Fleischmann & Brown, 1999b; Jesperson, 1998). In 1999, a video about the hotel was produced (Fleischmann & Brown, 1999a). And in 2002 in a debate in the House of Commons Dr. Fox, Member of the British Parliament for the Conservative Party, used the hotel as a positive model of community living:

> Hon. Members may be aware of examples such as the Hotel Magnus Stenbock, in Helsingborg, which is well known in mental health circles. It is a good example of what might be termed a halfway house for those moving between an institutionalised setting and the community. It has 21 single rooms and offers a balance between private and social space. It offers not just structure and crisis accommodation but a place of safety, and develops a sense of community and acceptance. It is run by RSMH, a multi-million pound organisation of mental health care users that sustains and nurtures self-help care models throughout Sweden (United Kingdom Parliament, 2002).

In 2004, the local social service took over the control of the hotel. This was not due to any criticism of the way the user organisation RSMH (the National Association for Social and Mental Health) had run it, but had to do with some complicated rules of the European Union concerning contractors. The politicians are pondering over giving it back to RSMH.

The hotel still looks much the same as when it was run by RSMH. The same people are working there with the same daily routines. But some fundamental changes have happened in its social structure. Since it is run by the authorities, it has ceased to be a self-help project which means that the democratic management is lost and the residents are no longer "shareholders." Also the volunteers and daily visits by other members of RSMH have disappeared— and with them the lively, social network, which was so important in offering new social contacts for the residents.

The Golden Days of Hotel Magnus Stenbock

Which were the principles guiding the project? What was the vision? How did it work in practice? What was the outcome?

The fundamental principle for the hotel was that living there shouldn't be seen as part of any rehabilitation process or anything like that. Living at the hotel was just one alternative among others. You should be able to chose this way of living without being forced to sign up for a whole plan of treatment and rehabilitation at the same time. The hotel was only a place of living, the other things were up to the persons themselves.

The official model is people should move on from the hotel, that an apartment of your own is the top stair to aim for. For many people, having an apartment on their own is not the best idea. Particularly if they are men over 60 living as single persons; given an apartment in the suburbs, they never tend to cook food. Persons in these situations may not benefit from an apartment. Maybe it's better for them to have a place where they can have social contacts.

At the hotel, there was no pressure on people to move on. This was a relief for many residents as they got stressed at other places after a while by the pressure to move on to "the next step in the rehabilitation programme." In an article about the hotel in the *BMA News*—the magazine of the British Medical Association—the journalist Neil Hallows summarised this principle in some striking words: "They can check in, but they don't have to check out" (2004).

Some people stayed at the hotel only for a couple of weeks, while sorting out some problems, but many stayed at the hotel for several years. Some elderly men moved in to the hotel and stayed there to the day they died.

The hotel was open for everyone. Many came directly from psychiatric institutions. Others were homeless people who came from a life on the streets or in common lodging-houses. A few came from prisons, where they had spent several years. But you didn't have to have a background in psychiatry or the social services or prisons to get a room at the hotel.

An 87-year old man, without any psychiatric or social problems, for example moved to the hotel after an operation on his legs left him unable to climb the stairs to his old apartment anymore. He hated the idea of moving into a nursing home. He preferred to live with younger people at the hotel and said: "I know they are mad, but that doesn't matter." He lived at the hotel for three years and celebrated his 90th birthday there, before he died.

At the hotel, we strived to have a balance between young and old and between men and women. We didn't want it to have that scent of common lodging-house for elderly bachelors, which places like this often have. Women and young people had priority in the queue.

In the beginning, we had big problems with people addicted to hard (illegal) drugs. Some used their room for selling drugs, some for prostituting their bodies. Some of these drug addicts and their customers were quite dangerous and occasionally threatened other people at the hotel with knives. We solved this problem by asking new residents for permission to check if they had heavy drug problems before giving them a room.

After a big fire, which almost demolished the entire hotel and could have caused deaths among the residents, we had to ask for permission also to check if new residents had a history of arson, before giving them a room. An investigation after the fire showed that four fire-setters were actually living at the hotel at that time. The one who put the hotel on fire had done this in other housing accommodations but nobody had informed us about it (Later this man committed suicide).

Problems with heavy drug addiction or arson were the only things we checked out with the authorities before giving a room to a newcomer—and we did it only with their own consent. On the other hand, we only gave out a room, when the consent was given.

We never had any problems with psychiatry. Actually, the chief psychiatrist thought Hotel Magnus Stenbock to be a very good place. As the hotel was only for living and not part of any treatment or rehabilitation plans, we didn't express any opinions about what kind of care or support the residents should or could have. It was their private business. Some were on psychiatric drugs, some not. Some were still psychiatric patients, while others had left psychiatry entirely. Of course, we supported persons who tried to get out of the psychiatric system and live a life without intervention from any authorities.

A hotel is a special place of living. It offers a private and anonymous life and, at the same time, a collective and social way of living. All residents could choose themselves if they wanted to live as a recluse or socialize with the other residents at the hotel. No one was forced to be social. Some of the residents lived completely on their own and we only saw them occasionally when they left their room to go out.

Living at a Hotel

Living at a hotel is actually an old tradition, which is now almost forgotten. As recently as the 1950s, there were many people who lived in hotels year-round, especially in big cities like Paris and New York. In general, a hotel has the advantage of being in the middle of the city, where everything is happening and you have all kinds of services just around the corner. Persons living at Hotel Magnus Stenbock were only 10 yards from a bank and the nearest shops, and only about 50 yards from the central railway-station and the ferries to Denmark, and the beach was only 100 yards away. And festivals or an open-air concerts were often taking place in the immediate surroundings.

People with mental health problems often get in trouble with neighbours when living in housing areas in the outskirt of the town. Living at a hotel in the centre doesn't cause this problem, because people who also live or have a shop in the city centre accept even the noise and disturbance from pubs and nightclubs; in comparison, the hotel residents pose very few problems.

As already mentioned, the hotel was emphatically a place to live rather than be treated. It had none of the feeling of authority found in a residential home run by the local authorities. There was none of the control. As a psychiatric patient, you have to be very careful what you are saying and doing because everything can turn up in your records and might have consequences for you. Patients tend to learn what to say and what not to say—they know what the doctor expects. They are playing a role. Once people are fixed in the roles of patients, they tend to continue in them. That is why, at Hotel Magnus Stenbock, the philosophy was to have no gap between clients and workers, aided by the fact that many people who lived at the hotel also worked there in various capacities.

The hotel had only two steady employees. They worked Monday-Friday during normal business hours, but could be called whenever the residents had a problem that needed to be solved immediately. This happened very seldom, because mostly the residents solved the problems themselves, including calling for an ambulance when somebody at the hotel was injured. We had decided on two employees without a training in the psychiatric or social field, because we didn't want to have any "professionals." Instead, both of the employees were craftsmen, which was very good, because there were often lots of things to repair at the hotel.

Besides the two employees, two of the residents of the hotel were working there, paid by the social services as part of the programme for "sheltered working-places." One of them worked at the reception desk. Also, some members of our local user group worked as volunteers at the hotel.

It was very important to have some of the residents working at the hotel, because we wanted to counteract the usual division in "we" and "them." In the hotel, the employees and the residents weren't two opposite groups, because one person could belong to both of them. The dividing line was not very clear. This non-dividing approach was important, because it was a way of breaking down the cemented role as patient, mentioned above.

A Hotel as a Self-help Project

The hotel was a self-help project. All residents could become members of our local user group, RSMH-Helsingborg, which ran the hotel. They had a direct influence on such things as the policy and rules of the hotel, as well as its finances and instructions for the employees. Many of the other members of the user group were former residents of the hotel, which meant that there was in-depth knowledge in the user group about the hotel.

At the annual meeting of RSMH-Helsingborg, its board was elected. As its members, the residents of the hotel took part in this voting. Some became members of the board, and in this position they were actually employers of the employees at the hotel where they were living. The president of RSMH-Helsingborg lived at the hotel himself (and still does) and he was the man who had the highest responsibility for everything concerning the hotel. All this means that the hotel was really run by the users/residents themselves.

Hotel Magnus Stenbock, named after an 18th century general, was built in 1898 and was entirely renovated in 1995 and classified as a three star-hotel. It has five floors, a cellar and a courtyard of its own; this helped to reduce any disturbances with neighbours. We had taken over the entire hotel with all its furniture. This allowed us to offer our members and other homeless people single-rooms with complete hotel-standard: toilet/shower in each room, bed with sheets, writing-desk, chairs, mirror, lamps, hair-drier, towels, alarm-clock/radio, TV-set with cable channels, telephone etc. We supplemented the rooms with refrigerators and coffee makers. If people wanted to furnish the room with their own furniture instead, we could remove the hotel-furniture.

In the beginning, we had 18 single-rooms. These rooms were in the three storeys at the top. They were supplemented with two single-rooms on the ground floor which were used for crisis-purposes or for visitors who just wanted to stay over night. Because of the high pressure from people who wanted to live at the hotel, we later converted the two single-rooms so they, too, could accommodate long-staying residents. We also converted some other rooms into hotel-rooms, which meant that, in later years, we had 22 single-rooms.

During the first years, we also had our PO-project ("Personal ombudsman" or "personal agent"—see my other contribution in this book) located in one room at the top of the hotel. The PO was working as a kind of "barefoot-lawyer" or advocate for our members and others.

The two storeys at the bottom of the hotel were used for daily activities, not only for the residents but also for other members of the user-group and for visitors. Previously the first floor was occupied by single-rooms, but we tore down some of the walls to get bigger rooms for social activities. RSMH-Helsingborg used this floor as its club-apartment, where you could be together with other members and with residents of the hotel, talk, smoke, watch TV, play billiards, dart or cards, borrow a book from the library, play music etc. We also had a little cafeteria there. At times, we organised parties, cultural or dance evenings, lectures, painting workshops, art exhibitions and so on. And our theatre-group—led by a director from the City Theatre—had rehearsals there. On the ground floor in front of the reception and office area we ran a small restaurant. The basement held the laundry room and a recording studio.

This social meeting place and activity centre was an important part of our vision from the beginning, because we didn't just want to offer rooms for living; we wanted to develop possibilities for friendships and private networks outside the psychiatric and social institutions. This was important, because some persons had very few contacts outside the institution—which was the main reason why some people, feeling lonely, went back to the institutions again.

Economically, the hotel was financed during the first three years with special project-money from the National Social Welfare Board in Stockholm and after that with grants from the local community. One third of the costs were financed in this way, while the remaining two thirds were financed by rents paid by the residents for the rooms.

How was it possible to persuade the local authorities to finance a project as big as the Hotel Magnus Stenbock? The decisive argument for the politicians was when they found out that this was not a project that they would have to spend a lot of money on. Instead, they were saving money, because for the same people, the local authorities would have to pay nearly 10 times as much if these persons stayed at a psychiatric institution or were sent to a private nursing home. As a newspaper headline at the time said: "Hotel Magnus Stenbock is a good bit of business for the town."

What was different about Hotel Magnus Stenbock was not only its structure, its organisation, or its management, but the social process going on inside. The hotel was not just about living or about offering accommodation for homeless people. It was about developing a real community for people who, for various reasons, are outsiders and find it very hard to build and sustain relations with other people.

Sources

Fleischmann, P., & Brown, G. (1999a). *Doing it ourselves Swedish style: A look at user run self-help services and how they operate in Sweden.* Video documentary. London: Brent Lund Alternatives in association with Cable Crouch Productions and Capricorn Productions.

Fleischmann, P., & Brown, G. (1999b). *Luxury hotels for the mentally ill! What the U.K. can learn from Swedish user-run mental health services.* Booklet. London: Brent Lund Alternatives in association with Cable Crouch Productions and Capricorn Productions.

Hallows, N. (2004, February 28). Three stars, no stigma. *BMA News,* 13-14.

Jesperson, M. (1997). Magnus Stenbock: A user-run hotel in Helsingborg. In L. Boone (Ed.), *20 jaar – ans – years Hand in Hand* (pp. 172-177). Gent: Hand in Hand.

Jesperson, M. (1998). Das Hotel Magnus Stenbock. Ein nutzerkontrolliertes Haus in Helsingborg. In K. Kempker (Ed.), *Flucht in die Wirklichkeit – Das Berliner Weglaufhaus* (pp. 71-76). Berlin: Antipsychiatrieverlag.

Jesperson, M. (2003). Das nutzer-kontrollierte Hotel Magnus Stenbock in Helsingborg. *Psychosoziale Umschau, 18*(3), 39-40.

United Kingdom Parliament (2002, June 25). Minutes. Column 757. Retrieved December 26, 2006, from United Kingdom Parliament Web site: www.publications.parliament.uk /pa/cm200102/cmhansrd/vo020625/debtext/20625-08.htm.

Michael Herrick, Anne Marie DiGiacomo and Scott Welsch

The Windhorse Project

The Windhorse Project was founded in 1981 by Edward Podvoll and a group of graduates of the Masters Program in Contemplative Psychology at Naropa University[1] in Boulder, Colorado. Podvoll had worked previously as a psy-

---

1 Naropa University was founded in 1974 by Chogyam Trungpa, Rinpoche, lineage holder of both the Kagyu and Nyingma Buddhist traditions of Tibet. The school is based on Nalanda University, which was characterized by its joining of intellect and intuition.

chiatrist in institutions such as Chestnut Lodge and Austen Riggs. He had also taken up Buddhist meditation practice and became a student of Chogyam Trungpa. Together they sought to bring a sane and compassionate approach to the care and healing of people living with extreme states of mind. Podvoll and his team came to believe that the integration of Western and Eastern psychologies could offer greater skilful means in assisting people who are severely distressed due to extraordinary life circumstances.

This early group of contemplative therapists began as Maitri Psychological Services (MPS), which became the first Windhorse therapeutic community (Maitri is Sanskrit for loving kindness / unlimited friendliness). The fundamental mission of MPS was to provide compassionate care to adults living in their own home and community.

In 1987, Podvoll left MPS to focus on writing a book that would be titled *The Seduction of Madness* where he presents his understanding of the evolution of psychosis and the journey of recovery and healing (Podvoll, 1990). This book was reissued with some new material in 2003 under the title *Recovering Sanity*. In 1991, two of the original founders, Jeffrey and Molly Fortuna, moved to Halifax, Nova Scotia and created Windhorse teams there. The Fortunas partnered with Connie Packard, a dedicated family advocate, and others to help Windhorse take root in New England. During the same period, Windhorse was also re-established in Boulder as Windhorse Community Services, which is a thriving presence in the Boulder/Denver area today.

Typically when people come to Windhorse they agree to stay at least six months to a year. The degree of daily therapeutic support depends on each individual, however Windhorse teams do not provide 24 hour support and people generally are able to spend some period of time during the day alone. Therapeutic support may increase during a time of severe distress. Windhorse is a private pay situation but health insurance is accepted and a certain degree of financial aid may be available upon request. Information regarding admissions and services can be accessed through the Windhorse website.

In addition to Windhorse organizations operating in the United States, Hans Kaufmann established a Windhorse organization in Vienna, Austria in

1995.[1] Kaufmann had met Podvoll in 1986 and was drawn both to his understanding of psychosis and to the Windhorse approach to care.

In the remainder of this chapter, we will present a brief description of Podvoll's working model of psychosis, the fundamental principles of the Windhorse approach and the therapeutic and contemplative practices of Windhorse.[2]

Working Model of Psychosis

In *Recovering Sanity*, Podvoll offers a model for understanding the genesis and development of psychosis. He describes certain causes and conditions that give rise to such an evolving process that ultimately leads to madness. He calls this "The Cocktail." "The 'Cocktail' consists of a Predicament, an Intention, Exertion, a Substance, and Mindlessness. Usually, all of these ingredients can be found to one degree or another in the production of a psychosis" (Podvoll, 2003, p. 173).

We briefly describe each element of this "Cocktail."

Predicament refers to the intense pressure of environmental circumstances, intractable dilemmas that threaten one's sense of safety and self. In the effort to escape the overwhelming weight of a profound predicament, one may "switch out" and enter realms of magic and power, undergoing radical self-transformation in a desperate attempt to resolve what seems unresolvable.

Intention refers to the powerful ambition to transcend the ordinary demands, responsibilities, and limitations of one's life as it is and attain a state of power and freedom beyond the pains of the earthly realm.

---

1   Addresses: Windhorse Associates, Inc., 211 North Street, Suite 1, Northampton, MA 01060, USA, tel. +1 (413) 586-0207 ext. 108, web sites www.windhorseassociates.org, www.windhorsecommunityservices.com, www.naropa.edu • Windhorse Gesellschaft, Zeltgasse 8/5, 1080 Vienna, Austria, tel. +43 (0)1 4080706, cell phone +43 (0)650 4080706, web site www.windhorse.at • Windhorse Frankenthal e.V., Postfach 1233, 67242 Lambsheim, Germany, tel. +49 (0)6233 506133, web site www.windhorse.de

2   Due to limited space in this chapter we were not able to include a first person narrative written by a client about his experience at Windhorse. This story is available online at www.windhorseassociates.org

Exertion refers to the great effort it takes to transform the self and so transcend one's predicament. This requires engaging in practices that desynchronize or dissociate the mind and body, as well as the mind-body from the environment.

Substance refers to the consumption of actual substances that alter consciousness and propel the effort toward self-transformation. This can include alcohol, marijuana, hallucinogens, amphetamines, etc. These further desynchronize mind and body and intensify the experience of a transcendent realm of power and freedom beyond the constraints of ordinary waking reality.

Mindlessness refers to the state that follows from fueling desynchronizing practices with substances and "switching out." As one gives increasing attention to and identifies more with the "other world," one loses touch with one's immediate environment, with other people, and even with the needs of the body. The mind becomes overwhelmingly preoccupied in an imaginary realm.

Considering these five elements provides a way to recognize the early stages of a developing psychosis and ideally offer support and alternative means for addressing an underlying predicament, and thus avoid catastrophe.

From a medical model point of view, a person suffering with psychosis is the victim of a pathological physical condition, i.e., a "brain disease." Other views may locate pathology elsewhere, i.e., in the family system or in the physical or cultural environment. Although Podvoll's model does not deny these possible contributors, it points to the active role that an individual plays in the development of their psychosis and challenges the notion that anyone is simply a victim. This view opens up the possibility for individuals to become more fully active agents in their own recovery. Although we recognize all of the toxic and traumatic circumstances that may contribute to the development of extreme states, we also recognize the power of individuals to take responsibility for their own experience, behavior, and recovery.

With recognition of all of these factors, Windhorse endeavors to provide a gentle and healing environment where impossible predicaments can be relaxed, practices of mind-body-environment synchronization can be engaged in, addiction to substances can be released, and ordinary life and full presence in the company of others can once again seem attractive.

Windhorse Principles

The foundation of the Windhorse approach is our faith that all beings possess intrinsic health and intelligence and that this can be accessed and utilized in overcoming any difficulty or challenge.

> The result of letting go is that you discover a bank of self-existing energy that is always available to you—beyond any circumstances. It is the energy of basic goodness. This self-existing energy is called Windhorse. The wind principle is that the energy of basic goodness is strong, exuberant, and brilliant. It can actually radiate tremendous power in your life. But at the same time, basic goodness can be ridden, which is the principle of the horse. So discovering Windhorse is, first of all, acknowledging the strength of basic goodness in yourself and then fearlessly projecting that state of mind to others (Trungpa, 1995).

Even amidst great illness and distress, Windhorse energy is available. Even when there are insurmountable physical or cognitive limitations, we can adapt, find meaning and purpose, and experience the joy of living. Because of Windhorse energy no person and no situation is unworkable.

Recovery is Possible

Following from the assumption that everyone possesses intrinsic health and intelligence, is our belief that recovery is possible. In fact, given the right environment, individual desire, discipline, and enough time, we have seen that it is more likely than not. While we believe that "recovery" must be defined by the person striving to attain it, we do hold a general vision of recovery. It entails the creation of a meaningful and satisfying life in which our needs are met and our potentials developed in four fundamental dimensions. Together these four dimensions make up the "whole person," as described next.

Whole Person

A whole person approach to understanding and responding to people in extreme states will recognize and include the following four fundamental dimensions of any person: physical, interpersonal, psychological, and environmental. At Windhorse we call these *body, speech, mind,* and *environment.* (These dimensions also correspond to the "four quadrants" as described by the American philosopher Ken Wilber. For a full elaboration of the quadrants see Ken Wilber's *Integral Psychology* [2000].) In contrast to reductionistic approaches that focus primarily on one dimension or another, a whole person perspective is curious about all four. It also sees them as vehicles for the radiant expression of spirit. We consider psychoses and other extreme states to be the result of imbalances within and between these four dimensions and that the path of recovery requires the means for addressing those imbalances.

Certainly we are critical of the prevailing bio-medical reductionism that sees psychosis as simply a brain disease, but we are also critical of theories that reduce the causes of distress to psychological, interpersonal, or environmental factors. While those who hold exclusively to one or the other of these explanations may argue over the "true cause" of "mental illness" and therefore the most effective responses, Windhorse believes that each perspective offers a piece of understanding as well as some skillful means. Alone, however, each is incomplete. We find that a whole person approach must weave all four together in a way that is finely tuned to the needs and capacities of each individual.

Contemplative Awareness

While a whole person perspective may allow us to understand those we serve in the broadest possible way, we find that even this scope is limited. What it leaves out is a perspective on oneself as a care provider. Windhorse was founded by contemplative practitioners who first examined their own minds and lives, holding to the understanding that self awareness provides the basis for offering anything useful to others. This remains at the heart of the Windhorse approach. Through contemplative practice, meditation in particular, we see that the seeds of psychosis are in every mind, that madness is only a matter of degree. In order to serve another, we must continually examine ourselves and cultivate our capacity for empathy and compassion.

Asylum Awareness

For most people, psychosis is an extremely threatening experience. It can feel as though one's life and very soul are on the line. Fear can be a common reaction both for persons experiencing psychosis and for those who encounter them. Much of the history of psychiatric care seems to be the fearful attempt to control people, to bring them under submission, i.e., through psychiatric drugs, electroshock, physical restraints, etc. (see Whitaker, 2002). Presumably these methods have come from benevolent intentions. However, Podvollhas described this process of exerting power to control people as "asylum mentality" (Podvoll, 2003, pp. 61-68). At Windhorse the practice of *asylum awareness* brings our attention to any blatant or subtle ways that we might be tempted to exert power over people in order to control them due to our own fear. Instead our first line of response is to cultivate empathic connection and provide a safe and healing environment to allay the fear and chaos of extreme states.

Islands of Clarity

The term "islands of clarity" (coined by Podvoll) points to the instances of health and sanity that occur even in the midst of the most extreme distress. While acknowledging confusion and difficulties, we practice looking for any expressions of courage, clarity, compassion, and insight. If we are not looking for them we can easily miss moments when someone wakes from the dream of psychosis and comes to their senses. These occasions can be fragile and fleeting. They need to be recognized, protected, and nurtured because they provide the sparks for recovery. The practice of basic attendance (described below) is designed to recognize and respond to islands of clarity and support and help stabilize them along the path of recovery.

Mutual Learning

A core aspect of our work at Windhorse is our acknowledgement that regardless of distinctions between the roles of "staff" or "client," in the words of Harry Stack Sullivan: "We are all much more human than otherwise." We are all on a path of growth and learning. We are not just providing treatment to those unfortunate others, but are simultaneously working on ourselves in the process. Or in the words of Lilla Watson, a Brisbane based Aboriginal educator and activist: "If you have come here to help me, you are wasting your time. If you come because your liberation is bound up with mine, then let us work together." We find that the attitude of mutual learning is an antidote to the arrogance that can give rise to asylum mentality.

Healing Happens through Authentic Relationship

Rather than seeing clinical staff as "change agents" that facilitate emotional and behavioral change in clients, we hold that necessary changes are the natural product of authentic relationships. In the words of Loren Mosher, we emphasize "being with" rather than "doing to." Certainly there are prudent boundaries inherent to any professional relationship. We maintain mindfulness of this while also embracing what Podvoll has called the "therapist-friend dilemma" (ibid., pp. 277-278). Essentially this requires showing up as fully human as possible and mutually negotiating the demands of relatedness. Since the lack of opportunity for healthy relations often contributes to the causes of extreme states, we believe that authentic relationship is one of the most important things that we can offer.

Households

Since a whole person approach recognizes the importance of environment, we believe that one's home should be pleasing and personalized to one's own taste. Each person lives in their own apartment (shared with a paid housemate) and anything that would make it feel like an "institution" is avoided. Attention is given to creating homes that are safe, functional, and beautiful according to the needs and preferences of those who actually live in them.

Community

Windhorse is a therapeutic community. We believe that recovery occurs not only through individual relationships, but through meaningful membership in a larger community. The Windhorse community includes clients, their families, staff members, and staff member's families. Through regular social events we provide opportunities for all to gather for learning, recreation, and celebration. Connection with the broader community beyond Windhorse is also important. This is why people live in their own apartments in town and basic attendance is done mostly out and about, rather than in an office setting.

Windhorse Therapeutic Practices

Basic Attendance

The Windhorse principles are embodied and manifest through the core practice of *basic attendance*. There are 10 skills of basic attendance which point
to the means necessary to properly attend to what arises in any situation.
These skills include: being present, letting in, bringing home, letting be,
bringing along, recognizing, finding energy, leaning in, discovering friendship, and mutual learning (ibid., pp. 247-284). Jeffrey Fortuna explained
these principles in an internal Windhorse document:

> Basic attendance is "basic" because it works with the most funda-
> mental situation: to synchronize body, mind and environment by
> gathering attention and sharpening perceptions with the ordinary
> activities of life. It is "attendane" because the therapist's intention
> and training is to be of compassionate service by tending to the
> needs of someone during the recovery process. We regard psycho-
> sis as a major disruption in the balance of the body-mind-environ-
> ment system that dislocates the person from the functional
> reference points of ordinary life. The mindful work of basic atten-
> dance brings the therapist's and the client's mind "back home" to
> the body and the immediate environment.

Windhorse Teams

Each Windhorse team member, including the clients themselves over time,
practices basic attendance. Fundamentally, the therapeutic work is collaborative in that the client is a full and participating member of the team. Their role
is to inform the team of their own needs and desires, engage whatever practices make sense to them, and voice concerns whenever team members are
more of a nuisance than a support.

When an individual's need for support is great, the team will include the
following roles. The *Housemate* provides an anchor within the Windhorse
household, living with the client as a companion within the context of community life and attending to environmental needs. The *Team Leader*, considered the organizing principle on the team, coordinates the schedules and

tasks of the team while also doing basic attendance and overseeing the domestic arena. The *Intensive Psychotherapist* is in partnership with the Team Leader, holding the big picture and attending to the "mind of the team" as well as meeting two to three times weekly with the client in individual therapy. The *Wellness Nurse* collaborates with the client regarding their overall health and well being (attending to diet, exercise, sleep, etc.) and liaisons with the psychiatrist, client and psychotherapist in monitoring medications. *Team Counselors* and *Peer Counselors* meet with the client for basic attendance once or twice a week. The Peer Counselor's own lived experience exemplifies the belief that recovery is possible. As the need for support decreases the team reduces in size. Over time it may be reduced to a single person who serves as a *Therapeutic Mentor*, a role that can be fulfilled by a Team Counselor or a Peer Counselor.

Windhorse also works with substance-use issues and the *Addiction Consultant,* who is typically a Windhorse therapist, oversees this area. The Windhorse view that recovery is possible includes clients, their families, and professionals. With this in mind there is a *Family Coordinator* position held by a senior therapist who provides support to the family members through phone contact, meetings, monthly support groups and written material.[1]

Windhorse Contemplative Practices

The contemplative practices engaged at Windhorse come from the fundamental ground of mindfulness-awareness meditation. This practice works with synchronizing body, mind and environment as a way of being present moment to moment in one's daily life.

Within the context of recovery, this basic practice is integral to the therapeutic life of clients, family members, and staff. The practices utilized at Windhorse include Quiet Moment, Group Contemplative Practice, Sending and Taking Practice, Body-Speech-Mind Supervision, and The Way of Council.

Quiet Moment is the simple practice of bringing mindful attention to the moment and leaving behind prior preoccupations in order to come into the

---

1   The Windhorse Family Guidelines are available on www.windhorseassociates.org

present situation with clarity and openness. This occurs at the beginning and end of all meetings and gatherings.

In addition to the requirement that staff have a personal contemplative practice, *Group Contemplative Practice (GCP)* supports staff in strengthening the mindfulness-awareness they bring to their therapeutic work. The basic meditation technique of focusing attention on the breath to synchronize body, speech and mind guides GCP.

Sending and Taking Practice, or "exchanging self for other," is a practice for cultivating compassion. It involves "letting in" the suffering of others as well as oneself with the in-breath and then sending out whatever is needed to ease the suffering with the out-breath. This practice is fundamental to the Windhorse way of being with clients and it is part of GCP.

Body-Speech-Mind Supervision is an integral part of the clinical supervision process at Windhorse. The primary intention of this approach is to decrease the therapist's tendency to interpret, analyze or judge a client's process while heightening the experience of exchanging self for other.

The Way of Council assists staff, clients, and family members in building strong and trusting relationships with each other in order to better handle conflict and discord as it unfolds in our day to day life together (Zimmerman & Coyle, 1997). We hold a seasonal All Staff Council and Community Council where the group sits together in a circle for an extended period, usually 2-3 hours, using a talking piece to allow full expression to take form while holding in mind the four intentions of Council: 1) speak from the heart; 2) listen from the heart; 3) be lean of expression; 4) be spontaneous.

Conclusion

It has been more than 25 years since Windhorse began working with people in their homes and communities with the genuine belief that recovery is possible. We have held that a whole person approach is essential and that mindfulness and contemplative practices provide the ground for our work and for recovery. As we strive to embody this way of being with others and ourselves, we have come to see that we are all more human than otherwise. The result has been a clear and unwavering commitment to respectful and compassionate care that fully nurtures and appreciates the health and sanity that is intrinsic to all beings. Hundreds of courageous individuals have walked this path of recovery. We honor them and are deeply grateful for the ways in which their lives and ours have been forever transformed.

Sources

Podvoll, E. (1990). *The seduction of madness.* New York: HarperCollins.

Podvoll, E. (2003). *Recovering sanity: A compassionate approach to understanding and treating psychosis.* Boston: Shambhala.

Trungpa, C. (1995). *The sacred path of the warrior.* Boston: Shambhala.

Trungpa, C. (2005). *The sanity we are born with.* Boston: Shambhala.

Wegela, K. K. (1996). *How to be a help instead of a nuisance.* Boston: Shambhala.

Whitaker, R. (2002). *Mad in America.* Cambridge: Perseus.

Wilber, K (2000). *Integral psychology.* Boston: Shambhala.

Zimmerman, J., & Coyle, V. (1997). *The way of council.* Putney, VT: Bramble Books.

Jeanne Dumont and Kristine Jones

The Crisis Hostel

Findings from a Consumer/Survivor-defined Alternative to Psychiatric Hospitalization[1]

Introduction

Having a place in Tompkins County, New York, where people could retreat if they viewed themselves in need and/or at risk of psychiatric hospitalization was the primary purpose of the Crisis Hostel Project. This place would consist of staff members who had "been there," a simple set of rules, meditation/ massage space, raging space and took many years of planning. The project

---

1 Adapted from *Outlook*, Spring 2002, pp. 4-6, a publication of NASMHPD (National Association of State Mental Health Program Directors) Research Institute

was sponsored by the Mental Health Association of Tompkins County beginning in 1994 with the goal of a spin off to a developing consumer/survivor
not-for-profit corporation. During its evolution we were awarded a Research
Demonstration Grant from the Federal Center of Mental Health Services to
operate and evaluate the Crisis Hostel. We are sad to say the hostel closed in
1996 when the federal grant monies ended and not enough operating funds
had been secured.

Our research showed that access to and actual use of the hostel significantly contributed to healing, empowerment and satisfaction with services.
In addition, we found that people who actually used the hostel spent less time
in psychiatric wards. This shift in acute care services use, coupled with the
lower per diem costs of the hostel compared with a day of psychiatric hospitalization, accounted for modest cost savings. Thus we conclude that the Crisis Hostel was an effective innovation. How is it then that such an effective
innovation is not currently in operation?

You may be familiar with the story of the *Three Little Pigs and the Wolf*
who blows their houses down. When we consider the gap between research
and services, often various versions may be told of what happens in translating particular findings into practice. Even with the Three Little Pigs there's
the story according to the Wolf you may not be aware of.[1] Mr. A. Wolf, as he
refers to himself, claims circumstances are what brought the houses down. A
bad cold, big sneezes. He was just looking to borrow a cup of sugar to make a
cake for his sick grandma. Although there was no Big Bad Wolf that blew the
hostel away, the research itself was both friend and foe. Foe in that vying for
continuing funds before all the results were in, the service was held to a
higher effectiveness standard than pre-existing services.

We would now like to describe the service and research components of the
project in further detail and, providing the evidence, we would like to discuss
the existence of such a hostel as a viable service option.

The Crisis Hostel, involving a five bed residence for short stays of less than
two weeks, operated in the mid 1990s for two years in the small city of Ithaca,
New York, as an alternative to psychiatric hospitalization. The Crisis Hostel

---

1   The author of this version is Jon Scieszka.

program consisted of two components, one that offered pre crisis planning and training in strategies for dealing with crisis including drop in support, and a second that provided overnight respite to persons who self defined the need and risk of hospitalization.

Throughout the project's planning and development, ex-patients and other consumers provided most of the initiative, expertise, concepts and staffing. The type of evaluation that was conducted should provide insight for consumers and payers who are searching to improve the existing delivery system of specialty mental health services.

The Crisis Hostel distinguished itself from conventional crisis services in its consumer/survivor involvement, voluntary non-medical model, self-definition of need, and foundation in peer support. The project's evaluation allowed entry to any County person who had had a psychiatric hospitalization in the past three years or who met criteria for having severe mental illness or severe distress. A sample of study participants was generated by inviting persons to participate and then randomly assigning to either an access (test) or a no access (control) to the Crisis Hostel group. While some people were homeless during the study period, and some expressedly had decided not to use medical model services, neither was a requirement to participate in the Crisis Hostel's evaluation.

This Crisis Hostel alternative was wanted to avoid the involuntary treatment system and the negative ramifications associated with inpatient hospitalization, e.g., disruption, loss of control, traumatizing treatment, avoidance of help, exaggeration of problems to get admitted and the unlikelihood of collaborative relationships. It was also felt that retreating to a supportive, healing and recovery focused environment surrounded by others who have experienced similar problems or who show an implicit understanding of the effect of the experience could help them learn from and work through a crisis.

Organizers believed that this alternative would result in less frequent and shorter durations of crisis service use—either of the Crisis Hostel itself or traditional hospital-based services. They predicted that persons with access to the Crisis Hostel would experience a movement toward recovery, a greater sense of empowerment and satisfaction with services than would persons without access to the hostel. They predicted that persons with access to the hostel would spend more days in paid or volunteer work than persons in the control group. They predicted that the reduction in use of crisis services would lower crisis service and total mental health treatment costs when compared to the usual treatment system.

Methods

Using a random design, the study investigated these outcomes for 265 participants having or not having access to the Crisis Hostel (CH). All study participants had been labeled with a DSM-III R *(Diagnostic and Statistical Manual of Mental Disorders)* diagnoses. They had experienced substantial hospital stays with a majority having had four or more admissions and a median "longest stay" of over one month. The median annual income was only $8,400.

Persons in the test group had access to all CH services. CH services included a preparatory hostel training, crisis services, on-going workshops, peer counseling, advocacy, entry to a rage or meditation/massage room, and access to overnight stays. Use of CH services was voluntary. During the grant period, guests were not charged for using crisis hostel services (in fact charging even a small amount was not permitted by the granting agency). Test group members also had access to usual services as did the study's control group. The control group was not able to avail themselves of CH services. Both groups were evenly distributed on all baseline variables.

Participants were assessed upon admission to the study, and both at six and 12 months with measures of empowerment, healing symptoms, hospital admissions and length of stay, job maintenance and satisfaction with services. They were also asked about stays in the Crisis Hostel, the local community hospital and state hospitals as well as about use of community-based specialty mental health services. Providers were contacted with the consent of participants to provide information concerning volume of service use. Each service category was assigned a unit cost estimate based on accounting data.

Results

Whole Sample Analyses

Looking at the results, the test group had better healing outcomes at the six month interval (p = 0.04)[1] and when a repeated analysis was conducted from baseline to 12 months (p = 0.05). With respect to empowerment, the test group had greater levels of empowerment than the control group at the 6-month interval (p = 0.02) and when a repeated analysis was conducted from baseline to 12 months (p = 0.01). Both groups reported the same number of hours spent in paid or volunteer employment over the entire study period.

Perhaps not surprising, the test group reported that the CH offered crisis services that were more timely and useful by more competent staff who respected the consumer's rights than persons receiving usual crisis services only. Greater levels of promotion of healing and self-care had been experienced by the test group than experienced by the control group. All in all, the test group had greater levels of service satisfaction than the control group (p = 0.00).

In the six months prior to entry into the study, a greater proportion of persons in the test group experienced hospital admissions (24.7% vs. 17.5%). Despite this, during the first six months, the proportion of the test group with any hospital admissions was a similar 11.9% as compared to the control group's admission rate of 12.6%. While not significantly different, in the second six-month period, the proportion for the test group was reduced to 7.7% as compared to a virtual no change in proportion of 13.2% for the control group.

When the length of stays associated with those who had hospital admissions was examined, those in the test group spent shorter periods of time in the hospital than the control group. Over the year, the average stay was 10.7

---

1   The editors: The p-value expresses the degree of likelihood that the measured difference is based on chance. A p-value below 0.05 for example indicates that the likelihood for a measured difference between two comparison groups to be based on chance is less than 5%.

days for the test group and 15.2 days for the control group. Hospital stays for those with hospital admissions in the control group were nearly 50% greater than the test group. This difference did not reach a level of significant difference. However, a repeated measure approach that took into account the entire sample did find a significant difference in mean hospital stay ($p = 0.02$).

Turning to whether or not a service system that includes a CH would result in lower costs, a comparison of the two groups psychiatric hospital costs (measured as inpatient stay costs and emergency room service costs) found that persons with access to the CH experienced significantly lower psychiatric hospital costs over the study period ($p = 0.05$). Their average costs were $1,057 while the control group's costs averaged $3,187. The control group's crisis service costs were over 200% greater than those of the test group's. Even when the CH costs are combined with the other crisis service costs the test group's average costs trended lower than the control group's. Their total crisis service average costs were just $2,018. Or, the test group's costs are slightly less than two-thirds of the average costs for the control group.

When all specialty mental health services are included—the crisis services costs as well as the expenditures on community mental health services and supportive housing programs, the test group was still associated with lower treatment costs. The test group's average cost for this expanded set of services was $9,088 and these costs averaged $13,919 for the control group. This represents a cost difference of $4,831 per person over just a year's time!

Crisis Hostel Overnight Stays

Within the test group, 66 persons made 169 overnight visits with an average stay of 7.79 days. These persons were asked about their reasons for their respective visits, what goals they had for the stay and about the helpfulness of the Crisis Hostel. Two strategies were used for guests[1] to report their reasons for initiating the visit. Guests were asked to respond to a check list of poten-

---

1 Initial language of hostel users was changed to guests because at least some hostel staff felt users implied that persons were using them while guests did not have that connotation.

tial symptoms; they also had an opportunity to state in their own words why they came.

Almost all guests reported feeling "nervous, tense, worried, frustrated, afraid." Only 7% of guests reported very mild or no such feelings. At 48% of visits, guests reported that the degree of these feeling was severe or very severe. Similarly reports of depression were also very common (38% reporting at least severe depression, 25% reporting at least a severe loss and 38% at least feeling a severe loneliness). Other common responses included feeling at least a severe sense of being overwhelmed or out of control (36%); feeling exhausted (34%) and having sleeping difficulties (40%).

A brief sampling of the words guests used to describe their reasons for an overnight stay are given below. In actuality, most persons gave more than one reason which may not be adequately conveyed in the following excerpts: "world riddled with strife," "dealing with too many dilemmas," "sleeping outside," "fear of hearing voices," "suicidal thoughts becoming overwhelming," "too much stress at home," "wanting to use drugs," "trying to keep control and keep from using drugs," "everything spinning out of control," "usual strategies not working," "freaking out," "everything falling down on me," "released from hospital and very panic stricken," "overwhelmed by everything," "living on street," "can't sleep."

Several themes emerged as guests identified their goals for coming to the hostel overnight. Among the most common goals were problem-solving and planning, respite and stress reduction, dealing with suicidal feelings, dealing with substance abuse, feelings of safety, housing or changing their living situations, becoming reconnected to mental health provider, jobs, dealing with feelings, and establishment of stable sleep patterns.

When guests left, 69% said that their visit resulted from a very or extremely urgent need to use the hostel and 66% said their feelings about their crisis had changed for the better since entering the hostel. In fact, in 66% of the visits, the guests reported that the hostel was either extremely or very important in working through their crisis. In 68% of the visits, the guests said that the hostel did a better job than the hospital of helping them work through their crisis.

Conclusions

In nearly all areas, persons who had been randomly assigned access to the CH were associated with both better outcomes and lower costs. Persons in the test group were associated with greater levels of healing, empowerment and satisfaction. They experienced no or less disruption in their work life. Hospital stays were relatively less frequent and shorter. Crisis service costs and total mental health service costs were lower for the test group than for the control group.

What do these findings suggest about the existence of a hostel as a viable service option? And can savings be realized even as persons are given the choice whether and when to use an overnight night hostel?

We found that persons' self assessment of their need to use the hostel ran the gamut from taking a time out to early prevention of a crisis to actually being in a crisis that in the past would have resulted in a hospitalization. People added the hostel to their service use or substituted the hostel for other service options such as the hospital.

During the study period the hostel was used as an early prevention option for many of the users. They made use of the hostel instead of doing whatever they would have done if the hostel didn't exist, in some cases nothing, either riding the crisis out or finding that it was exacerbated with time and more drastic or disruptive measures such as going into the hospital were realized, either on their own volition or through involuntary means. In some cases, the hostel was used in addition to the hospital. Usually persons went into the hospital and then subsequently used the hostel. On average hospital stays were comparatively shorter for persons with access to the hostel than for those without access.

If a hostel were to become a service option and not merely a temporary innovation during a grant period, we think that a hostel might continue to be used in a step down fashion; however, people would also more frequently turn to the hostel instead of hospitalization. This would be facilitated by people working at the hospital referring people to the hostel. In this project, attempts were made to facilitate hospital personnel seeing the hostel as a choice instead of a hospital admission, but we think it would be more likely to be realized if a hostel was in operation longer and positive findings from testing its effectiveness were better known.

Finally, we think that with a hostel operating for a longer duration and persons learning how best to use it to fit their individual needs, for example, having periodic short term overnight stays or making use of on-going trainings and drop in support, we would find that a hostel could be substituted for other service options, including high end residential support. Although cost savings are primarily realized through the substitution of hostel services for hospitalizations, the findings from the Crisis Hostel Project suggest that the comparatively low cost of a hostel would result in modest cost savings, even when a significant number of people add such an option to their support system or service utilization pattern.

The hostel stemmed from the expertise of consumer/survivors and their desire for an entirely voluntary choice based on their self-defined needs. Since the findings point to effectiveness and modest cost savings, we hope this will translate into the implementation of voluntary self-defined alternatives to hospitalization and to the practice of recovery principles.[1]

1   We want to acknowledge the many persons beside us involved in the Crisis Hostel Project which included the Crisis Hostel committee comprised of Olivia Armstrong, Lisa Baechtle, Jan Bridgeford-Smith, Mary Chapman, Jessica Curry, Harvey Fireside, Cathi Ganger, Jerry Gross, Stuart Halber, Myra Kovary, Larry Roberts, Carole Stone, and Joanne Zager; the research advisory group of Martha Ann Carey, Sharon Carpinello, Judi Chamberlin, Janet Chassman, Maureen Donohue-Smith, Beth Jenkins, Rhoda Linton, Julian Rappaport, David Shern, Tanya Tempkin and William Trochim; the research staff Lindy Costello, Edna Federer, Belinda Gross, CISER; the Crisis Hostel staff, Molly Brewton, Phoebe Brown, Catberry, David Elliot, Carmel Fusco, Joyce Hatch, Judi Hilman, Pat Shea, Surinder Sidhu and Maryann Sumner as well as the Mental Health Association of Tompkins County and all the participants.

Petra Hartmann and Stefan Bräunling

Finding Strength Together

The Berlin Runaway House

In recent decades, attempts have been made to change the practices of institutional and community psychiatry. Nevertheless, day to day life in the Runaway House is still overshadowed by earlier experiences of disempowerment and violations of personal rights in psychiatric treatment settings.

We also experience these type of degradations when dealing with the authorities and everyday situations as soon as any involvement with psychiatry or the existence of a psychiatric diagnosis becomes known. Whether a real estate agency cancels a viewing once they find out that the interested person has been in psychiatric care, whether the social welfare office refuses access to certain benefits on the basis of psychiatric diagnoses or based on a statement from a legal guardian—"Actually I get on very well with him and I think he's very nice but, well, he's psychotic … and so…"—such instances are usually followed by a curtailment of personal empowerment and the threat of coercive measures. These are only a few examples of the type of things that occur every day in the Runaway House.

The Runaway House is the ten-year old implementation of an experiment to offer people a refuge from these kind of disempowering and debasing experiences, and to take a clear political stand against this type of behaviour.

Crisis in Antipsychiatric Terms

The Runaway House is a place where it is possible to go through crazy states within the widest possible limits. We reject the notion that there might be such a thing as a disease of the mind. We don't diagnose nor do we inquire about those diagnoses that may have been given in the past. The consequences of psychiatric nosology are discrimination, stigmatisation, social devaluation and, in most cases, the administration of psychiatric drugs and the justification of coercive measures.

For us, crises are not an expression of a disease or a deficit but rather excessive demands on a person's strategies for dealing with stressful situations and the social environment. Even unusual behaviour has a function in the life of the person and can be an attempt to find a solution in conflict-ridden situations. In addition to individual factors, there are always societal and interpersonal causes that contribute to a crisis. These may be: limits on the opportunities to grow, refusal of access to resources, withdrawal of the means for survival and events experienced as existentially threatening. Crises are a normal part of life and an opportunity for constructive changes.

On the basis of this understanding of crises, the distinction between helpers and the person being helped must always be limited situationally and temporally. Everyone has a far greater wealth of experience, possibilities for action, and the potential for change than what may be apparent and available in a critically precarious situation.

Through experiences with violence and incapacitating attributions (e.g., psychiatric diagnoses), people are reduced to the status of objects and feel powerless and helpless. Every method of dealing with this experience must take account of this destructive core of violence. Our lesson from all this is that we must focus on re-establishing the capacity to and to avoid recurring situations of helplessness.

Our perspective is that the members of the Runaway House temporarily need help but they are adults capable of individuality and independence. We ask very carefully about what the members are feeling, about how they see themselves and their difficulties, about what they have experienced and what they think might be good for them in their current situation. Their descriptions of themselves are decisive. The members are the experts for their own situation. The outside evaluation of feelings and types of behaviour only aggravates crises and causes them to escalate.

To recognize violence for what it is the first step in regaining the status of an empowered person. Violence, even if it has been legitimised by society as part of psychiatric practice, is not a personal stigma, but an experience of injustice.

There are no doctors or nursing staff in the Runaway House. Psychiatrists are barred from entry. However, the Runaway House cannot be an exterritorial space in a psychiatrically organized world—involuntary commitments can still not be voided without the agreement of doctors or judges, and we cannot guarantee that individuals will not again end up in psychiatry.

The First 10 Years

The founding phase of the project which has lasted more than 10 years has been described in detail elsewhere.[1] The following is a discussion of a few of the central lines of development of the project in the course of its 10 years of operation.

The landmark Villa Stöckle is located in a quiet residential area of a northern Berlin suburb, near many wonderful walks and with easy access by commuter railway. Extensive renovations in the cellar (1998) and in the attic (2006) improved the living conditions. It can accommodate up to 13 people in lovely single or double rooms and large common areas. It is clear every day that this is a positive environment for the residents who have been shaken by crises. Unfortunately, the house is still not suitable for persons with physical disabilities even after the renovations.

From the start, the Runaway House served two needs: it provides antipsychiatric support and is also a part of a municipal organization that helps the homeless. In 2000, it was assigned to the new service category of "crises centres" within the Berlin homeless aid organization. Crisis centres are supposed to provide intensive support in acute crises quickly and relatively unbureaucratically, in order to forestall a lasting breakdown of the necessary supports and resources. However, the restrictive authorization practices and the pro-psychiatric attitude of many public offices result in serious limitations in the actual provision and sustainability of the help. Thus, the length of the stay has

---

1   See www.weglaufhaus.de/non_german.html

been reduced from an average of eight weeks in the past to approximately four weeks today.

Since opening on New Year's Day in 1996, more than 500 people have utilized the assistance offered at Villa Stöckle. Most of the residents are between 25 and 40; anyone over 18 can be admitted. So far, there have been somewhat more men than women. The vast majority of them were homeless or threatened with homelessness, unemployed, and in dire financial straits when they came to the Runaway House. Most of them were (ex-)users and survivors of psychiatry. Twenty-nine percent of the residents came directly from psychiatric hospitals. However, 13% did enter a psychiatric hospital from the Runaway House. A quarter of the residents moved to their own new apartment, and another quarter to a supported housing situation.

Fifteen paid staff plus students provide support around the clock. An important measure of quality control is the requirement that at least half of the staff must themselves be survivors of psychiatry. The team works without formal hierarchy, and the staff administers the project by themselves. In the beginning, a lot of people with a variety of professional training and experiences were involved; today, the Berlin Senate only allows the hiring of social workers. This limitation represents a severe restriction in the spectrum of life experience represented among team members. The gap between the residents and the staff is thus widened unnecessarily and the potential for former residents to become employed in the house is reduced.

Whether the antipsychiatric Runaway House is a part of the psychosocial service network (or even, cynically put, a part of community-based psychiatry) or whether it remains outside of it will always be a matter of controversy. The Runaway House has certainly received a great deal of acceptance within the psychosocial landscape and valuable co-operations have developed (e.g., with other homeless service providers). The Runaway House has good contacts with national and international organizations of (ex-)users and psychiatric survivors (European Network of [ex-]Users and Survivors of Psychiatry—ENUSP, World Network of Users and Survivors of Psychiatry—WNUSP, German Union of [ex-]users and survivors of psychiatry—BPE). Even necessary encounters with psychiatric inpatient units or community mental health agencies have on occasion proven to be useful. In the first years, an attempt was made to prevent the assessment of new residents by the community mental health services. Today this battle must be considered lost because these assessments have turned out to be necessary requirements by the social service administration for many prospective residents.

Support during withdrawal from psychiatric drugs is a particularly important service provided within the house. In the early days, the staff were not completely clear about what to do when individual residents didn't want to come off their drugs. We never recommend the use of psychiatric drugs for the treatment of psychological or social emergencies. In the case of residents who see this matter differently, the staff focuses primarily on promoting an informed use, rather than insisting on complete withdrawal. Other drugs and alcohol are approached in a similar fashion, although these substances have long been explicitly banned *within* the Villa Stöckle.

The financial situation of the project was precarious during the first three years, and serious savings had to be made on salaries. This was followed by three good years. From about 2002, the social welfare cuts imposed by the city of Berlin had an increasingly negative effect. Fortunately, the project receives donations from other sources in addition to the daily stipends provided by the authorities.

Help in Antipsychiatric Terms

Our basic antipsychiatric attitude results in a number of peculiarities in the communal life and mutual support within the house. These are not part of any particular antipsychiatric method, which we do not presume to exist. Contact between staff and residents is always intense, but does not follow a preconceived plan. At the core of our efforts is the desire to provide the residents with the best possible conditions for realizing their personal goals.

Everyday Life in a Residential Community

The residents and the staff on duty address the everyday demands together. A common kitty provides the necessary funds for purchasing food and other supplies. The residents are responsible for maintaining their own rooms, the common areas are cleaned by everyone together on Saturday morning. There is a schedule for chores such as cleaning the kitchen and shopping. Once a week, there is a house meeting to discuss organizational issues and any general conflicts.

There is almost no prescribed daily structure: communal breakfast is available and enjoyed by a few individuals; dinner preparation is generally a group activity; the nights must be quiet for those who want to sleep. A more precise structure derives from the reality outside of the house (appointments, business hours of authorities, doctors etc.) and has to be worked out individually. This is a problem for some, particularly when in phases of madness when all boundaries seem to dissolve. The lack of a structured schedule or a "rhythm" around which one can orient oneself can lead to complete confusion. On the other hand, specifying a schedule can make practicing self-reliance more difficult. The opportunity to "chill" and to ignore the pressures bearing down on a person is an important element in successfully dealing with a crisis. The resulting openness makes it often possible to rediscover desires and goals and to mobilize the energy to realize them. This may mean that someone does little other than smoking, listening to music or the like for quite some time—which might require some justification for a social welfare office that looks for quick results.

Residents support each other by exchanging experiences, giving practical help or undertaking recreational activities. This is a desirable but not compulsory element in the concept of the house; the mood can swing between a group that is completely at odds with each other to a very "tight-knit" group. After the social isolation that is a byproduct of psychiatrization, new friendships often form here and last beyond the time spent in the Runaway House.

Space for Mad Behaviour

Crises are permitted here, the atmosphere is marked by an extraordinary acceptance and tolerance of unusual experiences and behaviour. This tolerance is displayed both by the residents and the staff. It represents the conviction that crises and mad phases always have some sort of meaning, possibly in the way that the relationship to oneself and one's surroundings is being shifted away from its prior normality. Undoubtedly, this meaning may be hard to fathom, but when it is grasped, it provides an opportunity to understand unsolved conflicts or to work through past experiences which had been bottled up.

The fact that someone behaves in a mad way and that needs get all mixed up for a while (or break new ground), is not considered an expression of a need for therapy. Therefore, it would be wrong to offer a therapeutic program within the house. Obviously, some residents may want to get involved in psychotherapy outside of the Runaway House. They are given advice and support in planning this and in searching for a suitable therapist.

Orientation According to Individual Goals

Focusing on the individual goals of the residents makes it necessary to size these up accurately and to inquire about past experiences and current ideas as to how these goals might be achieved. Staff at the Runaway House cannot say, "I think this step is correct, therefore we will do it this way." They have to weigh carefully their role of professional helper and explain the options as comprehensively as possible. This applies equally to advice, recommendations, and support. Helpers must never present themselves as experts in the traditional sense of knowing everything better.

Withdrawing from Psychiatric Drugs

Supporting residents who want to come off psychiatric drugs is a service not offered in any other centre. Experience has shown that it is almost indispensable to be in a residential setting with round the clock care when going through this difficult process. It is accompanied by a wide variety of negative feelings, fears and withdrawal symptoms. We advise residents to come off the drugs in a gradual fashion. The experiences that residents and some staff members have gained by withdrawing form a valuable base to assure that gradual withdrawal is generally successful.

The process of gradual withdrawal takes time, usually a few weeks sometimes even months. The withdrawal from so-called atypical neuroleptics calls for particular care and prudence. This clashes with the time pressure that the social welfare services place on the residents.

Intensive Crisis Support

People always turn to the Runaway House in acute emergencies and extraordinary social difficulties including experiences with psychiatrization and homelessness. Some of them react to their complex problems by altering their behaviour and perceptions, many just cannot take it anymore and they run out of options to control inner or outer events. What happens when people become very upset, dejected, desperate, terrified, maybe or even extremely happy is highly individual. The main thing such crises have in common is that the (ex-)users and survivors of psychiatry need a great deal of attention and support.

Crises in the Runaway House can be attended in a number of ways. At first, residents are relieved of existential hardships, homelessness and being alone. The community in the house and the close contact to the staff help create a trusting atmosphere where people feel well looked after. There are always two staff members present, supplemented by a trainee during the day, which makes it possible to devote a fair amount of time to a resident with a particular need of support. Having two staff members available at night is particularly important since crises don't stick to a day-night rhythm; inner agitation, fears, sleeplessness or nightmares can be torture. Residents in need of special attention spend a lot of the time in the common areas or in the office. If necessary, they can share a room with one of the staff members. An exercise and romper room is also available, but no "soft room" like the one in Soteria projects exists in the Runaway House. The garden and nearby open fields are also important. For many residents, the long walks, alone or accompanied by one of the staff are practically the centerpiece of their experience at the house.

Situations which create an artificial distance between "helpers" and "clients" are avoided as much as possible. The decisive element of the support work in the Runaway House is the expectation of developing a personal, trusting relationship between staff and residents right from the first contact, which often takes place in a telephone conversation. It is remarkable that most people begin to trust in the behaviour and competence of the staff right from the time of the admission interview. The unprejudiced approach without any diagnostic schemes and the accepting atmosphere quickly enables people to see the Runaway House as a place where they can feel safe and well.

Staff members try to go some length in sharing the experience of a crisis, offering the kind of support that might relieve suffering and stabilizes the person. This includes listening, encouragement, handholding, assistance with eating, personal hygiene and sleep, providing a minimum of time structure, looking after health issues, those cherished walks and much more. Sometimes it also requires a certain degree of confrontation as a reminder of limits and a renewal of the link to reality. However, what actually happens comes out of each individual situation.

Empowerment

The overriding goal of the support provided in the Runaway House is to enable the residents to gain a maximal level of empowerment in their own lives. Obviously, this cannot be prescribed for them, the staff can only offer assistance towards to self-help.

The residents must always be aware of what is being done for them and with them. For this reason no help is being given without an explicit request. Everything done by the staff must be transparent and reversible. Everything kept in writing must be accessible to the resident it concerns. Any reports that are being prepared are always shared with the resident and discussed. There are no discussions with third parties without prior agreement by the resident. Instructions from third parties are not accepted without being discussed with the resident.

A basic prerequisite for this type of support is its voluntary nature. Needless to say, residents can leave at any time. Correspondingly, this means that they retain responsibility for their situation at all times. To meet this challenge demands a lot of courage—considering the extent to which (ex-)users and survivors of psychiatry have experienced disadvantages in aspects of their lives.

Repeated experiences of being labelled as "mentally ill" and institutionalized for it make it very difficult for many residents to again assume responsibility for their affairs. The kind of self-help that the Runaway House promotes means that others—including "society"—are always expected to meet their responsibilities too. Therefore. we find it proper that this project, although aimed primarily for the benefit of a small group of individuals, is also seen as a endeavour in political action.

Quality in Antipsychiatric Terms

The Runaway House grew out of the movement of (ex-)users and survivors of psychiatry. More than half of the staff in the Runaway House have themselves experienced psychiatry, and (ex-)users and survivors of psychiatry have a special position in the governing organization.

The key role of (ex-)users and survivors of psychiatry in the development of the services being offered, as well as in their implementation, is laid down in the articles of the association as well as in the program of the Runaway House.

In cooperation with two other Berlin projects, *Tauwetter* (Thaw) and *Wildwasser* (Wildwater) an "approach controlled by (ex-)users and survivors" has been formulated since 2004. Among other things, it describes in what way the fact that half of the staff of the Runaway House have themselves had experience with psychiatry is considered a particular indicator of quality:

The quality of staff with experience in psychiatry working in crisis intervention is based on the background of their own madness, their understanding of the damage caused by psychiatric attitudes and treatment methods, the experience of dealing successfully with their own crises, and the need for an accepting environment.

The key elements of the experience of staff who are survivors of psychiatry are structurally manifest in the Runaway House: in the relationships between residents and staff which deals transparently with hierarchies; in its range of supports which are guided by the needs and goals of the person and based on voluntary acceptance; and in a community where taking personal responsibility is expected and encouraged.

However, the Runaway House would not function as an institution just by virtue of applying these structures. Ultimately, this would lead to the dissolution of role distinctions between helpers and helped, which in turn would collide with the demands of the psychosocial system where needs and services, helpers and help-seekers are necessarily separated. The Runaway House attempts to respond to a dilemma inherent to the service system and expressed in its most radical form within psychiatry: that help and autonomy are exceedingly difficult to reconcile.

The balancing act between expecting residents to take responsibility for themselves and their need for support demands experience and a keen understanding of this dilemma. Self-determination comes about less through the acceptance of institutionalized help than through a process of becoming less dependent or fully emancipated from such help. The fact that the Runaway House grew out of the self-help movement and that many staff members have gone through this process facilitates the acceptance of and the emancipation from help.

However, some of the staff who work in the Runaway House are not survivors of psychiatry. The cooperation between both groups offers an opportunity to deconstruct differences. A first important step to resolve differences and misattributions in such a mixed group is to shift the perspective from that which separates to what is held in common in the experience of madness in a society that almost always reacts to mad behaviour with by the intervention of psychiatry. Due to the presence of survivors and those who have not experienced psychiatry firsthand, which often creates uncertainty as to who is in which group, attributions must automatically be challenged. This effects contact among persons within the house as well as persons from the outside. Such challenges provide an opportunity—along with the danger of renewed stereotypes—to dissolve these attributions or at least to destabilize them by demonstrating their absurdity and the fact that they are mere constructs.

In the attempt to keep that which separates the residents from staff to a minimum, it becomes apparent that by defining the criterion of being personally affected on the basis of psychiatric experience we engage in an evaluation of life experience that does not correspond with the rather complex nature of life experiences among the residents. Thus, there are ideas among the team to consider such factors as homelessness, imprisonment and a background of migration as equally relevant as psychiatric experience in establishing criteria for "being affected." However, this is a controversial discussion that should not interfere with the main objective of the project—to be a refuge from psychiatry.

... To the End

Given its long development phase and its intensive personnel and motivational requirements, the Runaway House (with only 13 places) is a rather extravagant project. It still enjoys a high degree of acceptance while facing a great deal of rejection and outrage. Considering the mountain of work and the turbulence of day to day life in the house, neither of these responses provide much distraction. Its persistence to this day is nonetheless impressive, given the fact that it had practically no predecessor models that might have provided guidance. The key to this lies in the fact that it was not primarily conceived on the basis of theoretical considerations but on the practical experience and the needs of those directly affected.

Through the collaboration of people with and without experience in psychiatry, based on the full respect of those who are in crisis and living out mad states with or without psychiatry, this project remains at the cutting edge of the psychosocial landscape. We are working tirelessly to make the Runaway House superfluous one day, having overcome mass homelessness and the dominance of psychiatry.

Translated from the German by Mary Murphy

Gisela Sartori

Second Opinion Society

Without Psychiatry in the Yukon

In 1990, Canada's Yukon territory had little contact with any critical approaches to madness or any alternatives to the mental health system. Three times larger than Germany, the Yukon is home to only 33,000 people. Athabaskan First Nations moved into the area thousands of years ago. In recent time, gold first brought white settlers in any number, and the need to open Alaska as a front in the second world war built the highway that now connects the Yukon to the "outside." In the 1970s and 80s, Whitehorse, the Yukon's capital, was growing rapidly as a government town, with a colonial model of social services keeping pace. Although the situation has improved somewhat with steps toward First Nations self-government, twenty years ago there was little recognition of any approaches to healing for individuals or communities beyond the imported social welfare, medical, and mental health industries.

As an alternative—and as a cry of protest—Second Opinion Society was founded in 1990 by three psychiatric survivors. SOS has been operating continuously since then, providing a critical voice for psychiatrized people in the Yukon. SOS runs a drop-in centre and offers access to resources for advocacy, support, and building community. Because the Yukon is so sparsely populated and so isolated, SOS has had a real influence not only in the lives of the people directly involved, but also in the larger community's approach to emotional crisis and the legal and social situation of people who have been diagnosed or otherwise labeled as mentally ill. As the only group active in this field in the Yukon, SOS has also been able to shift public opinion, influence legislators, give the media consistent and reliable access to an understanding of the issues psychiatrized people face, and sometimes take control of the public agenda in a way that it could not have in a larger community.

But the SOS approach has not been to just run a drop-in centre and provide a voice. We have tried to apply an integrative model, based on the emotional, spiritual, mental, and physical needs and capacities of people—the four points of the "medicine wheel." We have always seen people not just as individuals, but as individuals in a social context. SOS has tried to not only meet people's real needs, but to be a place where needs and interests are expressed and met within a community.

Of course, SOS has been vulnerable to many of the problems that have plagued the movement generally. The power of the medical and social welfare industries, the dominance of the medical model, and the way in which "the system" colonizes the consciousness of the individuals it draws in have complicated and interfered with SOS's work from the beginning. But this is not to detract from our successes: SOS has been a positive force in the community and in the lives of many individuals, has stood up whenever it could to "the system," and has actively promoted alternatives.

The Birth of SOS

In 1989, two psychiatric survivors, Stewart Jamieson and myself, got together in response to our dismay over the way the psychiatric agenda dominated the local media's portrayal of the "mentally ill." The informal public meeting we set up to discuss the issue—attended by a crowd of 64 people—was front-page news the following day. The ground was far more fertile than Stewart and I had imagined. This meeting was, in fact, the first time these issues had been discussed openly in the Yukon by people who had received psychiatric treatment at some time in their lives.

At the same time, the Yukon chapter of the Canadian Mental Health Association was promoting a housing project for "mentally ill" Yukoners. We were severely critical of the project, and the social-democratic government of the day invited the newly-formed SOS to provide a critique. The result was that the government deferred funding of the housing project, turning instead to the survivors group to carry out a participatory assessment of the needs of survivors and others involved with the mental health system.

SOS could hardly have been born under better circumstances. The survivors organization was entirely spontaneous, and clearly tapped into a strong need and consciousness in the community. The group's orientation from the outset was a critical response to the individualistic, illness-based model that held sway among professionals and the public. The needs assessment study, while supported by the territorial government, was carried out entirely by SOS as a group endeavour. Organization was an inherent part of the project. A series of public meetings, and a visit to the Yukon by anti-psychiatry activist Irit Shimrat, were vital to the study, which revealed that housing was not what Yukon survivors wanted. Rather, the needs we identified were primarily for a meeting place, and for a culture of mutual support in which survivors felt listened to and validated. Direct peer support, holistic alternatives to the psychiatric system, and rights protection and advocacy, were the other needs we identified.

The needs assessment, which was designed and carried out by SOS members, and the organizing that went along with it, took time. For over a year, we worked on the assessment, continued our advocacy work, and built the organization, and SOS's voice became stronger all the while. In 1992, on the basis of the needs assessment, SOS was funded by the territorial government to start a drop-in and resource centre, which we opened in 1993 in a small house in the older—and more working-class—neighbourhood of downtown Whitehorse.

We had chosen this part of town and a house rather than an office, because we wanted to be a genuinely accessible resource to SOS members. Alienation and isolation were what we were fighting with the drop-in centre; our aim was for integration of SOS and its members into a real community.

Starting the drop-in centre shifted SOS's focus. When we left the tiny office where we had spent a year organizing and moved into our new house, we created a home for many disenfranchised people. Our emphasis shifted from advocacy to community-building. Mutual support of individuals—including in situations of crisis—was part and parcel of the growing SOS community. It also meant we had less energy for some of the organizing, advocacy, and public agitation of the preceding two years. We still planned and carried out one public campaign after another, but the day-to-day focus shifted more toward the lives of individuals and the challenges of building the SOS community.

The SOS Approach

SOS's work is based on a recognition of the fundamental human rights of psychiatric survivors and patients. SOS challenges the biological and medical model of mental illness, and the institutional, medical, and pharmaceutical treatment approaches the medical model includes. The alternative approach SOS takes emphasizes community and connection instead of treatment, with a focus on self-help generally and specific attention to peer support and holistic healing alternatives. SOS actively promotes the recovery model, in which self-determination, choice, and independence are key.

Direct promotion of human rights issues for people who have been labeled as mentally ill is another emphasis for SOS. This means support for individuals in dealing with the specific legal threats of restraint, confinement, and treatment or transfer without consent. SOS is the only group in the Yukon which has ever taken a vigourous public stand in support of the rights of people who have been labeled by the medical and social-services system.

Advocating for rights and advancing alternatives also includes education to change negative attitudes and promote constructive alternatives. It also includes direct efforts to improve the quality of life of people who have been diagnosed or labeled by addressing specific needs such as housing, employment, and recreation. Combating discrimination in those areas, and in public life in general, as well as providing a recognized voice for people who have been diagnosed or labeled, is another essential part of the picture. This work includes a series of public actions and campaigns on electroshock, outpatient committal, psychiatric drugs, and other issues, as well as work with schools and Yukon College, and media campaigns.

In practice, SOS's efforts in peer support have included, first of all, providing a place for people to gather and call their own, a place where feelings can be expressed freely without the threat of being shut down, drugged up, or locked up. We have always seen SOS as a place where people could work through emotional pain, with the support of others who are willing to be present, to listen, to validate.

Support also includes access to a variety of practical resources. SOS has provided reliable and completely free services to meet many of the needs of people with few economic resources, including laundry, a kitchen, internet and e-mail. At the drop-in centre, people can find support with housing, employment, and dealing with social workers, doctors, and the rest of the "system," as well as a friendly place to simply relax and socialize. The drop-in centre also provides flexible short-term crisis support. SOS has been the only resource in the community for emotional crisis support in the evenings and on weekends and holidays, and the only place where freedom from coercion has been guaranteed. For instance, SOS nearly had its government funding withdrawn because of our non-interventionist stance on suicide, a point on which we refused to compromise.

The SOS drop-in centre has been run by its users, with the first goal of providing an environment where people can be safe from the threat of labeling, coercion, or manipulation. A basic SOS principle has been minimal intrusion in people's live, and SOS keeps no files on individuals, doesn't use and actively discourages pathologizing language, and minimizes administrative self-importance. The life of the SOS house is centred in the big living room/ kitchen area, and while some space is set aside for administration, SOS has no real office. Neither has SOS made hard-and-fast distinctions between "professionals" and the rest of the SOS community. We have all tried to be ourselves, that is, human beings struggling with human issues, with as little hiding behind masks as possible. There has been little distinction between "professional lives" and "user lives," and SOS has tried, whenever possible, to deal with difficult issues and problems as a group. The input of professionals or other non-survivors has, as much as possible, been a sharing of expertise rather than top-down direction.

Social action efforts have included a number of campaigns on public issues of immediate concern to SOS members. When a psychiatrist wanted to begin giving electroshock treatments at the Whitehorse hospital, SOS organized a week of protest. We brought Leonard Frank, a renowned anti-electroshock activist, to the Yukon, and marched through downtown Whitehorse to the territorial legislature, where a passionate crowd not only listened to speeches, but also shared spontaneous and moving recollections of their own experiences and those of family members. The anti-shock campaign generated enormous public attention, including several front-page stories and a four-page feature in the local newspaper, letters to the editor from the Yukon and internationally, and supportive comments from people in grocery-store queues and local judges. When the Canadian Medical Association held its national conference in Whitehorse, SOS brought David Oaks to the territory, and held public meetings, a demonstration, and a march through the capital to bring public attention to the spread of outpatient committal statutes in Canada. SOS has also agitated continuously for changes to the territory's mental health legislation, and was recently part of the consultation process which brought in new legislation to eliminate the mental health review board in favour of a new process which looks at all substitute consent decisions equally.

Beyond agitating for political change, SOS also supports individuals dealing with threats to their rights and liberty. This includes working with people facing committal and involuntary treatment, and dealing with the variety of social services and social workers SOS members encounter. SOS lobbies to get better legal support for psychiatrized people, and publishes guides for patients trying to avoid committal and involuntary treatment.

The SOS drop-in centre is also home to the Yukon's best collection of publications on madness, the psychiatric system, and alternatives. The library is not only a resource for SOS members, but attracts students, professionals, and interested members of the public. As part of its public education work, SOS has hosted seminars and educational events which have included SOS members, the public, and professionals. Presenters have included Judi Chamberlin, Peter Breggin, Leonard Frank, David Oaks, and Michael Perlin, and have covered topics from organizing against psychiatry to mental health law. The emphasis has always been to bring SOS members, the public, and professionals into a joint process of education and consciousness-raising.

Healing Alternatives

Since its inception, SOS has been active in promoting alternatives to psychiatric treatment, and in working with other holistic health practitioners and groups in the community. For many years, SOS has run a regular series on holistic alternatives, called Healing the Hurting Soul. Led by local practitioners, these weekly workshops are practical introductions to a wide range of techniques from acupressure to writing as a tool for healing.

Some workshops were so popular that they were extended and developed a devoted following. Indeed, these workshops and our deepening public education work began to draw in many non-survivors, and this was the time when SOS really began to have a consistent influence in the larger community. The SOS community changed too, with growing participation of not just survivors, but a range of individuals seeking community and alternatives.

Similar public education initiatives have included weekly yoga sessions for SOS members and more extensive contacts with specific local practitioners. SOS is also an active participant in the Yukon Holistic Health Network, and has presented and held information sessions at every significant holistic and First Nations health fair held in Whitehorse.

Regular peer support and self-development sessions have also been part of SOS's work. These have included ongoing peer support workshops, conflict resolution training seminars, and intensive workshops on a range of self-development issues like personal-boundary-setting and interpersonal communications. Two years ago, SOS also offered its members a certificate training course in working with individuals in emotional crisis.

SOS has always believed that community social life was essential to advocacy and the pursuit of alternatives. The Thursday Soup Lunch, open to all, has for many years been the focus of SOS social life. The soup lunch has been attended over the years by a vast range of people including SOS members, guest speakers, politicians, local holistic health practitioners, tourists, visiting mystics, social workers, people staying at SOS during periods of intense crisis, and neighbours. Beyond the soup lunch, SOS has never failed to celebrate an important birthday or other life event, and SOS holiday dinners always attract a diverse and lively crowd. Located for 14 years at the same address on a quiet residential street, SOS is also a valued part of the neighbourhood. For most of the last several years, the principal SOS fundraiser has been a day-long street festival; local musicians perform, home-cooked food is served, prizes are given out, and the neighbours join in. SOS was a founding member of the Whitehorse community garden, and the garden not only provides the food for Thursday lunches in summer and fall, but is also another activity that integrates SOS into the neighbourhood and the community.

One aspect of community that matters especially in the Yukon is the life of the many small villages in the territory. SOS has tried to develop and promote a model of community approach to emotional crisis. This approach is in direct contrast to the outside-expert model, where social workers and medical professionals frame and direct the process. Along with a respected First Nations healer, I traveled through the Yukon to meet with people in the territory's predominantly First Nations rural communities. Phil Gatensby and I talked with people about the value of meeting crisis by connecting with others, about the traditional ways of seeking support in the community instead of waiting for and depending on the "experts." The response was enthusiastic, but the challenges for funding and actualizing further work were enormous.

This area—community approach to crisis—is one that we have long felt is vital in the Yukon.

One thing that became clear as the SOS community grew was that psychiatrized people, and others at the margins of Yukon society, had little access to the benefits of outdoor recreation. Whitehorse is small, and surrounded by woods, lakes, and rivers, and from early on outdoor recreation has been an important part of life at SOS. Winters have included daily cross-country skiing lessons and trips, while running, camping, canoeing, fishing, and berry-picking have been regular summer activities. SOS even smokes its own fish, caught on trips to the coast. SOS also regularly participates in organized community recreation activities like the elder games, and for four years fielded a ten-person team for the grueling Skagway-to-Whitehorse Running relay which attracts more than a thousand serious runners from all over North America. All of these endeavours, which have included survivors and non-survivors, brought not only very real physical benefits, but also the satisfaction of involvement in activities most wouldn't normally have felt confident enough to be part of.

Involvement with the larger community has also been essential to SOS from the beginning. We have built relationships with other groups in the Yukon, principally those involved in social justice, community, and healing. SOS has always been active in the Yukon Anti-Poverty Coalition, for example, and in groups like the Holistic Health Network, the Council on Disabilities, and the Whitehorse Community Garden. Situating SOS and SOS members in the larger struggle has also been a constant. SOS has always seen itself as part of a larger movement, learning from and participating in the National Association of Rights Protection and Advocacy (NARPA), the International Network Toward Alternatives and Recovery (INTAR), and Mind-Freedom International.

Challenges

Like every other such organization, SOS has faced and continues to face challenges from every side. Although SOS has gained some recognition and respect in the local community, society's prevailing mentalism undermines the work at every turn. While the local psychiatrist—there has never been more than one working full-time in the Yukon—and doctors have to occasionally deal with patients who demand SOS involvement in their treatment, the medical system in the Yukon is just like the medical system everywhere else in North America. In other words, people in the Yukon who are diagnosed as mentally ill still face committal, involuntary drugging, forced transfer to psychiatric hospitals in other parts of the country, and sometimes electroshock. SOS members and constituents are often involved with the social welfare system, and while some Whitehorse social workers support SOS, most continue to label and stereotype and systematically demean clients they have labeled as mentally ill. SOS has also experienced direct attacks from politicians and professionals, and some SOS political campaigns have made permanent enemies.

SOS continues to receive core funding from the territorial government. Government support has brought with it a number of predictable problems, but it has given the organization a basis for its work and the stability to maintain its position in the community. Outside of specific programs for First Nations, SOS is the only such community project with government funding. This has not only given SOS unique influence in the community, but also enough political leverage to withstand threats to the funding itself. At the same time, funding has often been a struggle. Sometimes party politics have threatened funding, while at other junctures the danger has come from internal ministry machinations. The funding was reduced about 10 years ago, and has been constant, with no increase for inflation, since. This has squeezed programming, and meant that the two staff members who share co-ordination duties are paid less than they deserve, with very little in the way of benefits or security.

Government funding has also never covered more than the basic, minimum expenses. All of SOS's projects and campaigns have depended on donations, funding from other sources, and volunteer effort. Over the years, SOS has found it easier to get funding from outside sources, because of our solid track record in doing good work, even when much of it challenged the system. SOS's work has also depended on fundraising, too, with a range of volunteer activities throughout the year for bringing in more financial support.

Some of SOS's challenges are particular to the Yukon. The population is very transient, SOS has seen many involved members simply move away, in pursuit of work, for family reasons, or when the seasons change. While our isolation has brought us some advantages, it has also meant that SOS is far from similar groups, resources, and supportive social connections. People who have been locked up are also usually transferred, against their will and often against the will of their families and communities, for long periods to psychiatric hospitals "outside"—that is, 2,000 kilometers (about 1250 miles) or more from their homes. This is a feature of the Yukon's mental health legislation SOS has been unable to do anything about, and it means that people involved with SOS sometimes just disappear. They then find themselves in unfamiliar urban situations where they have no support and where they become career mental patients. This is especially grievous for First Nations individuals who may have spent little time away from the Yukon, and have no family or social support networks at all in Edmonton or Vancouver.

One of the challenge that SOS faces is that of colonization from within. Many of SOS's constituents are significantly involved with the medical and social services systems, and have been for years. They find themselves on the cycle of dependency and despair when the effort they put into self-determination becomes challenging, the system offers powerful incentives to return to dependency. Even when individual social workers or even medical professionals are supportive, the only thing the system can really deliver is welfare cheques, medication, debilitating side-effects, and a mind-numbing labyrinth of rules. Many people have cycled from SOS, back to the system, back to SOS, around and around. Others reach a turning point, but then keep running back to the system, which always welcomes them with open arms. At the same time, SOS has been a home and a resource for many people who do not want to be involved in the system, and very definitely do not want psychiatric treatment. Indeed, this has been one of SOS's accomplishments. For many, SOS has been a very supportive alternative to the system, outside the system.

We like to think that SOS's successes demonstrate the value of what we have tried to maintain as our principles, that in the face of a disempowering and depersonalizing system, what matters is mutual support, community, and standing up for rights.

Shery Mead

Trauma-informed Peer Run Crisis Alternatives

> In the hospital, I was treated as though I deserved to be punished.
> People treat their animals better than many psychiatric patients are
> treated. Any self-respect I had quickly disappeared. As a result of a
> rather long hospitalization, I lost my well-paid management job,
> custody of one of my children, my friends and social supports, and
> ended up having to rely on benefits, the food-bank and other chari-
> ties. It has taken me many, many years to regain my sense of self,
> and to this day I still struggle with the sense of shame and "other-
> ness" this experience created. The sad thing is that if someone had
> lent me a caring ear and helped me to see the options, none of this
> would have happened (Survivor of psychiatry, 2006).

There are many losses that come with psychiatric hospitalization but perhaps
the greatest loss of all is our sense of self-in-community. We are literally
transported out of our lives and when we return we are reconfigured as damaged, fragile, dangerous, vulnerable and "ill." In other words, we may be out
of the hospital but it's often a long battle to get the hospital out of us. In this
paper, we suggest that trauma informed peer run crisis alternatives to psychiatric hospitals and/or forced treatment will ultimately contribute to stronger,
healthier, more compassionate and inclusive communities.

   More and more research is emerging on peer run crisis alternatives. In their
Crisis Hostel research project, Dumont and Jones (2002) found that the test
group (who could choose between the hostel and hospitalization), had better
healing outcomes, greater levels of empowerment, higher levels of self care,
and a reduction in traditional crisis services than the control group who could
only access the hospital (see the chapter by Dumont and Jones in this book).
MacNeil and Mead (2005) studied changes in the narratives of people who

had many previous hospitalizations and were now using a trauma-informed peer run crisis alternative. They found that, where many people had taken on a strong identity of "mental patient" after repeated hospitalizations, the alternative outcome included "critical learning" (e.g., redefining one's role, and *not* seeing one's self as "crazy"). If we are to systematically shift the way that crisis is conceptualized and responded to, we will need to think about the components that are required.

Why Trauma-informed Peer Run Crisis Alternatives?

Trauma-informed peer run crisis alternatives (TIPRCA) operate from a completely different set of assumptions than traditional services. Where traditional services diagnose and treat illnesses, TIPRCA focuses on the construction of meaning people have made of their experience, building mutually responsible relationships, and creating "new stories." To be trauma-informed is to recognize that past trauma (including psychiatric hospitalization) results in a way of seeing and relating that leaves people disconnected, isolated, and shamed. It is having an awareness of how people's individual painful life experiences (physical, sexual and emotional abuse, major loss, disaster, war, forced treatment, etc.) impact every aspect of their lives.

TIPRCA establishes no strong hierarchy (patient/expert), no particular framework for interpreting experience, and best of all it can all happen (with a little groundwork laid) in community. There are currently three of these programs operating in the U.S. (New Hampshire, Maine, and North Carolina), and other countries are investigating this approach.

On the surface, it would appear that peer support is quite simple (you and I sharing our experiences) and qualitatively different than other approaches to mental health. What we tend to forget is that many people doing peer support have received traditional services for a long time, and through this process, have accumulated a lot of information about "help." Without a unifying framework, peer supporters may find themselves "doing what was done to them." To evolve something unique and new means building some common understanding and the capacity to evaluate it. Following are some suggested standards for trauma-informed peer support:

Because trauma-informed peer support suggests that we know what we know in a context; that things have happened to us influencing how we see, relate, make sense, and act, there is no assessment or evaluation of a "problem" (MacNeil & Mead, 2005; Bloom, 1997; Copeland & Mead, 2004). Instead, people strive for mutual responsibility and communication that allows them to express their needs to each other without threat or coercion. An example of this might include a negotiation of how to talk about difficult feelings without scaring each other ("Is there another way you could talk about this? It scares me when you talk about feeling suicidal.").

Trauma-informed peer support does not operate from a medical framework. Instead, we build relationships that support learning and growth across whole lives. This might, at times, take the form of challenging each other's language or assumptions in order to stimulate a different conversation. Having these different conversations requires a different response.

Trauma-informed peer support assumes reciprocity. There are no static roles of helper and helpee. Although this may not be surprising, reciprocity is the key to building natural community connections. This is an enormous shift for people who have learned to think about community as a series of services.

Trauma-informed peer support is about mutual responsibility which assumes that
- both people learn from each other
- both people figure out the rules of the relationship
- power structures are always on the table and negotiated.

In traditional helping relationships, it is assumed that the primary responsibility for making the relationship work is up to the helper. When things are not working so well this kind of dynamic has led helpers to feel like they're "doing something wrong," or to blame the other person for not trying. The worker may stop saying what they see, what they need and then begin to disconnect, falling into an assessment and evaluation rather than working through difficulties together. On the other hand, many of us, as users and survivors, have been implicitly taught that we cannot or don't have to take responsibility in a helping relationship. We fall into believing that we are victim to our own reactions and then wonder why people disconnect or take over when we say things like "I'm suicidal."

We cannot talk about doing something fundamentally different until we re-define the notion of safety. In traditional mental health services, safety has come to simply mean risk assessment. We've been asked, "Are you safe, will you be safe, will you sign a safety contract?" As recipients this has left many of us feeling quite fragile, out of control, and has left us thinking that safety is about soothing someone else's discomfort. If we don't begin to address issues of risk and power, we cannot help but replicate many of these dynamics in peer support.

For most people a sense of safety happens in the context of mutually responsible, trusting relationships. A sense of safety happens when we don't judge or make assumptions about each other. A sense of safety happens when someone trusts/believes in us (even when they're uncomfortable), and it happens when we are honest with each other and own our own discomfort. With this interpretation of safety, we can begin to take risks and practice alternative ways of responding. We can choose who to be with, when we can be there, and we can begin to talk about shared risk. Sharing risk in peer support tackles the issue of power, what it's like to lose it, abuse it, or balance it. We talk about how we each are likely to react when we feel untrusting or disconnected. We begin to pave the way for negotiating the relationship during potentially difficult situations. This level of honesty works well in trusting relationships but is critical to the health of a trauma-informed peer support initiative.

How Can Trauma-informed Peer Support be Applied?

Proactive crisis interviewing serves as both an introduction and as a type of advance directive. The process of proactive interviewing is, in fact, a model for "doing" trauma-informed peer support (Mead, 2006). In other words, when there is no particular framework, dialogue is stimulated about both people's understandings of the purpose and the type of relationship, and a template is created that both people inform. This initiates a mutually responsible relationship where both people's needs, thoughts, and feelings are part of the ongoing conversation.

The proactive interview is not without structure. Interviewers are taught to engage in these conversations as a way of modeling the process of trauma-informed support. They have some basic questions that guide them, and are taught to offer their understandings of the process as a way to stimulate questions and dialogue. An example of this type of conversation might start with information about:

1. What a TIPRCA is and what it's not (not about treatment, people not seen as ill, but seen as responsible adults trying to learn something).
2. Relationships and the importance of mutual healing (it needs to work both ways, exploring how mutual relationships have been helpful and/or taken our power).
3. Facilitate a non-illness story (building on a person's subjective experience and language).
4. Thinking "from a distance" (How might someone else describe your difficult experiences)?
5. Think together about the kinds of things that make a difference (Crisis as opportunity for growth rather than returning to baseline).

After the basic introduction is built, some guideline questions are suggested:

1. If you use crisis respite instead of another crisis service, and it worked really well for you, what would be different in your life? What are some other things in your life that have already led to that kind of difference?
2. Can you describe a positive experience you've had in which people were able to challenge you into trying new things? Who were the people involved? What were they doing? What do you need in order to "hear" that challenge from people here?
3. How will you challenge us if you feel that we're "stuck?"
4. Imagine that there is no mental health language. Describe yourself on a really good day (what are you feeling, what are you doing, with whom?). Describe yourself on a really bad day.
5. Can you describe a time when you were headed towards a really bad time and you decided, and then were able, to turn it around? Who or what helped? What did they do? When you've turned it around, what were you able to accomplish?
6. What would you be willing to try when you're using crisis respite? How will you/we know if you're trying it? What do you want to make sure we're doing while you're in respite? How will you/we know if we're try-

ing? (Note: Even though this appears to be too many questions, interviewers are taught how to do this in the context of a supportive dialogue with the person.)

When people experience extreme emotional distress, regardless of cause, attempts to negotiate and relate are challenging. Understanding that this situation is a language with meaning and emotion, no matter what's happening, grounds the supporters in understanding that the first priority is to help the person feel welcome, safe and heard. Contradiction, challenge or refutation build unhelpful power dynamics, and create relationships that lead to secrecy and control. Rather, it is essential to allow a person to talk about their perception of the experience in as much detail as is necessary without having the perception labeled, assessed, or interpreted (Mead & Hilton, 2003).

While the crisis worker is intently listening, he or she must also be aware of the extent to which his or her meaning is being imposed. If the two people are unfamiliar with each other and this is their first interaction, it is crucial to build a relationship that doesn't foster old power dynamics. Traditionally with "expert/patient" roles, both people end up stuck.

> The process of *stepping in* while *stepping back* is at the core of building new responses to crisis. It provides an opportunity to mutually explore the "essence" of the experience relationally while creating the groundwork for a meaningful relationship oriented towards the learning and growing of both people (ibid., p. 6).

A Few Thoughts on Structure

Although it's not a bad idea to have a physical space for people, leaving home at a point of crisis is not necessarily the ideal situation for everyone. In attempting to create an alternative venue, we don't want to inadvertently set up another institution (albeit run by peers). If we think of this trauma-informed process as a type of dialogic response, we can adapt the structure to fit the need (e.g., meeting people in their homes, talking on the phone, meeting in a coffee shop, or as a last resort, having them come to a peer run crisis alternative program. However this is implemented, crisis workers should not be acting in isolation. This process is new, often painful and can be emotionally draining, and although somewhat mutual is not meant to address the immediate needs of the worker. Co-supervision can help workers critically reflect on their experiences and help build a knowledge base from which everyone can learn.

Though this way of thinking has potential, like other challenges to' the dominant ways of knowing, there is a natural tendency to move back towards what we know; the things that are socially supported, and to the power dynamics that maintain certain roles. Many people are recipients of traditional services as well as members of peer support initiatives. This has sometimes led to the dilemma of conflicting paradigms. In other words, some people have found that when they start challenging the medical version of their evolving story, they are told (by their treatment providers) that they're in denial, that they're in danger, or even told that their treatment may get cut off. This kind of conflict has also led many peer support initiatives to get pulled into very traditional practices in order to sustain their sense of legitimacy.

Conclusion

Historically there has been no better time to implement these types of crisis alternatives. In 2006, the United Nations adopted the convention on the rights of persons with disabilities, a potentially powerful landmark in how we view and deal with situations of significant crisis. A paradigm shift has been heralded internationally that demands individuals be viewed as having legal capacity and in need of differing levels of support at different times. The Convention also states that "persons with disabilities have a right to physical and mental integrity." In practical terms, both of these statements potentially open a door to challenging and working towards the reduction and elimination of forced treatment and guardianship. It is also a legal "lever" to promote and develop other ways of dealing with crisis that don't involve force and are proven to be effective.

Even without the convention, this type of process is not unknown, but has been a natural part of many small communities: basically people are understood and supported in context of their environment. In thinking more systemically, we see this response as not one that just supports individuals, but rather one that looks at the social problems from which many of these inci-

dents stem (violence and abuse). In other words, healing becomes inextrica-
bly linked with social action and social change.

Sources

Bloom, S. (1997). *Creating sanctuary: Toward the evolution of sane societies.* New York:
Routledge.

Copeland, M. E., & Mead, S. (2004). *Wellness recovery action plan & peer support: Personal, group and program development.* Dummerston, VT: Peach Press.

Dumont, J., & Jones, K. (2004). Findings from a consumer/survivor defined alternative to
psychiatric hospitalization. *Outlook,* Spring, 4-6.

MacNeil, C., & Mead, S. (2005). A narrative approach to developing standards for trauma
informed peer support. *American Journal of Evaluation, 26*(2), 231-244.

Mead, S. (2006). *Peer support: An alternative approach.* Plainfield, NH: Self publication.

Mead, S., & Hilton, D. (2003). Crisis and connection. *Psychiatric Rehabilitation Journal,
27*(1), 87-94.

Giuseppe Bucalo

A Sicilian Way to Antipsychiatry: *La Cura*
(Rules Do Not Exist, Only Exceptions Do)

Antipsychiatry is not a theory, but a set of practical and daily actions that
human beings put into effect in order to defend themselves from psychiatric
violence and to manage their own existence.

The antipsychiatric experience which I have witnessed for 20 years in Sicily, is rooted in the cultural tradition of my country which is based on tolerance, acceptance and social solidarity. The Sicilian culture is naturally an
antipsychiatric culture because it wants to include the diversities rather than
to isolate them in the asylum. Our experience is one of active solidarity promoted by common people without professionals, but with volunteers whom
they have chosen to create a network to support people who want to live their
own madness, beyond every idea of "disease" and "mental cure."

This network supplies acceptance and shelter 24 hours and seven days a week to persons who want to escape from psychiatric cures. Everyone who comes is granted the possibility to share their own experiences with others and/or to find a place to live and an independent job. The social emergency network does not address users and survivors of psychiatry as a separated category, but is open to accepting and supporting anyone who is found to be in a situation of serious social marginalization. We not believe that we must find "alternatives" to psychiatry, since we do not believe that "alternatives" to this torture can exist. The goal of the network in Sicily is to bring people living without psychiatry.

The Board of Antipsychiatric Initiatives

The history of antipsychiatry in Italy comes to terms with a particular situation created by the approval of Law 180 in 1978, which sanctioned the closure of the asylums. The Law, which many people thought of as revolutionary, was in reality nothing more than new clothes for the Emperor.

Italian psychiatry tends to call itself an alternative. But it is an alternative for whom and to what? Whereas in the past it certainly was an alternative to the asylum and its methods, today it is an alternative to those older psychiatric practices, but it shares with them the same tools, medical concepts, and vocabulary.

The history of antipsychiatry in Sicily is linked to the story of the Board of Antipsychiatric Initiatives, the association founded by other members and myself in 1986 in Furci Siculo, a small village of 3,000 souls near Messina. We were volunteers and social workers with professional training working in the mental hospital of Messina.[1] There every one of us met the horror of psychiatry, the absurdity of its diagnoses and the violence of its therapies, while developing the will to act in order to free the people from this oppression. The Board was born with a few simple ideas:

1. Mental illness does not exist. There are infinite ways of being, of thinking and acting, and everybody has the right to live in this world. Words,

---

1 Address: Comitato d'Iniziativa Antipsichiatrica, via dell'agro n. 3, 98028 S. Teresa di Riva (Messina), Italy, e-mail bucalo@tao.it, www.ecn.org/antipsichiatria

thoughts and actions of every person are the expressions of his/her will and responsibility. They can be judged on an ethical, penal and moral level, but not on a medical level.

2. Patients of psychiatry are not people *with* problems, but people who *create* problems.

3. The function of psychiatry is not to treat mental illness, but to prevent the patients from creating trouble and problems for their families and society because of the way they live, feel and act.

4. Psychiatric "horror" does not involve only the doctors, who become the persecutors of other human beings, and their victims, but also the community which, due to its intolerance, is the true instigator of psychiatric detention and treatment.

If one is not a psychiatric victim (nor persecutor) one is consequentially left in the role of instigator. Without instigators, without the back-up of so-called public opinion, psychiatrists could not act in such an openly violent way against their patients. In fact, we share with the psychiatrists the same idea of normality. What is unusual makes us uncomfortable, tense and scared. Psychiatry lets us sleep well and provides absolution from our sins.

Our experience starts from the awareness that it is our ordinary way of being that "puts to death" those who live in an unusual way. To stop the psychiatric horror is possible only if we do not refer to psychiatric practice; it is possible only if we are honest and accept that the problem is not some sort of illness inside somebody's head, but it is the *conflict* among people who live, think and act in different ways.

The antipsychiatric revolution in Sicily is capable of understanding that the right tool is not to fight against psychiatry and its methods of mental annihilation and destruction, not to care for or defend its victims, but it *is the refusal to adopt a normal behaviour*. Ordinary men and women stopped being the instigators of psychiatric detentions and treatment, accepted an active role in this revolution and asked their friends and relatives to do the same.

What did we do in Sicily? We made our town and ourselves face the facts. We organized public meetings where we asked for example: Why did we allow Giovanni's hospitalization? What has he done, or better, what has he done against us? We took all those people who advocated for psychiatric wards to visit those places themselves. Using local radio we allowed people who lived in isolation because they were regarded as dangerous, to talk and share their views with the people of the town. We defended and openly supported the unusual positions of the people who were under psychiatric treatment, and helped them to get out from a position of inferiority. In other words, we gave everybody the opportunity to be accepted, heard and recognized, because this opportunity is the basis of being understood and respected as human beings, conscious and responsible for their actions.

What did we achieve? The result was the end of coercive psychiatric hospitalization. In two years of daily activity, the Board prevented all the coercive psychiatric treatments proposed by the doctors. The story of the Furci Siculo antipsychiatric experience ended in 1994, but it left us with the knowledge that it is possible to experiment successfully with new forms of individual and general self-management of extra-ordinary experiences.

The disappearance of psychiatric practice is not the solution to a problem but is a fundamental condition. It is the first step toward the acceptance of every human being's right to live his/her own experiences.

Since the early nineties the Antipsychiatric Board has started two initiatives in the cities of Catania, Messina and Palermo. The first initiative, called *Telefono Viola* (Purple Telephone) is a phone line against psychiatric assault. The second initiative, called *La Sindrome Associativa* (The Associative Syndrome), represents the first attempt of self-management for unusual experiences.

Telefono Viola aims to provide useful legal strategies to avoid coercive hospitalization. These legal strategies have been subsequently used successfully by other Italian antipsychiatry organizations. The most important strategy is the legal possibility to fight to coercive psychiatric hospitalization. In Italy the law allows for a person to be interned in a psychiatric unit against their will, if he or she became seriously "mentally ill" and refuses treatment. The admission is arranged by the Mayor of the community where the person resides and has a duration of seven days. If a person interned against its will declares to accept the treatment they will be discharged immediately and can choose freely where and by whom they want to be treated. The "declaration of acceptance of psychiatric treatment," developed by the lawyers of the Telefono Viola, has helped many people to get rid of coercive treatments and to be discharged from the psychiatric hospital.

Associative Syndrome, on the other hand, promotes the sharing and exchange of practical knowledge by people with unusual experiences. This self-management group is formed by people with different extra-ordinary experiences and shows that with free and impartial discussion it is possible to come out from the psychiatric circle and to improve people's quality of life. The group particularly reflects on "hearing voices" and independently draws conclusions similar to those that were reached in the same period by other European groups.

The only fundamental difference is that this action starts from the bottom and is the result of the work of both psychiatric patients and non-professional psychosocial volunteers. This is not a therapeutic strategy but a practical knowledge built up by those who experience these extra-ordinary conditions and those who are interested in exploring the infinite paths of human capacities.

The intention of the Board was not to create separate knowledge or to deny the claims of (psychiatrists or antipsychiatry) experts. At the core of our initiative is that the people can give expression to themselves, to their own experiences and problems. Our task is to make this possible, defending people's right to choose freely and make their own decisions.

Penelope and Social Emergency Network

Associazione Penelope (Penelope's Association) has inherited antipsychiatry from the Board. Founded in 1996, this Sicilian group acts locally to put the antipsychiatric theory into practice.[1]

If it is true that people receive psychiatric treatments because of the problems they cause to those who are close to them and live with them; if it is true that the majority of psychiatric treatments against patients, in Italy, is justi-

---

1   Address: Associazione Penelope, via Philip Cluverio 24, 98039 Taormina (Messina), Italy, tel. +39 (0)942 550058, Fax +39 (0)942 571269, e-mail ass.penelope@tin.it, www.associazionepenelope.it

fied by the urgency to guarantee these people the same adequate conditions of life and to protect them from social marginalization, then the creation of practical possibilities of life is for these people the chance of escaping from coercive environments and to experiment for themselves in total freedom, escaping from psychiatric stigma. In our "antipsychiatry genes" is the belief that specific places and professionals imply the existence of individuals with mental illness in need of special treatments and structures. Mental illness does not exist, hence the category of mentally ill people does not exist either. Grouping these people into a category acts to reproduce the dichotomy sane/insane, patient/healer, and normal/unusual.

Association Penelope is a net that gives to these people a place to live, a place to eat, to be heard, but also a place where they can wash themselves, can obtain clothing, find a job and a place to live, or where they can lay back and go on a journey within themselves. This net is open to all the people who do not want to or cannot live with their families. This is not an alternative service aimed at psychiatric patients, but is a practical example for general use. By weaving this net, Associazione Penelope has extended the opportunities offered to all of those who are in difficult situations.

The headquarter for this net is *La Cura* (The Cure), an emergency social service open 365 days a year, 24 hours a day. La Cura gives hospitality to all the people with no home and/or help from their families. Admission is immediate and not selective, according to the number of places available and the practical conditions. The center is "de-psychiatrized," which means that mental health workers are not allowed in the center and the guests are free to choose whether they want to be under pharmacological treatment or not.

The provocative name, "The Cure," is intended to denounce the improper use that psychiatry, and medicine in general, give to the term. The "cure" proposed by these two disciplines is, in fact, very far from taking real care of the people.

The centre can host 16 people (currently 10 men and 6 women) and from 2002 until now more than 400 people with different backgrounds have lived there (female victims of violence, migrants, alcoholics, homeless people, patients of psychiatric services...). The centre provides free meals, showers, laundry service and clothes. There is an office for social service that offers jobs to those who want to become independent.

There is no fixed time for admission. Admission is discussed for every case. Guests do not pay any fee; they have no restrictions for going out or to come back at night. Internal rules are kept to a minimum. It is not allowed to introduce weapons or to act violently against other guests. It is not allowed to keep alcohol and street drugs, but there is no entry ban for those who come back drunk or under the effect of street drugs. The centre has no educative purpose. It does not aim to change the guests' behaviour and choices. The centre just represents an opportunity for everybody to experiment for themselves in total freedom.

The administration of the centre has always been self-funded, supported by private structures and awards from the public services. No funds are asked or accepted from psychiatric services, nor do they derive from the care of psychiatric patients. People can be admitted to the centre only if they are below the subsistence level. Associazione Penelope and its experience show every day that it is possible to live without psychiatric practice and to give practical solutions to the conflicts among people.

The main reason behind the greater part of psychiatric hospitalization is that it is difficult to live with a psychiatric patient and it is difficult for a psychiatric patient to live on his/her own. These are practical troubles that need practical answers. Having found an antipsychiatric alternative to the family and hospitalization is for us the right way to avoid psychiatry without reproducing its practices. If what I said seems impossible, well, bear in mind that the impossible is our aim.

Jaakko Seikkula and Birgitta Alakare

Open Dialogues

Can you imagine a psychiatric practice, in which, concerning a psychotic or other severe crisis in the family, the first meeting is organized within one day after the contact; in which both the patient and family members are invited to participate in the first meeting and throughout the treatment process for as long as needed; in which all relevant professionals—from primary care, from psychiatry, from social care, etc.—who have some contact to this family are invited to participate in the same meetings and share openly all their thoughts and opinions about the crisis and what should be done? And that the professionals would stay the same for as long as help is needed? And that all discussions and treatment decisions are made openly while the patient and family members are present?

These are the basic guiding principles of the Open Dialogue approach, a new treatment method centred around family and social networks, that has been put into practice in the Western part of Finnish Lapland. The development of the new approach started in the early 1980s. Jaakko (first author) became a psychologist in the Keropudas hospital in 1981, one year after the chief psychiatrist Jyrki Keränen had taken charge as the chief of the hospital. Birgitta (second author) started her career as medical doctor in 1982 in the Keropudas hospital. Later, she specialized in psychiatry. Birgitta has been working as the chief psychiatrist in the health district for years. One important member of the team, psychologist Kauko Haarakangas, came in 1986 and is presently working as the chief psychologist. Along with several newer team members we came up with the idea of building a family centred system and luckily had the control of treatment planning for admitted patients and could thus initiate new practices and ensure their continuation.

The new approach did not emerge automatically from one decision, but developed by analysing problems in our practice and trying to find solutions to them by re-organizing the system. There were different phases in the process of developing open dialogues, with the following critical steps: (1) in 1984, open family treatment meetings began to take the place of systemic family therapy in the hospital; (2) in 1987, a crisis clinic was founded to organize case-specific teams for inpatient referrals; and (3) in 1990, all the mental health outpatient clinics started to organize mobile crisis interventions teams. This meant that since early 1990s the entire psychiatric system in the small Länsi-Pohja province located in the South Western part of Finnish Lapland has followed the ideas described here. In this paper, we describe the basic ideas of Open Dialogues. We include the approach in Western Lapland and add some elements that are applied in different contexts in many countries where the ideas of Open Dialogues have been adopted.

Before Opening the Boundaries

When we began to develop the acute psychiatric inpatient system at Keropudas hospital in Tornio we had two primary interests. First, we were interested in individual psychotherapy of patients diagnosed with schizophrenia. This is not a big surprise since the Keropudas hospital was at that time occupied with dozens of long term patients who had been considered "incurable" and were thus transferred to the B-mental hospital which was designated to receive patients who needed long term inpatient treatment. In shifting to a more acute treatment, the Keropudas staff had to learn how to work with the psychological resources of the patients with psychotic problems.

In Finland, psychotherapeutic practice has been conducted as one part of public health care. Especially important has been the program and research developed in a Turku psychiatric clinic since the 1960s by professor Yrjö Alanen and his team. Starting with individual psychodynamic psychotherapy, the Turku team integrated family perspectives into their treatments in the late 1970s and called the approach Need-adapted Treatment to emphasize that every treatment process is unique and should be adapted to the varying needs of each patient.

Systematizing their ideas in the context of the Finnish National Schizophrenia Project in the 1980s Need-adapted Treatment emphasized (1) rapid early intervention; (2) treatment planning to meet the changing and case specific needs of each patient and family; (3) attention to therapeutic attitude in both examination and treatment; (4) seeing treatment as a continuous process, integrating different therapeutic methods; and (5) constantly monitoring treatment progress and outcomes (Alanen, 1997; Alanen, *et al.*, 1991). Taking into account the long tradition of schizophrenia treatment in Finland, in Western Lapland the Open Dialogue (OD) idea meant that psychotherapeutic treatment is organized for all patients within their own particular support systems.

What is Open Dialogue?

The name Open Dialogue was first used in 1996 to describe the entire family-
and social network centred treatment. It includes two aspects: first, the meetings in which all relevant members participate from the outset to generate
new understanding by dialogue; secondly the entire system of psychiatric
practice is contained in one geographic catchment area.

The main forum for dialogues is the treatment meeting where the major
participants in the problematic situation join with the patient to discuss all the
relevant issues. All management plans and decisions are made with everyone
present. According to Alanen (1997) the treatment meeting has three functions: (1) to gather information about the problem, (2) to build a treatment
plan and make all decisions necessary on the basis of the problem which was
described in the conversation, and (3) to generate a psychotherapeutic dialogue. On the whole, the focus is on strengthening the adult side of the patient
and on normalizing the situation instead of focusing on regressive behaviour
(Àlanen, et al., 1991). The starting point for treatment is the language of the
family, how each family has, in their own language, described the patient's
problem. Problems are seen as a social construct reformulated in every conversation (Bakhtin, 1984; Gergen, 1994; 1999; Shotter, 1993a; 1993b). All
persons present speak in their own voices—and, as Anderson (1997) has
noted, listening becomes more important than the manner of interviewing.
Team members can comment on what they hear to each other as a reflective
discussion while the family listens (Andersen, 1995).

The meeting takes place in an open forum. All participants sit in a circle in
the same room. The team members who have taken the initiative for calling
the meeting take charge of leading the dialogue. On some occasions, there is
no prior planning regarding who will take charge of the questioning and thus
all staff members can participate in interviewing. On other occasions, the
team can decide in advance who will conduct the interview. This is the best
option when the treatment unit is accustomed to conducting family meetings
in a structured way. The first questions are as open ended as possible, to guarantee that family members and the rest of the social network can begin to
speak about the issues that are most relevant at the moment. The team does

not plan the themes of the meeting in advance. From the very beginning the task of the interviewer(s) is to adapt their answers to whatever the clients say. Most often, the team's answer takes the form of a further question, which means that subsequent questions from team members are based on and have to take into account what the client and family members have said. If the patient does not want to join the meeting, we discuss with family members whether or not to continue the meeting. If the family wants to continue a staff member informs the patient that s/he can return if s/he wants. During this discussion we do not make decisions concerning the patient. If we hear something so dangerous that we feel required to act, we inform the patient before doing so.

Everyone present has the right to comment whenever s/he is willing to do so. Comments should not interrupt an ongoing dialogue. Every new speaker should adapt his/her statement to what was previously said. For the professionals this means they can comment either by inquiring further about the theme under discussion, or by commenting reflectively to the other professionals about their thoughts in response to what is being said. Most often, in those comments, specific phrases are introduced to describe the client's most difficult experiences. When the staff members have to remind the family of their obligations, it is advisable to focus on these issues toward the end of the meeting, after family members have spoken about what are the most compelling issues for them. After deciding that the important issues for the meeting have been addressed, the team member in charge suggests that the meeting be adjourned. It is important, however, to close the meeting by referring to the clients' own words, by asking, for instance, "I wonder if we could begin to close the meeting. Before doing so, however, is there anything else we should discuss?"

At the end of the meeting it is helpful to briefly summarize the themes of the meeting, especially whether or not decisions have been made, and if so, what they were. The length of meetings can vary, but usually 90 minutes is adequate.

Practical Guidelines

In Finland, several effectiveness and treatment process evaluations of the Open Dialogue approach have been completed employing an action research methodology (Aaltonen, *et al.*, 1997; Haarakangas, 1997; Keränen, 1992; Seikkula, 1991; 1994; Seikkula, *et al.*, 2003; 2006) By summarizing the observations in these studies, seven main principles emerged: 1) immediate support; 2) a social networks perspective; 3) flexibility and mobility; 4) responsibility; 5) psychological continuity; 6) tolerance of uncertainty and 7) dialogism.

It is worth noting that these principles came out of the research and were not principles planned before and then followed. Later on, more general ideas about good treatment were added. In the following, we will describe the principles as guidelines for treatment focusing on dialogue. Although most of the studies have focused on the treatment of psychotic problems, they are not diagnosis specific, but describe an entire network-based treatment that is especially practical in crisis situations.

Responding Immediately

The best start in a crisis is to act immediately, and not, for instance, to wait for the patient with psychosis to become more coherent before a family meeting. It is preferred that the first response be initiated within 24 hours. The staff of the response unit should arrange a meeting regardless of who first contacted the response unit. In addition, a 24-hour crisis service ought to be set up. One aim of the immediate response is to prevent hospitalization in as many cases as possible. All, including the patient, participate in the very first meetings during the most intense psychotic period.

A common observation seems to be that patients experience something that is unappreciated by the rest of the family. Although patients' comments may sound incomprehensible in the first meetings, after a while it becomes apparent that the patient was actually speaking of real incidents in their lives. Often these incidents include some terrifying elements or a threat that they have not been able to articulate before the crisis. Psychotic experiences most often include real incidents and the patient is bringing forth themes that have not previously been verbalized. This is also the case in other forms of difficult be-haviour. In extreme anger, or depression, or anxiety, the patient is speaking of themes that have not previously been aired. In this way, the main person in the crisis, the patient, reaches for something unreachable by others in their surroundings. The aim of the treatment becomes the expression of experiences that did not have words or a shared language.

During the first couple of days of a crisis, it seems possible to speak of things that are difficult to discuss later. In the first days, hallucinations may be handled and reflected upon, but they easily fade away, and the opportunity to deal with them may not reappear until after several months of individual therapy. It is as if the window for these extreme experiences only stays open for the first few days. If the team manages to create a safe enough atmosphere by responding rapidly and listening carefully to all the themes the clients bring up, then critical themes may find a space where they can be handled and the prognosis improves.

Including the Social Network

The patients, their families, and other key members of their social network are always invited to the first meetings to mobilize support for the patient and the family. The other key members may be representatives of other agencies, such as State employment health insurance agencies, vocational rehabilitation services, fellow workers or the supervisor at the patient's workplace, neighbours or friends.

Social networks can be seen as relevant in defining the problem itself. A problem becomes a problem after it has been defined as one in the language of either those closest to the patient or by the patients themselves. In the most severe crises, the first notion of a problem often emerges in the definition of those closest to the patients after they note that some forms of behaviour no longer conform to their expectations: for example, if a young member of the family is suspected of using drugs. The young person will seldom see using drugs as a problem, but their parents can be terrified by the first signs of possible drug abuse. Anderson and Goolishian (1992) said that the one seeing the problem becomes a part of the problem-defining system. From a network perspective, all these individuals should be included in the process, because the problem is resolved only if everyone who all has defined it as a problem no longer refers to it as such.

It is helpful to adopt a simple way of deciding who should be invited to meetings. It can be done, for instance, by asking the person who made the contact in the crisis: 1) Who knows of the situation or who has been involved? 2) Who could be of help and is able to participate in the first meeting? And 3) who would be the best person to invite them, the one who contacted the services or the treatment team?

By doing it this way, the participation of those closest to the patient is suggested as part of an everyday conversation, which decreases any possible suspicion about the invitation. Also, the one who has made contact with the services can decide who they do not want to participate in the meetings. If the proposal for a joint meeting is done in an official tone, by asking, for instance, "Will you allow us to contact your family and invite them to a meeting?" problems may arise in motivating both the patients and those close to them. Another factor in deciding about the relevant participants is to find out whether the clients have contacted any other professionals either in connection with the current situation or previously. All of these parties should be invited sooner rather than later. If the other professionals cannot attend the first meetings, a joint meeting can be arranged later.

The social relations of our clients can be included in many forms. They can be present, or if some of them cannot manage to attend meetings, then the clients can be asked if they want to invite others who know of their situation and who could possibly help. Some member of the network can be given a task of contacting them after the meeting and relaying the absent persons' comments in the next joint meeting. Those present can be asked, for instance, "What would Uncle Matti have said if he was present in this conversation? What would your answer be? And what would he say to that?"

Adapting Flexibly to Specific and Varying Needs

Flexibility is guaranteed by adapting the treatment response to the specific and changing needs of each patient and his/her family using therapeutic methods best suited to each family. Each patient needs to be treated in a way that best suits their specific language, way of living, possibilities for making use of specific therapeutic methods, and the length of treatment time that fits the actual problem, instead of applying a generic program without variation from case to case. During the first 10-12 days of a crisis, the need is quite different compared to three weeks later. For instance, during the most acute phase, it is advisable to have the possibility of meeting every day, which will no longer be necessary once the situation has stabilized. In that later period, families generally know how frequently they should be meeting.

The meeting place should be jointly selected. If the family approves, the best place might be the patient's home; in other situations, it might be an emergency department or a psychiatric outpatient clinic, if the family sees that as more suitable. Home meetings seem to prevent unnecessary hospitalisations, since the family's own resources are more available in a home setting (Keränen, 1992; Seikkula, 1991).

New ideas for psycho-social treatment of psychosis have recently been developed. Most new programs still follow an illness model, in which psychotic reactions are seen as signs of an illness that families would benefit learning about so as to avoid over-stimulation and relapses. In these approaches, psychoeducational models are used. Families are informed about the illness and family members are trained in managing stressful interactions. In most cases, it involves a therapeutic program that is followed similarly in each case. Such programs are relatively easy to evaluate scientifically, but the problem of adapting them to individual needs remains. Families can easily refuse to participate (Friis, *et al.*, 2003). To avoid this, the need-adapted approach seems better at taking into account the uniqueness of each treatment process. It seems to suit the Nordic system, in which every psychiatric unit has total responsibility for all clients in its catchment area.

Taking Responsibility

Organizing a crisis service in a catchment area is difficult if all the professionals involved are not committed to providing an immediate response. A good rule of thumb is to follow the principle that whoever is contacted takes responsibility for organizing the first meeting and inviting the team. The one contacting the professional may be the patient herself, a family member, a referring practitioner or other authorities, such as a school nurse, for instance.

Organizing a specific crisis intervention or acute team is one possibility. Thus all staff members will know who to contact if clients have contacted them. This principle means that it would no longer be possible to answer a request for help by saying "this has nothing to do with us, please contact the other clinic." Instead, one can say, for instance, "It sounds like, to me, that alcohol abuse may be involved in your son's problem. Would you allow me to invite someone from the alcohol abuse clinic to join us in the meeting tomorrow?"

In the meetings, decisions are made as to who will best form the team that will be responsible for the treatment. In multi-problem situations, the best team is formed with professionals from different units, for instance, one from social care, one from a psychiatric outpatient clinic and one from the hospital ward.

The team mobilized for the first meeting should take all the responsibility needed for analysing the current problem and planning the treatment. Everything needed for an adequate response is available in the room, there is no other authority elsewhere that will know better what to do. This means that all team members should take care of gathering the information they need for the best possible decisions to be made. If the doctor was not able to attend the meetings, s/he should be consulted by phone, and if there is a difference of opinion about certain decisions, a joint meeting is advisable to discuss the choices in the presence of the family. This empowers family members to participate more in the decision-making.

Guaranteeing Psychological Continuity

The team takes responsibility for the treatment for as long as needed in both outpatient and inpatient settings. This is the best way to guarantee psychological continuity. Forming a multi-disciplinary team early increases the possibilities for crossing boundaries of different treatment facilities and preventing drop outs.

In the first meeting, it is impossible to know how long the treatment will continue. In some instances, one or two meetings are enough, but in others, intensive treatment for two years may be needed. Problems may occur if the crisis intervention team meet three or five times and then refer the patient to other authorities. In these circumstances, even in the first meetings, too much focus is on the actions that are taken and not on the process itself. Representatives of the patient's social network participate in the treatment meetings for the entire treatment sequence, including when other therapeutic methods are applied.

One part of psychological continuity is to integrate different therapeutic methods into a cohesive treatment process where these methods complement each other. For instance, if individual psychotherapy is recommend for the patient, psychological continuity is easily guaranteed by having one of the team members act as the individual psychotherapist. If this is not possible or advisable, the psychotherapist could be invited to one or two joint meetings, in which ideas are generated that can serve as the basis in for an individual therapy process. The therapist should be invited every now and then to meetings with the team and the family. Problems may occur if the individual psychotherapist does not want to participate in the joint meetings. This can intensify the family's suspicion towards the therapy, sometimes affecting the entire joint treatment process. This is particularly important to consider in the case of children and adolescents.

Tolerating Uncertainty

The first task for professionals in a crisis is to increase the safety of the situation, when no one yet knows the answers to the actual problem. The aim is to mobilize the psychological resources of the patient and those nearest to him or her so as to increase the agency in their own life, by generating new stories about their most extreme experiences. This is furthered by building up a sense of trust in the joint process. For instance, in psychotic crises, an adequate sense of security can be generated by meeting every day at least for the first 10-12 days. After this, meetings can be organized on a regular basis according to the wishes of the family. Usually no detailed therapeutic contract is made in the crisis phase, but instead, at every meeting it is decided if and when the next meeting will take place. In this way, premature conclusions and treatment decisions are avoided. For instance, neuroleptic drugs are not commenced during the first few weeks. This allows for more time to understand the problem and the whole situation. There is also time for spontaneous recovery and, in some cases, the problem can dissolve by itself. Recommendation of neuroleptic drugs should be discussed at least in three meetings before implementation if we think the drugs are necessary.

In contrast, illness-oriented approaches during the early phase of treatment focus on decreasing or ameliorating symptoms with psychiatric drugs. For psychotic patients, these are typically neuroleptics. Psychiatric drugs can help, of course, but the risk is that they, decrease psychological resources at the same time. Neuroleptic drugs have a sedative effect that calms psychological activity and thus may be a hindrance to psychological work. The challenge is to create a process that, increases safety and encourages personal work. It is helpful to consider maintenance psychiatric drugs at least two or three meetings before starting them. This conclusion is verified in the studies we will describe later. In our study, only 29% of acutely psychotic patients used neuroleptic drugs during the five year follow-up period.

Besides the practical aspect of seeing that the family is not left alone with its problems, increasing safety means generating a quality in the therapeutic conversation such that everyone can be heard. Working as a team is one prerequisite in guaranteeing safety in a crisis with loaded emotions. To return to our example: One team member may start to listen more carefully to what the son says when he is saying that he does not have any problems, it is his parents who need the treatment. The other team member may become more interested in the family's burden of not being successful at stopping his drug abuse. Already in the very first meeting, it is good to reserve some time for reflective discussion among the team apart from these different or even contradictory perspectives. If the team members can listen to each other, it may increase the possibility for the family members to listen to each other as well.

A situation in which professionals are in a hurry to get to the next meeting and therefore propose a rapid decision is not the best use of the family members' psychological resources. It would be better to note that important issues have been discussed, but no firm conclusions can be made and thus the situation is defined as open. One way to put it into words might be: "We have now discussed this for about an hour, but we have not reached any firm understanding of what this is all about or the best option to address it. However, we have discussed very important issues. Why not leave this open and continue tomorrow?"

After that, concrete steps should be agreed on before the next meeting to guarantee that family members know what they should do if they need help.

Dialogicity (Promoting Dialogue)

In meetings, the focus is primarily on promoting dialogue and secondarily on promoting change in the patient or in the family. Dialogue is seen as a forum through which families and patients are able to acquire more agency in their own lives by discussing the problems (Haarakangas, 1997; Holma & Aaltonen, 1997). A new understanding is generated in dialogue. (Bakhtin, 1984; Voloshinov, 1996; Andersen, 1995). For a professional, this means eliciting new aspects of being an expert in whom clients can trust. Professionals have to become skilful in promoting dialogues through which their specific expert knowledge becomes rooted in the context.

Effectiveness of Open Dialogues

In Western Lapland, the effectiveness of Open Dialogue has been assessed in follow-up studies for first-episode psychotic patients. The results compared to treatment as usual are promising (Seikkula & Arnkil, 2006). In comparing *the treatment outcomes* of patients diagnosed with schizophrenia between Open Dialogue and treatment as usual, the following differences were noted at the two-year follow-up (Seikkula, *et al.*, 2003):

- In the comparison group, the patients were hospitalised significantly longer (approximately 117 days compared to 14 days in the Open Dialogue (OD) group.
- All the patients in the comparison group used neuroleptic drugs compared to one third in OD.
- Fewer family treatment meetings were organized in the comparison group (approximately 9 compared to 26 in OD). The variation was large in each group, in the OD group from 0 to 99 and in the comparison group from 0 to 23.

Treatment as usual seemed to emphasize the controlling aspects of treatment, such as hospitalization and the use of neuroleptic drugs. Family members were invited to the discussion in most cases, but family meetings were not focused as much as in Open Dialogue. Individual psychotherapy was used with equal frequency in each group—in about half of the treatments—which indicates that the integration of different therapeutic methods is taking place in both traditional as well as in Open Dialogue treatment.

When comparing *the outcomes*, Open Dialogue patients diagnosed with schizophrenia seem to recover better from their crises. The following differences emerged at the two-year follow-up:

- At least one relapse occurred in 71% of comparison group patients compared to 24% in the OD group.
- Comparison group patients had significantly more residual psychotic symptoms compared to the OD group. Some 50% of comparison group patients had at least occasional mild symptoms, compared to 17% of OD patients.
- The employment outcome was better with OD patients, of whom only 19% were living on a disability pension compared to 57% of the comparison group patients.

The results with Open Dialogue patients remained positive at the five-year follow-up (Seikkula, *et al.*, 2006). Only 29% of OD patients experienced one or more relapses (39% in the comparison group). Recovery from psychosis occurred equally in both groups. After five years, 82% of OD patients (76% in the comparison group) had no residual psychotic symptoms. Employment status was better than in any other outcome studies, with 86% of the OD patients (72% in the comparison group) returning to their studies, work, or to active job-search.

Conclusions and Reflections

The outcome results actually show a remarkable change in psychiatry. As one known professor of psychiatry noted in a personal communication, "we have not previously seen any of these kinds of results with psychosis." In the small province in Western Lapland, first signs have emerged that the incidence of schizophrenia has decreased, from 33 new patients per year per

100,000 inhabitants in 1985 to two during the first years of 2000s. A research project has been undertaken to analyse this phenomenon and its relations to the new treatment approach.

The above information suggests that our approach to psychiatric crisis has changed. We are used to thinking of psychosis as a sign of schizophrenia and as a relatively stable state that afflicts the patient throughout his/her entire life. For instance, 1/3 of the patients with schizophrenia are said to need on-going treatment, 1/3 will need intermittent treatment, and 1/3 will fully recover and actively work. In the few long-term follow-up studies of first time psychotic patients, after five years more than a half, often about 60% are said to be living on a disability pension (Svedberg, *et al.*, 2001; Lenior, *et al.*, 2001).

The positive outcomes in Open Dialogue may indicate that psychosis no longer needs to be seen as a sign of illness, but can be viewed as one way of dealing with a crisis and after this crisis, many or most people are capable of returning to their active social life. And when so few actually need neuroleptic drugs, we can ask whether our understanding of the problem itself should be changed. Perhaps it is not the biochemical state of the brain that causes hallucinations, but, instead, hallucinations include real incidents of life and are one possible response to severe stress. This can occur in every one of us and no specific biological vulnerability is needed.

New ways of thinking about psychoses seem to have emerged in the new practice. Does this mean that we should re-think the way psychiatric services are organized? Instead of primarily focusing on having control over the symptoms and removing the symptoms as rapidly as possible, the attention could be on organizing meetings, for those involved, including family members and other relevant individuals from the private social network and the professionals sphere. And it may mean that in these meetings we should be more interested in generating dialogues by following what family members are saying than in planning interventions aimed at change in the patient or in the family. If so, the training of professionals should be restructured to include new aspects: not only to read books about medical interventions, but also to reflect upon the philosophy of our human views, of the possibilities how to generate dialogue and how to listen to people instead of dominating the therapeutic process. Currently, in Western Lapland, every staff member can attend three years of training in dialogical family therapy for free. These suggestions are relevant questions for any psychiatric context. But Open Dialogue is not a model that should be followed uniformly from place to place. We actually are against the idea of generalized models for psychiatric treatment, and would argue that each practice should follow the local conditions and culture. As any treatment process with a single patient always is a unique process, the treatment system should also be unique.

Sources

Aaltonen, J., Seikkula, J., Alakare, B., Haarakangas, K., Keränen, J., & Sutela, M. (1997). Western Lapland project: A comprehensive family- and network centered community psychiatric project. In ISPS, *Abstracts and lectures 12-16 October 1997* (pp. 124-129). London: ISPS.

Alanen, Y. (1997). *Schizophrenia: Its origins and need-adapted-treatment.* London: Karnac Books.

Alanen, Y., Lehtinen, K., Räkköläinen, V., & Aaltonen J. (1991). Need-adapted treatment of new schizophrenic patients: Experiences and results of the Turku Project. *Acta Psychiatrica Scandinavica, 83,* 363-372.

Andersen, T. (1995). Reflecting processes: Acts of informing and forming. In S. Friedman (Ed.), *The reflective team in action* (pp. 11-37). New York: Guilford.

Anderson, H. (1997). *Conversation, language, and possibilities.* New York: Basic Books.

Anderson, H., & Goolishian, H. (1992). The client is the expert: A not-knowing approach to therapy. In S. MacNamee, & K. Gergen (Eds.), *Therapy as social construction* (54-68). London: Sage.

Bakhtin, M. (1984). *Problems of Dostojevskij's poetics.* Manchester: Manchester University Press.

Berger, P., & Luckmann, T. (1966). *The social construction of reality.* New York: Doubleday / Anchor 1966.

Gergen, K. (1994). *Realities and relationships: Soundings in social construction.* Cambridge, MA: Harvard University Press.

Gergen, K. (1999). *An invitation to social construction.* London: Sage.

Haarakangas, K. (1997). Hoitokokouksen äänet [The voices in treatment meeting: A dialogical analysis of the treatment meeting conversations in family-centred psychiatric treatment process in regard to the team activity. English summary]. *Jyväskylä Studies in Education, Psychology and Social Research, 130,* 119-126.

Holma, J., & Aaltonen, J. (1997). The sense of agency and the search for a narrative in acute psychosis. *Contemporary Family Therapy, 19,* 463-477.

Keränen, J. (1992). The choice between outpatient and inpatient treatment in a family centred psychiatric treatment system [English summary]. *Jyväskylä Studies in Education, Psychology and Social Research, 93,* 124-129.

Salokangas, R., Räkköläinen, V., & Stengård, E. (1991). Uusien skitsofreniapotilaiden hoito ja ennuste. V: Viiden vuoden seuranta [Treatment and prognosis of new schizophrenia patients. V: 5-years follow-up. English summary]. *Reports of Psychiatrica Fennica, 96.*

Seikkula, J. (1991). Family-hospital boundary system in the social network [English summary]. *Jyväskylä Studies in Education, Psychology and Social Research, 80,* 227-232.

Seikkula, J. (1994). When the boundary opens: Family and hospital in co-evolution. *Journal of Family Therapy, 16,* 401-414.

Seikkula, J., Alakare, B., Aaltonen, J., Holma, J., Rasinkangas, A., & Lehtinen, V. (2003). Open dialogue approach: Treatment principles and preliminary results of a two-year follow-up on first episode schizophrenia. *Ethical Human Sciences and Services, 5*(3), 163-182.

Seikkula, J., Aaltonen, J., Alakare, B., Haarakangas, K., Keränen, J., & Lehtinen, K. (2006). Five-year experiences of first-episode non-affective psychosis in open dialogue-approach: Treatment principles, follow-up outcomes, and two case studies. *Psychotherapy Research, Vol. 16*(2), 214-228.

Seikkula, J., & Arnkil, T. E. (2006). *Dialogical meetings in social networks.* London: Karnac Books.

Shotter, J. (1993a). *Conversational realities. Constructing life through language.* London: Sage Publications.

Shotter, J. (1993b). *Cultural politics of everyday life: Social constructionism, rhetoric, and knowing of the third kind.* Toronto: University of Toronto Press / Milton Keynes: Open University Press.

Svedberg, B., Mesterton, A., & Cullberg, J. (2001). First-episode non-affective psychosis in a total urban population: A 5-year follow-up. *Social Psychiatry, 36,* 332-337.

Voloshinov, V. (1996). *Marxism and the philosophy of language.* Cambridge, MA: Harvard University Press.

Theodor Itten

Psychotherapy Instead of Psychiatry? A No-brainer

About Psychotherapy

Psychotherapy as a science is a wide field. There are a number of complementary modalities. Several schools of therapy emerged during Sigmund Freud's lifetime and after his death in 1939. Psychotherapy may be individual or group therapy. In every form of psychotherapy, no matter what method, the therapeutic relationship is the vessel for the transformation of emotions. A psychotherapist who tackles the issues of the client is, like the court jester, the only one obliged to the naked truth that reveals itself.

The idea behind psychotherapy is to try and understand one's own world, the acquired way of living, the actual lifestyle and—if one is suffering—to change. As a patient and as a psychotherapist, I try to recognize which feelings, images and impulses I can sense within myself. Am I open, am I closed, do I repress, am I cut off from my feelings? As a patient, I try to share my inner perceptions in the form of verbal associations with my therapist.

Psychotherapy is an continuous examination of the inner world and a process that attempts to achieve a social diagnosis (literally to see through the social situation). Psychotherapy is a way of rehearsing the feelings that are lived in other relationships. As a patient I can be honest, truthful and learn new things about myself in the presence of a therapist. I may realize painfully how my world has been formed in false and self-protective ways. What kind of story goes along with my "false-self" system that I have acquired in order to survive my primary, ready-made family and social situation? What kinds of limiting addictive habits have I developed to protect myself?

Symptoms are the necessary pointers on the path to finding my own emotional truth. The experience gained in therapy about a new integration of body, self and soul enables a fresh approach to life: the therapeutic experience as a patient allows me to distance myself from the story that has shaped the current phase of my life and discern a new life plan. As a dejected, over-burdened and melancholy person, I experience myself as a prisoner held in a small room. Emotionally trapped and restrained as I am telling my life-story to the therapist, we can find a way out of this room together.

The therapist asks himself: what is he concealing for the time being? What is taboo? What traumatic experiences are fraught with emotions that create a fear of being overwhelmed? As a patient, I do not want to know at this moment, why I ended up in this room, rather, I am more interested in knowing how I can get out again. Once outside, I can find enough room to breathe and feel safe, then I can start to explore this question. Now I find out why I entered this space. What was the meaning of my melancholy? How was it that I didn't recognize the signals of my emotional fragmentation? If I recognized them, why didn't I take my early warning signs seriously as a saving, helpful *blink* (Gladwell, 2005)?

Nine out of 100 people experience injuries before they learn to speak. Many mental disorders are the result of early trauma in relationships—emotional wounds. In psychotherapy, I can explore why, as an adult, I continue to carry these injuries around with me like a story that has not come to an end. Some colleagues describe psychotherapy as a journey charged with the re-kindling of the soul. We all need our own metaphors. I can flip out, freak out, become "psychotic" so that I no longer have to consciously feel my inner emotional pain, especially when it becomes too bad and gets the better of me. Or I take no notice of the signs of things that might be good for me—singing or running around for instance—and become inhibited once again. I become further alienated in order to conform. Neurosis or stomach pains are the price to pay, and I submit to a social morale whose ethics limits my vitality.

The sources of my healing are within me, but repressed. Slow means quicker, less is more. To linger in creative idleness so that something can emerge from within. At the beginning, there is always some form of contact, often physical, eye contact. body-rhythm, depth and fullness of breath. Feeling the presence or absence of vitality. To listen inside of myself. With this inner foundation, I can use the bridge of therapy to get from my past, where trauma and existential fears rule, towards resourcefulness and the ability to live.

In Therapy

Throughout early family history and childhood, everyone has developed a form of protection that ensures their own survival. This turns into a particular character style as one grows older. The emotional context of life is found, as a person comes into the world, at a particular time and in a particular place. The inner attributes remain. Whether this first fold and the diversity of life are experienced as a blemish or as the source of vital energy and meaningfulness— can be influenced. A person in psychotherapy gets to know the source of his/ her feelings and again has the opportunity to choose a path other than the familiar and trusted one. In this way, we can develop a new habit to replace the old one that causes suffering and step into our own future.

We psychotherapists love the world of the soul and have developed our own therapeutic styles. After undergraduate studies in the humanities and social sciences, and occasionally in medicine, we were all initially patients during our training therapy. Modern therapeutic training is organized in one of the four basic modalities (depth psychological/psychoanalytic, behavioral, body-oriented, or humanistic) and lasts about five to six years including a clinical internship year.

The therapeutic relationship accounts for 30% of the curative effect. The life circumstances of the patient, his or her awareness, language, education, work and class status contribute to 40% of the curative effect. The placebo effect, i.e., the belief in the healing powers of psychotherapy, contributes 15 percent, as significant as the specific psychotherapeutic method (Lambert & Bergin, 1994; Tschuschke & Kächele, 1998).

Psychotherapy is an art of healing the soul. As in any professional field there are of course those who have chosen the wrong profession. Those looking for help must, therefore, keep their eyes open, allow their trust to grow and pay attention to their own perceptions. Entering into relationships always carries a risk of negative experiences (see Märtens & Petzold, 2002).

Individuals who become involved in psychotherapy actively observe their life situation, their way of experiencing and behaving, and their childhood and life patterns. Psychotherapy functions as a support when making the choice of going down a new path.

There is time and space for your own wishes, your own rhythm and lifestyle. Psychotherapy is based on a commitment in the relationship to repairing? the fracture of the soul, the emotional vulnerability.

Psychotherapy Versus Psychiatry

Psychiatry is a medical service practiced within the social context. Quite a few practicing doctors have broken their Hippocratic oath: *Primum nil nocere*—First do no harm. Academic psychiatry dominated the helping professions at the beginning of the 19th century with its motto "mental illnesses are diseases of the brain," and in doing so relegated psychotherapy for people with serious mental problems and diagnoses such as "schizophrenia" to a less than helpful role. Psychotherapy would be of better use if psychiatry recognized its role in enhancing compliance and helping formulate diagnoses. Apart from that, the respective psychiatric methods of the time were supposed to be used. Such an approach does not reengage the patient in communication (Retzer, 2004).

Electroshock and neuroleptics lead to many varieties of harm among the recipients and the traumatizing effects of coercive treatment can also cause lifelong damage.

Modern psychiatric work consists of making physically healthy people ill with so-called "medications," that are basically toxic synthetic substances. In-depth, uncovering psychotherapeutic methods are thereby curtailed right from the start, the power of self-healing is undercut and psychotic processes are frozen. Psychiatrists such as Klaus Ernst of the University Clinic Zurich came to this conclusion when, at the beginning of the 1950s they conducted systematic self-experiments with the neuroleptic prototype chlorpromazine (trade names Chloractil, Largactil, Thorazine etc.). After testing it on himself and his wife Cécile, Ernst pointed out the double-edge effects of modern neuroleptic symptom suppression; his detailed description gives an idea of why the opportunity of successfully conducting a psychotherapy that aims at resolving conflicts under psychiatric drugs, especially neuroleptics is so compromised:

We are especially concerned about the creation of—as far as we can tell today—a reversible localized organic brain syndrome (familiar to us from lobotomy and characterized by disinhibition, aimless activity as well as apathy, lack of initiative, awkwardness, emotional indifference, affective flattening, euphorically tinged lack of judgment, tactlessness and egocentricity—Th. I.). Assuming that this occurs raises the question about its relationship to adjunct occupational rehabilitation and psychotherapy. Regarding the first we can be brief. The Largactil cure fits in nicely with every type of routine work therapy. After only a few days, the patients get up of their own accord and are able to work without any serious orthostatic problems (which might occur while working in an upright position). Needless to say, we are talking about light work under staff supervision. The problem of combining Largactil with psychotherapy is more complicated. Remembering our self-experiments we can barely imagine that psychotherapy could have taken place at the same time...Furthermore, we have to distinguish between supportive and uncovering psychotherapy. The relaxing effect of the medication is a good prerequisite for the former. But it is certain that the drug suppresses the entire affective spectrum and not merely its pathological elements. Such a broad suppression might also affect impulses issuing from our self-healing tendencies. Individual, albeit, irreproducible impressions of acute patients led us to wonder whether the medicinally caused apathy did not in fact lead to a solidification of the psychotic development, affecting both relapse and remission (Ernst, 1954, p. 588).

What was true for the first neuroleptic, chlorpromazine—the affective blunting and the development of an artificial "thick skin" applies basically just as much to the neuroleptics that came to market more recently. Their effect is similarly based on the impairment and modulation of central nervous and intrapsychic processes as characterized by Ernst.

To conclude, modern psychiatry, especially academic psychiatric, is one great labeling lie. It has very little to do with the mind. More and more psychotherapy units from the time of social and community psychiatry (for example in England from 1960s onwards) are being closed down while psychotherapists and psychologists are being let go. Human suffering is disappearing into a medical explanatory model. Psychiatrists, suffering from a scientific inferiority complex, consider themselves and people with mental problems as objects with defective genes and disturbed neuronal networks. Their diagnostic look blocks any possible empathic fellowship with other human beings as equals.

Bertram P. Karon, professor of psychology at Michigan State University and author of a ground-breaking book, *Psychotherapy of Schizophrenia* (1994), has devoted more time than anyone else to the reasons why psychiatrists are so reluctant to endorse psychotherapy for people who have been diagnosed with schizophrenia. As early as the 1950s, he demonstrated a positive effect of psychotherapy for people considered acutely schizophrenic. He addressed this in a speech at the Washington School of Psychiatry in March 2001:

> ... schizophrenia is a human experience with meaning, meaning that is hard to uncover, but it only takes patience, kindness, a tolerance for not understanding, a willingness to understand the human condition at its most painful, a tolerance for desperate defenses, and a willingness to take psychoanalytic ideas seriously when patients talk about them. Understanding persons with schizophrenia means facing facts about ourselves, our families, and our society that we do not want to know, or to know again (in the case of repressed feelings and experiences)...The real tragedy of schizophrenia is not the severity of the symptoms and the suffering that results for patients and for their families, but that we know psychoanalytic therapies that work and we are not using them. Families and patients are settling for treatments that aim at making the patient a lifelong cripple who is not too disturbing. Psychoeducational programs, which could be helpful, usually give false information which makes worse the burdens of both patients and their families (2003, p. 90).

Karon repeatedly critized the untruth of the apparent superiority of biological psychiatric methods such as psychiatric drugs and electric shocks over psychotherapeutic methods:

> Sometimes it is argued that research shows psychotherapy is not helpful. However, when the Michigan State Psychotherapy Project

(Karon and VandenBos, 1981) randomly assigned schizophrenic patients to (a) an average of 70 sessions of psychoanalytic psychotherapy per patient, (b) medication used effectively, or (c) a combination of the two, blind evaluation showed that psychotherapy alone, or with initial medication that was withdrawn as the patients could tolerate it, led to earlier discharge from the hospital, kept the patients out of the hospital, and improved their thought disorders more than medication did, and the patients lived a more human life in a variety of ways. Psychotherapy with maintenance medication was better than medication alone, but not as good in the long run as psychotherapy alone or with initial medication that was withdrawn. Because of the hospitalization and particularly re-hospitalization findings, psychotherapy was much less expensive over a four-year period than traditional treatment with medications... With schizophrenics, the treatment of choice is psychotherapy with a competent therapist who has relevant experience or training. If the patient, the therapist, and the setting can tolerate it the psychotherapy is best conducted without medication. If the patient asks for it, or the therapist is uncomfortable talking with disorganized patients, or the setting requires it, medication can be used, but it should be withdrawn as rapidly as the patient can tolerate (ibid., pp. 97/106).

According to Karon, biological psychiatric methods have the advantage over elaborate psychotherapeutic ones in that it is not necessary to engage with the individual problems of the patients. The psychotherapist Karon did not just speak about the conveniences for psychiatrists but also about their interest in earning money:

Today, medication is the predominant treatment that does not require understanding symptoms of schizophrenia. Medication reduces disturbing affect and some of its immediate consequences; some of the patients' behavior improves; and they become more compliant. This is sometimes very helpful because other people almost always fear schizophrenics. People tend to be cruel when they are afraid. Because cruelty makes schizophrenic people more schizophrenic, there are advantages to making schizophrenic people less frightening...A study funded by the American Psychiatric

Association reported that psychiatrists who practice psychotherapy cannot make much more than $100,000 per year, but that a practice confined to medication and evaluation will yield $300,000 certainly a strong incentive (ibid., pp. 100-101).

Just like Karon, the psychotherapist Arnold Retzer, former medical director of the Department of Psychoanalytic Research and Family Therapy at the University of Heidelberg, who has devoted himself to family systems therapy, spoke about the positive results achieved with psychotherapy for people diagnosed with "schizophrenia." In an extensive study, a total of 60 families were examined three years after the completion of family therapy; the patients who had been diagnosed as manic-depressive, schizoaffective, and schizophrenic (his terminology) showed a significant reduction in relapses and furthermore

... a reduction of prescriptions for medications and a positive effect on vocational and educational outcomes. A far-reaching dissolution of the disease concept among patient and family members is associated with positive developments in the above mentioned areas. It is sensible and potentially successful to conduct systematic family therapy with psychotic patients and their families as early as possible (Retzer, 2004, p. 189).

The Poetry of Experience without Psychiatric Drugs

The Scottish psychoanalyst Ronald David Laing (1927-1989) was considered a radical psychiatrist during his lifetime, as well as paragon and teacher of many psychotherapists. He believed "...that to give serious consideration to the issues that arise from seeing the same differently itself contributes to lessening some of the fear, pain, madness and folly in the world" (Laing, 1985, p. X).

Taking a look at your life even when things get quite confused at times is a good idea and helps protect you against becoming dogmatic. If I am mentally disturbed or if my soul is in turmoil it may be that I can't manage my usual everyday life and all the things I have to do. To arrive at a useful clarity and to obtain temporary emotional and social protection I can turn to psychotherapy—particularly if I cannot manage to help myself. If I become unbearable for others, for whatever reason, then I need a safe place, a place of calm, a place where I can rest up, such as in the therapeutic communities of the Philadelphia Association, London, the various Soteria Houses and other communal therapeutic centers. Meals are provided, I have a roof over my head, a bed I can crawl into and the assurance of being able to pursue my healing process at my own pace. The therapeutic staff in these type of settings are there for me, accompany me on my path which may be off the beaten track with respect to the normal world. Being with others in a respectful manner, honoring my own and the boundaries of others, and the wisdom of the heart are the basis of this healing art. Space and time are made available, so that I might be accommodated in my potential speechlessness and that I can be seen as a person. It is only when my needs are understood and dealt with that I can reach my goal of becoming emotionally healthy.

Laing described how patients occasionally use the therapeutic space: "They wanted to enact some sort of drama, with me there but not interfering, not stopping them, or trying to change them by 'making interpretations,' hypnosis, or other techniques designed to change them" (Laing, 1985, p. 131). Everyone has their own metaphor, thought Laing, with whom I spent much time over a 14-year period. With his undivided attention and empathic presence he enabled others to arrive at a calmer, more balanced, better integrated healthy emotional state. An example:

A 9-year old girl, who has been mute for several months at home, is brought by her father to see Laing. Once into the consulting room, Laing tells the father to come back in one hour to fetch her. It was a one-off session as the parents had already seen and consulted a school psychologist, an educational psychotherapist, and a psychiatrist. But nothing had worked so far. The child would not speak. So her parents thought of taking her to this rather famous but also strange psychiatrist and try him as a last resort before she sending her to a clinic. So she comes to meet Laing. This is a case story he told us students, and as far as I know it has not been published by him. After her father had left, Laing said to the 9-year old girl, once he was sitting comfortably in his chair and the girl was still standing in the middle of the room:

> You may do whatever you can and want, but you don't have to do anything. You may be silent here and You don't have to speak to me, you don't have to perform, stay with me for 50 minutes, as I'm

staying with you, and we'll just see what happens. So let's just relax (Laing, 1980).

He realized that the girl was taking this in and she was walking slowly towards him with her arms raised parallel in front of her, and the palms of her
hands facing Laing. So Laing put his hands up as well, to mirror and receive
her hands. They touched and he closed his eyes. Laing followed the slow
movements of her small hands, circling up and down, forward and back, like
a playful dance of the hands. The whole thing lasted almost the entire 50 minutes. When the father came to pick up the girl he paid Laing 70 £ right away,
which was rather a lot of money in the early 1970s, when a standard session
would cost around 30 £. The father was a bit startled, but he paid up and they
left.

Laing forgot about the girl. But when he went to a party in the mid 1970s, a
young women came up to him, introduced herself and said: Can you remember the small girl who was brought to you mute by her father for a consultation 12 years ago? No, said he, I can't remember. What was the occasion and
situation? She said, I was the girl with the dancing hands: Wow, he said, now
I remember, I was always curious what happened to you. She said: Well, my
father was rather cross with you about the large fee and once we drove off he
asked me: What did he do with you for this kind of money? So I said: it is
none of your business. At first he wanted to smack me, but then he became
overjoyed when he suddenly realized that I was speaking again. Laing and
the young woman toasted to life.

This brief episode demonstrates how important it is to experience a good fit
in psychotherapy, in other words, the chemistry between the patient and therapist must be right. Good therapists accept what comes from the patients and
adjust to it. They know that psychiatric drugs alter the personality and hinder
or preclude a useful and effective psychotherapy just like other psycho-active substances like hashish or alcohol. They trust that their own soul can
tune in and join the other person in their confusion without abandoning their
own position. The little girl in Laing's example had not been diagnosed as
psychotic, but the path to that diagnosis and the corresponding prescription
of psychiatric drugs was already in progress.

I would like to add a modest example of help for someone who had been
psychiatrically diagnosed and who became a patient of mine: a farmer's wife

who had been suffering from summer depression for more than 20 years was referred to me by her family doctor. She had tried almost everything, had been in analytical psychotherapy, in a variety of psychiatric hospitals, had been given medication and behavior therapy. These interventions all helped her to live with her depression for a while. But she and her husband were at the end of the road. I asked her: what do you need after having had all these therapies and attempts to find a cure? What do you want from me as your new psychotherapist? She answered after thinking for a while: I want to spend the sessions in a café. One week you choose the place and the following it will be my turn. I want to tell you about my life over a cup of coffee. Alright, I thought, that is a version of the extended consulting room. After two years and approximately 65 café visits, during which we had spoken about her hurt soul which had retreated deep down into herself, and she had told me about her experiences in psychiatry and we were able to bring closure to these stories and find space for her desires for her life, she wanted to finish the therapy. "I think" she said one afternoon, "this therapy does not go deep enough. We sit here in cafés and chat about my life, I drive my car again, I have new part-time job, I don't need to kill myself anymore, I have lost the weight that I had gained from taking medication, I can speak better with my husband and my children, I dream well and I go dancing again." After that we had two final sessions in my practice to look back at the course of the therapy once more. Later I saw her occasionally in town and she was never again pathologically depressed.

This is an example of "being with" and of following that which was lying dormant in the patient as a healing response and which she expressed as her desire. As simple as dancing in your dreams. To be fully alert to what happens in the therapeutic encounter.

Summary

These brief examples are only intended to demonstrate what was discussed above: only by taking people seriously, by dealing with the complexities of people's life histories and by leading the excommunicated back into communication can we really assist people in trying to tackle difficult problems of life and support them in their inner emotional pain. As serious and committed psychotherapists we meet our patients with goodwill, honesty and integrity. Presuming they have the opportunity to make a decision and see no other way out then in should not be too difficult to decide on psychotherapy.[1]

Sources

Ernst, K. (1954). Psychopathologische Wirkungen des Phenothiazinderivates "Largactil" (= "Megaphen") im Selbstversuch und bei Kranken. *Archiv für Psychiatrie und Nervenkrankheiten, 192,* 573-590.

Gladwell, M. (2005). *Blink: The power of thinking without thinking.* London: Little, Brown & Co.

Karon, B. P. (2003). The tragedy of schizophrenia without psychotherapy. *Journal of The American Academy of Psychoanalysis and Dynamic Psychiatry, 31*(1), 89-118.

Karon, B. P., & VandenBos, G. R. (1994). *Psychotherapy of schizophrenia.* Northvale, NJ: Jason Aronson.

Laing, R. D. (1980). Case history at the Philadelphia Association seminar in London. Unpublished.

Laing, R. D. (1985). *Wisdom, madness and folly.* London: MacMillan.

Lambert, M. J., & Bergin, A. E. (1994). The effectiveness of psychotherapy, In A. E. Bergin, & S. L. Garfield (Eds.), *Handbook of psychotherapy and behaviour change* (pp. 143-189). New York: Wiley & Sons.

Märtens, M., & Petzold, H. (Eds.) (2002). *Therapieschäden – Risiken und Nebenwirkungen von Psychotherapie.* Mainz: Matthias Grünewald.

Retzer, A. (2004). *Systemische Familientherapie der Psychosen.* Göttingen / Berne / Toronto / Seattle: Hogrefe.

Tschuschke, V., & Kächele, H. (1998). Was leistet Psychotherapie? Zur Diskussion um differentielle Effekte unterschiedlicher Behandlungskonzepte. In: M. Fäh, & G. Fischer (Eds.), *Sinn und Unsinn in der Psychotherapieforschung* (pp. 137-162). Gießen: Psychosozial-Verlag.

Translated from the German by Mary Murphy

---

1   I would like to thank Evelyne Gottwalz, Kerstin Kempker, Peter Lehmann and Martin Urban for their helpful suggestions and critical collaboration I received in the preparation of this chapter.

General and Specific Beneficiaries of Alternative Approaches

Introduction

We could only make a limited selection from the large number of different groups who, with their specific problems, have become the object of patronizing and damaging psychiatric treatment. More and more children, who are not in a position to make their own decisions, are being given psychiatric drugs in order to adapt them through chemical means to a hostile environment. More and more defenceless older people are given these substances as a way of making up for deficiencies in their care. An increasing number of women are being given psychiatric drugs to chemically neutralize their disruptive reactions to a silencing and restrictive patriarchal environment. Ever greater numbers of people who come into conflict with the law are given psychiatric drugs in order to keep them quiet in prisons or to break their resistance to deportation. People with disturbing handicaps, members of minority groups and people with deviating sexual orientations…there is almost no limit to the number of groups who have become targets of psychiatry.

The debate about the psychiatric problems of gay men should not overshadow the discussion about the problems of women in psychiatry. Since women and their supporters have been speaking out about alternative approaches for years, we want to talk here about the issue of men in psychiatry: men who have been psychiatrized because of their sexual orientation and their refusal or failure to adapt successfully to the male stereotype. We see the included contribution by Guy Holmes and Geoff Hardy as a first step towards an alternative approach—whenever "the men" are finally ready—for men who develop psychiatric problems because they have been driven crazy by male role expectations.

The problems experienced by relatives of people caught up in psychiatry are complex: despair when experiencing the misery of psychiatric treatment from close up, excessive worries or a need to dominate, feelings of guilt, family constellations that can drive someone mad, intra-family aggression, the influence of pharmaceutical sponsorship and much more means that cooperation with relatives and (ex-)users and survivors of psychiatry in the area of self-help is not exactly easy. For this reason, the constructively critical approach practiced in Canada in an exemplary manner should be an impetus for the desperately needed development towards tackling the multiplicity of psychosocial problems in a cooperative and independent fashion.

Increasing migration in almost all countries of the world has led to a need for alternative approaches to psychosocial support for migrants. The example from the U.K. demonstrates clearly that the basics of effective support must be sought in the culture and traditions of the migrants themselves and not the other way around. This applies for children and adolescents as well as for elderly people with emotional distress. When we look at these approaches we realize that we are only beginning to rethink our way of doing things. The following contributions should act as encouragement for this project.

Translated from the German by Mary Murphy

Karyn Baker

Families: A Help or Hindrance in Recovery?

This articles outlines how traditionally families have not been given adequate information or strategies for helping them in the recovery process. As a result, families have tended to unwittingly become a hindrance in their relative's recovery. The Family Outreach and Response Program in Toronto, Canada has created a program that teaches and supports families in developing a critical perspective of the mental health system and to create a recovery environment in their family. The group was originally started by a group of family members whose relatives were patients at a provincial psychiatric hospital in 1996. The families wanted to provide each other with support and to advocate for changes within the hospital.

Background

Families of those recovering from serious mental health issues are probably among the last groups within the mental health community to embrace the vision of recovery. Their experience of the mental health system is one of despair, shame, hopelessness, helplessness, alienation, isolation and discrimination. Families are often told by psychiatrists and family support programs to grieve the loss of their loved one as they knew them, to lower all expectations of their relative's future and to make sure their family member takes their medications. This leads to a family environment that does not promote recovery but rather may hinder the recovery process. How can a family nurture a recovery atmosphere when they feel their lives are full of hopelessness, sadness, anger and power struggles?

Traditionally, family support and education programs mostly focus on teaching families about diagnosis, symptoms, psychiatric treatments, mental health resources, crisis intervention, communication skills and self-care. There is little, if any, mention of recovery and no critical examination of the mental health system from a trauma-informed and anti-oppression perspective. These programs created like-minded thinking between families and mental health professionals, which further reinforced the limiting idea that severe mental distress is an illness and brain disease and must be treated with medication or otherwise recovery is not possible.

In North America, the alliance of mental health professionals and family organizations has become entrenched in the medical model of mental health distress and has led to an extreme over-reliance on psychiatric medications and coercive mental health interventions as well as legislation. A collateral damaging consequence has been the divisiveness between the psychiatric survivor organizations and family groups. Psychiatric survivors have been highly skeptical of family involvement in the recovery movement. Often survivors have felt both the controlling and paternalistic (and sometimes traumatizing) experience of both their own families as well as those of large family advocacy organizations. However, most people who are in extreme distress want the love and support of their families and most families want to be helpful in a caring way. This is the underlying principle of the Family Outreach and Response Program (FOR). FOR believes that families can be exceedingly helpful in their relative's recovery when given education, support and skills based on a critical recovery perspective.

A Family and Recovery Approach

The Family Outreach and Response Program is a non-profit, community family initiative located in Toronto. Since its inception in 1997, the program has worked together with consumer/survivor advocacy organizations and fought against coercive mental health legislation and refused any funds from the pharmaceutical industry. However, the program's values of self-determination, choice, respect, and anti-oppression did not always fit well into its practice with families on an individual or group level. Like many of its fellow family programs, FOR had fallen into the net of using traditional "best practice" family psychoeducational approaches.

In 2001, FOR decided to create a family education and support program that would be based on both a recovery approach and a critical perspective of psychiatry. A staff team comprised of a psychiatric survivor and a family member began by conducting a literature review on recovery and critique of psychiatry. The only article they could find written about families and recovery was the *Windhorse Guide for Families*, by Constance Packard.[1] This article which was published on the Windhorse Associates website gave FOR the basic foundation for a curriculum. The Guide speaks about the disservice the medical model does to families and gives a clear message to families that recovery is possible and, most importantly that their attitudes, beliefs and behaviors are essential to that recovery process. The article suggests that families can develop an attitude of acceptance, respect and hope. FOR sifted through literature primarily from the USA, the U.K. and New Zealand. The program based its recovery content on longitudinal studies of researchers

---

1 See www.windhorseassociates.org/index.php?id=33

such as Courtney M. Harding and colleagues (1987); on the narratives of us-ers/survivors of psychiatry such as Pat Deegan (1993), Shery Mead and Mary Ellen Copeland (2000), Mary O'Hagan (undated), Priscilla Ridgway (2001) and Ronald Bassman (2001); and on critical perspectives of psychia-try, including the work of Philip Thomas (Thomas & Bracken, 2006), Phil Barker (2003) and Loren Mosher (Mosher, *et al.*, 2004; Read, *et al.*, 2004).

FOR's course content was based on the research and stories of what psy-chiatric survivors said they needed to recover: *hope*—the belief that recovery is possible; *self-determination*—people need to be in charge of their own re-covery journey; *choice*—people need to have real choices about their sup-ports; *recovery education*—knowledge and tools/strategies for recovery; *support*—to give and receive support.

The course has been structured into a 10 week, two hour program which uses a number of adult education strategies—lectures, small and large group discussions and exercises, role plays, videos, self reflection exercises, home-work and readings. Almost all of the resources used have been written or produced by psychiatric survivors. The maximum number of family mem-bers is 12 per group. The definition of family member is broad and includes any significant person in the life of someone recovering from extreme emo-tional distress. The majority of participants have been parents. Typically, a psychiatric survivor and a family member co-facilitate the group.

The program uses two textbooks for the course: *A Mental Health Recovery Reader for Providers, Survivors and Families* (Thompson, 2006) and *Path-ways to Recovery Self-help Workbook* (Ridgway, *et al.*, 2002). The course outline includes: Introduction to Mental Health Recovery—what are people recovering from? / Pathways to Recovery and Barriers / Hopelessness and the Power of Hope / Role of Family and Tapping Resilience / Power and the Role of Family / Understanding, Motivation and Stages of Change / Having a Strengths Perspective / Self-reflection and Self-care / Family Recovery Ac-tion Planning / Recovery—the Evidence and the Practice.

Results

The *key messages* that families report taking away from the course are:
• to view madness as a human experience

- hope is the cornerstone to recovery—it is almost impossible to recover without hope and the family's role is to "hold the hope"
- to avoid creating learned helplessness by being overly-involved
- to support also risk-taking and giving the relative the dignity and freedom to fail like any other human being
- to let go of controlling relatives' choices—this is their recovery journey
- to stop viewing everything from a problem orientation and start building on strengths
- not to use coercion or forced treatment
- explore alternatives and use advanced directives
- recovery is possible even without any professional intervention (for many families this is the first time they have heard this message).

Families also have reflected back on the importance of the group process in learning about recovery and their own behavior. They want a place that does not perpetuate their guilt or shame about their own role in their relative's journey into unwellness but helps them to acknowledge their role and behavior and to make changes in a safe environment. Many families acknowledge that they started this journey as either uninformed or misinformed and that often their natural intuitions about how to be helpful was actually counter-productive. Families in their sincere effort to help can often become over-protective and deny their relative the opportunity to take risks and learn from their mistakes which is the way most people grow. Families also become aware of their own internalized discrimination or mentalism about people with mental health issues. Families learn to use language that does not hurt or hinder recovery. The program uses two tools to measure the shift in recovery attitude and specifically the family's level of hope (Snyder, *et al.*, 1991).

Future Challenges

Toronto is one of the most diverse multicultural cities in the world, with over 100 languages spoken. This poses challenges for understanding family structures, dynamics, beliefs and attitudes that are different from the dominant culture particularly with respect to notions of autonomy, extended family and community. FOR is now partnering with specific multicultural communities to learn more about what recovery means in their communities.

The program also needs to create ongoing mechanisms for recovery education and support. Like all of us who work from a critical perspective, families confront opposition and sometimes hostility from the mental health system. They need support to maintain their hope, strength and resilience to create a recovery environment at home and to make change in the system. FOR has seen the transformation of individual families adopting a recovery approach. Families learn that the most important tool they have for recovery is a positive relationship with their relative. Family members have healthier relationships as power stuggles are greatly reduced. These family members know that their relatives are in charge of their own recovery and as a result there is less coercion to use unwanted medications or to force hospital admissions. FOR believes that these families can make useful allies with survivors in creating change within the mental health system.

Sources

Barker, P. (2003). The tidal model: Psychiatric colonization, recovery and the paradigm shift in mental health care. *International Journal of Mental Health Nursing, 12,* 96-102.

Bassman, R. (2001). Whose reality is it anyway? Consumers/survivors/ex-patients can speak for themselves. *Journal of Humanistic Psychology, 41*(4), 11-35.

Bassman, R. (2007). *A fight to be: A psychologist's experience from both sides of the locked door.* Albany, NY: Tantamount Press.

Deegan, P. E. (1993). Recovering our sense of value after being labeled. *Journal of Psychosocial Nursing, 31*(4), 7-11.

Harding, C. M, Brooks G. W., Ashikaga, T., Strauss, J. S., & Breier, A. (1987). The Vermont longitudinal study of persons with severe mental illness, II: Long-term outcome of subjects who retrospectively met DSM-III criteria for schizophrenia. *American Journal of Psychiatry, 144,* 727-735.

Mead, S., Copeland, M. E. (2000). What recovery means to us: Consumers' perspectives. *Community Mental Health Journal, 36*(3), 315-328.

Mosher, L. R., Hendrix, V. with D. C. Fort (2004). *Soteria: Through madness to deliverance.* Philadelphia: Xlibris Corporation.

O'Hagan, M. (undated). A call to open the door. Retrieved March 5, 2007, from www. dinf.ne.jp/doc/japanese/resource/right/acallto_eng.html.

Read, J., Mosher, L. R., & Bentall, R. (Eds.) (2004). *Models of madness: Psychological, social and biological approaches to schizophrenia.* Hove: Brunner-Routledge.

Ridgway, P. (2001). Restorying psychiatric disability: Learning from first person recovery narratives. *Psychiatric Rehabilitation Journal, 24*(4), 335-343.

Ridgway, P., McDiarmid, D., Davidson, L., Bayes, J., & Ratzlaff, S. (2002). *Pathways to recovery self-help workbook.* Lawrence: University of Kansas School of Social Welfare.

Snyder C. R., Harris C., Anderson J. R., Holleran, S. A., Irving, L. M., Sigmon, S. T., Yoshinobu, L., Gibb, J., Langelle, C., & Harney, P. (1991). The will and the ways: Development and validation of an individual-differences measure of hope. *Journal of Personality and Social Psychology, 60*(4), 570-585 (Appendix: The Recovery attitudes questionnaire 16 from "Can we measure recovery? A compendium of recovery and recovery-related instruments and The Hope Scale").

Thomas, P., & Bracken, P. (2006). *Postpsychiatry: Mental health in a postmodern world.* Oxford: Oxford University Press.

Thompson, A. (2006). *A mental health recovery reader for providers, survivors and families.* Toronto: Canadian Scholars' Press.

Philip Thomas and Salma Yasmeen

Choice and Diversity

Developing Real Alternatives for People from Non-Western (and Western) Cultures

There is a paradox at the heart of this chapter. Its title implies that there is a need to provide something special, or different, for people from non-Western cultures as an alternative to psychiatry. This is true to a point. The history of the relationship between psychiatry and people from non-Western cultures is a tragic and unhappy one. It ranges from *drapetomania*, the expression coined by the 19th century American psychiatrist, Samuel A. Cartwright (1851) to describe as madness the actions of slaves who ran away from the "civilising" influence of the slave masters. The natural desire for freedom had to be interpreted as madness, a fear of the "rationalising" and "civilising" impulse of Western slave owners, to be treated with a mixture of care and punishment (Fernando, 1991). It emerged, too, through colonialism, the ideology of which resulted in the imposition of systems of mental health care in

South East Asia (and elsewhere) that undermined local understandings of distress and support systems rooted in these understandings (Higginbotham & Marsella, 1988), resulting in poorer care for people in these communities. Finally, in the 20th century, it emerged in Britain in the form of inequalities in health rooted in institutional racism in terms of diagnosis, treatment, and access to services. All this suggests that choice and alternatives to psychiatry are a necessity for people from non-Western cultures who experience distress.

At the same time, however, this argument holds for all people regardless of their culture of origin. The plane of resistance opened up by the voices of the survivor movement in Britain and elsewhere, the struggle to assert an opposed truth, lies at the heart of the cry for alternatives to psychiatry. This struggle assumes a particular saliency for people from non-Western cultures, where histories of colonialism and slavery must be reckoned with.

That said there is also a need for complexity and sophistication in developing these arguments. For too long people from non-Western cultures have been saddled with third rate derivatives of Western bureaucracy and science, largely as a result of the inequalities in wealth between economically advantaged (EA) and economically disadvantaged (ED) countries. This chapter is *not* a call to dismantle science and technology, neither is it a call to reduce all to a common level of mediocrity. People wherever they live have the right to access the best available medical care, or for that matter, real alternatives to biomedical psychiatry. For this reason we want to place this contribution in a global context that recognises that as far as real alternatives to psychiatry are concerned, both EA and ED countries have much to learn from each other, on moral grounds, and in terms of economic realities. For example, Western models of support that rely extensively on expensive professional resources raise doubts as to their sustainability in ED countries (Thomas, *et al.*, 2005).

There is, finally, another powerful reason to argue that people from non-Western cultures have specific needs that are unmet by mainstream mental health services dominated by biomedical psychiatry. This concerns the underlying philosophical assumptions upon which the practice of psychiatry, psychology, therapy and counselling are based. The cultural ground of Western psychiatry is one that sits comfortably with the autonomous, rational and reflexive self situated at the core of Western identity, and the formulations of moral agency and autonomy that follow from this. However, when we move to the cultural and spiritual traditions of South Asia, Africa and the Caribbean, this identity becomes highly problematic. Without wishing to reduce the great variety of non-Western cultures to a single monolithic entity, in broad terms they share a decentred notion of self with strong ties to family, community and faith traditions. This makes it difficult for people from exclusively Western traditions to provide appropriate responses for people from non-Western traditions. For this reason we will argue that it is essential that people from these communities are involved in the search for and delivery of alternatives.

In this chapter, we outline the historical inequalities in the experiences of mental health services by people from Black and Minority Ethnic communities in Britain. We talk about the situation here, although we believe that similar conditions apply to other migrant groups in host communities, as well as Black and Latino Americans. Then we consider a conceptual critique of mental health theory and practice to help understand the problems that Western psychiatry poses for people from non-Western cultures. This critique, sometimes referred to as postpsychiatry, does not in itself provide answers, but it raises questions about the values that underpin the responses we envision for ourselves when we experience madness or distress. Finally, we propose the use of a community development approach as a way forward.[1] We outline the principles of community development, and describe how these principles have been applied through *Sharing Voices Bradford*, a community development project with which we are both closely associated. We emphasise the importance of creative and spiritually relevant approaches in this work, and the importance of linking together so-called bottom-up approaches that let ordinary people have a say in their lives. A vital part of this work is the belief that community development is a democratic approach that has the potential

---

1 In Britain, community development is a long-established way of working with poor and marginalised communities. The Department of Health in the British Government uses the expression Community Engagement to describe a particular way of working with Black and Minority Ethnic communities originally in the field of substance misuse, but more recently in mental health. Although the two have different origins, they share much in common.

to enable ordinary people to have a say in the sort of help and support they want in times of crisis.

Why Has Psychiatry Failed People from BME Communities?

This question is important because if we answer it we may find ways of rectifying the situation. Psychiatry is a modernist enterprise. By this we mean that its origins can be traced back to the European Enlightenment and the ideas of Descartes, Kant and Newton, and the belief that human life and society can be progressed through the rational application of scientific thought and knowledge. The Enlightenment has had a profound influence on our modern way of life, and although many controversies exist amongst historians about the period (Porter, 1990, gives an excellent overview) it is possible to discern a number of key themes that emerge from it. In particular, Bracken and Thomas (2005) have described two key preoccupations emerged from Enlightenment and have directly influenced psychiatry, psychology and psychotherapies. These are the importance of reason, and a focus on the individual self, particularly its depths. As far as psychiatry is concerned, three significant developments arose out of these Enlightenment preoccupations: the promotion of an orderly society, a belief in the importance of technological solutions to complex human problems, and the exploration of individual subjectivity and its depths. These relationships are summarised in the figure on the next page.

These features are deeply embedded within Western culture, so much so that we take them for granted and rarely think about them. They are an important feature of contemporary psychiatry (Bracken & Thomas, 2005). The professional expertise embodied in psychiatry plays a central role, through state legislation, in excluding and controlling madness, and thus promoting an orderly society. Its theories provide the principal way of framing and accounting for emotional problems, and locate the origins of madness deep within the individual self, whether in the form of psychoanalysis, cognitive theory or phenomenology.[1] We question the relevance of these assumptions

---

1 Here we are speaking of the type of phenomenology that dominates psychiatry in the

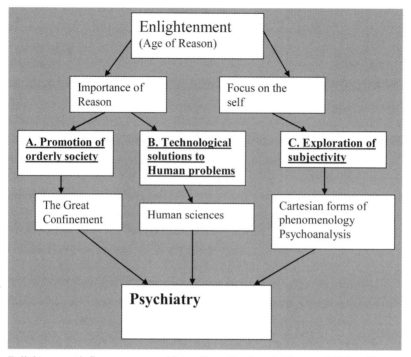

Enlightenment influences on psychiatry (from Bracken & Thomas, 2005, p. 7)

for cultural groups who do not share this Enlightenment heritage, and who instead attach greater importance to family, community, faith or spirituality.

The practical implication of this is that we must think in radically different terms if we are to treat people from Black and Minority Ethnic (BME) communities equally and fairly, and in ways that respect their cultural traditions. Until recently, policy in Britain for meeting the mental health needs of these communities hinged on the idea that if you provided mental health services and psychological therapies in South Asian languages, and offered appropriate diet and places to pray, then their needs would be met. There remains a

guise of "descriptive psychopathology." It is important in passing to note that there are "interpretative" or hermeneutic phenomenologies (e.g., Mosher, *et al.*, 1994; Thomas, *et al.*, 2004) that differ radically from descriptive phenomenology.

common belief that all services have to do to respond to the needs of BME communities, and thus "tick" the diversity box, is to provide cognitive behavioural therapy for South Asian communities by South Asian practitioners, speaking South Asian languages. This belief overlooks the fact that non-Western cultures have different conceptions and understandings of the nature of the self that is the focus of therapy. It also disregards the historical and political contexts of colonialism and slavery, and the implications of this for the relationship between Black people in mental health services that are staffed largely by white professionals.

In any case, there is a growing disenchantment in Western culture with the sterility of the materialistic assumptions that underpin biomedical interpretations of mental health, and especially the experience of psychosis. Many people in the West cry out for spiritual or humanistic approaches to psychosis and madness, and responses to these states that reflect these understandings (see, for example, Rufus May's account in this volume). The question then arises as to what sort of responses do people from non-Western cultures value at times of despair and distress, and how can social and health care systems ensure that these responses are made available to them. How can mental health inequalities be tackled? How can genuine choices be offered to people from non-Western cultures who experience severe distress? This is where, within a British context, community development has been invaluable.

Community Development: A British Perspective

In Britain, community development (CD) is rooted in a tradition of philanthropic self-help that extends back at least 100 years (Gilchrist, 2004). After the Second World War community work saw itself as the preventative branch of social work and it featured prominently in its training. It also became politicised, challenging established power structures on issues such as welfare rights. A more liberal strand supported citizen participation in the planning of public services. In the 1960s, "communities of interest" such as people with disabilities and Black communities started to organise themselves separately and gain political influence. They offered specific expertise and sought to shift the balance of resources and power in their favour. As multiple inequalities and sources of oppression within society were highlighted, there was recognition that anti-oppressive strategies should be incorporated into community development.

There is, however, limited experience in the use of CD in mental health. It has been used in mental health promotion (SCMH, 2000) and community care. Despite this, there are strong arguments for its value in mental health from a critical perspective. It is fundamentally democratic in nature, and it values peer support whilst reducing dependency on others (Henderson & Thomas, 2002). It has a commitment to building civil society and democracy, responding to the challenge of social exclusion (Henderson, 2005). It is also a powerful way of investing in social capital. Robert Putnam (1996), whose work has popularised the idea of social capital, argues that "... for a variety of reasons, life is easier in communities blessed with a substantial stock of social capital." Kwame McKenzie, an academic psychiatrist working in London, and colleagues point out that it may also play a positive role in mental health, because "... it offers a way of thinking about potentially important but difficult to quantify aspects of community that may be associated with health" (McKenzie, *et al.*, 2002).

Community development helps to foster social capital by promoting a sense of belonging and influence within public and voluntary services. It supports an understanding of difference, greater fairness for all groups and use of democratic processes to reduce the risk of violent protest. The notion of "safe" spaces plays an important part in this. These are places where people can meet to express themselves in ways that are not possible in the networks that surround them. They are meeting places where people with different perspectives can explore common ground (Community Development Foundation, 2004).

Community Development and Sharing Voices Bradford

Sharing Voices Bradford (SVB) is a community development project that focuses on mental health, grounded in a critical analysis of mental health theory and practice (Bracken & Thomas, 2005). It was set up in 2002, funded by the local service commissioners (Bradford City Teaching Primary Care Trust). It anticipated by two or three years a string of government policies aimed at rectifying inequalities in mental health experienced by people from BME communities (Walls & Sashidharan, 2003; Sainsbury Centre for Mental Health,

2002; Department of Health, 2005). These policies set out an ambitious vision: reducing the fear of services in these communities, increasing their satisfaction, and offering a more balanced range of therapies and a more active role for BME service users in service development and delivery. The government chose community development (community engagement in its parlance) as a means of achieving this.

SVB (see www.sharingvoices.org.uk/index.htm) was established to work with BME communities in inner city Bradford (population approximately 155,000, 55% of whom are from BME communities, largely but not exclusively South Asian) and to find new forms of support for those experiencing distress. At the heart of its work is the view that poverty, racism, loneliness, relationship difficulties, domestic violence, sexual abuse and spiritual dilemmas are at the heart of most mental health crises. The project has five staff, including two community development workers, one community engagement worker and a co-ordinator It works across all black and Asian communities, identifying common concerns while respecting differences. This resonates deeply in Bradford where communities, even within the majority Pakistani population, have been described as fragmented and suspicious of each other. CD lies at the heart of many activities aimed at building community cohesion in the city following the riots of 1995 and 2001. SVB aims include:

1. Enabling people who experience distress, their families and others to develop sustainable solutions within the community.
2. Liaison with statutory service providers to improve the range and quality of services.
3. Stimulating a wider debate locally, nationally and internationally about the nature of distress, and the importance of diverse cultural perspectives.

One of the most important aspects of the project's work is to foster the development of peer support groups. Although the project offers one to one support, the main objective is the development of collective support networks to achieve social change through social action. The workers have successfully engaged a wide variety of individuals, families and communities, including key gatekeepers and existing voluntary/statutory sector organisations that focus on mental health, and many that work outside the traditionally defined boundaries of "mental health," such as the countryside services, youth organisations and sports and recreation services. This requires perseverance; much time is spent listening and talking to people in many locations, including informal and small local networks, often with no immediately obvious outcome. Attending traditional ceremonies such as weddings and funerals has proved a particularly valuable way of establishing links with communities and gaining trust. Over time the workers have developed relationships built on trust, with an open and honest approach that acknowledges the limitations of mainstream mental health services. This has resulted in the development of several community groups. Many of these are gender and faith specific. Hamdard, a community based self-help group in Bradford, for example, is run by and for South Asian women who have experienced distress, and who found a road to recovery in their Islamic faith and peer support. On the other hand, the Creative Expressions group has brought together culturally diverse women, to share their experiences of distress and oppression, and to express this through poetry and painting.

SVB has been evaluated using participatory action research. Community volunteers from six community groups supported by SVB were trained by the project team in qualitative research methodology, questionnaire and semi-structured interview design, interviewing skills and research ethics. They established contact with 126 people in the community from a variety of backgrounds, all of whom had experienced mental distress and had had contact either with SVB or with the mental health services. The researchers set up focus groups and/or undertook in depth interviews with their peers. The evaluation (Sainsbury Centre, 2005; Thomas, *et al.*, 2006) found that participants in the project valued the culturally and spiritually relevant support they received, but felt that more opportunities were needed for training and employment. They also demanded greater representation on the project's management committee, and greater awareness of the project in the community. External stakeholders in statutory services felt that the project gained credibility from its community base and valued its ability to work across faith traditions and cultures. It was also seen as successful in acting as a bridge between the communities and statutory services, although there were concerns about the project's relationship with frontline services.

Conclusions

The model of community development (CD) established by SVB in 2002, is now playing a significant role in shaping British Government policy for tackling the health inequalities in mental health experienced by many people from BME communities. The government has established 17 focused implementation sites to fast track the implementation of its Delivering Race Equality policy and to accelerate the process of carrying forward the equalities agenda. At the time of writing (April 2007), many of these projects are embryonic, but significant developments are emerging. CD is helping to shape and change service provision. It is increasingly seen as a valuable tool by communities, service providers, and commissioners. As a result, new partnerships are beginning to emerge between the statutory and voluntary sector, in recognition of the vital role to be played by projects like SVB in the recovery and social inclusion of people from BME communities who experience distress. CD workers can also support the participation of marginalised voices in the planning and redesign of services.

The encouraging sign in British mental health policy at the time of writing is the way in which Delivering Race Equality provides a coherent framework for action on all levels whilst placing the voices of BME communities at the heart of the change process. The Focused Implementation Sites act as a bridge between disenfranchised and marginalised individuals and groups, statutory mental health services and the voluntary sector.

There are two caveats. One concerns the extent to which statutory services can genuinely allow CD projects to function autonomously by placing them fully in the non-statutory sector, rather than under the control of services. The latter option is clearly safer from the services' perspective, but means that CD projects thus affected are much less able to represent the interests of communities, and thus foster the development of genuine alternatives to mainstream services. The former option means that services may well have to accept risks by, for example, embracing cultural forms of knowledge and interventions that have in the past been pathologised within mental health services, such as the use of Hakims and spiritual healers. The final point concerns sustainability. Those projects not placed within mainstream services (like SVB) have to fight for financial survival. This, together with concerns about the sustainability of Delivering Race Equality, means that the future of these alternatives remains uncertain.

Sources

Bracken, P., & Thomas, P. (2005). *Postpsychiatry: Mental health in a postmodern world.* Oxford, Oxford University Press.

Cartwright, S. (1851). Report on the diseases and physical peculiarities of the Negro race. *New Orleans Medical and Surgical Journal,* May, 691-715. Reprinted in A. Caplan, H. Engelhardt, & J. McCartney (Eds.), *Concepts of health and disease.* Reading, MA: Addison-Wesley, 1981.

Department of Health (2005). *Delivering race equality in mental health care: An action plan for reform inside and outside services and the government's response to the independent inquiry into the death of David Bennett.* London: Department of Health.

Fernando, S. (1991). *Mental health, race & culture.* London / Basingstoke: Macmillan / London: Mind Publications.

Gilchrist, A. (2004). *The well-connected community: A networking approach to community development.* Bristol: The Policy Press.

Henderson, P., & Thomas, D. N. (2002). *Skills in neighbourhood work.* London / New York: Routledge.

Henderson, P. (2005). *Including the excluded: From practice to policy in European community development.* Bristol: The Policy Press.

Higginbotham, N., & Marsella, A. (1988). International consultation and the homogenization of psychiatry in Southeast Asia. *Social Science and Medicine, 27,* 553-561.

McKenzie, K., Whitley, R., & Weich, S. (2002). Social capital and mental health. *British Journal of Psychiatry, 181,* 280-283.

Mosher, L. R., & Hendrix, V., und die Beteiligten des Soteria-Projektes mit D. C. Fort (1994). *Dabeisein. Das Manual zur Praxis in der Soteria.* Bonn: Psychiatrie-Verlag.

Porter, R. (1990). *The Enlightenment.* London / Basingstoke: Macmillan.

Putnam, R. B. (1996). The strange disappearance of civic America. *The American Prospect, 7,* 1-8.

Sainsbury Centre for Mental Health (2000). *On your doorstep: Community organisations and mental health.* London: SCMH.

Sainsbury Centre for Mental Health (2002). *Breaking the circles of fear: A review of the relationship between mental health services and African and Caribbean communities.* London: SCMH.

Sainsbury Centre for Mental Health (2005). *Together we will change: Community development, mental health and diversity.* London: SCMH.

Thomas, P., Bracken, P., & Leudar, I. (2004). Hearing voices:A phenomenological-hermeneutic approach. *Cognitive Neuropsychiatry, 9,* 13-23.

Thomas, P., Bracken, P., Cutler, P., Hayward, R., May, R., & Yasmeen, S. (2005). Challenging the globalisation of biomedical psychiatry. *Journal of Public Mental Health, 4,* 23-32.

Thomas, P., Seebohm, P., Henderson, P., Munn-Giddings, C. & Yasmeen, S. (2006). Tackling race inequalities: Community development, mental health and diversity. *Journal of Public Mental Health, 5,* 13-19.

Walls, P., & Sashidharan, S. (2003). *Real voices: Survey findings from a series of community consultation events involving black and minority ethnic groups in England.* London: Department of Health.

Bruce E. Levine

Troubled Children and Teens

Commonsense Solutions without Psychiatric Drugs or Manipulations

When I mention oppositional defiant disorder (ODD) to the media and the general public, people often chuckle and say, "Oppositional defiant disorder—that sounds like something from George Orwell's *1984.* Are ODD kids what we used to call juvenile delinquents?" No, I respond, illegal activities constitute another DSM disorder called "conduct disorder," and I then list some of the DSM symptoms of "oppositional defiant disorder": often angry with adults, argues with adults, refuses to comply with adults. At which point they often exclaim, "Don't psychiatrists know that it is normal for kids to rebel against authority?"

While today, overt rebellions by young people are increasingly medicalized (as exemplified by "oppositional defiant disorder and conduct disorder"), historically, mental health professionals have routinely pathologized subtle rebellions. Studies show that virtually all "attention deficit hyperactivity disorder" (ADHD) diagnosed children will pay attention to activities that they enjoy or they have chosen and when it is stimulating to them. In other words, when ADHD-labeled kids are in control and having a good time, the "disease" goes away. ADHD is not the only subtle rebellion against authority that has been pathologized. I have talked to many psychiatric survivors who had been, earlier in life, diagnosed with schizophrenia or depression, and who now recognize that their "symptoms" had in fact been a kind of resistance to the demands of an oppressive environment.

Powerlessness is one cause for troubled and troubling children, but not the only one. Other major reasons for emotional crisis and disruptive behaviors include boredom, attention starvation, emotional pain, revenge for injustice, lack of life skills, loss of respect, parental emotional difficulties, physical deprivations, and lack of community. For each commonsense cause, there is a commonsense solution.

Commonsense Causes and Solutions

1. Powerlessness: The American school critic Jonathan Kozol wrote that children are often given choices "among a thousand paths of impotence, but none of power." Powerless children often impulsively find an easy way to make an impact, and what's impulsive and easy is also often destructive to themselves and others—and gets diagnosed as a mental disorder.

The solution: The solution begins with a helper—a parent, teacher, coach, or therapist—*not* being horrified by a child's need for power. A horrified adult is often a controlling and shaming one. The need for power is a natural need. For some of us, power is an extremely strong need.

The message a helper needs to deliver is, "Your need for power and dignity is quite reasonable, but some of the things that you are doing are destructive to yourself and others." While this message is quite simple, establishing the respect and credibility to be heard is more difficult. Effective helpers recall periods in their own lives when they felt powerless, and this allows them to authentically empathize.

If these young people sense that a helper respects their need for power and dignity, they will usually listen to that helper. If they learn from a helper how to achieve power in constructive ways (e.g., legally earning money), a helper will gain respect and be taken seriously when that helper confronts destructive behaviors.

2. Boredom: Young people so often announce, "I'm bored," that many adults fail to take it seriously. Boredom can lead to poor attention and annoying actions that get diagnosed as ADHD, or it may be behind over-eating resulting in obesity, or result in vandalism (which will get classified as "conduct disorder").

The solution: A helper needs to recognize that bored young people often seek unhealthy stimuli such as TV, video games, and other consumer behaviors that fail to provide useful life skills. Bored children need to know that they are not "bad kids" for seeking such stimulation, and they need help in discovering that which is both interesting and truly nourishing.

Life for many children has become increasingly sterile and hyper-organized, and also less spontaneous—and boring. For many children, school is a boring place, and for some it is intolerably boring. Alternative schools or home schooling are sometimes solutions.

For bored young people, it's especially important that helpers are authentic and spontaneous. Many mental health professionals have so much fear around their professional images that they become unstimulating, nonspontaneous bores. If helpers are authentic and spontaneous, they are more likely to get these children's attention—a prerequisite for forming a helping relationship.

3. Attention starvation: Feeling deprived of attention, some children will do *anything* to get it. If a child is desperate for attention, the easiest way to get it is to annoy parents, teachers, and others—this routinely resulting in some kind of "disruptive disorder" diagnosis.

The solution: Classic behavior modification techniques (e.g., positively reinforcing desired behaviors and not paying attention to problematic ones) may work—but often only temporarily. Children can feel manipulated by these techniques and ultimately rebel. Behavior modification is often ineffective in the long term because it is not addressing the core issue: what is not getting enough attention is who that young person really is.

Consider a neglected 15-year old girl who allows herself to be sexually exploited in order to gain attention, or a 17-year old boy who becomes a drug dealer to gain attention from his peers. Behavior modification and lectures will be impotent forces in the face of their need for attention.

I have sat across from many attention-starved children who were unhappy or annoying, but when they believed that I was genuinely trying to understand them, they became quite fun. Paying attention to a child's being will result not only in a happier and more cooperative child, but will provide a helper with energy and joy.

A good therapist also attempts to help parents better attend to their child's joys, pains, worries, hopes and dreams. If parents are incapable of doing so, a good therapist helps the child deal with this loss.

4. Emotional pain: Why do young people mutilate themselves or purposely provoke others? While it is true that some children are simply trying to gain attention, many other young people are seeking intense stimulation to distract them from terrifying emotional pain, especially the pain of neglect or abuse and the accompanying shame.

The solution: Shame is a nasty fuel that powers all kinds of destructive compulsions. Shame-fueled compulsive behaviors will not be helped by behavior modification, and while psychiatric drugs can temporarily dampen emotional pain and perhaps its accompanying compulsivity, long-term use often results in drug tolerance and troubling adverse effects.

Deep wounds need healing, which neither behavior modification nor psychiatric drugs provide. For healing to occur, children need to be open about the source of their wounds. This requires trust building, which often requires patience. With kindness, gentleness, trust, respect, and love, healing will naturally take place.

While there are many healing paths, one powerful one is a relationship with a respected person with whom one feels safe. True healers are non-manipulative and unafraid of emotional pain. While mental health professionals are trained to focus on symptoms, genuine healers refuse to be distracted by the dumb things people do. Instead, healers care about the whole person.

5. Revenge over injustice: Children are very aware of unfairness, and they can be so resentful over injustices that they take revenge, aggressively or passive-aggressively.

The solution: A helper needs to gain awareness of a child's experience of injustice. However, these children often refuse to talk about it. For a shutdown child, a starting point of helping could be to say something like, "I think the behaviors that you are getting in trouble for are motivated by hurt and a feeling of unfairness." Sometimes unresponsive children may open up when they hear helpers talk about what in their lives made them feel angry. Helpers also need to ask others who have contact with the child for clues about sources of resentment.

When children open up, it is important that they feel genuine care and that they see heartfelt efforts at correcting injustices.

6. Lack of life skills: Fewer expectations and demands will be made on children who have persuaded parents and teachers that they are incapable, and so some children have an incentive to act immaturely and goofy. For this "strategy" to work well, children must actually believe that they are inadequate.

The solution: Human beings need to feel useful and know how to solve practical problems, and often school doesn't give children that experience. A century ago, children learned many useful skills on the farm, and in pre-industrial societies, young people became virtually self-reliant by their teens. Children who behave problematically because of felt inadequacy can turn around after they have learned *anything* useful (e.g., simple construction or cooking skills).

All children have talents, and it is the responsibility of adults to recognize these talents and help children see them. A young person who is behaving problematically because of felt inadequacy is usually afraid of failing and is not a self-starter—and so often needs to be pushed. What's critical when pushing children is knowing them well enough to push them toward something that fits them.

7. Loss of respect: While it's natural to be frustrated and even angry with parental limit setting, it is also natural for children to want to respect their parents. When children have lost respect for their parents, parents have almost always brought this on themselves.

The solution: Young people consider adults who need to be constantly liked to be childlike—and not to be taken seriously. After enough disrespect, often these same parents will explode into a temper tantrum, another child-like behavior. Young people respect authentic, non-manipulative, calm assertions, and helpers need to teach parents these parenting skills.

Children also resent parental limit setting when the parent-child bond is a weak one due to parents not having spent enough time with their child or because the time together is meaningless. To strengthen the parent-child bond, parents often need to begin spending their time with their child in one-on-one, meaningful activities such as projects and conversations that will result in greater mutual understanding.

As a clinical psychologist, I often work with single parents—especially single mothers and their teenager sons—where respect has broken down. These mothers are often afraid that if they are authentic (e.g., strongly expressing disappointment with their son for lying), their child will say "I'm going to live with Dad." These parents need support to gain confidence that if they are authentic and truly caring, they will not permanently lose their relationships with their children because of limit setting.

Increasingly, I see parents who lost their children's respect because these parents complied with school or medical authorities and accepted a mental diagnosis and drug treatment for a behavioral problem. Sometimes it is necessary for parents to apologize to their children for making a mistake. It is my experience that children almost always accept these apologies if they are heartfelt, this often resulting in reconciliation and restoration of respect.

8. Parental emotional difficulties: When parents are afraid or ashamed of their own emotions, they can't calmly set limits on their child's emotional outbursts. Children may stop maturing because they are terrified of taking on the burden of having to "parent their parents."

The solution: Anger is an emotion that many parents have difficulty with because they have never made the distinction between anger and violence. Often these parents themselves had parents who became violent with their anger, and so they cannot effectively communicate to their own children that anger is okay but that violence and destructive behaviors are not.

A significant part of parenting is instilling an acceptance of all emotions while at the same time setting limits on destructive behaviors. Parents who cannot both nurture emotions and set limits on behavior often need healing so as to accept their own emotionality.

9. Physical deprivations: Many children do not get required nutrition, physical activity, or sleep. If adults can become miserable and bratty with these deprivations, so, of course, can children. This should be obvious, but in the current era of assembly-line medicine, these basic needs are routinely not checked.

The solution: Nowadays, it is not uncommon for a child to receive psychiatric drugs or be behavior modified for ADHD symptoms when the original problem was a lack of physical activity or fresh air, resulting in a child who stayed up until 2 a.m., got up for school at 6 a.m., and was sleep deprived.

Studies reveal what should be common sense: sleep deprivation is associated with anger, irritability, and unhappiness; children who have even a marginally nutritious breakfast have better attention spans and happier moods; and a bare minimum of exercise results in decreased depression.

10. Lack of Community: Sometimes good parents, try as they might, have difficulty relating to their child's personality. Almost always this is because the child's personality is dramatically different than the parent's.

The solution: Children who feel that there is at least one adult who has deep respect and affection for them are usually happy and likely to be well-behaved. Good parents feel guilty when they have difficulty relating to their child. But all of us—including teachers and doctors—are human, and we all need to admit our limitations. In a rehumanized society, if a parent had difficulty relating, there would be at least one grandparent, uncle, aunt, friend, or other adult in the community who could easily relate.

This might be the most difficult problem of all because the real solution requires a transformation of our society. In our disconnected society, there are increasingly numbers of children who do not have even one adult who has an understanding and affection for them. We need to rebuild genuine community for our children.

Why Psychiatric Drugs and Behavioral Manipulations are Counterproductive

Psychiatric drugs can make a disruptive child more manageable, and bribes, negative reinforcements, and punishments can also result in compliance; but behavior changes from drugs and manipulations are often temporary and can result in severe biological, psychological, and relational adverse effects. Long-term solutions have to do with respectful and trusting relationships, and psychiatric drugs and manipulations can interfere with healthy relationships. From a risk-benefit analysis, as I document in Commonsense Rebellion (2003), psychiatric drugs and behavioral manipulations are bad ideas.

Long term, psychiatric drugs and manipulations do not have great success. The U.S. Surgeon General's 1999 report on mental health stated with respect to ADHD, "Psychostimulants do not appear to achieve long-term changes in outcomes such as peer relationships, social or academic skills, or school achievement." Jerrold Maxmen and Nicholas Ward's psychiatry textbook notes, "In treating depressed children ADs [antidepressants are] not proven to be better than placebo" (1995, p. 94); and Robert Julien's book, A Primer of Drug Action, reports,

> Studies suggest that TCAs [tricyclic antidepressants] are no more effective than a placebo for the treatment of major depressive disorder in children and adolescents...[and] a double-blind, placebo controlled study [on depressed adolescents] did not find significant differences between a placebo and fluoxetine [Prozac] (1998, p. 205).

Many critics of behavior modification, including Alfie Kohn in Punished by Rewards (1993), have documented how behavior modification is ultimately ineffective and counterproductive when it comes to raising a caring, generous, and well-behaved child.

Even the most enthusiastic drug prescribers admit that there are biological adverse effects associated with psychiatric drugs, but they often fail to mention the psychological adverse effects, which include children coming to believe that the psychiatric drugs rather than themselves are responsible for their actions. There are also psychological adverse effects for behavioral manipulations, especially relationship resentments.

For the helpers themselves, there are also adverse effects associated with psychiatric drug and behavior modification interventions. Medicating and manipulating often result in hostile resistance by those who feel that they are being controlled. Hostility from those whom one is charged with helping can cause therapists, teachers, and parents to feel "burned out." In contrast, the non-controlling solutions that have been described in this chapter are energizing and vitalizing. These solutions are not only effective but also improve rather than damage the helper's relationship with the child.

It is natural for very young children to be self-absorbed and not to care about their impact on others. In a healthy society, children would have contact with at least one adult who cares about them and respects them. This caring and respect feels good, and children come to care about and respect someone who cares about and respects them. Naturally, such children begin to care about the impact of their behaviors on such people. And naturally, children will often model the behavior of someone for whom they respect. This natural process of maturing from a self-absorbed disruptive small child to a well-behaved young person who cares about others is subverted by both psychiatric drugs and behavioral manipulations.

I've talked to hundreds of children who have taken psychiatric drugs, and none have ever told me, "When I was on my Risperdal *(neuroleptic, active ingredient risperidone, marketed also as Ridal, etc.)* or Ritalin *(psychostimulant, active ingredient methylphenidate, marketed also as Attenta, Concerta, Daytrana, Equasym, Metadate, Rubifen, etc.)*, I cared more about other people's feelings and my impact on them." Most of these children have told me just the opposite, that the psychiatric drugs made them care less about their own and others' feelings (and the research that I document in *Commonsense Rebellion* supports this).

Psychotropic drugs dampen the intensity of emotional experience. People often call such dampening "taking the edge off." Research shows that even when parents and teachers report psychiatric drugs as working, the children have become more manageable often because they have become more apathetic. They no longer care about their powerlessness, boredom, attention starvation, emotional pain, perceived injustices, lack of life skills, loss of respect, parental emotional difficulties, physical deprivations, or lack of community. Only a barbaric culture would consider induced apathy resulting in greater manageability to be a successful outcome.

Behavioral manipulations are also counterproductive to healthy, trusting human relationships. When children experience only control and do not experience caring and respect, they are not likely to reciprocally care and respect. Instead, they are likely to learn how to be manipulative. Moreover, when the adult world is exploiting its knowledge of a child's joys and pains for purposes of control, children learn to shut down about their true joys and pains. Such children are routinely difficult to engage because they have learned to be guarded about their true self for fear of it being used against them.

Even the most talented and skilled helper cannot help every young person, and so therapists, parents, and teachers need to have humility. Absent of such humility, helpers who find themselves with an unreceptive child will jack up the severity of a diagnosis, escalate behavioral manipulations, or administer psychiatric drugs. With humility, helpers will have faith that for any given child, some other helper may be better suited than they are.

Sources

Julien, R. M. (1998). *A primer of drug action.* 8th edition. New York: Freeman & Co.

Kohn, A. (1993). *Punished by rewards.* Boston: Houghton Mifflin.

Levine, B. E. (2003). *Commonsense rebellion.* New York: Continuum.

Maxmen, J. S., & Ward, N. G. (1995). *Psychotropic drugs: Fast facts.* New York: Norton & Co.

U.S. Department of Health and Human Services: Mental Health (1999). *A report of the surgeon general: Executive summary.* Rockville, MD: U.S. Department of Health and Human Services.

Erich Schützendorf

When a Slice of Sausage Turns into a Lens-cleaning Cloth

To Respect and Support People with Dementia

Elderly people sometimes evolve in rather interesting ways. For example, an elderly woman tries to clean her eyeglasses with a slice of sausage while eating her breakfast.

A person seeing this behavior, perhaps the son, caregiver or visitor, may react in very different ways.

- The woman's behavior makes the person sad. He looks away and hopes that this does not happen to him one day.
- The person would like to help the old lady. He takes the glasses from her and puts the sausage aside.
- He smiles at the crazy behavior and allows the woman to proceed.
- He explains to the woman that the sausage is there to eat, and hands her a cloth to wipe her glasses.
- He advises the woman not to do "something like this" again.
- He wonders if the situation can be dealt with using medication.

At first glance, the case is clear. The son feels responsible for his mother. To him, his mother's actions are abnormal or sick; he can tolerate them, but not approve or respect them. For her wellbeing, he sees himself as authorized, perhaps even called upon, to intervene and make things right again. The glasses are cleaned, the slice of sausage disposed of and the plate with the remaining sausage is placed out of reach. Now there is a chance that the mother, due to her cognitive deterioration, will not be willing to abandon her new predilection. Her son considers how to prevent this kind of mistake in the future. Eventually there will be no other choice for him than to supervise the mother's breakfast every day, and to stop her from playing with the sausage. This is a recipe for further conflict. The mother wants to clean the glasses, the son wants to prevent it, the mother insists. In the end, when everything runs awry, the mother will be sedated with psychiatric drugs.

What would happen if one recognized the old woman not as a sick, demented patient with no control over her senses, but rather as an aging human being who is behaving in accordance with her world? What if one could grant her the right to self-determination even for the kind of behavior that is not determined by common sense, and respect her pointless and playful aspects of her actions as reasonable behavior? She might then no longer be the irrational, perhaps compulsive old invalid, who must be guided, protected, supervised and attended to, but rather a human being who can be supported in her willfull actions. This change in perspective is not hard to achieve when one stops viewing dementia as an incurable sickness that is associated with deterioration, loss, and destruction, and instead accepts that people affected by organic changes in the brain develop a new relationship to their world, and as a result perceive the world in a new way. It could very well be that certain cognitive structures develop within the brain of a person with dementia that facilitate a particular relationship to the world.

Many decades ago the developmental psychologist Jean Piaget described the development of a child's cognitive abilities. Cognitive structures are built through assimilation and accommodation that allow growing children to better understand the world in their own unique fashion. The small child is not yet able to draw logical conclusions or to recognize relationships between objects in different locations or at different times. This skill is developed over time, until at last, as a sort of a crowning achievement, the child is able to understand complex contexts and is capable of thinking on a high level of abstraction. Now imagine that for people with dementia, the cognitive abilities are perhaps dwindling away in reverse order from the way they have been gained in childhood, then one has an idea of how people with dementia perceive the environment and relate to it.

The ability for abstract reasoning is among the first to be lost, followed by thinking in complex contexts. The person once again thinks more concretely. The meaning of images, for example, can no longer be understood. The phrase "The apple doesn't fall far from the tree" no longer refers to children resembling their parents, but rather they imagine that the apple falls off and comes to rest next to the tree trunk.

Or the meaning of a newspaper article can no longer be understood, even though the person can still read it word for word. Soon words in a sentence can no longer be understood as a meaningful sequence. The sentence, "a man was bitten by a dog" goes from passive to active: "A man bit a dog." At some point only individual words are understood but not their context. The sentence "Father, would you like to drink some water?" becomes simply an accumulation of words. The person with dementia picks out the word "father" from the sentence and says for example, "Yes, certainly" (I am your father), or he takes the word "water" and sings "water is here for washing, tralala" or the word "drink": "I like to drink" he responds to the question without answering it, and when the water sits before him, he says, "I'm not thirsty."

At some point over the course of his cognitive changes, the person with dementia will cease to perceive the newspaper as such. They see objects before them and try to manufacture a reference for them. They grasp for the object (the newspaper), and now an ingrained act, in this case the years-old practice of reading a newspaper, is repeated. They leaf through the newspaper, fold it, and turn it over. These actions have nothing to do with what we normally would consider as reading a newspaper. It could be pure chance that these ingrained actions are repeated with the newspaper. The person might as well be folding a napkin, leaf through it or consider it intently, as if they were reading.

When one considers the development of a person with dementia not as pathological alterations, but rather as an expression of individualistic behavior, then a respectful encounter becomes possible. Older folks relate to their world, they act within it. No one should deprive them of the possibility to act, for instance by swiping the newspaper or the napkin.

An old person may perceive the newspaper as a "case" and pack their glasses inside. The respectful companion will perceive this deed as a sensible act and only intervene when the person looks for his or her glasses and can't find them. He or she will behave exactly the same way with the sausage that served as a lens-cloth. They admire the old man, who cleans his glasses with great care and when he tries putting them on his nose, the companion takes them and cleans them again using their own methods.

The old person who holds a newspaper in their hands might also rip it up. They discover a sound through this action that they might like or want to re-create again and again. They act, they play, they experiment. They may touch their drinking glass, discover its contents, and splash the liquid over the table. By the way they do this, the companion recognizes earlier behaviors of the person. The companion may interpret the actions as making a mark. The old person spills the coffee across the table, and the companion recognizes within this action the attempt to water flowers. The companion observes the behavior in order to find an approach to discover a meaning that is at first elusive. This must be done with reserve, caution and attentiveness. Under no circumstances should they interrupt or hinder the behaviour, unless the old person was about to put himself or others in danger. When people with dementia are understood as pursuing sensible actions, then protecting and safeguarding them are no longer in the foreground, but rather the creation of possibilities and the granting of room to maneuver. In this way, the person's actions are seen as much less dangerous and menacing, and a life-affirming risk becomes worth taking without resorting to the sedative effects of psychiatric drugs.

There are people with dementia that seem to live in one eternal moment, without foothold or security. They are restless, they scream, they whine or wail, they ask the same questions repeatedly, they perform the same acts over and over, they wander about. At first glance these people are pitiable and worthy of bemoaning. One tries to help them by distracting, pleasing, or freeing them from their agitated melancholia or anxiety through psychiatric drugs. Perhaps even those people might be able to create their own structure that could give them a foothold, a framework, a chance of survival in a disintegrating world. They walk, for example, to and fro along the railing, scratch the edge of a table with their fingernails, or continuously roll a glass in a circle on the table. This puts them, at least temporarily, in a situation of relative ease. They are holding on to something for a little while. Why should they be relieved of such a situation? Because their supporter cannot stand the monotony? A person that has found their own mental framework does not need stimulation, or engagement, distracting conversations and group work. These well intended offers will disturb him. A respectful companion sits with the person, observes him and avoids taking the lead. Maybe the older person responds to the closeness of the other and seeks security by holding on to him, making eye contact and communicating. He might find that the companion provides a stable counterpart, at least for a while. Other people with dementia find relative security by repeating the same words: "Back again. Back again. Back again." You don't have to ask them anything, except letting them know that you are here, and sometimes they will say: "I'm glad you're here." Then they pick up the familiar pattern once more: "Back again" The duty of the companion is plain and simple, to stand by the person, to be there. The old person with dementia is the principal, he sets the pace, he is in charge. The companion reacts or intervenes only in emergency situations, e.g., with essential nursing duties.

This type of companionship sounds a bit strange, because the current care giving system in rich countries like Germany for people with dementia is medically oriented and relies on traditional nursing care. However, medical science is a bit at loss since it cannot cure organic brain alterations. That's why it focuses on the medical conditions alongside dementia, even though the administration of a whole mess of symptom-suppressing and unpredictably interacting drugs is anything but agreeable for the metabolism and the organs of an older person.

Nursing care does not have much to add by merely providing functional support, and has therefore begun to engage in relational work. The meager results of these efforts are seen in home care as well as in residential settings. Ambulatory services have very few strategies of caring for these persons, the structures in the nursing homes are unhelpful and the care providers are soon overextended.

These sad circumstances are reason enough to move into new directions by replacing supportive care with caring support.

The difference between care and support is demonstrated by some everyday examples:

- Mrs. Schmitz searches her memory every time someone asks her something. She does this while pacing around her home or along the hallway of a residence. After a while, an answer occurs to her, but not always the right one. Then she turns around and responds to the previous question.

  The caring daughter or the anxious caregiver doesn't recognize this active searching. They see a woman straying aimlessly and ask: "Do you have to go to the bathroom?", "Did you take your drops?", "Would you like something to drink?"

  The respectful companion waits for Mrs. Schmitz and is there when she, can give him an answer once she has completed her search.

- Mrs. Schmitz likes to take her skirt off to make herself more comfortable.

  The daughter pulls the skirt back up, and the caregiver takes her away from the other residents when she does this. If the woman resists or refuses to leave, the caregivers wonder how she can be "protected" from her new affliction.

  The companion offers her a footstool so that she may put her feet up and make herself comfortable. Or he watches how the lady "folds" her skirt and searches for a place where she can work or rest.

- Mrs. Schmitz crouches down to urinate. Lifts herself up, takes a few steps and crouches down again, letting a few more drops fall on the floor, gets up again, and continues in this manner.

  The old woman has an urge to urinate, but clearly doesn't exactly know where she is.

  The son or caregiver may use an adult diaper to manage her incontinence. By doing this, they accept the fact that the essential function of holding or letting out urine is being eliminated. Resources and capacities are being ignored because they might create more work for the caregivers.

  The companion wonders whether he can offer the woman another option instead of a toilet: a bucket, bushes, a box with sand, an organic toilet.

- Mrs. Schmitz is searching for structure and asks constantly: "What should I do now? What should I do now?"

  The daughter or caregiver is irritated and begs the doctor to prescribe a sedating agent.

  The companion knows that the constant pressure that disturbs him will not go away, and that he will not be able to do anything about it. He stands by the lady and offers his support, but accomplishes nothing. At best, the woman makes contact with him.

- Mrs. Schmitz declares that something isn't right with her, and makes a circle around her head with her hand, saying, "Here. You can have all of this." The son or the caregiver worries about Mrs. Schmitz and wants to help her with psychiatric drugs.
  The companion listens and tries to figure out what Mrs. Schmitz wants to communicate. She probably wants to explain that something in her head doesn't feel right. She says: "Everything is rattling in my head." This is her way of describes the dementia. The companion understands her concern and confirms that this must be a very disturbing feeling.

Without a doubt, mentally and cognitively transforming individuals often extract much energy from their companions. A companion may be able to understand the person, but they are generally hard to deal with, especially over the long term.

When one thinks of a person transformed by mental or cognitive changes as someone at sea with risk of drowning then the companion requires lifeboats, floodgates and islands (see Schützendorf, 2006). Lifeboats help them to keep a safe ground underfoot. Floodgates to manage various pressures, and islands for charging up the engine. The companion must realize the need for these survival tools and utilize them appropriately.

Lifeboats prevent drowning, but the companion has to check when it might be appropriate to step off that boat again, whose purpose is pragmatic, goal-oriented and functional. Floodgates are vital, but how to use them intelligently for reassurance, communication and balance, rather than merely to isolate oneself from others? Islands are essential places for retreat. But is it possible to set up islands that enable the companion to stay with people without being immediately available? A companion might lie in a hammock that appears like a cocoon. She is separated from the people around her but still near them. She shares her own time with the old person.

Personal attendants who are well versed in pedagogy and psychology and who are capable of understanding and taking care of themselves, having learned to identify their own needs in relationship to people with dementia, know that they have to take as much time as they need to look after and even pamper themselves. This will enable them to negotiate a compromise in which neither the older person nor they themselves comes up too short. The person with dementia might suffer for a little while, as the companion is recharging his batteries for their next encounter. The person with dementia keeps acting, and the companion decides how long they can take this person. When they can no longer stand the calling, the clinging, the weeping and all the other sounds, they should remove themselves. The person left behind might scream and cry because he has lost his social bearings. The companion needs to accept this, because he knows that he will be returning soon, and if it goes well, will become reengaged in a relationship that is borne by aimlessness, play and sensuality. Together they can munch on sweets, squash chocolate kisses, sway along and listen to music, make noise and faces. The companion can perform magic tricks, dance, do anything they might enjoy and which helps him to stay with the other person without pulling him out of his world.

Source

Schützendorf, E. (2006). *Wer pflegt, muss sich pflegen*. Vienna: Springer

Translated from the German by Katy E. McNally

Guy Holmes and Geoff Hardy

The Shame of "Not Being a Man"

Experiences of Gay, Straight and Bisexual Men

The shame cycle (see next page) is a model of how "not being a man" can result in behaviours that get medicalised and treated by psychiatry. Being gay, effeminate, not standing up for yourself, revealing vulnerabilities or dependence—in fact any behaviours that involve difference from the male norm,

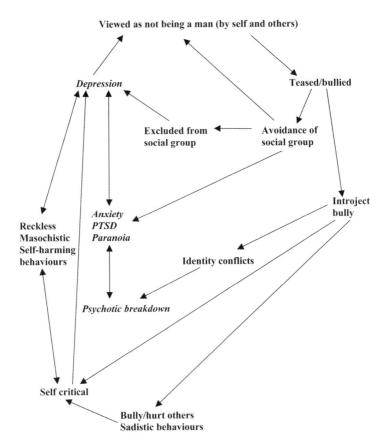

Figure: The Shame Cycle

even being ineffectual at sports or fighting—can lead to teasing and bullying by male peers who try to exclude the "different" person from the group. In group theory, this is referred to as scapegoating. The scapegoat is ostracized because he demonstrates traits that other group members reject as a result of socialisation (e.g., homophobia) or as an attempt to remove from consciousness aspects of the self that disturb group members (e.g., feminine aspects of character). Potential allies avoid the scapegoat and stick with the excluders for fear of being tarnished and consequently teased and bullied themselves. The bullied person isolates himself and avoids others. This is common in schools and many workplaces, especially those with dominant male cultures. People in positions of authority frequently neglect their duties to protect people and often add to the process. Geoff for example recalls being publicly taunted by a teacher at school: "Hardy, you run like a girl, a pansy!"

Paul Gilbert, Professor of Clinical Psychology at the University of Derby in Great Britain, has written about evolutionary processes that make rank critical—the male who is "not a man" is pushed to the bottom of the rank, scapegoated and excluded from the "pack." Shame and depression ensue. The person internalizes the bully, putting himself down for not being "man enough" and the so-called inner critic takes command. Avoidance as a survival strategy leads to people living more in their inner worlds which can exacerbate realistic fear into paranoia. A person can come to question who they are; core identity issues such as sexuality and even gender can become confusing: *Am I a man? Am I gay? What's wrong with me? Am I in the wrong body?*

Identity problems can lead to psychotic breakdowns as a person is caught in Laingian-type knots—unable to be "a man" and fit in but unable to survive as a different kind of man due to lack of societal and practical support for that identity. Bizarre identities based on fantasy can develop. Inner conflicts, isolation and loathing can combine to induce self-harm or necessitate escape through drugs and alcohol. People who have not been valued can find it hard to value themselves or others, and can become reckless regarding their own and other people's health and safety. Bullied people learn how to bully and sometimes behave sadistically to others, acting out the experiences that they have endured, giving others a taste of what it has been like to be them. Many of these factors lead to depression, and for men who loathe the appearance of being vulnerable ("weak"), the cycle of being further viewed by themselves and others as not being "man enough" continues.

People Who Don't Fit: Geoff's Story

As there were no images about gay sexuality in my time, I grew up knowing what I *wasn't* rather than what I *was* or *might be*. I was socialized into a very rigid idea of being a man. But I realized gradually that my feelings towards some boys were "not alright." In my teenage years, I tried to cover this by acquiring and flaunting girlfriends, yet people noticed, threatened me, called me "sissy" and taunted me with "Backs to the wall, Hardy's coming." I felt terribly alone, that I had no one to turn to. I was often physically sick on the journey to school.

I "came out" through Gay Liberation Front in 1971 whilst training to be a teacher. The sense of "arriving home"—meeting others like me—is still with me. I was the first "out" student at college. I experienced prejudice at Halls of Residence and ridicule at discos when I danced with my partner. But I was enabled to see it as *their* problem, even though I had to deal with the situation. I later went to see my G.P. because of relationship difficulties. He diagnosed me as depressed and referred me to the college psychiatrist who recommended therapy at the Maudsley Hospital (London) to assist me overcome my sexuality! Later, as an openly gay teacher, I was accused of "flaunting." Gay News was often found in the bin. It seemed like all eyes were on me and I had to be exemplary. But it felt then, and still does, important to be open. Apart from reducing misplaced shame, I believe I changed perceptions of gays for all students, straight and gay. For the latter, I hope it gave encouragement and a sense of *okayness*—there is nothing to be ashamed of.

People Who Don't Fit: Guy's Story

In my early twenties, I had a breakdown. I did not eat or talk for 10 days and could feel and see an additional head growing out of the back of my neck that resembled a ferocious-looking Easter Island statue. Many factors coalesced to bring about this breakdown, some of which are relevant to this chapter. Throughout school I lived a very male existence, preoccupied with sports, and escaped bullying by being sufficiently "hard." But at college, after years living with feminists whose views I greatly admired, my ideas about men became wrapped up with knowledge and (what I now recognize as misplaced) guilt about the awful things that men do. With my thinking clouded by massive consumption of alcohol, I subsequently became uncomfortable with my new-found attraction to and sexual involvement with men as it clashed with my upbringing and "manly" persona, and equally uncomfortable with my sexual feelings for women which I equated with misogyny—viewing women purely as sex objects. I recall a longstanding wish to exist as a sexless, genderless "blob."

Subsequently I fell in love with a woman who was in a long-term abusive relationship with a very macho and domineering man who said he had an iron bar in his car that he would use if he ever saw us together. On reflection, when she left me to return to being with him, I believe I repressed many feelings that subsequently manifested themselves in the emergence of the Easter Island head: the hurt ("it's not manly to cry"); anger ("to get angry would be to get violent like the man I resented and be like all abusive men"); the envy ("me, envious of the kind of man I rejected as a role model?!"). It took several years to get over this, to find a settled male identity and sexuality, and to become the kind of man who was less reckless and damaging to himself and others. Non-directive, exploratory counselling was helpful, as was keeping away from the kind of doctors who had given my grandfather ECT, but what was most helpful was support and guidance from gay, straight and bisexual friends.

The Way Forward

Psychiatry and clinical psychology, with their focus on individual people's symptoms of what we have argued are the results of damaging social structures and cultures, clearly have limited scope to bring about effective change. We believe that the whole psychiatric endeavour of identifying, labelling/ pathologising and treating people who are "different" has to be stopped. Below are examples of some things that we have been involved in that illustrate alternatives to mainstream mental health approaches.

The examples mostly focus on gay men because we feel that in many ways more has been done by the gay community than straight community in this area, and the selected examples point the way for *all* men regarding the topics of this chapter:

(i) "Being Out"

Homosexuality is no longer classified as a mental illness as a result of activism (e.g., demonstrations at psychiatric conferences) and the coming out of gay psychiatrists: the authors of the DSM *(Diagnostic and Statistical Manual of Mental Disorders)* struggled to think of their esteemed, gay, psychiatric colleagues as mentally ill and a paradigm shift occurred.[1] We think that the more gay men who come out, the quicker cultural change will occur. Similarly, the more men who are openly bisexual or straight but behave in ways that challenge the rigid male norm, the quicker a set of more fluid male identities will become accepted and not feared or pathologised. The shame cycle will be broken.

(ii) Activism, Community Work and Prevention

Gay activism—e.g., Gay Pride events; lobbying local and national government—has led to many changes in public attitudes and in the law. The British government recently launched *Stand Up For Us,* a national strategy to reduce homophobia.[2] Getting children involved in anti-bullying schemes, conflict resolution and mentoring in schools has great promise. Nationally, *Childline*[3] helps bullied children; locally we have joined the Homophobia in Education Steering Group, a body that aims to link up people involved in education in order to employ preventative strategies to reduce bullying, prevent the shame cycle and hopefully lessen the number of people who end up diagnosed as mentally ill in adulthood.

(iii) Use of the Media

Although the media can reaffirm stereotypes (e.g., "Lad's Mags"), a myriad of films and other forms of art and media where men are seen in a kaleidoscope of images in terms of male behaviour, sexuality and roles is likely to be helpful in terms of enabling acceptance of new male identities in the 21st century. If there could be democratisation of the media, taking it out of the domination of a small number of powerful elites with vested interests, change would be quicker and more effective. In December 2006, Shrewsbury held its first lesbian and gay film festival at a local independent cinema. The films

---

1   See Kutchins, H., & Kirk, S. (1997). *Making Us Crazy*. London: Constable.

2   Information on the internet at www.wiredforhealth.gov.uk

3   Information on the internet at www.childline.org.uk

were chosen to reflect the varied nature of the gay community with the aim of helping gay people and gay culture become more visible in what is a relatively conservative provincial English town, and with an aim of reducing societal and self-oppression of men who are different from stereotypic male norms.

(iv) Community Groups

Groups, drop-ins, clubs and bars provide a sense of community and belonging, help acceptance and self-esteem related problems, combat isolation and provide focal points for outreach workers to disseminate information. Locally, Geoff has helped set up various drop-ins and support groups in community settings for gay men aimed at combating the effects of the shame cycle. Examples include: *The Older Men's Group*—a support group that helps people damaged by extreme acts of prejudice, many of which occurred decades ago; *The Fruit Bowl*—a monthly drop-in for people who do not fit into a fashion-conscious gay scene, that attracts men aged 16 to 70 and offers a safe, friendly environment to come out and obtain support. Men's groups not specifically aimed at the gay community are rare, but there has been a long-running local group that has been open to all men wishing to explore issues of sexuality and gender. A significant proportion of men who attend these groups have had previous contact with mental health services—often unhelpful or harmful experiences. Members of these groups report benefits from being accepted for whom they are (rather than being treated for having problems), and therapeutic effects (e.g. being less self-critical and less depressed) paradoxically being aided by the groups not being identified as therapy groups.

(v) Mental Health Services

There is evidence that men in general, and especially gay men, are dissatisfied with existing mental health services.[1] A radical re-think is needed to provide services that men will turn up to and benefit from. Guy has facilitated men's groups for people with long histories of involvement with psychiatric

---

1   See MIND Factsheets: Men's Mental Health—www.mind.org.uk

services. Repetitive themes have included: the impact on members of bullying and violence; how diagnoses (especially of schizophrenia) and long-term involvement with psychiatric services have provided additional stigma to the stigmatising effects of "not being a man," not having a job, not having a partner, etc; and the inappropriateness and lack of effectiveness of "treating" the symptoms of social causes of distress (How can medication stop someone feeling scared of being assaulted for "being a wimp"? How can ECT stop someone feeling depressed about not being a "bread winner" due to them being terrified to return to the bullying environments of factory work?). Bringing about change is not easy from within services (can mental health services lessen work-related bullying?). However, sensitively delivered individual and group therapies have enabled some men to break the shame cycle, become more comfortable and open regarding their ways of being a man, and ease some of the distress that they suffer and cause others.

(vi) Mentoring and Crisis Support

Over the past 20 years, with our partners, we have mentored and sometimes opened up our homes to many men who have been in crisis with the kinds of problems highlighted in this chapter. This can be extremely challenging but has also led to deep bonds with people who otherwise would have become much more involved with psychiatric services—people who have been suicidal, stigmatised and bullied, confused about their sexuality, people who have been psychotic. Key factors for meaningful support seem to be: a safe place to stay in a world that can be cruel; a pressure-free environment; a non-judgmental attitude; and an openness to distressed men being able to reveal their fears, vulnerabilities and secrets.

If these things can be done in small, conservative-minded British towns they can be done anywhere.

Realizing Alternatives and Humane Treatment

Introduction

In the USA, a national meeting with participants from all 50 states and the four territories has been held annually for more than 20 years under the name "Alternatives Conference." These meetings are very well attended and illustrate just how important the search for non-psychiatric alternatives is for (ex-)users and survivors of psychiatry and their supporters. Unfortunately the gap between desire and reality is as wide as ever. People are forced to accept what psychiatry has to offer which usually means stigmatizing diagnoses, psychiatric drugs, involuntary admission to psychiatric institutions and even being subjected to electroshock.

This situation is similar all over the world. Self-help centers, which have been set up everywhere, are quickly pushed to the breaking point in their attempt to help people in severe crises because of their extremely limited financial and personnel resources.

If we take a closer look at history and even at current developments we can find a series of very successful approaches that reject psychiatric dogma and have the potential of transforming the system if they were systematically implemented. These encompass the development of alternatives outside of psychiatry, as well as—in particular through the successful application of human rights—qualitative changes within the existing system.

Unfortunately, there are severe obstacles blocking such widespread implementation. In cooperation with the pharmaceutical industry, health insurance companies, hospitals and other institutions of authority, psychiatry, as an instrument of power in the cloak of biomedicine, has succeeded in keeping effective alternative projects deprived of funding opportunities. The previous chapters have shown that these projects manage to help largely without psychiatric drugs, hospital admissions, coercion or force.

The following contributions point to potential strategies for promoting and disseminating alternatives and for achieving human rights. We will introduce examples of interdisciplinary advocacy services or customized person-centered supports such as the personal ombudsman. You will have the opportunity to read about initiatives and individuals that employ lawsuits, advance directives and other strategies to enforce the rights to physical inviolability and to alternatives to psychiatry or alternative methods of treatment. The experiences of MindFreedom International clearly illustrate the prospects for the success of a persistent and united defense of human rights whether the activists are in Africa or in the United Nations in New York. The multiple interests of (ex-)users and survivors of psychiatry can be advanced with user-led research into psychiatric incompetence or refusal to help, by demonstrating the effectiveness of user-oriented alternatives, and with training provided by (ex-)users and survivors of psychiatry.

This holds true whether the objective is increased representation in committees, more effective work in the area of self-help, or competent participation in research and teaching. The fundamental rule, whereby common interests are best achieved through cooperative work is demonstrated in the coming together of people and groups within organizations such as INTAR, which represents many of the most important alternatives to psychiatry, or in organizations of (ex-)users and survivors of psychiatry and their supporters that use new methods of communication to exchange experiences, spread information and encourage each other. All these are working on the development of a sorely needed counterweight constituting of realistic choices outside the realm of psychiatry.

Translation by Mary Murphy

Maths Jesperson

Personal Ombudsman in Skåne

A User-controlled Service with Personal Agents

On 13 December 2006, the General Assembly of the United Nations adopted the first human rights treaty of the 21st century, the historic *Convention on the Rights of Persons with Disabilities*. One of the most groundbreaking parts of this convention is §12 on legal capacity. It says "that persons with disabilities enjoy legal capacity on an equal basis with others in all aspects of life" and shouldn't be prevented from "exercising their legal capacity." According to this statement, all forms of guardianship must be abolished.

During the preparation of the convention, this paragraph was much debated at the United Nations. In the beginning, the majority wanted to exclude persons with severe psychosocial disabilities or learning disabilities from this right. These persons were seen as being too confused to be able to exercise their legal capacity. It was said that such a person could be substituted by a guardian in legal matters—as "a last resort."

This opinion was much criticized by the disability movement, including users/survivors of psychiatry, as legal capacity is a fundamental element of the dignity and rights of every human being. It was acknowledged that there are some persons who have difficulties expressing and communicating their wishes, but this is no argument for depriving them of basic human rights. As an alternative to *substituted decision-making,* the disability movement suggested *supported decision-making*. Instead of guardians who have proxy decision making authority for the person, they suggested that people who are close friends or personal supporters could just help these persons express and communicate their own decisions.

In January 2006, this idea was presented at a seminar in the UN-building in New York. The seminar was persuasive, because afterwards the majority of the delegates changed their opinions and embraced supported decision-making as a solution for abolishing guardianship completely.

At the seminar, some practical examples of supported decision-making were presented. One of these examples was PO-Skåne (Personal Ombudsman in Skåne)[1], a user-controlled service with personal agents which has grown out of the Swedish psychiatric reform of 1995.

A PO (personal ombudsman) is a professional, highly skilled person, who works 100% on behalf of his client. The PO is not in alliance with psychiatry or the social services or any other authority, and neither with the client's relatives or anyone in his surroundings.

The PO doesn't act according to what he thinks is "for his client's own good." He only carries out what his client tells him to do. All decisions are made by the client himself and the PO just helps him to express and implement them.

This might sound like little more than plain common sense, but this way of supporting people with severe psychosocial disabilities is actually revolutionary. It turns the whole paradigm within the field of psychiatry and social services upside down. It not only helps to counteract coercion, but also all forms of paternalism. The client who is used to being at the hierarchical bottom is suddenly the chief at the top, who makes the decisions and gives orders, which the PO helps him to express and communicate to the authorities. Because of this functional difference, the client no longer has to adapt to the plans and theories of psychiatry and the social services, rather, the service providers must adapt their measures to what the client thinks are the most important steps in the direction of a better life.

This makes the service offered by PO-Skåne a good example of supported decision-making. PO-Skåne is one of the pioneers in developing this new kind of support but, in Sweden, services with POs are now being started in many places all over the country. Most of them are run by the local communi-

---

1   The Swedish phrase "personligt ombud" (PO) can be translated as "personal ombudsman" or "personal agent", and of course the agent can also be a woman. This is a new profession that didn't exist before 1995. It came as a solution to a problem that previously existed without any strategies of how to handle it. For more information see www.po-skane.org

ties, but there are some besides PO-Skåne which are run by non-governmental organisations. We think it's important that the POs are not employed by the local community or any other authorities. To avoid the problem with "double loyalties" the POs must be employed by a non-governmental organisation.

Skåne is the most southern province of Sweden. It has about 1.2 million inhabitants. One third of them live in Malmö, which is the third largest city in Sweden. PO-Skåne operates as a contractor in 10 of the 33 local communities in the province. Two thirds of the funding for this service comes from grants by the state and one third from the local community.

PO-Skåne is an organisation, founded in 2000 by the regional divisions in Skåne, that is part of large user organisation RSMH (Swedish National Association for Social and Mental Health) and the family organisation IFS (Schizophrenia Fellowship). Between 1995 and 2000, RSMH-Skåne ran a project with personal agents in three towns. In 2000, it became a permanent user-run service—with personal agents operating in all parts of Skåne.

Only regional divisions and local groups in Skåne of RSMH and IFS can be members of PO-Skåne. Representatives of these groups (users or family members) assemble once a year at the annual general meeting of PO-Skåne where they elect the board of PO-Skåne. Half of the members of the board are appointed by RSMH and the other half by IFS, which means that the board consists of users and family members. The board is the employer of the managing director and the 25 personal agents. This means that although PO-Skåne is a professional service, it is user-controlled and working according to the users' guidelines. Being a board-member is a voluntary commitment but the director and the personal agents are paid with a monthly salary, the service is free for the clients.

Most of the POs are trained social workers, but there are also some who have a background as lawyers. It is important that the POs have much knowledge about the legal system, the laws, the administration and the way the authorities work. Because this knowledge is so important, we employ persons with some kind of academic education in these fields. The other skills we are looking for when employing people is their attitude towards the clients and their ability to communicate with this group of people. These skills are personal qualities and are not really able to be learned at any school. To ensure that the new POs have the desirable qualities, they are first employed on a trial basis for six months.

A new PO is assigned an experienced mentor and supervisor during the first months. He or she is also trained in this new profession through a series of work shops, seminars, and lectures. One of the important things is to "forget" their old profession as a social worker or lawyer. They shouldn't bring their old roles with them into this new profession. A new PO starts with only one or two clients and doesn't have to reach the total number of clients (approximately 12 to 15 per PO) until several months later.

The PO does only what his client wants him to do. There are only two exceptions from this fundamental rule. If the PO finds out that one of their clients has children who are being mistreated, the PO has to report this even if the client doesn't want this done (according to the law about the protection of children). The PO can also refuse to carry out some tasks which are in conflict with his or her deepest moral beliefs, like supporting the client in committing suicide, having sexual intercourse with the client or buying weapons on behalf of the client. Fortunately those exceptional situations almost never occur.

As it can take a long time—sometimes several months—before the client knows and dares to tell what kind of help he wants, the PO has to wait, even though a lot of things may be chaotic and in a mess. This means that the PO has to develop a long-term engagement for his clients, usually over several years. This is a necessary condition for developing a trustful relationship and for getting into more essential matters.

The service is primarily offering supported decision-making for persons with psychosocial problems of the most difficult sort (for example people who live entirely in a symbolic world of their own, are barricaded in their apartment, or homeless in the streets).

In other services, it is usually the clients who have to adjust to a bureaucratic system, but PO-Skåne works in the opposite way and tries to adjust itself to this very special group of persons. This means that the POs have to be very flexible, creative, and unconventional in their work.

As many clients are very suspicious or hostile towards strangers—or hard to reach for other reasons—the PO has to go out and find them where they are. If you just sit and wait for clients to come, only the most active users get the benefits of a PO. This would mean that once again the person who is in most need of support and who nobody cares about might be missed.

The PO tries to reach the person through a series of steps: make contact, develop a communication, establish a relationship, start a dialogue, get instructions. Each of these steps can take a long time to complete. Just to make contact can sometimes take several months. It can mean going out and start talking with a homeless, psychotic person in a park, or talking through the mail drop with someone who lives a very barricaded life. Sometimes the communication for a long time only occurs via SMS, internet or letters. Not until a relationship is established and a dialogue created can the PO start getting specific instructions from his client.

There should be no bureaucratic procedure to get a PO. If a form had to be signed or an admission note were necessary, many psychiatric users would back out and never get a PO—and it would probably be the persons who need a PO most. To get a PO from PO-Skåne doesn't involve any formal procedure. When a connection is made, the PO just asks "Do you want me to be your PO?" If the answer is "Yes" the whole thing is settled.

The PO doesn't have an office, because an "office is power." The PO works from his own home with the help of telephone and internet—and he or she meets their clients in their homes or at neutral places in town.

The PO doesn't limit his/her work to Monday-Friday office hours. The week has seven days and each day 24 hours—and the PO must be prepared to work at all these various hours, because their clients' problems are not limited to normal business hours and some clients are easier to reach on evenings and weekends. The PO has to work 40 hours a week within a flexible schedule according to the wishes of their clients.

The PO should be able to support the client in all kind of matters. The priorities of the client are usually not the same as the priorities of the authorities or the relatives. According to 10 years of experience, the clients' priorities are usually not housing or occupation, but existential matters (Why should I live? Why has my life became the life of a mental patient? Is there any hope for change?), sexuality, and problems with relatives. A PO must be able to spend a lot of time talking with their client about these kinds of issues as well—and not just try to "fix" things.

The clients have the right to stay anonymous with regard to the authorities. If they don't want their PO to tell anybody that they have a PO, this must be respected. PO-Skåne gets money from the community for the service, but there is a paragraph in the contract that says that the PO could refuse to reveal the name of their clients to the community.

The PO doesn't keep any records or notes. All papers belong to the client. When their relationship is terminated, the PO must either give all papers to the client or burn or destroy them another way in the presence of the client.

Peter Rippmann

PSYCHEX: A Swiss Experiment

PSYCHEX is an association of lawyers, doctors, journalists and survivors of psychiatry founded in 1987. Simply put, PSYCHEX can be described as the practical center of the Swiss antipsychiatry movement which began during the 1970s. The association is a response to the lack of human rights in the treatment and care of people who exhibit mental disturbances or those who have been classified as ill by dogmatic and conservative medical professionals and by a society that displays a lack of understanding.

Nowhere else is there a higher proportion of the population that has been involuntarily committed to psychiatric institutions than in Switzerland. These people are not criminals but victims of coercive orders that have been euphemistically called a "caring deprivation of liberty" by Swiss legislators. Those affected are in fact members of society who don't fit in, who don't wish to or cannot adapt to the notion of a decent human being held by the "silent majority." Such individuals keep disappearing into the closed wards of psychiatric hospitals where they are subjected to involuntary administration of psychiatric drugs, if necessary through brutal force.

PSYCHEX is committed to providing unbureaucratic help: "One telephone call will suffice (044 241769) to get the association involved," is how they put it; furthermore:

> We find advocates for those incarcerated from the social, medical and legal sector, we intervene at the psychiatric institutions and the courts, collect addresses of people who can provide or help obtain accommodation and jobs for our clients, we provide guidance for self-help and if necessary organize care for those who have been discharged. The organizational and practical activities of the association have the backup of an office with fulltime staff. Services and referrals on the part of PSYCHEX are free of charge. The association is, therefore, dependent on donations to finance its activities.[1]

All forcibly incarcerated individuals, and not just those receiving direct support from the association, benefit from its commitment: by using the available legal instruments PSYCHEX has solved many cases which have led to a general change in practice. A few examples:

In the 1980s, petitioners who were incarcerated against their will had to wait up to six months before the responsible judge bothered to come to a decision on a release from such "caring deprivation of liberty." Through the steadfast insistence of the association regarding the applicability of the decisions by the Humans Rights Court in Strasburg, the so-called fast-track provision has led to a reduction of this waiting period to four days. Of similar importance was the success of the association in arguing that those wanting to be released can apply to the court without stating a reason. Rather, the burden of proof was placed on the psychiatric hospital wishing to uphold the commitment order.

Developments in the Canton of Zurich are especially interesting. The three-person court-appointed commission was dominated by two psychiatrists. One of them visited the petitioner, prepared a report, circulated it to the

---

1 Address: PSYCHEX, Postfach 2006, CH-8026 Zurich, Switzerland, Tel. +41 44 2417969 or +41 44 8180870, Fax +41 44 8180871, e-mail info@psychex.org, web site: http://psychex.org; PSYCHEX romand, BP 3508, CH-1211 Geneve 3, Switzerland, Tel. +41 22 3106060, Fax +41 22 3106068, e-mail romand@psychex.org

other two and they simply endorsed it. In the first eight years of the court's operation (1981-1989), only about 10 of the 250 to 300 petitions for release per year were granted. PSYCHEX demanded that all three members of the psychiatric court commission personally examine the petitioner. The Federal Court initially rejected this application, but accepted it later after the association persisted with its position in another case. Regardless, once again only one medical expert was present at the next court hearing. The association had to appeal four times to the Federal Court before the governing council of the canton finally decided to revise the court directive. In the first six months after this decision, more than 40 people who had been forcibly incarcerated were released by the courts. In the following year, the number released increased to 110 people.

The open-ended detentions as practiced in Swiss psychiatric institutions lost their legal basis and thus became unlawful. The judicial route had been a farce because instead of a court, only an administrative body overseeing the mental institutions could be petitioned. PSYCHEX succeeded in obtaining an *obiter dictum* decision from the Federal Court, which is a partial judicial decision not directly relevant for the adjudication of individual cases, but which contains additional pertinent legal considerations:

> Forced drugging is *a priori* to be reserved for serious emergencies and to be used only during acute situations for a limited period of time. Longer administration of drugs or actual (forced) therapy is unconstitutional and is in absolutely not permitted by tested Canton law. The Canton law directive which describes the limits of the treatment in rather imprecise terms is thus to be understood in this narrow context.

Following this judgment, the Swiss cantons quickly enacted legal directives which stipulated, among other things, an obligation to document the proceedings and that the *habeas corpus* judge serve as the instance of appeal. Hence, the officials of the psychiatric institutions have become far more cautious in issuing orders for coercive treatment.

Telephone contacts of inmates in psychiatric institutions had been limited to certain times of day. On two occasions, a canton government determined that this practice was in contradiction of the European Convention on Human Rights. In fact, Article 10 promises everyone "the freedom to receive and send messages or ideas without any intervention on the part of the public authorities."

Numerous other examples could be cited. The association has a collection of no less than 150 court decisions considered to be precedents.

Many similar-minded people rallied around PSYCHEX, not least among them the few psychiatrists who fought against the current of conservative medicine, such as Marc Rufer from Zurich, author of *Irrsinn Psychiatrie (Insane Psychiatry,* 1997) or Bierens de Haan, editor of a *Dictionnaire critique de psychiatrie (Critical Dictionary of Psychiatry,* 1986). The promoters of the movement also included several anonymous helpers, some themselves survivors of psychiatry who had gained their freedom and who had suffered the same fate and were in solidarity with those still held in hospitals.

Of particular importance are the lawyers who mirrored the unconventional approach of many PSYCHEX staff and took up the legal fight to free incarcerated patients, following the lead of the Zurich lawyer Edmund Schönenberger. As the prime initiator of the movement Schönenberger developed a comprehensive strategy based on constitutional principles to fight incorrect constitutional developments—occasionally with resounding success. (For example, a case before the Zurich courts resulted in the payment of a six-figure sum to a client who had been wrongfully incarcerated for many years; see Rufer, 1996). Occasionally, there were also apparent failures, as when the highest court in Switzerland did not agree to outlaw the use of forced drugging.

This was only an apparent failure, since not only the pursuit of the law to its fullest extent, but indeed every engagement of the legal system has a prophylactic effect. The unconditional solidarity with the victims of forced incarceration as demonstrated by the lawyers working for PSYCHEX necessarily triggers adversarial reactions on the part of their opponents—even if such reactions consist only of trying to avoid such procedural annoyances. It is certainly a matter of conjecture whether the trend noted in recent years towards shorter hospital stays has come about as a results of new treatment approaches or whether this is not at least in part a response to the struggle fought by individuals in the antipsychiatric movement.

Sources

de Haan, B. (1986). *Dictionnaire critique de Psychiatrie.* 2nd edition. Paris / Lausanne: Favre.

Rufer, M. (1997). *Irrsinn Psychiatrie.* 3rd, worked-over editon. Berne: Zytglogge.

Rufer, M. (1996). Zu Tode "behandelt!" Der Fall Franz Schnyder und die Psychiatrie. In A. Bultmann (Ed.), *Vergiftet und alleingelassen. Die Opfer von Giftstoffen in den Mühlen von Wissenschaft und Justiz* (pp. 119-138). Munich: Knaur. Retrieved March 1, 2007, from www.antipsychiatrieverlag.de/artikel/gesundheit/rufer_schnyder.htm.

Translated from the German by Mary Murphy

James B. Gottstein

Money, Rights and Alternatives

Enforcing Legal Rights as a Mechanism for Creating Non-medical Model Alternatives

In the USA, the Law Project for Psychiatric Rights (PsychRights) is mounting a coordinated litigation campaign aimed at substantially reducing forced psychiatry and at creating non-coercive, non-medical model alternatives.[1] The primary instruments being attacked are involuntary commitment, which is the medico-legal term for psychiatric imprisonment, forced psychiatric drugging and forced electroshock. While this legal campaign is being mounted in the USA, the basic concepts can be applied to other regions and countries.

---

1 Law Project for Psychiatric Rights (PsychRights), 406 G Street, Suite 206, Anchorage, Alaska 99501, USA, tel. +1 (907) 274-7686, Fax +1 (907) 274-9493, e-mail jim.gottstein @PsychRights.org, web site www.PsychRights.org

Within the USA, there are over 50 legal jurisdictions, all with at least somewhat—and often significantly—different legal criteria and procedures. One unifying feature in the USA is its constitutional Bill of Rights, which provides at least theoretical rights against forced psychiatry with which all states are required to comply. There are some existing and proposed international conventions and accords which can essentially serve the same purpose.

The Setting: Rights Dishonored as a Matter of Course

Under the U.S. Constitution, while fundamental rights, such as freedom from confinement, are not absolute, (1) there must be a compelling governmental interest in infringing them, (2) the infringement must accomplish the governmental interest, and (3) there must be no less restrictive (or intrusive) alternative. Being free from psychiatric imprisonment[1] and forced psychiatric drugging[2] are such fundamental rights, to which these principles apply.

The justifications for psychiatric imprisonment under the U.S. Constitution are: the person is a danger to self or others as a result of mental illness and the "treatment" one receives during such psychiatric imprisonment will benefit the person. The danger needs to be both serious (e.g., grievous bodily harm or death) and there needs to be some immediacy to the prospective harm, although it doesn't necessarily have to be "imminent." The justification for forced drugging, other than in "emergencies," is that it is in the person's best interest. Put another way, psychiatric imprisonment and forced drugging and electroshock are justified on the grounds that if the person wasn't crazy, she would know this is good for her.

The courts, prosecutors, and most tragically, the lawyers assigned to represent people facing psychiatric imprisonment and forced drugging, act on the premise that they won't let people's pesky legal rights get in the way of doing to them what they believe to be in their best interests.

Because psychiatric defendants do not get vigorous representation by their appointed attorneys, the legal proceedings are essentially shams. Obtaining

---

1   *Addington v. Texas*, 441 U.S. 418 (1979)

2   *Mills v. Rogers*, 457 U.S. 291 (1982); *Washington v. Harper*, 494 U.S. 210 (1990); *Riggins v. Nevada*, 504 U.S. 127 (1992); and *Sell v. United States*, 539 U.S. 166 (2003)

psychiatric imprisonment and forced drugging court orders is by far the path of least resistance for government psychiatrists.

It is beyond the scope of this chapter to discuss the various potential steps that PsychRights has identified to try and obtain vigorous legal representation. Suffice it to say this is a key issue and it may ultimately go to the U.S. Supreme Court.

Change Elements

Three critical elements must be simultaneously addressed to change this state of affairs: Creation of Alternatives, Public Education, and Strategic Litigation (Honoring Rights).

Each reinforces the others in ways that can lead to meaningful system change and can be depicted as in the figure beside.

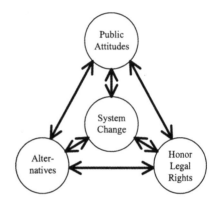

Changing Public Attitudes ⇔ Honoring Legal Rights

Clearly, the judges and attorneys believe, as does the rest of society that hospitalization and psychiatric drugs are good things; both for the person involved and for society in general. Therefore, to the extent that public attitudes change to include an understanding of the counter-productive and harmful results of psychiatric imprisonment, forced drugging and electroshock, judges and lawyers will tend to be more attentive to people's rights. Similarly, just as the landmark U.S. Supreme Court case of *Brown v. Board of Education*[1], was instrumental in changing public attitudes against legal segregation, vigorous legal efforts in exposing the moral and scientific horrors of psychiatric imprisonment, forced drugging and electroshock can help change public attitudes.

---

1   347 U.S. 483 (1954)

Changing Public Attitudes ⇔ Creation of Alternatives

By the same token, to the extent public attitudes incorporate an understanding that alternatives to coercion, alternatives to the medical model, and alternatives to psychiatric imprisonment, forced drugging and electroshock can lead to much better outcomes for both the people who would otherwise be forcibly "treated," and society, in general, the creation of such alternatives will tend to be encouraged. It also runs the other way; to the extent that alternatives demonstrating these facts become known, it will tend to change public attitudes in favor of the creation of such alternatives.

Honoring Legal Rights ⇔ Creation of Alternatives

The same type of positive feedback loop occurs with respect to Honoring Legal Rights and the Creation of Alternatives. Recall that one of the key constitutional principles in the USA is that psychiatric imprisonment, forced drugging and electroshock are not allowed if there is a less intrusive alternative. This restriction technically applies even if no actual alternative exists. In other words, under this legal doctrine if the government wants to psychiatrically imprison and/or force drug or electroshock someone, but it *could provide a less intrusive alternative*, it is not allowed to force drug or electroshock the person even though the government has not chosen to make the alternative available. This can serve as a powerful impetus to create such alternatives. As a practical matter, however, judges will be very reluctant to release someone they consider dangerous and/or in need of psychiatric drugs because of a non-existent, theoretical alternative. Thus, having such alternatives available will greatly increase the likelihood that people will not be ordered psychiatrically imprisoned or forcibly drugged or electroshocked.

There is another mechanism by which vigorous legal action encourages the availability of alternatives. Currently, due to the sham nature of most legal proceedings for psychiatric imprisonment, forced drugging and electroshock, obtaining such orders through the legal process is by far the easiest course of action for government psychiatrists. To the extent these proceedings are truly contested through vigorous representation (as is the person's right), legal psychiatric imprisonment, forced drugging and electroshock become considerably more burdensome to accomplish and other approaches become more attractive to government psychiatrists.

Alaska: A Testbed

For various reasons, with some nascent success, the State of Alaska has become a testbed for the three-pronged approach described here.[1]

In late 2002, PsychRights was founded to mount a strategic litigation campaign against forced drugging and electroshock. Robert Whitaker, author of the seminal book *Mad in America* (2002), was invited by PsychRights to speak to the Alaska Mental Health board at a time when Jim Gottstein (co-founder of PsychRights and author here) was one of its members. Psych-Rights gave copies of *Mad in America* to every member of the Alaska Mental Health Board, and the Alaska Mental Health Trust Authority.[2]

In early 2003, two non-governmental organizations, Soteria-Alaska and CHOICES, Inc., were formed to provide non-coercive, non-medical model alternatives to psychiatric hospitalization and in the community. Soteria-Alaska was envisioned as a replication of the original Soteria-House, an alternative to hospitalization, proven as humane and effective by the dearly missed Loren Mosher (see the chapter about Soteria by Aderhold, Stastny and Lehmann in this book). CHOICES, Inc. aims to provide the community-based support services set forth in Dr. Mosher's and Dr. Lorenzo Burti's *Community Mental Health: A Practical Guide* (1994). The consistent message presented by these two organizations is that people should have non-co-

---

1 A more detailed description of these efforts is available on the internet at http:// PsychRights. org/Articles/AKEffortsRevAug06.pdf

2 The Alaska Mental Health Trust Authority was created as a result of litigation over the state of Alaska's misappropriation of one million acres of federal land granted in trust for Alaska's mental health program. In addition to having the ability to spend its earnings as it decides in the best interests of its beneficiaries, the Mental Health Trust Authority formally advises the State of Alaska what should be included in its mental health program. This has made Alaska's mental health program unique in the USA in its ability to influence a state's mental health program.

ercive, non-medical model choices and that they are entitled to such choices in lieu of involuntary commitment and psychiatric drugs.

From the middle of March 2003, until early July, PsychRights waged an all-out legal battle at the trial court level on behalf of a patient's (Faith Myers') right to not be forcibly drugged, the likes of which had never before been experienced by the hospital.[1] While technically losing at the trial court early on, the forced drugging order never became effective due to a stay being granted and the case being appealed to the Alaska Supreme Court. Ms. Myers chose to have the trial open to the public which resulted in some local newspaper articles. One result of the legal battle has been that PsychRights has subsequently obtained the release of people from the hospital with just a phone call or an e-mail. This is attributed to the hospital recognizing that when PsychRights represents someone, they will not have such an easy time psychiatrically imprisoning and/or forcibly drugging that person. (Forced electroshock is not allowed in Alaska.)

On appeal, PsychRights argued that under the Alaska and U.S. constitutions (as set forth above), that the government can't force someone to take drugs against their will unless it can at least prove it is in the person's best interest and there are no less restrictive (or intrusive) alternatives. The oral argument in this case resulted in a couple of stories in local papers. The consistent message given in all of these by PsychRights was that people have the right to a non-drug choice.

In September 2003, PsychRights sponsored a two-day seminar on Mental Disability Law, which Robert Whitaker opened and the remainder of the seminar was presented by the internationally known expert and New York Law School professor, Michael L. Perlin. This seminar was attended by lawyers, clinicians and judges as well as policy makers, users and psychiatric survivors. Perlin remarked on this, saying it presented a unique opportunity for interaction between these groups of people. After Whitaker's talk, the Executive Director of the Alaska Mental Health Trust Authority noted that

---

1   A fairly detailed description of the Myers' trial court legal battle, as well as all of the important documents are available on the internet at http://PsychRights.org/States/Alaska/CaseOne.htm

the implication of Whitaker's information was that there should be non-drug choices and these choices were not available in Alaska's mental health system.

In August 2004, after additional work with the Alaska Mental Health Board, it recommended to the Alaska Mental Health Trust Authority that Soteria-Alaska be a number one priority for funding as a new program. The Alaska Mental Health Trust Authority generally expressed interest and support, but did not approve Soteria-Alaska for funding during the funding cycle it was considering at that time. However, the Mental Health Trust Authority did provide increasing amount of seed money to further develop the Soteria-Alaska proposal.

In November 2005, the local newspaper ran a front page feature story on Jim Gottstein, the president of PsychRights, Soteria-Alaska and CHOICES, Inc., regarding these efforts.[1] In this story, the Executive Director of the Alaska Mental Health Trust Authority is quoted as saying, "Ten years ago, there was no way you would get anyone on the medical staff of that hospital to even understand what Jim is talking about. Now the issue is how will we get there."

In 2005, PsychRights also filed an appeal in the *Wetherhorn* case seeking to have the Alaska Supreme Court require attorneys assigned to psychiatric defendants to vigorously represent them. On January 12, 2007, the court ruled an appeal was not the way to challenge whether people were represented properly, but also held people can not be involuntarily committed for being "gravely disabled," unless they are "unable to survive safely in freedom."[2]

In early 2006, CHOICES, Inc., after a number of unsuccessful attempts, received a small grant to provide independent case management and flexible support services, which it is attempting to leverage into a sustainable program.

---

1 This story is available on the internet at http://PsychRights.org/News/ADN11-6-05 GottsteinEfforts.html

2 The decision is at http://PsychRights.org/States/Alaska/CaseFour/WetherhornIsp-6091. pdf

At the end of June 2006, the Alaska Supreme Court issued its decision in *Myers v. Alaska Psychiatric Institute*[1], in which it held Alaska's forced psychiatric drugging regime unlawful under the Alaska Constitution, requiring that before a court could issue a forced drugging order, in addition to all of the statutory requirements, it must find, by clear and convincing evidence that the forced drugging is in the person's best interest and there is no less intrusive alternative available.

In September 2006, the Alaska Mental Health Trust Authority formally adopted the opening of Soteria-Alaska as a goal, including committing its money to continuing the development of the program and to commence operations. Recognizing that in order for Soteria-Alaska to be successful it has to be part of the state's mental health program, the Mental Health Trust Authority also formally recommended that the State of Alaska use its money to fund its continued operation. The Legislature failed to do so, but in May 2007, the Mental Health Trust Authority decided to use its additional Trust funds to open Soteria-Alaska in 2008, provided the State indicates it will support the project.

It can hopefully be seen that as a result of the strategic litigation, public education and promotion of alternatives in Alaska, that non-medical model choices are now likely to become available in Alaska in the near term. Over the course of the four years this effort has been pursued, one can see how public policy makers were moved from merely taking in information to active support. It is fair to say the prevailing opinion has gone from one of "drugs for everyone" to one in which non-drug choices are recognized as desirable, even necessary. The *Myers* case ruled people are constitutionally entitled to a non-drug approach and Soteria-Alaska and CHOICES, Inc., are poised to offer such approaches. Over the course of the four years this effort has been pursued, one can see how public policy makers were moved from merely taking in information, to active support. It is fair to say the prevailing opinion has gone from one of "drugs, of course (for everyone)" to one in which non-drug choices are recognized as desirable, even necessary. The

---

1   138 P.3d 238 (Alaska 2006)

Myers case ruled people are constitutionally entitled to a non-drug approach and Soteria-Alaska and CHOICES, Inc., are poised to offer such approaches.

Application Outside of the USA

This raises the question of the applicability of the concepts and approach presented here to countries other than the USA. To be sure, the legal settings range from only somewhat different to completely different, but the three pronged approach set forth here should be adaptable to local situations. Even in countries that don't require courts to get involved in psychiatric imprisonment and forced drugging, public education about the superiority of non-medical model approaches, and exposing the inhumane current practices used by psychiatry can be used to create such rights. In the USA, courts began ruling that people were entitled to court hearings as recently as the early 1970s with respect to psychiatric imprisonment, and the early 1980s with respect to forced drugging. These developments were in no small part influenced by the revelations of inhumane treatment.[1]

Users and survivors of psychiatry have recently become very active in seeking international protocols calling for the legal protection of persons that governments want to psychiatrically imprison, drug and electroshock against their will. On 13 December 2006, The Plenary of the General Assembly of the United Nations adopted by consensus the Convention on the Rights of Persons with Disabilities.[2] The European Union (EU) is considering a mental health policy document which includes:

---

1   International human rights pressure has been brought to bear in Turkey against un-anaesthetized electroshock, cage beds in the Czech Republic, Slovenia, Hungary and Slovakia, and similar human rights abuses in Kosovo, Peru, Hungary and Mexico to some effect already.

2   This Convention recognizes the right of people with disabilities to free and informed consent with no discrimination based on disability, guarantees the right to make their own decisions (legal capacity) on an equal basis with others, and requires governments to provide access to non-coercive support in decision-making, for those who need such support. More information can be found at www.un.org/disabilities/convention.

[C]oercion is extremely counterproductive in treating mental ill health...compulsory in-patient and/or community-based care should be applied only once less restrictive, voluntary alternatives have failed...effective mechanisms to respect people's fundamental rights, must be included in the processes and procedures relating to compulsory admission and treatment (Bowis, 2006, p. 18).

Especially the EU effort, if adopted, can provide an international law basis for strategic litigation aimed at promoting non-medical model choices as outlined here, with language that is very similar to U.S. constitutional requirements. Already, the United Nations and European conventions on Human Rights may provide a basis for asserting such rights outside the USA. On the other hand, the "Recommendation of the Committee of the Ministers to the member states concerning the protection of the human rights and dignity of persons with mental disorders" (see www.enusp.org/wp), which was accepted by the European Council in 2004 and which declares forced outpatient treatment, forced administration of electroshock and forced admission without a decision of a judge as ethical, shows how far the way to human rights within the psychiatric system is and how important it is to enforce legal rights as a mechanism for creating non-medical model alternatives by ourselves.

Sources

Bowis, J. (2006, July 18). Report on improving the mental health of the population: Towards a strategy on mental health for the European Union.

Mosher, L. R., & Burti, L. (1989). *Community mental health: A practical guide.* New York: Norton & Co.

Perlin, M. L. (1993/94). The ADA and persons with mental disabilities: Can sanist attitudes be undone? *Journal of Law and Health, 8,* 15-45.

Whitaker, R. (2002). *Mad in America: Bad science, bad medicine and the enduring mistreatment of the mentally ill.* Cambridge: Perseus Publishing.

Laura Ziegler

Upholding Psychiatric Advance Directives

"The Rights of a Flea"

Psychiatric advance directives are of increasing interest to people who wish to retain autonomy when interacting with the mental health system. While they can be collaborations between patients and clinicians, their origin and the few reported court decisions on their use demonstrates their adversarial potential.

Advance directives are legal instruments designed to preserve the rights of competent individuals to choose or refuse health care. They may document specific choices or appoint agents to make decisions. Through these prior instructions, people can still assert control over psychiatric treatment when they are considered incapable. Even where the law does not clearly recognize psychiatric advance directives, a person who executes one and insists that it be honored will sometimes prevail.

Advance directive statutes often include restrictions that maintain the power of institutional psychiatry. This is ironic, because the first advance directive was conceived as a means of protection from that very power. In 1964, Mary Ellen Redfield self-published *Will for Living Body*, a draft contract with doctors and lawyers that authorizes them to act as temporary guardians if she becomes comatose or of unsound mind. They are pledged to "secure immediate remedial legal aid" should she fall into the power of doctors who will not honor its terms: refusal of all forms of psychiatric treatment, including those not yet invented. She exempts and welcomes consensual psychotherapy, and invalidates any consent given while drugged or of unsound mind. Declaring "NO FAITH" in psychiatry she prohibits imposed alteration of her mind, in the expressed faith that she is sovereign over her psyche and soul.

Her faith had been tested by mind-altering psychiatric institutions. *Terror on Tuesdays and Thursdays* describes the assembly-line, unaenesthetized ECT she endured for two years while confined in a state hospital. It concludes: "Memory returns partially. Most of the details of my past life never did" (Redfield, 1964a, p. 8).

Upholding Advance Refusal

K. v. Departement de l'Action Sociale et de la Santé

The idea of using advance directives to control psychiatric treatment only began to attract significant public attention in the early 1980s, when Thomas Szasz proposed the "psychiatric will" (1982). Theresja Krummenacher, a determined activist living in Geneva, Switzerland, put his proposal to use. In 1995, she achieved a ground-breaking legal decision.

Krummenacher's disabilities were primarily physical, yet she was caught in a revolving door of psychiatric internments and coerced neuroleptics. Her withdrawal symptoms were interpreted as relapse by the psychiatrists at the local psychiatric hospital Bel-Air, who believed she required a life-long prescription. After spending a year in a zombie-like state from one depot injection of Haldol, she resolved to defend herself. With support from other former members of the activist group AUDUPSY in 1985, she began a campaign, which lasted 10 years, to establish her right to refuse neuroleptic drugs.

She wrote to the Commission for the Surveillance of Medical Activities and filed a complaint with the Department of Public Health, objecting to the hospital's use of neuroleptics against her will. The Commission found no gross negligence or professional misconduct but questioned the disregard for her refusals, and asked administrators to clarify to the medical staff the importance of taking them into account.

In 1987, she was again admitted involuntarily at Bel-Air and administered the neuroleptic zuclopenthixol (Clopixol) against her will. She filed a criminal complaint against two doctors. The Federal Tribunal applied the mental health laws and ruled that it was legal to forcibly treat patients who were involuntarily admitted. A psychiatrist subsequently wrote a medical certificate stating that Krummenacher had shown intolerance of all psychotropic drugs, particularly neuroleptics, which were detrimental to her health. This was put into her file at Bel-Air. She requested confirmation that the hospital would refrain from any future administration of neuroleptics. The reply was a quote from the Federal Tribunal's decision, stating that the hospital's treatment conformed to medical science and to the law. Krummenacher filed a complaint with the Department of Social Action and Health in Geneva, asking that it be clarified that no forced neuroleptics would be authorized if she was involuntarily interned in the future. The Department dismissed her complaint.

On appeal, the Tribunal Administratif cited the Geneva law requiring informed consent for medical treatment[1] and found it applied equally to psychiatric patients, without excluding involuntary patients. The only legal exception was life-saving treatment when a person could not express her wishes.

Krummenacher had executed a psychiatric testament in which she appointed legal representatives (agents) and refused all neuroleptics, shock treatment and psychosurgery. Her presumed wishes were therefore clear. In case of necessity, Krummenacher preferred being locked in a room to being forcibly administered neuroleptics. She argued that to use them on her would violate the principle of proportionality. When questioned, the Bel-Air doctors could not say that neuroleptics had been the only way to save her life during past interments and admitted that she posed no danger to other patients.

Although the hospital found physical restraint objectionable, it was clearly a life-saving alternative which Krummenacher had declared herself willing to accept. The Tribunal noted that her intense opposition to neuroleptics made it likely that physical restraint would have to be used to administer them. It found the law would not permit imposing neuroleptics when physical restraint alone could both save her life and conform to her will. The "life-saving" exception was therefore set aside. It also found Krummenacher had a legal interest in the issuance of a declaratory decision concerning her rights, and ruled that in the future the hospital would have to respect her will not re-

---

1 Law of the Canton of Geneva of 6 December 1987, Article 5

ceive neuroleptics even if she was incompetent.[1] After 10 years, Krummenacher had an advance directive recognized by law (Krummenacher, 2006).

Matter of Rosa M.

The first reported court decision on a psychiatric advance directive occurred in 1991, when a New York court denied a petition to authorize use of electroshock (ECT) on Rosa M., a patient confined at Manhattan Psychiatric Center. It deferred to her prior competent wishes expressed in a brief signed statement: "I am withdrawing my consent to electroconvulsive therapy and am refusing any more treatments with this procedure." The court rejected the State's argument that this was "ambiguous." It also noted that 19 days earlier Rosa M. had signed a consent form for ECT, countersigned by a physician who claimed she understood its nature and purpose. There was no evidence that her ability to make a reasoned decision had diminished in that interval.

I was involved in events leading to the case, having met Rosa M. while interviewing potential witnesses in another lawsuit. Rosa brought up ECT: she complained it was erasing her memory of her college education and said she did not want to receive that form of treatment. I communicated this to a hospital administrator and was told that ECT was court ordered. A review of her medical record showed the court order had expired, at which point she signed consent to more ECT. Rosa explained she had thought she had no choice. I informed her that under New York law she did have a choice, and helped her to formalize her decision in writing.

Her signed statement was not an advance directive as defined by the state statute. But it was sufficient evidence. The court ruled: "Absent an overriding state interest, a hospital or medical facility must give continued respect to a patient's competent rejection of certain medical procedures even after a patient loses competence."[2]

---

1 Decision of the Administrative Tribunal of the Canton of Geneva on 7 March, 1995 in *K. v. Departement de l'Action Sociale et de la Santé*, A(702) 1992—ASAN], translated by Padma Meier

2 *Matter of Rosa M.*, 155 Misc. 2d 103 (NY Sup. Ct. 1991)

In re Hatsuye T.

Six years later, in the case of *Hatsuye T.,* an Illinois appellate court upheld an advance directive that barred an agent from consenting to ECT.[1] The order was voided on appeal. Hatsuye T. had appointed an agent under a power of attorney for health care. After she refused ECT, a trial court granted her agent's petition to become her guardian[2], and furthermore issued an order authorizing the agent to consent to have ECT forcibly administered to Mrs. T. The order authorizing the guardian to consent to forced ECT was voided on appeal. Before a guardian could intervene in a decision covered by a power of attorney, Illinois law required a court to find that her agent's actions or inactions had caused or threatened serious harm to Mrs. T. *in a manner that she had not authorized or intended.* The appellate court cited this unmet requirement, and found that the "harm" of preventing her agent from consenting to ECT was exactly what Mrs. T. intended.

These cases provide a glimpse through the institutional keyhole at what passes for informed consent. As a voluntary patient, Hatsuye T. had agreed to undergo ECT after her doctor misinformed her that the sole alternative was immediate discharge to a nursing home, where she feared she would die. Hours later, with two attorneys witnessing, she revoked consent and amended her advance directive to prohibit ECT. Like Rosa M., she asserted refusal only with on-site assistance from an advocate.

Competent to Consent, Incompetent to Refuse

The tendency of clinicians to equate disagreement with incapacity is well known (Stefan, 2004; see also Mazenauer, 1987, p. 211). Testifying on Ontario's Substitute Decisions Act, geriatrician David Molloy described how capacity is only questioned when treatment is refused, in order to make people do what doctors think they should do (Molloy, 1996). The New York State Office of Mental Health enshrines its double standard in rules that per-

---

1   *In re Hatsuye T.*, 689 N.E.2d 248 (Ill. App. Div. 1997)

2   A guardian's role is different from an agent's. A principal appoints an agent to represent her, while a guardian is someone appointed by a court to make decisions for her.

mit hospital staff, after formally finding a refusing patient incapable and petitioning for court-authorized forced treatment, to continue to "explain" prescribed treatment in an attempt to obtain that patient's assent.[1]

How might these practices affect advance directives? People may be pressured to execute or revoke them. Their activation may depend on tainted capacity determinations that reflect doctors' level of discomfort with the instructions or agents. More insidiously, doctors may attempt to bypass an advance refusal or a health care agent's role by soliciting a principal's incapable agreement (Priaulx, 2003).

R. R. and Xenia Williams v. Vermont State Hospital

Psychiatric advance directives have been a subject of legal controversy in Vermont since 1997, when R. R. and her agent Xenia Williams filed suit against the State Hospital for its refusal to honor a durable power of attorney for health care (DPOA).

R. R.'s instructions were to refuse ECT and the administration of any drug against her will. But throughout multiple admissions her DPOA was disregarded. Williams was banned from visiting R. R. for months after coming to see her with an attorney. Staff asserted R. R. was competent, which by law would inactivate the DPOA. Meanwhile R. R., who had severe tardive dyskinesia, was subjected to a series of psychotropic drugs at high doses and in multiple combinations, sometimes crushed to "increase compliance." She reported being repeatedly pressured by the hospital psychiatrists to revoke her DPOA.

The State argued that a health care agent had no authority when a principal was in the custody of the Mental Health Commissioner. The judge found this a "tortured reading of the statutes" that would "tremendously increase the power of the Commissioner by inferential leaps" and permit him to "isolate R., involuntarily medicate and treat R., and revoke or suspend R.'s power of attorney, all without formally being appointed R.'s guardian."[2] He ordered

1   14 NYCRR 527.8 (c)(4) (ii)(a)

2   *R. R. and Xenia Williams v. Vermont State Hospital*, Docket No. 414-7-97 Wncv (unpublished). Entry order, November 13, 1998

that Williams be granted access to R. R.'s medical records. When the case was settled in late 1999, R. R. received $30,000, and an agreement was signed detailing how the hospital would comply with her DPOA.

Williams is a formidable advocate in the role of agent. But when asked what kind of impact a strong agent would have, she replied: "Almost none, if the agent was without significant legal back-up" (Williams, 2006). Before the settlement, R. R. commented on the State's failure to respect her advance directive: "Xenia has been protecting my rights for six years. I have often said, though, 'I have the rights of a flea' because the system overpowered Xenia's desire and mine to be a real live human being" (R. R., 1999).

Hargrave v. State of Vermont

In 1998, the Vermont legislature changed the law to limit the effectiveness of a DPOA to 45 days if a person had been committed and was the subject of a forced drugging petition. Unless it found "significant clinical improvement," a court could override it (Act 114).[1]

In 1999, Nancy Hargrave executed a DPOA in which she refused consent to psychiatric drugs or ECT. She then filed suit in federal court challenging the new law. In a press release, Hargrave, who had been diagnosed with cancer, stated: "It strikes me as fundamentally unfair that I can choose or refuse chemotherapy, which is saving my life, but I don't have the same right to choose or refuse psychiatric medication."[2]

The District Court agreed, and permanently enjoined sections of the statute as violating the Americans with Disabilities Act (ADA). It observed that Vermont law did not compel incompetent people with physical disabilities to undergo treatment contrary to a DPOA even if this might result in death, and refused to find that if an incompetent person with a psychiatric disability endangered herself, her prior refusal of treatment could be ignored.[3] On appeal,

---

1   1997, No. 114 (Adj. Sess.), §4 (codified as 18 V.S.A. §§7624-7628). See on the internet at www.leg.state.vt.us/DOCS/1998/ACTS/ACT114.HTM and www.leg.state.vt.us/statutes/fullsection.cfm?Title=18&Chapter=181&Section=07626

2   Cited in Access New England (1999)

3   *Hargrave v. State of Vermont*, No. 2:99-CV-128 (2001)

the Second Circuit Court affirmed that the law was discriminatory. It rejected the State's argument that since Act 114 only applied to people who were civilly committed, the members of the plaintiff class posed a "direct threat" to others and were therefore not protected by the ADA. It distinguished danger to self (a basis for civil commitment) from danger to others (required for "direct threat"), and found that "...defendants have offered no evidence that a period of commitment would not significantly mitigate—if not eliminate—the 'threat' posed by most patients."[1]

Despite the *Hargrave* decision, discriminatory statutes have proliferated in the U.S. Most permit advance directives to be overridden if the principal is committed and treatment ordered by a court or its equivalent. In England and Wales, advance directives can be disregarded when people are detained and subject to compulsory treatment under the Mental Health Act.

Upholding Advance Consent

In *Cohen v. Bolduc*, the Massachusetts Supreme Court upheld an agent's authority to consent to her principal's voluntary admission to a psychiatric hospital, finding this would enhance patient autonomy. It ruled that Helen Bolduc's due process rights had not been violated, since she could object to her confinement and was presumed competent to revoke her advance directive.[2]

However, due process would hinge on an incapable, hospitalized elderly woman asserting her rights. Attorney Nadell Hill, who represented Bolduc, confirmed that when people are unable to convey their objections in a way that is legally recognized, they can remain indefinitely in "voluntary" limbo (Hill, 2006).[3]

In many jurisdictions an advance directive cannot be revoked unless a principal has capacity. Statutes tend to be vague about implementing an irrevocable directive, although in Ontario and the Yukon a principal can authorize an agent to use force to evaluate her capacity, take her to a care facility, and

---

1 *Hargrave v. State of Vermont*, 340 F.3d 27 (2nd Cir. 2003)

2 *Cohen v. Bolduc*, 455 Mass. 608, 760 N.E.2d 714 (2002)

3 See also *Zinermon v. Burch*, 494 U.S. 113, 494 U.S. 113, at 134,135 (1990); *HL v. United Kingdom*, 40 EHRR 32 ECHR (2003)

admit, detain and restrain her there. She may also waive in advance her right to apply to an administrative board for review of a finding of incapacity.[1] Whether this is a permissible waiver of due process has yet to be decided.[2]

Partial Justice

Since 1990, four people have chosen me as agent. One signed her advance directive wearing handcuffs, in a courthouse conference room on hospital grounds, as her hearing on the State's applications for retention and forced drugging was about to begin. Another became the target of a forced drugging petition by a hospital that had failed to contact or acknowledge me as decision maker. When I wrote to the judge informing him of my role and instructions, the petition was withdrawn. As advocates have reported, "Often just the threat of legal action is all that is required to obtain compliance by hospitals" (Priaulx, 2003).

But will judges impartially apply the law? Kathy Kosnoff, an attorney with Minnesota's Mental Health Law Project, observed how courts "look for ways to avoid the advance directive and order treatment against the patient's wishes" (cited in Perling, 1993). Scholars of mental health law are also skeptical. According to Nottingham University Law Professor Peter Bartlett, the evidence suggests that courts manipulate standards so that treatment can be imposed, and "bend over backwards to find reasons why [advance directives] don't apply" (Bartlett, 2006). Michael Perlin, director of New York Law

---

1   Substitute Decisions Act, S.O. 1992, c. 30, s. 50 (2); Care Consent Act, S.Y. 2003, c. 21, schedule B s. 30

2   Editor's note: The psychiatric will (advance directive) used in Germany since 1987 includes a provision stating that any revocations of directives at a time when persons are under the control of psychiatry should a priori be considered invalid (Rolshoven & Rudel, 1993). This is meant to protect the principals from attempts at coercion into any type of agreements on the part of psychiatrists. On the other hand, principals are restricting their options by executing such a directive—if it were indeed upheld—to change their opinions at any time they choose; in other words, such directives curtail the freedom of opinion and self determination. Finally, this also suggests that due to the impossibility of covering all eventualities in advance, there can be no perfect formula for advance directives.

School's International Mental Disability Law Reform Project, has described the corruption of mental health legal proceedings by courts' "pretextual" acceptance of dishonest testimony and application of dishonest, and often specious, reasoning (Perlin, 2003).

Courts and legislatures may share clinicians' biases, enacting inequitable laws and dispensing unequal justice to people perceived as mentally disabled. The law on advance directives may not be agreed on or adhered to; nor will it be consistent from one jurisdiction to the next. At best, advance directives are limited and uncertain instruments. But as the reported cases show, it is sometimes possible to uphold autonomy through the judicial system, and to overturn discriminatory statutes. In the hands of persistent advocates, advance directives have extraordinary potential in the struggle for self determination.[1]

Sources

Adaptive Environments, Inc. (1999). Class action suit filed regarding Vermont's forced drugging law. *Access New England Newsletter, 3*(4). Retrieved July 11, 2007, from www.adaptiveenvironments. org/newsletter/summer99.php.

Bartlett, P. (2006). Human rights? Of course... but what does that mean? In T. Minkowitz, *No-force advocacy by users and survivors of psychiatry* (pp. 23-29). Wellington: Mental Health Commission. Retrieved May 5, 2007, from www.mhc.govt.nz/publications/2006/ No%20Force%20Advocacy.pdf.

Hill, N. (2006, October 16). Personal communication.

Krummenacher, T. (2006, November). Personal communications. Translated by Katherine Zurcher.

Mazenauer, B. (1987). Kontrolle über die "Psychiatrie" einer öffentlichen Psychiatrischen Klinik. In P. Tercier (Ed.), *Aspects du droit medical (3e cycle de droit 1986)* (pp. 207-225). Freiburg (Switzerland): Editions Universitaires.

Molloy, D. (1996, February 21). Testimony before the Standing Committee on Administration of Justice, Legislative Assembly of Ontario. Retrieved July 26, 2007, from www.ontla.on.ca/web/ committee-proceedings/committee_transcripts_details.do?locale=en&Date=1996-02-21&Parl

---

1 To the author's knowledge, a comprehensive international review of the legal status of psychiatric advance directives has yet to be undertaken. Further sharing of news and information on this subject would be welcome. See http://psychrights.org/Countries/ AdvanceDirectives.htm

CommID=39&BillID=&Business=Bill+19%2C+Advocacy%2C+Consent+and+Substitute+
Decisions+Statute+Law+ Amendment+Act%2C+1995

Perlin, M. L. (2003). "Things have changed": Looking at non-institutional mental disability law through the sanism filter. *New York Law School Law Review, 46,* 535-545. Retrieved July 11, 2007, from www.nyls.edu/pdfs/v46n3-4p535-545.pdf.

Perling, L. J. (1993). Health care advance directives: Implications for Florida mental
health patients. *Miami University Law Review, 48,* 193–228.

Priaulx, E. (2003). Enforcing advance directives. *Protection and Advocacy News, 1*(1).
Retrieved July 11, 2007, from www.ndrn.org/pub/PANews/0303advdir.htm.

R., R. (1999). Letter to the editor. *Counterpoint—News forum published by Vermont Psychiatric Survivors, Inc.,* Winter / Spring 1999.

Redfield, M. E. [Field, E.] (1964a). Terror on Tuesdays. In E. Field, *The white shirts* (pp.
6-8). Los Angeles: Self publication.

Redfield, M. E. [Field, E.] (1964b). Will for living body. In E. Field, *The white shirts* (pp.
15-16). Los Angeles: Self publication.

Stefan, S. (2004). *Competence issues in self-directed care.* Newton: Center for Public
Representation.

Szasz, T. S. (1982). The psychiatric will: A new mechanism for protecting persons against
"psychosis" and psychiatry. *American Psychologist, 37,* 762-770.

Williams, X. (2006, September). Personal communications.

David W. Oaks

MindFreedom International

Activism for Human Rights as the Basis for a Nonviolent Revolution in the Mental Health System

This is a call for a nonviolent revolution in the mental health system. Yes, reform is important. But we call for more. We call for a nonviolent revolution
of freedom, equality, truth and human rights throughout the entire mental
health system.

What is Your Choice: Reform or Nonviolent Revolution?

In spring 2006, I visited Istanbul and there I met something, which showed me again, why our movement is so important. I had the opportunity to give a workshop to a room full of psychiatric survivors on behalf of the organization Mental Disability Rights International. The workshop was in a psychiatric community center with art on the wall and, as is the custom in Turkey, a great deal of tobacco smoke in the air. I was deeply emotionally moved as I heard several psychiatric survivors in the workshop tell a similar story one after another. These psychiatric survivors had experienced involuntary electroshock in horrible psychiatric institutions. Against their will and without any anesthesia, they were held down fully conscious as electricity pulsed through their brains until they had a convulsion. The procedure was repeated over and over for days and weeks. Although anesthesia would not have protected their brains from the blast of electricity, this kind of "direct electroshock" meant they were held down on the table with their eyes wide open while they were fully conscious of what was going on. Is this not torture?

Some of these psychiatric survivors said they had also experienced physical beatings in the institution. Now that they are out of the institution their oppression continues. Every one of them faces joblessness and loneliness. They are treated as different and separate from the population.

This severe abuse is why the World Health Organization (WHO) officially declared there is a "global emergency" of human rights violations throughout the mental health system. WHO emphasizes that this global emergency is in both rich countries and poor countries. Little or no advocacy is available in many institutions internationally as captives routinely face solitary confinement, restraints, electroshock, psychiatric experimentation, and much more.

Psychiatric human rights violations inside institutions have spread out of institutions and into our own homes and our communities and our neighborhoods. Psychiatric labeling often leads to a lifetime of segregation, discrimination, poverty and stereotyping that falsely portrays those of us with psychiatric labels as dangerous.

The unfair influence of the psychiatric drug industry adds to these human rights violations. We support personal choice in mental health care. Many of those in our movement choose to take prescribed psychiatric drugs and that is their personal decision. However, psychiatric drug corporations use fraud, force and fear to violate the human rights of clients.

For example, the drug companies have manipulated media, advertising and research to convince the public and mental health professionals that those of us with mental health problems have a chemical imbalance. When I personally went through the mental health system in the 1970s, I was almost broken by the experience. The forced drug injections in solitary confinement certainly wore me down. The most powerful blow, though, was when a psychiatrist sat down with me, looked me in the eyes and claimed that I had a chemical imbalance, and therefore I must take psychiatric drugs the rest of my life. That psychiatrist was wrong. I was able to quit psychiatric drugs, and I have been off of them for 30 years. If you the reader personally believe in a chemical balance that is your right, and I respect your right. However, there is no scientific proof of a genetic or biological basis for any psychiatric diagnosis.

Drug companies also use fraud by routinely covering up information that their products can be harmful and can even kill. There are more and more scientific studies showing that common psychiatric drugs such as antidepressants can frequently lead to the very opposite of their intended effect, including influencing people toward a path of aggression or even suicide.

The Psychiatric Drug Industry Pushes a Domination Model

The main family of psychiatric drugs used in forced psychiatry is called the neuroleptics or antipsychotics. The first neuroleptic was chlorpromazine. Now there are newer neuroleptics such as Risperdal and Zyprexa. Scientific studies show that neuroleptics, especially when administered in high dosages over a long time, can cause structural brain changes including shrinkage of the frontal lobes of the brain that is so extreme it is visible in brain scans and autopsies. Before anyone blames "mental illness" for these brain changes, please understand that neuroleptic-induced brain change can be replicated in animal experiments. Drug-caused brain changes like this can make it especially hard to quit psychiatric drugs.

These drug-induced brain changes mean that neuroleptics, especially when given at a high dosage for a long time, are in the same general category as psychosurgery, which nearly everyone agrees ought to never be given forcibly. And yet, forced drugging is growing. Psychiatric drug companies fund organizations that lobby the government to make it easier to force the products these drug companies manufacture into customers. Today, 43 of the 50 states in the USA, along with regions of several nations such as Canada and Australia, have laws allowing courts to order us to take psychiatric drugs against our will even while living peacefully in our own homes.

While fraud and force are fairly easy to view as human rights violations, the most pervasive and subtle human rights violation in the mental health system is fear, a fear that there is no alternative to force and drugs. There ought to be a full range of voluntary, humane, safe options and alternatives offered to all who choose to use them, including mutual support, jobs, housing, peer run programs, nutrition, advocacy, quality counseling, and other holistic approaches. A range of choices to achieve mental and emotional well being is not just a good idea, choice in mental health care is a human right. Unfortunately, everywhere we look the mental health industry is narrowing the range of choices available.

In one of the most disturbing developments, psychiatric drugging, labeling and electroshock are all globalizing into poor and developing nations as never before. This Western style mental health system is often called a "medical model." More accurately, we ought to call this approach a "domination model," because its main effect is to squeeze out all other options from mental health care. When the government of a poor and developing country has been convinced to base its mental health system on the West, they quickly discover that psychiatric drugs are expensive. Since electricity is almost everywhere, this globalization of the western psychiatric system into poorer nations is leading to more and more of electroshock without anesthesia. We are against all use of electroshock in all circumstances because it is so intrusive and has so irreversible damages. And the rise of forced electroshock without anesthesia in Turkey, India and other poorer countries is especially horrifying and alarming.

Those who simply call for "more money" to export the western mental health system into poor and developing countries imply that the main barrier is funding. But the real problem is not just money. Several studies by the

World Health Organization (WHO) found that individuals diagnosed with so-called serious psychiatric disorders such as schizophrenia were about twice as likely to recover if they lived in poorer developing countries rather than in richer developed countries!

A Mad, Mad World Ought to Hear from the Experts: Psychiatric Survivors

Before billions of more dollars are pumped into the mental health system, the first step in winning the right to choice is to be certain that the voices of those on the receiving end of mental health care are heard. Since about 1970 psychiatric survivors and their allies have organized together to fight for major changes in the mental health system. This little-known but powerful social justice movement has united with the larger cross-disability movement.

There ought to be an enormous united initiative throughout the health, human rights and disability fields to provide support and technical assistance so that the voices of psychiatric survivors can be heard, especially in poor and developing countries. We also need to hear from allies such as advocates, attorneys, dissident mental health workers, and concerned family members who question the current mental health system. One thing that has changed in my 30 years as a human rights activist is that today this struggle is not about a small minority. Today, just about every family is impacted by the mental health system. More generally, the issue of mental and emotional well being affects every human being. Our issue is mainstream.

Just a few decades ago, the general population was intimidated by complex issues such as energy policy, urban sprawl, international trade agreements, discrimination based on gender preference and foreign affairs. Just a few decades ago, the public was more likely than now to defer to "experts" on these topics and to stay silent. Today, it is more common for the average citizen to explore and take a stand on these issues, though of course society has a long way to go.

We are in the very beginning of the public becoming confident about addressing the subject of mental and emotional well being. Democracy as a whole must learn to get hands-on with the mental health care system!

I believe society has been slow to critically examine mental health care because the topic can seem overwhelmingly complex and because each citizen is personally threatened by it. For a moment, let's look at the big picture about why society seems so reluctant to address our concerns, and why a human rights perspective may help break the silence.

If leaving the definition and control of what is normal to a few unelected experts in white coats was truly necessary for the survival and well being of humanity, perhaps there could at least be an argument in favor of the violence those of us called "mad" are suffering. But as we know, what is called "normality" is in fact threatening—such as through human-caused disasters like the greenhouse effect—the very ecological fabric of our planet. Martin Luther King, Jr. said many times, "Human salvation lies in the hands of the creatively maladjusted." Society ought to turn to those who have survived and recovered from extreme trauma to discover the tools and skills that humanity needs to survive today.

In fact, the best scientific experts are confirming what our social change movement has said for decades. The best of modern science suggests that the mind apparently emerges from extremely complex feedback systems on the edge between chaos and order. The only true "chemical balance" is death. The best of modern science is finding that the idea of normality itself is unscientific. With the study of quantum and string theory, leading scientists are discovering that reality is far weirder than generally imagined, that no one has an absolute grip on reality, and in fact it may be impossible to ever have an absolute grip on reality.

In other words, what is generally called madness may be at the very core of the human experience. The border between mad and normal is not absolute, that border is shifting, it is changing and it is porous. We are, all of us, in the same mad boat. Taking a human rights stand on the mental health system is one way to focus on the equality, rather than on the difference, between those labeled mad and not mad.

The ideal of uniting a wide diversity of people and groups from throughout society for a nonviolent revolution in mental health care is reflected in our practical work in MindFreedom International (MFI).

MindFreedom International Unites to Win Human Rights

Our project began in 1986 as a newsletter. In 1990, readers of our publication held a counter-conference and protest of the American Psychiatric Association (APA) Annual Meeting in New York City. At the end of our event, representatives from 13 movement groups formed Support Coalition International. We changed our name to MFI in 2005.[1] We have won many campaigns for human rights in mental health, and we now (June 2007) unite 100 grassroots sponsor and affiliate groups internationally. MFI is the only group of its kind to have accreditation by the United Nations as a Non-Governmental Organization (NGO) with Consultative Roster Status. We are proud that our UN team of psychiatric survivors, led by MFI board president Celia Brown, has frequently attended meetings inside the UN headquarters for several years to argue for our human rights, and this process has led to a proposed international binding treaty about disability and human rights.

Here are a few other specific examples of MFI campaigns:

- An MFI hunger strike exposed how the APA uses fraud to promote its chemical imbalance myth.
- Activism against forced electroshock convinced the WHO to endorse, in writing, a ban of the practice.
- An MFI human rights alert e-mail network[2] reaches more than 10,000 people who take action and complain to government authorities about abuse.
- MFI coordinates Mad Pride cultural events in now six nations, including Ghana, to celebrate the spirit of the psychiatric survivor movement.

MFI is one of the very few independent groups in the mental health field with no funding from the mental health system, governments, religions, or drug companies. MFI is funded by members, sales, sponsor groups and foundation grants. While we are proud of our independence, this is not a criticism of

---

1 Address: MindFreedom International, 454 Willamette, Suite 216 – POB 11284, Eugene, OR 97440-3484 USA, www.mindfreedom.org, office@mindfreedom.org, phone +1 (541) 345-9106, Fax +1 (541) 345-3737, member services toll free in USA: 1-877-MAD-PRIDE or 1-877-623-7743

2 www.intenex.net/lists/listinfo/mindfreedom-news

groups that accept funding from the mental health system and the government. System funding is absolutely necessary to accomplish the goals of our movement. However, those groups that do receive government and mental health funds ought to acknowledge, appreciate and nurture the independent movement. After all, what would the environmental movement be if all ecology groups were funded by the government and the oil industry?

MFI seeks to work in a spirit of mutual cooperation. While most of us are psychiatric survivors, we are open to all who support human rights. We have mental health workers, family members, attorneys and the general public among our active leaders. Values that have helped sustain MFI are unity and mutual respect. We take a stand against abuse between one another inside our organization, and we take a stand for civility and nonviolence even when interacting with opponents.

We see the center mission of our movement and MFI as linking up with other movements for justice. Our movement originated within the ferment of oppressed people in the poor people's movement, the peace movement, the prison justice movement, the women's movement and more. As never before, we need to link up with groups and movements in other fields that are also seeking a nonviolent revolution.

The mind is one of the most complex topics humanity has ever studied. The psychiatric industry is one of the most profitable in the history of the planet. While science has never found a chemical imbalance in our brains, our movement has discovered an imbalance—an enormous power imbalance in society itself. A focus on human rights activism is one way those who are oppressed can unify and activate a wide diversity of concerned people against this overwhelming tyranny. Readers of this chapter may have an astoundingly varied range of opinions about questions such as "What is madness?" and "What is normality?" and "Should I ever take a psychiatric drug?" However, whatever your perspectives on these fascinating topics, we can all unite around basic principles of human rights, empowerment, self-determination, choice and supporting the voices of psychiatric survivors.

Whatever action you take as an individual or in a group can have a powerful influence. Whether or not you are an official member of MFI, we look forward to working together in a united way. If you are interested in becoming a member of MFI, please see our web site listed below, and consider joining one of our campaigns. Your group may join as a sponsor group, or you may start a regional affiliate using the MFI name in your area.

When enough individuals and groups work effectively together in a spirit of mutual cooperation, we know that the kind of torture faced by those psychiatric survivors in Turkey will end, forever. Please join our movement for a nonviolent revolution in mental health care!

Dan Taylor

MindFreedom Ghana

Fighting for Basic Human Conditions of Psychiatric Patients

In Ghana, there are three major psychiatric hospitals. The Accra Psychiatric Hospital, located in our capital city and almost 100 years old, has 24 wards with 1,162 patients currently admitted. It was built like a prison by the then British colonial government to house patients who were considered wild and/or uncontrollable. The high walls and other prison vestiges still remain as painful reminders of how people with severe mental distress—which here are called mentally ill—were treated during the colonial days. All three hospitals are located in Southern Ghana. In these circumstances, all patients have to be brought from the middle and northern parts of the country for treatment.

About (ex-)Users and Survivors of Psychiatry in Ghana

Many Ghanaians believe that when you have psychiatric problems, it means that you have offended the gods. They therefore run to shrines or spiritual camps before coming to the hospital. Illiterates and literates alike do that. They often overlook the fact that stress and too much work cause depression and various other types of mental distress. People in the fashion and design industry break down a lot during festive occasions or seasons like Christmas.

The Typical Situation of Patients

Cases of maltreatment of persons with altered mental states within the communities are so widespread that space would not allow us to enumerate. A few occurrences that can be cited relate to stoning and throwing of harmful objects at such persons in severe mental distress, making mockery, jeering and calling of names. These harassments are done by both adults and children. Another violation of the rights and dignity of such persons is engaging them in menial and tedious jobs for no pay whatsoever. All that they are given are some food leftovers which ought to be given to animals.

Sometimes relatives chain the patients and send them to fetish shrines or spiritual camps where they are placed in the scorching sun when they get uncontrollable or wild. The chains sometimes cause wounds which left untreated can lead to tetanus infections and, in some cases, gangrene. These then may culminate in amputation or even cause the death of the patient.

Patients on admission wards are fed three times a day with fruits being added to their diet. It is, however, sad to relate that, too often, due to inadequate funds, the hospitals are unable to provide enough food and fruits to satisfy the patients. In these circumstances, relatives/friends have to bring along food to supplement what are given. Those who do not have any relative seeing to their welfare tend to force their way out or sneak out to look for more food items to supplement what is given them.

The hospitals have to give out various types of clothing to patients whose relatives fail to provide these when they are admitted. Mostly this applies to warm clothing for their upkeep. When such clothing is not available, patients have to go about almost naked or in tattered clothes.

Malaria is a tropical pandemic disease that has to be prevented. Most often the hospitals are unable to provide either insecticides or bed nets to ward off the mosquitoes, which carry the malaria. Consequently, most patients contract the disease and when treatment is not expedited, it can result in complications or death.

Insufficient beds in the wards force some patients to sleep either on the bare floor or on mats spread about. In some cases, when there are no spaces in the wards, patients are forced to sleep on the balcony, exposing them to the vagaries of the weather potentially deadly mosquito bites. Aside from these woeful situations, patients have had to live with pests such as rats, mice, cockroaches etc.

About MindFreedom Ghana

Our group was founded in September 2004 by Nii Lartey Addico, Dan Taylor and Janet Amegatcher. Currently (August 2007) based and operating primarily in Accra, due to limited finances, membership of MFGh is about 20 persons including survivors.[1] These are people with varied backgrounds in law, psychology, marketing, teaching, farming etc. Source of funding for MFGh's activities has been from its members and donations. MFGh obtained its formal statutory certification to operate as an NGO in Ghana in November 2005.

We project to spread our operations nationwide when our financial position improves. It must be stressed that inadequate funding has made our continued operations extremely difficult.

The total efforts of the organization must be directed towards improving the mental health and especially the lives of (ex-)users and survivors of psychiatry in Ghana. Our objectives are

- support and assist people with severe mental distress to receive the treatment they want or get protected from a treatment they do not agree with
- create and provide a forum for addressing the needs and concerns of (ex-) users and survivors of psychiatry
- support and assist in rehabilitative schemes for the people in recovery from severe mental distress and psychiatric treatment
- seek to improve upon the social, moral and economic conditions of people of (ex-)users and survivors of psychiatry and deal with the stigma they suffer
- develop and embark upon educational activities meant to avert various conditions that precipitate severe mental distress

---

1   Address: MindFreedom Ghana, P.O. Box CT3415, Cantonments – Accra, Ghana, Tel. +233 20 211 2228 / +233 277 483 188 / +233 277 421 207, Fax +233 21 760 142, e-mail mindfreedomghana@yahoo.co.uk

- promote activities and schemes that would give persons with mental disabilities a sense of belonging and acceptance into the larger society
- advocate for conditions that would not infringe on their human rights and dignity.

Our programmes are:

- counselling
- organizing public sensitisation forums on severe mental distress and psychiatric treatment for societal attitudinal change towards (ex-)users and survivors of psychiatry
- counselling services to (ex-)users and survivors of psychiatry
- material assistance and other relief services to (ex-)users and survivors of psychiatry and their families
- formation of "Friends of Psychosocial Sufferers Clubs" in schools and communities
- reaching out to the public with information through research, articles and publications on severe mental distress, self-help of (ex-)users and survivors of psychiatry and on alternatives beyond psychiatry
- promoting rights and dignity of (ex-)users and survivors of psychiatry
- organizing community preventive education outreach on severe mental distress
- facilitating provision of occupational therapy for survivors.

Some other programmes undertaken by MFGh in the recent past had been the 1st Mad Pride Event Ghana organized in July 2006 and a symposium. Activities organized during the Mad Pride Event with the theme "Free Minds at Ease," were radio, and TV discussions, community rallies and culminated with a street march involving about 300 people after which a petition was presented to Ghana's Minister of Health.

We have had some success in the following areas:

- counselling some people who were depressed and managed to get them out of their sullen mood and downward trend
- capacity building of users and survivors of psychiatry
- recognition from the Government
- a good working relationship with the professionals

- collaboration and networking with local and international organizations in the field of disability work and
- participation in local conferences of disability movement.

Our aim is to develop and facilitate the provision of rehabilitative schemes that would ease the re-integration of the (ex-)users and survivors of psychiatry into society and hence assure them of means of dignified sustainable livelihood. One example of our work is the support for a woman, who otherwise probably would have been lost because of the lack of psychosocial support in our country. Named Abena Nyarko, she hailed from Agona Nyarkrom, a village about 55 km (about 35 miles) from Accra. She had migrated to Accra to work in a restaurant as a dish washer. Not being able to afford a room to stay in, she stayed with a friend who was occupying a kiosk at a place nearby. According to Abena, she fell in love with an auto mechanic who lived around the area. After a short time, she got pregnant. When she mentioned it to her boyfriend, he flatly denied responsibility and beat her on two occasions when she asked for money to attend prenatal clinic. Faced with this predicament and having no relative in Accra to intervene on her behalf, she had to care for the pregnancy with her meagre salary for the nine months. Not long after giving birth in April 2005, she got into serious financial difficulties where she couldn't get money to buy food to feed the baby. She had to go begging from well-wishers to get some money to care for herself and the baby. It must be mentioned that Abena was laid off from her restaurant job just after childbirth. In the midst of these serious challenges, she broke down mentally and some good samaritans found her, took her to hospital and someone among them proffered to care for her baby when she got admitted. At the time our members met Abena, she had recovered from her condition and remembered every aspect of her family background and personal life. She was due to be discharged from the hospital but no relative showed up. This lack of support, coupled with her apparent reluctance to move out of the hospital for fear of being maltreated, made discharge an unlikely option. Upon counselling from our members, Abena agreed to be discharged from the hospital and go back to her village to resettle there. It was also prevailed upon her that her child will also be given back to her. As far as the work she'd like to do to sustain herself and her child, she mentioned trading in food stuffs such as yams, plantain, cassava, maize etc. MFGh was able to mobilize the equivalent of 225 Pounds Sterling from our members which was used to take her to her village and as start-up capital for her trading business. It is refreshing to report that Abena is currently pursuing her trade diligently and has been happily accepted back to where she came from.

We of MFGh feel profoundly proud and elated to have been of assistance to this young lady whose life would have been ruined due to no fault of her own. The inner satisfaction can be greater if and only if our finances improve thereby enabling us to do more of such things in our activities.

Our future programmes are: MFGh intends in the short-term to identify with such persons by reaching out and fighting for them to be re-admitted to their previous workplaces or facilitating their employment into new jobs. MFGh will be a strong advocate for the human rights of (ex-)users and survivors of psychiatry.

We project as a long-term programme to start a day centre where members can come and have recreational facilities and occupational therapy. There will be a library and farming activities. It must be stated that transportation will be needed to make it easy for users to get to the centre and back.

This part of our integration scheme will ultimately make facilities available for (ex-)users and survivors of psychiatry to engage themselves in vocational skills such carpentry, basket weaving, sewing and needlework etc.

With the facilities also serving as a recreational centre, the users shall have access to a library, computer centre, indoor games and other forms of entertainment. As much as possible, the centre shall not be residential. In extreme cases, consideration will be given to any user(s) who has genuinely lost touch with his/her relatives.

We plan to exchange information and study visits to other analogous organizations both locally and internationally to gain and share experiences. MFGh seeks to foster and strengthen links with analogous minded organizations both locally and internationally to harmonize their operations and explore diverse forms of cooperation and assistance geared towards helping (ex-)users and survivors of psychiatry. We also plan to produce a quarterly newsletter.

Our future focus will be on human rights and dignity of (ex-)users and survivors of psychiatry: ensuring that the general public is fully committed with the issues and concerns of users and survivors of psychiatry, raising funds to facilitate and smoothen the activities of MFGh and making sure that the abilities and skills of users and survivors are acknowledged and used in proper ways.

Jan Wallcraft

User-led Research to Develop an Evidence Base for Alternative Approaches

The Role of Research in Mental Health

Mental health research does not appear from a void, but is carried out by people with a life-history and a set of beliefs and motivations. The purpose of mental health research is to create a solid foundation of knowledge, on which to base treatment and services. But knowledge can never be free from value-judgements, beliefs, attitudes and experiences. I have found it useful to look at the models (otherwise known as paradigms, world-views, or discourses) that underpin mental health research, as that enables better awareness of the political aspects of research, and the power struggles over what knowledge will be most socially valued and receive the greatest funding.

The most influential model is the biomedical model of mental illness, which still dominates most funded research. The biomedical model has been described as a mechanistic and reductionist model, based on Cartesian philosophy and Newtonian science (Capra, 1982). Research is as far as possible carried out in clinical settings where treatments can be tested without interference from extraneous factors. Research is largely based on statistical methods.

The psychosocial model of mental health and illness which is more holistic and dynamic and includes a wider range of interacting factors, is gaining ground as, in most countries, large asylums are being closed and people with mental health problems are living most of their lives in the community. Psychologists, community psychiatric nurses, occupational therapists, social workers and other professionals are gaining status in relation to doctors and many are carrying out research using a psychosocial model. Qualitative research based on interviews and questionnaires is more likely to be used in the psychosocial model.

The third, emerging model, I call the self-advocacy model, developed by service users/survivors and their allies, challenges the power of professionals and their right to define and treat so-called mental illness. It emphasises the value of personal experience in knowledge creation and the importance of regaining power and control over one's own life. Many people who have survived severe mental health problems have been able to find meaning in their experiences and have worked to create and research alternatives to psychiatry. Self-advocacy research often needs more empowering methods of doing research, and some have been found in the work of the disability movement, which has developed concepts of emancipatory research. This, at its best, ensures true power sharing, so that research workers and research subjects are paid equally for their time. Everyone shares in developing the research, carrying it out, writing and publishing it, so that all gain power and knowledge from the process. Methods include action research, narrative research, indepth interviews and focus groups.

Service user/survivor researchers do not all have the same knowledge and beliefs, but we usually share a commitment to addressing the power imbalance between researcher and subject, and between doctor and patient. Some of us are academically qualified, others have learned research skills in short courses or simply by doing it. Some started out as researchers and then became service users; some, like me, began as service users and learned to do research to understand our experiences better.

We usually seek to remove the mystery from psychiatry and to find out what psychiatrists know. We also want to understand the limits of their knowledge. We explore different forms of support and help in real life contexts rather than merely comparing the difference between one drug with another drug in treating clinically-defined symptoms. Clinical trial methods are criticised by service user/survivor researchers because they limit the kinds of questions that can be asked, and the outcome measures that can be used. In clinical trials, the aspects of "mental illness" and recovery that can be numerically or statistically measured become the most important aspects, simply because they are measurable and not because they are necessarily the most important to service users/survivors.

My own path to becoming a researcher was part of my journey towards reclaiming my own life. Ten years after I left the mental health system, I went to college to get a degree. Having spent years trying to piece together my shattered memories, I was curious to know more about the effects of ECT on the brain. The medical literature I read rarely questioned the ethics of electrocuting mad brains, but I found a wonderful book in a socialist bookshop, *The History of Shock Treatment*, by a survivor from the US, Leonard Roy Frank (Frank, 1978). This is a collection of writings from every perspective about shock treatments from insulin coma onwards, including many personal testimonies and writings by service users/survivors. I learned from Frank that there is no simple path towards scientific truth, especially in such a complex field as psychiatry. At one point, early in the history of ECT, 52 different medical theories about how it worked were listed. The problem is that, in conventional psychiatry, the patient's perspective has been automatically discounted because within the discourse of "mental illness" we are not regarded as reasoning human beings.

It is only since service users/survivors of psychiatry became an international movement that we have been able to demand our legitimate place in knowledge creation, but our movement is not yet strong enough to call for a revision of the accumulated psychiatric knowledge of the past 150 years or to force a major change in the methods of doing research.

At college and outside it, I began to meet other people with personal experience of psychiatry. Women were saying that the hospital is not safe for them. Many (like me) had experienced sexual abuse in hospital (in my case by a psychiatrist), so I became concerned with how we can help ourselves without psychiatry. I studied alternative therapies and became a qualified aromatherapist and healer. I learned co-counselling and joined self-help groups. I tried various forms of psychotherapy and counselling. I helped to set up a "women only" crisis service. I learned that both men and women have the same needs for respect, dignity, safety, self-esteem, empowerment, and trusting relationships.

I heard and read hundreds of service user/survivor stories over the years and I learned that we could help each other to cope even with the most severe mental health problems. I went on to do a Ph.D. in which I developed my skills as a service user/survivor researcher. In the U.K., there are a growing number of service users/survivor researchers within and outside the academic system. Service user/survivor led research has been supported by voluntary organisations such as MIND, the Mental Health Foundation, and the Sainsbury Centre for Mental Health.

I have been involved in several pieces of research alternatives to psychiatry. The biggest and most influential project was the four-year Strategies for Living service user/survivor research programme at the Mental Health Foundation (Faulkner & Layzell, 2000). This was managed by a service user/survivor researcher, Alison Faulkner . Funding came from the National Lottery. The research was overseen by an advisory group of service users/survivors.

The first stage of this programme was a large survey called *Knowing Our Own Minds* (Faulkner, 1997) about what people with mental health problems think about mental health treatments and therapies, and what kinds of personal self-help strategies they find helpful. Over 400 responses were received. Based on the findings, the Strategies for Living research was designed to find out more about how people with mental health problems managed their own lives.

I was appointed to lead a team of researchers, all of whom were service users/survivors, to carry out 71 in-depth interviews with service users/survivors around the U.K. about the supports and strategies they found helpful. We developed a topic guide with a series of open-ended questions about the role of mental health services, talking therapies, complementary and alternative therapies, spirituality and other forms of help. The interviews were taped, transcribed and analysed.

The strongest theme to emerge from the research was the importance of relationships with other people, in all their different forms, including relationships with professionals. Other strategies and supports found helpful were:

medication, complementary therapies, religious and spiritual beliefs, self-help strategies, sport and physical exercise, and creative expression. We asked what was most important about these different supports, and the main themes were: being accepted, sharing experience, finding meaning or purpose, and finding ways to take more control over one's life, and achieve peace of mind. Coping strategies could be grouped into categories: on-going survival strategies, crisis or life-saving strategies, symptom management, and healing strategies. Different types of support would fit different types of strategy. We were able to show that people create their own strategies for living with mental health problems.

The report recommended that mental health professionals, service providers and policy makers should recognise that persons with mental health problems develop their own expertise based on personal experience. This expertise must be supported and valued. Mental health organisations were urged to disseminate information about the strategies that people find helpful and to encourage and support people in managing their own lives.

The Strategies for Living programme (Nicholls, 2001) also funded, trained and supported service users/survivors to carry out small scale research projects. These included:

- An evaluation of peer support at a drop-in centre. People said the drop-in centre motivated them to go out and meet others. They valued relationships, companionship and the empathy and understanding they received.
- A study of ear acupuncture at a women's mental health drop in. Women found the treatment helped them relax and gain confidence. Two participants came off antidepressants during treatment. Several said the treatment had raised their awareness of the possibility of alternatives.
- An evaluation of the role of attending mosque in the lives of Muslim men with mental health problems, mosque was seen as an important place for men to connect with others of shared faith and prayer was soothing to the mind and heart.

A larger service user/survivor-led project supported by Strategies for Living was *Life's Labour's Lost* (Bodman, *et al.*, 2003). This was a survey of 56person's experiences with losing employment due to mental health problems. It looked at the importance of employment in people's lives, how the loss of occupation affects people, how they re-form their lives and what helps them to find new occupation.

The report found that support was needed to help people understand and cope with their mental health problems to re-establish an "ordinary" life, find activities and occupations, try new things and regain hope and confidence. They also valued practical support with the stress of going back to work. People's stories told of difficult journeys with many ups and downs along the way. A particular job might be appropriate at one stage but not at another. A surprising finding was that many persons' sense of self changed for the better despite, and because of, their experiences. Some people reported positive changes in their values and priorities: they became clearer about what is important in their lives, developed greater understanding of others, and drew on their inner strength to create and rebuild more balanced and healthier lives. The researchers said that "such outcomes might be more common in society if people with mental health problems were included and supported more effectively. This would mean more people could contribute at less personal and social cost."

For the service user/survivor researchers who carried out the small projects, this was an important learning experience. Most of those involved in this programme were new to research, and they valued the training they received and the confidence and sense of competence they gained from doing the work. Several went on to do more training, others assumed new roles in local voluntary projects or paid work. Some have continued to develop their own personal coping strategies and help others to do so.

Another work that emerged from the Strategies for Living project was a report, *Healing Minds* (Wallcraft, 1998). I examined the evidence for a range of complementary and alternative therapies in mental health, including acupuncture, homeopathy, nutritional remedies, aromatherapy, massage and spiritual healing. I found clear evidence that service users/survivors wanted alternatives and valued them when they received them, in particular the lack of so-called side effects, improved feelings of relaxation, optimism and well-being, and being treated as a whole person. I found that despite some research showing that complementary therapies can reduce the need for psychiatric drugs, there is currently not much investment in doing more research, or in providing complementary therapies.

One problem is that randomised, controlled trials cannot easily demonstrate the aspects of complementary therapies that are most valued, for instance, the aspects of empowerment, choice, respect, individual treatment and healing partnership that come from working with a holistic practitioner. The dominance of the biomedical and psychosocial model in research makes it difficult to demonstrate the value of these therapies, and the lack of evidence for their value means that service providers do not provide them. However, in the U.K., there are signs that attitudes towards research in mental health are changing, with more qualitative methods being used and more involvement of service users/survivors in research priority setting.

I was involved as a research consultant in a recent investigation of coming off psychiatric drugs. This was a service user/survivor-led research project commissioned by the national organisation MIND (Read, 2005). As in the Strategies for Living project, a team of service user/survivor researchers were recruited to do the work. The team carried out 204 short telephone interviews, and interviewed 46 people in depth using a topic guide.

SSRIs (selective serotonin re-uptake inhibitors) are supposed to be easy to withdraw from; however, the researchers found that people had more difficulty coming off these antidepressive drugs than those on mood stabilisers (e.g., lithium or carbamazepine) or neuroleptics. The longer people were on any type of psychiatric drugs, the harder it was to come off.

Two-thirds of those who came off neuroleptics or mood stabilisers did so against their doctor's advice or without telling their doctor It was found that doctors could not predict which patients would be able to come off successfully. Those who stopped taking psychiatric drugs against their doctors' advice were just as likely to succeed as those who came off with physician agreement.

The forms of support found most helpful were: support from a counsellor, a support group or a complementary therapist, peer support, information from the internet or from books, and activities such as relaxation, meditation and exercise. Doctors were found to be the least helpful group to those who wanted to reduce or come off psychiatric drugs.

The benefits of coming off psychiatric drugs included: better mental ability, taking back personal power and control, feeling more alive, and feeling good about managing without psychiatric drugs.

Following this study MIND (the organisation who commissioned it) has changed its standard advice to patients. Historically, their advice was not to come off psychiatric drugs without consulting a doctor first. MIND now advises people to seek information and support from a wide variety of sources. MIND also gave evidence based on this report to a government committee looking at mental health legislation, and plans to use the report to support the case against compulsory treatment in the community. The results of the MIND study confirm the international reports of experiences, which Peter Lehmann as editor gathered in *Coming off Psychiatric Drugs: Successful Withdrawal from Neuroleptics, Antidepressants, Lithium, Carbamazepine and Tranquilizers* (1998); this was the first book on this topic to be published in the world.

Conclusions

Knowledge created by service user/survivor researchers is based on a different value system from that of professionals. The key values for service user/survivor-led research include a commitment to change, expertise based on personal experience, countering stigma, redressing power imbalances, and desired outcomes such as self management and recovery of a satisfying life.

Involving service users/survivors in setting priorities, designing and carrying out research is likely to result in better quality research on more relevant topics. Service user/survivor-led research such as Strategies for Living can ask questions that are independent of existing services and treatments. For instance, spirituality and mental health emerged as important to people and led to further work on the subject. There is some evidence that people interviewed by service user/survivor interviewers have a better experience of the research process, feel more heard and understood, and are more likely to open up and give more information. Service users/survivors often find the process of doing research empowering:

> By focusing on the research process as much as on the outcomes, it
> aims to enable service users/survivors to take part in carrying out

research while gaining skills and confidence in the process. It aims to be inclusive and informative, ensuring that people who take part as research participants are kept fully informed of the results and of any action subsequently taken. This is rarely the case with traditional research (Faulkner & Thomas, 2002, p. 2).

Methods, such as narrative research carried out by service users/survivors who are likely to listen with genuine understanding and empathy, can get closer to the meaning of people's experiences. Experiences, such as hearing voices, cannot be objectively measured and diagnoses often explain little about individual differences, strengths and weaknesses that might be needed to ensure the most relevant support.

Service users/survivors in the U.K. are slowly gaining the confidence to challenge in particular the dominant biomedical model of mental health. As more of us gain qualifications in research, we are finding the courage and the support to carry out research with different underlying assumptions about the causes of mental distress. We take our own expertise through experience as a starting point. In doing this, we adapt research methods to fit an attitude of partnership and equality with those we involve as researchers and participants. Service user/survivor-led research into alternatives is one of the means by which we contest the discourse of psychiatry which negates our human rights.

Sources

Bodman, R., Davies, R., Frankel, N., Minton, L., Mitchell, L., Pacé, C., Sayers, R., & Faulkner, A. (1997). *Knowing our own minds*. London: Mental Health Foundation.

Faulkner, A., & Layzell, S. (2000). *Strategies for living*. London: Mental Health Foundation.

Faulkner, A., &Thomas, P. (2002). User-led research and evidence-based medicine. *British Journal of Psychiatry, 180,* 1-3

Frank L. R. (1978). *The history of shock treatment*. San Francisco: Self-publication

Lehmann, P. (Ed.) (1998). *Psychopharmaka absetzen. Erfolgreiches Absetzen von Neuroleptika, Antidepressiva, Lithium, Carbamazepin und Tranquilizern*. Berlin: Antipsychiatrieverlag [English edition: *Coming off psychiatric drugs: Successful withdrawal from neuroleptics, antidepressants, lithium, carbamazepine and tranquilizers*. Berlin / Eugene / Shrewsbury: Peter Lehmann Publishing 2004].

Nicholls, V. (2001). *Doing research ourselves*. London: Mental Health Foundation.

Read, J. (2005). *Coping with coming off.* London: Mind Publications.

Tibbs, N., Tovey, Z., & Unger, E. (2003). *Life's labour's lost.* London: Mental Health Foundation.

Wallcraft, J. (1998). *Healing minds.* London: Mental Health Foundation.

Andrew Hughes

Preparing People for User/Survivor Involvement Work in Mental Health and Social Care

After some stays in psychiatric hospitals, which included compulsory treatment, I began to be involved in the self-advocacy movement and to provide the occasional "patient perspective" and critique of mental health service provision during this time at conferences and training events. Involvement in local MIND organisations followed in 1988, and then, together with Anne Plumb and Tony Riley, I founded the Distress Awareness Training Agency (DATA), currently the U.K.'s longest established survivor training group.

I am happy to base my use of the term user involvement on the definition developed for the *On Our Own Terms* report, written by Jan Wallcraft and her colleagues:

> The use of the term "user involvement" is used in this report to mean the various ways in which mental health service users/survivors are helping to change mental health and social services. This often works through service users/survivors becoming members of committees along with professionals and people from voluntary organisations, though it can include a number of other ways, such as conferences, discussion forums, open days, service users/survivors acting as paid consultants, or professionals visiting user/survivor groups (Wallcraft, *et al.*, 2003, Appendix 1).

To these activities I would add the training of mental health workers and students by service users/survivors, and service users/survivors auditing, monitoring and researching mental health and social services.

That report used the term "service users" to refer to those who use mental health services and was more concerned with service reform and improvement than with a radical challenge. It also defined the term survivor as implying "that the person has come through traumatic experiences, related to their mental health and/or mental health services, and is committed to campaigning for change. In some cases it is used by people who no longer depend on services."

From the 1980s and particularly since the introduction of the National Health Service (NHS) and Community Care Act (1990), user involvement has increased in terms of the levels of activity and their scope. Additionally, the National Service Framework for Mental Health states that "service users...should be involved in planning, providing and evaluating education and training." Since the mid-1990s there has been a substantial increase in the number of opportunities for people with personal experience of mental distress to become involved in the planning and development of mental health and social services, in designing and delivering training to mental health workers and students, and in auditing, monitoring and researching mental health and social services.

It is now a widely shared principle that users of services should be involved in decisions that affect those services and therefore themselves and their peers. There are, of course, difficulties regarding the form user involvement should take and how it should be implemented practically.

Several studies have identified some of the components likely to promote effective user involvement. These can include: clear policies, an infrastructure to support ongoing user involvement, effective mechanisms for feedback on projects, the involvement of senior staff members who are credible to their colleagues and service users, and administrative, training and financial support.

I have been fortunate enough to play a role in helping to prepare and support some of the service users and survivors who have taken advantage of these increased opportunities. I have approached this role from my own background as a survivor of mental health services.

Most of my work in this area has been paid for by the NHS Mental Health Trusts and the Local Authorities, the same organisations which have the chief responsibility for delivering mental health services in the U.K. The fact that the service providers are also responsible for offering resources to user involvement has clear implications in terms of the amounts and continuity of funding for supporting user involvement activity. Additionally, it can be argued that there may be some conflicts of interest, especially in areas like their support for user focused monitoring.[1]

In helping to support people towards more effective user involvement, I have focused on four areas primarily

- Training people in the necessary skills: personal, facilitative, technical etc.
- Providing a working knowledge of the organisation in which they will be involved, especially the relevant structures for planning and delivering services
- Building people's confidence
- Supporting people into suitable future opportunities to practice their skills and enhance their confidence.

Training People in the Necessary Skills

For most of the activities in which people may want to become more involved, there are a range of skills that are likely to be useful in that role. It is always useful when possible to carry out some form of skills and needs analysis before setting out to train people. For representative and committee work, the skills most people will find useful include

- Managing priorities, managing time, preparation and planning for attending meetings, note taking for meetings, facilitating meetings, chairing meetings

---

1   User focused monitoring is a dynamic approach for evaluating mental health services that places the subjective experience of the service user at the heart of the process. Users of mental health services are the people best placed to comment on the services they receive, and the user focused monitoring methodology was developed to access these opinions and views. The first user focused monitoring project based on the model developed by the Sainsbury Centre for Mental Health was carried out in the London areas of Kensington, Chelsea and Westminster as a pilot project in 1996 by Diana Rose.

- Using body and voice to present a message, listening techniques, planning and giving presentations, using equipment such as flip charts, white boards, overhead and digital projectors, being an effective representative, and dealing with conflict assertively.

Other useful skills include using computers for writing text documents, for the internet and email, for desktop publishing, and for presentation software.

Sometimes rather more specialised skills are needed; e.g., working with the media, influencing politicians, carrying out public consultations and other specific projects. It is always useful to spend time helping service users/survivors examine their existing skills and identify their skill requirements. However, it is one aspect of my work that is often not recognised as necessary by commissioning agencies, which sometimes prefer to make assumptions about the needs of their service users. One of the difficulties in such skills analysis can be that service users/survivors are unaware of the nature of the role they will fill in user involvement. It can be useful to have some service users/survivors in a group of trainees with more experience; it can also be useful to share some of my experiences when I was active in user involvement, though the roles available have changed somewhat since then.

For Leeds Involvement Project as part of their Leeds Locality Development Scheme, I have been fortunate to collaborate in developing some accredited training programmes[1] for disabled people, not only service users/survivors, who wish to participate more in user involvement. The first programmes of training which have now been delivered on three occasions had two units: Service User Involvement Work and Equality and Group Development Work. Some of the sessions from that programme aimed at providing people with necessary skills included

- Recognising skills for user involvement work
- Understand the benefits of user involvement
- Understand how diversity brings value to user involvement
- Understanding how to develop a group

---

1 Accreditation was through the National Open College Network (OCN) with support from the OCN West & North Yorkshire, now OCN Yorkshire & Humber; information at www.nocn.org.uk

- Understanding key points of equality legislation
- Understanding anti-discriminatory practice
- Developing a presentation.

For South West Yorkshire Mental Health services NHS trust, the survivor trainer group to which I belong, DATA, designed and delivered a programme we called Moving On Training, aimed at service users/survivors who wanted to move towards further education, employment or user involvement activity. Some of the daily sessions and their contents included

- Working with others: active listening; negotiation; working to our strengths.
- Having good meetings: looking after ourselves in training and involvement; Why we go to meetings? meetings that are effective.
- Communicating your message: Who is listening? What do I want to say? What methods can I use?
- Getting your message across: presentation skills; tips and techniques for working with small groups; using equipment.

For Wakefield Metropolitan District Council, DATA supported an evaluation of a range of community mental health services through the Pioneers Project. A 14-member strong workgroup of local service users/survivors was set up to carry out a piece of user focused monitoring. The main learning points we aimed to get across were

- Build a team; understand user monitoring and evaluation; develop, practise and use skills in listening, planning, evaluation, report writing, facilitation, recording, analysis, independence and interviewing; develop and use skills and procedures to ensure confidentiality and impartiality by the pioneer team during the evaluation; develop and implement a user monitoring methodology for the Wakefield District user evaluation.

Also in the Wakefield area, I prepared some training for a social enterprise, Pioneers Education, Training and Research Agency. Their programme to equip them for user focused monitoring work included

- Introduction to research and user focused monitoring; interview skills; different types of questions and how to ask them; designing interviews; recording information; good reporting; looking after ourselves and participants; ethics, payments, consent, confidentiality, safety; other matters: contracts, control, context etc.

Providing a Working Knowledge of Organisations and Their Structures

Mental health trusts have a surprisingly wide range of planning and management structures. Typically, service users/survivors may be involved collectively in a number of forums with varying levels of influence.

There are local meetings, based around a service, which are mainly concerned with allowing the exchange of information, often referred to as "talking shops." Such informal networks may be useful stepping stones for people wanting to get involved, but are often frustrating in the longer term for service users/survivors due to the limitations of affecting change from such meetings. These gatherings are often quite informal making it easy for anyone to access them regardless of their levels of experience or confidence. Many are facilitated by a member of staff. This can inhibit some service users/survivors from expressing honest opinions about services and other matters. Some are facilitated by members of the service user group, though this can sometimes lead to feelings of inequity, as the facilitator is seen as being in a more privileged position.

There are meetings which aim to serve a larger geographical area, perhaps a town or part of a city. These meetings may send representatives to the main service user decision making body for an NHS trust. As the configuration of health services in the U.K. has changed so much in recent years, and given the patchwork nature of the development of user involvement and user groups, there are often considerable differences at this town level about how representation takes place. This can make it very difficult to have a clear and democratic way of moving that representation up to the trust wide or regional or national level. In the Leeds Involvement Project unit, "Service User Involvement Work," there is one session entitled, "Understand how health and social care services are delivered" which aims to provide insight into how health and social care services were planned and delivered across the city of Leeds and how the funding of those services worked at the national, regional and local level. To meet the assessment criteria for the level two award learners had to "Explain three different ways in which users of community care services can be involved in the development of those services and describe their impact."

Building People's Confidence for Participation in User Involvement

This aspect of the work I do is very important for many people and for me, very satisfying. I feel sure that the fact I have experienced mental distress for myself and received services, the fact I have experienced the same types of discrimination as many learners and the fact my own confidence has been melted away at times in my past, is helpful for the people whose confidence levels I am trying to build up and sustain. The level one programme, Moving On training, included the following sessions and content

- Aiming for recovery: What skills do I have and how can I use them?; feeling good about myself; planning a personal project.
- Communicating clearly and safely: Making my point; dealing with panic; dealing with criticism.

It is clear that the ideas for rebuilding confidence can often hinge on the same issues that people tackle when using the recovery approach (see Copeland, 1997) to achieve and maintain their well being. I am often told this aspect of the training is enjoyable, useful and very empowering. Oddly, I sometimes find myself arguing with the commissioners of the work I do that these sessions and similar ones are not straying too far into the territory of therapeutic work, for which the agencies have their own large staff groups, of course!

Opportunities

The provision of future opportunities for people to practise their new skills in realistic settings and roles is probably the single most important aspect in ensuring that service users/survivors can maintain their personal participation in user involvement. Regrettably, it is the area over which I usually have the least influence. I make a point of discussing this issue when I am negotiating for new pieces of work to support user involvement. I am often told that funding will be sought to advance the involvement opportunities that will follow on from my work, or that "the plan is to develop further opportunities." In reality, the budgets for these types of initiatives are very vulnerable. Many trusts and such organisations see increased user involvement as a luxury. I suspect that at the highest levels within organisations there is still reluctance if not fear at the prospect of service users/survivors taking a bigger role in the future planning and development of mental health, social care and other health services. The battle to establish the benefits of user involvement over the difficulties in the perception of health and social care leaders is one that service users/survivors are engaged in at international, national and local levels, with a variety of levels of success.

Some Lessons Learned and Problems Encountered

There are a number of factors that are influential in making sure that service users/survivors are most likely to be effective in their user involvement "careers" and in making user involvement influential at a local level:

• In each locality, there are likely to be particular directions in which service users/survivors wish to develop their services. Following these specific priorities in planning support for user involvement can mean that people are equipped for a role with which they already have considerable motivation to continue.

• The resources to sustain user involvement initiatives should have been identified and reserved ahead of the work. Quite often such resource allocation will only come about after clear policy statements have been made about an organisation's commitment to user involvement. Service users/survivors and their groups already involved may like to note that establishing such clear policies can be a valuable stepping stone to increased and improved user involvement.

• It is useful to ensure that some principles are built into user involvement at these early stages. In particular, ensuring that there is equality of opportunity is likely to provide a good basis for continued widening of the user involvement role. While the service user and survivor movement is quite good at including people with a wide variety of experiences of mental distress, it has not yet developed a great record in terms of including people who are service users/survivors and also gay, lesbian and bisexual, from Black and Minority Ethnic groups, who are young people, who have physical or sensory impairments, and people from numerous other backgrounds.

• It is helpful where there are systems put in place for continuous monitoring and evaluation of the user involvement landscape. The existence or development of local user focused monitoring groups can be useful in this respect. Independent service users/survivors groups from other localities may also have a role to play here.

* One of the greatest potential barriers to effective and enjoyable user involvement is fragmentation. Organisations and services can keep user involvement activities in separate pockets reducing the overall impact. Local service user groups can sometimes fail to find ways to collaborate and again this reduces the total energy going into change and probably reduces the goodwill among organisational leaderships for promoting further user involvement developments.

Sources

Copeland, M. E. (1997). *Wellness recovery action plan.* Dummerston, VT: Peach Press.
Wallcraft, J., Read, J., & Sweeney, A. (2003). *On our own terms.* London: Sainsbury Centre for Mental Health.

Laurie Ahern, Peter Stastny and Chris Stevenson

INTAR
The International Network Toward Alternatives and Recovery[1]

The International Network Toward Alternatives and Recovery was founded in 2003 by a group of U.S. practitioners and advocates in mental health recovery, including world renowned psychiatrists, people who have recovered from mental distress, psychologists, family members and other mental health

---

1 This chapter represents exclusively the personal views of the authors, and should not be construed as a statement by the organization or any other participant in the 2004 & 2005 INTAR meetings. Acknowledgment: The authors wish to thank Will Hall and Kim Hopper for their helpful comments regarding this manuscript.

professionals (www.intar.org). The international organization grew out of the shared experience and expert body of research that demonstrates a strong need to promote non-medical humane, non-coercive ways of helping people in emotional crisis. INTAR is a key international organization dedicated to advancing the knowledge and availability of alternative approaches for individuals experiencing severe mental distress.

In an era of so-called "evidence-based treatments" and "best practices," people who experience extreme states of mind, traditionally labeled mental illness, are still being subjected to predominantly bio-medical and involuntary treatments, often including repeated or prolonged hospitalizations, high dosages and multiple combinations of powerful psychiatric drugs, along with a lack of recovery-oriented services and opportunities in the community. People treated with traditional mental health services, and their families, have become increasingly more disillusioned with the results of conventional psychiatry and seek alternative practitioners and forms of assistance. The research literature supports their skepticism. A recent review of the literature demonstrates that a considerable percentage (40-60%, depending on the study) of individuals who experience a psychotic episode would recover without neuroleptics if they participate in active psychosocial treatment, while short- and long-term damage from these drugs is very common (Aderhold & Stastny, 2007). This greatly increases the need to amplify and search for alternative approaches that enable individuals to recover without undue harm to their bodies and minds.

Individually, INTAR members have experienced substantial success in advancing self-help programs and alternate clinical approaches that help put the person's distress into context, thereby respecting and acknowledging the entirety of the person and the experience. As a result, the work of INTAR members has assisted people to regain control over their lives without debilitating treatments meant to cure them. One INTAR member, a recovery researcher, described the drastic difference in outcomes when a non-medical, person-centered approach is used to help a person through distress:

> Take two wonderful, happy, smart young men. Both were in college, living on their own—testing the waters—testing themselves. New friends, new freedoms, new loves, new ideas, new temptations—new everything. Both had the world at their feet and were

limited only by their own imaginations of what their lives might be about, might become.

Then crash.

Jack is a child I have known for his entire lifetime. I watched him take his first steps and say his first words. I watched and I'm still watching.

Karl I met just months ago. The parallels between these two young men are eerie—yet the outcomes so different—so frighteningly different.

Crash, crash, crash. It seems to happen at that age. Eighteen to mid-twenties. And it happened to Jack and Karl.

Jack was at a college in New England and Karl was in school out on the West Coast. When Jack was 15 years old, he and a friend were car-jacked at knife-point. Even though they caught the man—and he was sentenced to seven years in prison—Jack never seemed to quite get over it. He would not stay alone in his house at night, always locked his car doors no matter where he was going, and would not travel without a cell phone.

Karl told me about a time when he was an exchange student in high school, how he had been held up—mugged—alone in a foreign country—and had never been so terrified in his life.

Jack has always wanted to be a journalist and Karl, he told me that music has been his passion since as long as he could remember. Both had such high hopes, such big dreams. Only one dreamer remains. The other dreamer died with his dreams when he was labeled "mentally ill."

Each experimented with drugs for the first time in college—Jack went to a concert and tried LSD. Karl started smoking marijuana with the band he formed in college. Pandora's box was now open. Paranoia and fear trickled in, replacing logic. Men were after them, people were talking about them. They could not sleep, they could not eat. Fear was the dominating factor in their lives. The drugs were gone, the high was over, the trip had ceased—but the demons remained.

Jack called home and Karl's friends called his parents. This is where the road divides. This is where the similarities end. This is where one has a breakdown and the other has a breakthrough.

Jack's mother knew he was frightened. She told him to leave college and come home. She felt she needed to help him feel safe again—the only way to bring him out of this fearful place.

Karl's parents told him to come home. They too knew he was frightened, needed help. They brought him to the best psychiatrist. He was hospitalized. He was medicated. He was told he had a chemical imbalance of the brain. He was labeled. He was told that college was too stressful for him. He could never return. He tried to commit suicide. He lived, but his dreams, his dreams died.

Jack's mother and friends stayed home with him, listened to the fears. He went off caffeine, ate healthy foods and took long, warm baths. He had acupuncture, massages, and found a therapist who did not label him. They took walks together, they talked. Slowly, very slowly, he felt safe enough to come back. And then they worked on why he left, why this reality was so frightening that he needed to leave it in the first place.

Jack—well, Jack is back living at college. He started working out and volunteers in a home for mentally retarded adults. He told me several things since his breakthrough: "This is the most painful thing I have ever experienced in my life and I would not wish it on anyone—but I would not change a thing. Better I deal with these issues now then wait until I'm 40 or 50. I feel stronger than I ever have. I've learned so much about myself, I still have fears but I control them—they no longer control me."

Karl—who once dreamt of being a musician—called me after he walked home from his last day at the day treatment program. "I saw a sign on a restaurant window—they were looking for a dishwasher. Do you think I could handle that?"

The participants in the INTAR meetings expressed a common belief. In their research, practices or advocacy they try to provide safe, caring and non-stigmatizing assistance to those in crisis or emotional distress. Although the work of INTAR participants from around the world is as diverse as the countries they are from, they espouse the same values and can frequently demonstrate better outcomes than traditional psychiatric treatment. During the first international INTAR summit held in the U.S. in November 2005, practitioners from Canada, Finland, Germany, Ireland, U.K., Austria and the United States came together to share information, research findings and their own personal experiences in non-medical approaches in helping people in extreme emotional states. As one INTAR member stated:

> It is our experience that even people diagnosed/labeled with the most severe mental illness can lead independent and self-directed lives without lifelong psychiatric treatment. When you look at a person's life experiences and history rather than looking at these problems as a disease people can get better.

Over the course of the three-day summit, INTAR members found affirmation for what they knew (i.e., for the values and beliefs that guide their individual work). Specifically, these include, among others:

- to do no harm
- create safe spaces
- no coercion
- accepting people's thoughts and feelings
- appreciation of altered states
- accepting different or unusual ways of being
- attempting to understand context but also accepting the limits of such understanding
- inspiring hope and possibility
- integrate self-determination
- reframing
- protection of human rights and dignity
- and bearing witness.

The second international summit in Ireland produced a network of work groups to explore a variety of practices/processes. The most important outcome of both summits was the conviction that there is a critical and pressing need to continue the work of the group and to continue sharing information on alternative practices and approaches.

To that end, the participants in the third international summit in Canada in May 2007 focused on formulating concrete ways in which INTAR could disseminate the groups' collective experience and knowledge to a wider audience. Additionally, INTAR held a public panel discussion at Malaspina University in Nanaimo, British Columbia, which again demonstrated the public's hunger for alternatives to traditional mental health services.

What are the Opportunities and Challenges for Promoting Alternatives through the Work of INTAR?

First of all, practitioners in alternative methods are very busy making sure that they can sustain themselves and their organizations. They have little time to promote their own approaches on the world psychiatric stage, much less engage in general advocacy to promote humane alternatives of many kinds. It is quite characteristic of many alternatives that they remain the sole example of their generally quite successful approach. For example, after 15 years of operation, there is still only one substantial Windhorse program in operation (in Northampton, MA), with three much smaller programs in Vienna, Austria; Lambsheim near Ludwigshafen, Germany; and Boulder, CO. The Runaway House in Berlin is still the only example of its kind in Germany, and probably in the world. Related approaches have been established in New Hampshire (Stepping Stone). A family-outreach program that does not espouse the medical model has been established in Toronto, Canada, but so far has not been replicated elsewhere. With INTAR, there is the possibility that these efforts will cross-fertilize and their positive results will become disseminated to a wider audience, thus encouraging further dissemination.

It is also possible that these often fairly insular approaches require charismatic leadership for their own successes, and that such leadership cannot be easily transplanted. Windhorse and the Runaway House have taken many years and a highly dedicated group of people to become relatively firmly established. It is possible that the necessary ingredients (beyond charismatic leadership) of these approaches can be identified and disseminated more easily. The obstacles that alternatives are facing in most communities have less to do with the lack of buy-in to the principles they are espousing, but are rather tied to a whole host of economic disincentives that are exceedingly difficult to overcome. In the USA, for example, hospitals and psychiatric emergency departments have totally cornered the market on crisis intervention, especially in urban communities (with few notable exceptions: San Francisco and San Diego, CA). This is the primary reason why programs such as

SOTERIA that provide non-hospital, largely drug-free interventions for individuals experiencing psychosis, have rarely been replicated successfully. It is our hope that organizations such as INTAR can affect a turning of the tide by affirming that there are safe and effective alternatives to hospital-based/biomedical interventions.

How Will INTAR Synthesize Charisma and Successful Alternatives to Traditional Psychiatry for More General Consumption?

INTAR embodies wisdom, creativity and practical experience, but without being self-congratulatory. The group is not homogeneous; it represents diversity in hearts and minds and language. The group has hands across oceans and a shifting population; as new alternative projects come on board, that adds to the diversity. Through this, INTAR is a spring of richness. Thus far, INTAR functions in a supportive and formative way. It breathes life into and feeds the soul of those who are fighting the good recovery fight, whether experts by experience or those offering a service, or those who are in both positions. The people who constitute INTAR make human to human connections and talk about their different treatment alternatives. As the group works with a flattened hierarchy—we all have expertise but there is no single expert— there is a pattern of operation—tentative, deeply respectful, tolerant and patient. There is a sense of the group "feeling its way in the light."

It remains a challenge to galvanise a loose collective towards producing outcomes. But much is at stake. If there is no concerted effort to proffer rational arguments for these and many other successful alternatives, then they are fated to remain the exceptions that prove the rule: hospitals and psychiatric drugs will remain the only available options for individuals experiencing acute psychiatric problems. Peer support and psychotherapy will be seen as nothing more than adjunctive interventions that are likely to be priced out of the market, especially for people considered to have serious psychiatric conditions. Holistic alternatives and techniques will remain the purview of rich self-payers and never reach the vast majority of those who could benefit from them. Therefore, an organization like INTAR must lead the way in providing the following essential services:

1. Creating and strengthening a world-wide network of like-minded providers of non-traditional mental health services.
2. Developing and disseminating an evidence base that derives from the collective experiences of non-traditional mental health programs.
3. Working in conjunction with other advocacy organizations, such as Mind-Freedom International and Mental Disability Rights International, to promote the widespread availability of effective alternatives.
4. Creating an international network of consultants who would be available for individual and organizational consultations, through discussion forums, mailing lists, video-links and other means of real-time communication.
5. Engaging with major professional and family organizations that are traditionally opposed to alternative treatments, but that are equally committed to finding ways of helping people who eschew the prevalent methods of mental health systems.

Source

Aderhold, V., & Stastny, P. (2007). Full disclosure: Toward a participatory and risk-limiting approach to neuroleptic drugs. *Ethical Human Psychology and Psychiatry, 9*(1), 35-61.

Peter Lehmann and Maths Jesperson

Self-help, Difference in Opinion and User Control in the Age of the Internet

Self-help and its facilitation and promotion are of fundamental interest for (ex-)users and survivors of psychiatry. Without the enhancement of self-help resources there will never be any progress in therapy or in recovery or in the ability to live a self-determined life. This is the message of organised (ex-)users and survivors of psychiatry from all over the world. Self-help is also the foundation for self reflection about the so-called symptoms of mental illness.

Self-help and professional support do not exclude each other. Often problems cannot be solved with self-help alone. But how can professional support in the mental health system be effective when individual self-help resources are not activated?

In our article, we try to answer the question how (ex-)users and survivors of psychiatry are organised and how they cooperate internationally, which includes the resolution of conflicts, with a particular emphasis on the role of the internet in reaching their goals.

The International Movement of (ex-)Users and Survivors of Psychiatry

Since the beginning of the 1990s, (ex-)users and survivors of psychiatry have organized themselves on the international level. In 1991, a European network—an association of member-organisations—was formed, followed two years later by the World Network of Users and Survivors of Psychiatry (WNUSP).

To form an international movement seemed, at first, to be an impossible project, not only due to economical and geographical obstacles, but also because of the great variety of opinions about psychiatry and its methods among (ex-)users and survivors of psychiatry. However, it turned out that these differences were actually not that great. It was, on the contrary, amazing to realize that our experiences of psychiatry and our opinions were rather similar not only in various western countries, but also in the formerly Stalinist countries of Eastern Europe, as well as in so-called developing countries in Africa, Asia and Latin America. It was especially easy to gather around a human and civil rights perspective. Our experiences of paternalism, stigmatisation and oppression within the psychiatric system as well as in society as a whole are very similar everywhere in the world, even if the forms these might take are rather different.

We also have differences regarding psychiatry's medical model and its treatment methods, but the differences are not that substantial. Nobody loves psychiatry, but some find aspects of it helpful and supportive, while others find it basically despicable.

Within the movement of (ex-)users and survivors of psychiatry in general, there is respect for these divergent opinions; most of the constituents are fed up with the superior attitudes in psychiatry, the constituents have experienced the negative effects of the psychiatric treatment methods in their own bodies. Like everywhere else, dogmatism and sectarianism exists among (ex-)users and survivors of psychiatry; there are also louts, windbags, machos and other unpleasant contemporaries. And there are the attempts of Scientology (via the so-called Citizen's Commission for Human Rights) and the drug companies to engage self-help groups, family-organisations and prominent critics of psychiatry in their own agendas either through direct financial sponsorship or other measures.

First Common Positions

At the first conference of the European Network of Users and Ex-Users in Mental Health in 1991, the 39 representatives of 16 European countries endorsed the cornerstones of the common position called *The Zandvoort Declaration on Common Interests*, which is still valid today:

- The European Network opposes the medical unilateral approach to, and stigmatisation of, mental and emotional distress, human suffering and unconventional behaviour.
- The European Network supports users' autonomy and responsibility in making their own decisions (self-determination).

Further areas of interests are

- to influence the treatment in psychiatry.
- to create and support alternatives to psychiatric treatment.
- to act against all kinds of discrimination in society concerning people who went through the psychiatric system.
- to work on abolishing compulsory treatment.
- to increase users' influence on their own treatment (e.g., right to describe or define their own case, right to refuse professional "aid," right to make correction of their own record).
- to secure that users receive adequate information about their treatment and their rights (e.g., right to receive written information about all possible risks of the treatment, the users' right to establish independent advocacy).

- to support and promote the right to professional drug free support.
- to support of user groups setting up alternatives to medical psychiatry.
- to support and promote the right to establish user controlled initiatives inside and outside psychiatry.
- to fight psychiatric stigma.
- to get work for a proper salary.
- to fight for proper housing.
- to monitor European or national legislation on aspects of discriminating laws.[1]

To reflect the current differences of opinion towards psychiatry in their own terminology, the independent organisations active internationally have adopted the term "(ex-)users and survivors of psychiatry." In 1997, the European Network of Users and Ex-Users in Mental Health decided to call itself "European Network of (ex-)Users and Survivors of Psychiatry (ENUSP)." This term has by now become more or less established among professionals as well, especially in English-speaking countries, although the USA and Australia/Oceania favours "consumers and survivors."

The term "user and survivors of psychiatry" shows the potential for conflict inherent in this cooperation which is based on a great variety of individual experiences and opinions. "Users" might refer to people who have experienced (1) (coercive) commitment that they believe saved their life, (2) they were relieved by getting a psychiatric diagnosis and (3) they cannot exist in their current life-circumstances without taking psychiatric drugs, and therefore they define psychiatry as useful to them. "Survivors of psychiatry" in turn refers to those who have experienced (1) coercive commitment as arbitrary and harmful detention, (2) psychiatric diagnosis as a distortion of their experience and/or a basis for discrimination and commitment; and/or (3) psychiatric treatment as representing a danger to their life and wellbeing. Considering these vast differences, constructive cooperation cannot be rated highly enough.

ENUSP and WNUSP have grown rapidly over the years. Currently (August 2007), ENUSP has members in 39 European countries, from Belarus to Ireland, from Portugal to Iceland.

---

1   See www.enusp.org/congresses/zandvoort-declaration.htm

In 2004, the Danish town of Vejle hosted the first real world congress of (ex-)users and survivors of psychiatry. Delegates and participants from 50 countries in all continents were present.[1] The participants from Africa formed a continental network, Pan African Network of Users and Survivors of Psychiatry (PANUSP). Further continental networks are not being considered at this time.

Beside these organisations that exclusively represent (ex-)users and survivors of psychiatry, there is MindFreedom International, which has been fighting for human rights of (ex-)users and survivors of psychiatry since 1990. Representatives of 13 initiatives came together and founded the Support Coalition in New York; this mixed organisation changed its name to MindFreedom International (MFI) in 2005. Its members, staff and board identify themselves as psychiatric survivors, though they are open to all. MFI is accredited at the United Nations as an advisory NGO (see the chapter by David Oaks in this book).

In June 2007, the first collective by ENUSP, WNUSP and MFI took place in Dresden at the World Psychiatric Association's conference, *Coercive Treatment in Psychiatry: A Comprehensive Review.* Within a few days (via the internet), the *Declaration of Dresden Against Coerced Psychiatric Treatment* was written and confirmed; its central message: "We stand united in calling for an end to all forced and coerced psychiatric procedures and for the development of alternatives to psychiatry."[2]

Together and Against Each Other in Self-help

Many longstanding activists know that if we want to change something and if we want to be understood, we must respect each other. We need to enter into a cooperation where we see the variety of ways to overcome emotional problems not as something that divides us, but as our common strength. To believe that our opinion is the only correct one, invariably leads to a dogmatic position that precludes acting in solidarity with each other. What good would

---

1   See www.enusp.org/congresses/vejle/index.htm

2   See www.enusp.org/dresden/dde.pdf

all the structures do that users and survivors are building if they constantly challenged our very essence, our solidarity with each other, by overemphasizing our disagreements? We certainly share the fact that we were once subjected to psychiatric diagnoses and treatments. But beside this, we are different in our origins, beliefs, political interests and personal preferences. If we base the answers to political questions about psychiatry exclusively on the experience of psychiatrization (an experience initiated by others, not ourselves), then political divergences and fights are programmed as soon as we emerge from basic critiques to concrete demands and actions. Therefore it is extremely helpful to consider the major differences of opinion within the movement between "users" of psychiatry and "survivors" early on.

Moreover, if we want to be respected, no matter by whom, we have to respect each other and treat those who think differently with equal respect, even if we do not share or understand their opinions. This is especially true when we run the risk of replacing the other person with an image that comes from our own imagination. This risk is particularly great in international communication, where different cultural backgrounds and languages can easily result in misunderstandings.

As much as we demand choices and possibilities for situations when we need help, we have to concede to each other the right to desire the kinds of changes in psychiatry and/or the kinds of alternatives that in our estimation appear most reasonable to us. As long as we are looking for more humanity, equality under the law, and better living conditions, why should different approaches lead to irreconcilable differences? The discrimination of (ex-)users and survivors of psychiatry in society is still so massive, that demands for change can only carry weight if we articulate them together.

Vejle Declaration

Mutual respect was the central theme of the *Declaration of Vejle*[1] which was approved unanimously by the General Assemblies of ENUSPand WNUSP at the world congress held in this Danish town (see next page).

---

1 See www.enusp.org/congresses/vejle/declaration.htm

Vejle Declaration

How We Propose to Deal with Each Other

In all organisations we should:

- build a constructive, welcoming, friendly, attractive atmosphere, respectful of all the opinions of others, not trying to decide what is good for them and support each other in developing our individual and creative capacities
- underline the importance of transparency, good governance and responsibility in financial matters
- integrate minorities in a proactive way and combat any discrimination, whether is based on origin, gender, age, disability, economy, religious or sexual orientation
- be patient with each other, try to see the whole person behind the label and emotional and physical problems, and try not to judge others
- be careful in the election of representatives and consider their experiences in self-help organizations; work to prevent burnout in ourselves and our colleagues to avoid departures from the organization.
- appreciate the work of all people who honestly try to improve psychosocial treatment as well as those who work to establish alternatives to psychiatry and resist any unilateral approach to the understanding of mental health problems
- respect the work of volunteers and recognize the need for paid jobs; look for allies as we face a vast and complex task.
- demand that psychosocial services are made for the (ex-)users / clients / survivors / people in recovery, under our input and with respect to our equal rights as citizens in a democratic society.

Because the goods in this world are distributed rather unevenly and because human beings are different from each other, including their experiences with psychiatry, and because their conflicts and the way to cope with them are as different as their personal biographies and resources, a reflection of these actual differences is no less important than the consideration of commonalities. These differences of opinions center primarily around such questions as whether the psychiatric system can be reformed from inside, whether self-help groups should take money from drug companies[1] and whether psychiatric drugs are more helpful or more damaging.

User Control via the Internet

A substantial contribution to international networking is made via the internet, which is largely free from censorship and the exertion of power—except in totalitarian countries like China. (Ex-)users and survivors of psychiatry from all countries can communicate with each other as easily as otherwise lonely and isolated individuals.

The co-operation among groups of common interests representing other discriminated persons, for example people with disabilities, has increased considerably over the last few years. A rapid exchange of information and its inexpensive dissemination to the media as well as to political decision-makers, can be seen as an important step toward user control in all areas that are relevant to (ex-)users and survivors of psychiatry.

However, there is still an under-use of the internet. Today there are tools such as wiki, web-based discussions, uploading photographs and videos on Google and YouTube, SecondLife, videoconferencing, audio, blogs, text messaging, podcasts, content management system web sites, open source software, etc., that (ex-)users and survivors of psychiatry do not use very much. Compared to the youngsters who grow up with these media, they use blogs, videos, networking, etc., rather poorly. And there are not enough active and competent activists in the movement to cover all possibilities and tasks.

---

1   ENUSP rejects money from Big Pharma on principle and it supports the position paper by the European Public Health Alliance from 2001 about the independence of patients' organisations: all organizations that accept funds from the pharmaceutical industry should, at a minimum, determine an upper limit to the proportion of industry sponsorship and their total income; they should also articulate clearly the role of the sponsoring body in relation to sponsored projects and to the organisation as a whole in their statutes (see www.enusp.org/documents/epha-participation.htm).

Needless to say, declarations or the internet cannot by themselves solve internal problems which beset even the self-help movement. There are always know-it-alls who claim a hold onto the truth or those who want to appear as "most concerned." Better funding of certain organizations or a linguistic predominance of English-speakers on international communication lists can put people working under less favourable conditions at a disadvantage. Some folks use communication lists as a vehicle for self-promotion, and the limited knowledge of English by (ex-)users and survivors of psychiatry from countries where only small proportions of the population learn this language, is not always taken into consideration. Many (ex-)users and survivors of psychiatry are thus thoughtlessly excluded from the international internet discussion. Therefore, ENUSP informs the participants of its mailing list of the following:

> English is one language within the European Network. Other languages spoken by a lot of members are Russian, German, French, Spanish, Croatian, Serbian, Greek, Rumanian, etc. Please always be aware that writing in English may be very easy for native English speakers, but very hard for all others if they want to communicate on the same level. Therefore, non-native English writers should be supported by the use of concise communications with short sentences, simple words, no slang, and no abbreviations other than well known ones like ENUSP, WNUSP, WHO, USA, UN. A short summary at the head of a document might also be very helpful, especially when distributing long texts.[1]

Due to the fact that user control is never a goal of psychiatric reforms, its promotion is left exclusively to the movement of (ex-)users and survivors or psychiatry. The following two examples show how the internet can be used as a medium for approaches to user control.

Examples of Effective User Control

The critical response of many (ex-)user/survivor-organizations and their supporters to the European Parliament "Draft Recommendation of the Com-

---

1   See www.enusp.org/discussion

mittee of Ministers to member States to ensure the protection of the human rights and dignity of people with mental disorder, especially those placed as involuntary patients in a psychiatric establishment" clearly demonstrated the value of the internet for user control. The blueprint of this so-called ethics convention by the European Parliament from 2000 included the right of psychiatry to commit people to psychiatric hospitals without court order, employ forced electroshock, and impose involuntary treatment even in the privacy of a person's home. Even though psychiatry did ultimately succeed at having these human rights violations covered by the convention, the user/survivor protests delayed its ratification for quite a long time. This revealed rather starkly the reactionary positions taken by relatives' organizations sponsored by the pharmaceutical industry, who felt that even these endorsements of psychiatric power did not go far enough.[1]

Another example is the struggle against the introduction of outpatient commitment statutes in Germany, which is still going strong. The rapid distribution of critical documents to the media and politicians played an equally central role in this fight; the nearly simultaneous overview and documentation of the relevant discussions presented on the autonomous website of the German Union of (ex)-users and survivors of psychiatry also played a meaningful role.[2]

Elitist Internet?

The argument that the internet is a rather elitist business favoured by well-off young people of primarily male gender and white skin which has little to do with the immediate interests of (ex-)users and survivors of psychiatry, is brought forth frequently. This might indeed be true for many people who are impoverished, elderly, or lacking education and/or internet access, or who may live in places where the internet is still not commonly available. But we should not underestimate people's ability to learn in general and in particular the capacity of people in Africa, South America and Asia (especially in India and Japan) to use the internet. We know that its use is quite widespread there

1 See www.enusp.org/wp
2 See www.bpe-online.de/1/bremen.htm

with regional variations. And everywhere there are helpful individuals who are eager to share their knowledge with others.

Given these often inadequate conditions, the following consequences should be considered:

- Self-help groups should facilitate the use of the internet medium.
- We have to demand continuous internet access in psychiatric facilities, especially locked units, but also day treatment centres and community residences.
- Occupational therapy should no longer engage in basket weaving, but rather assist people in gaining access to the worldwide web, etc.
- Telecommunication in psychiatric units should not be limited to a public phone that affords no privacy, but rather offer computers around the clock with internet access, sound cards, loudspeakers and microphones that enable an exchange with self-help groups, relatives, friends and other supporters, as well as contacts with advocacy organizations and ombudsmen and -women.

Peter Lehmann, one of the co-authors of this article, has presented the demand for equipping psychiatric institutions with internet access at the plenary session of the World Health Organization on the occasion of World Health Day in April 2001. He had been invited along with Gregoire Ahongbonon, representative of the group "The Voice of the Voiceless" from the Ivory Coast, as the spokespersons of (ex-)users and survivors of psychiatry from around the world.[1] Gregoire Ahongbonon reported about mad people who had been chained by their relatives to trees for many years, locked in chicken coops, or tortured in other ways, thereby reinforcing the worldwide campaign towards a guarantee of the human rights of (ex-)users and survivors of psychiatry.

There are some examples of successful internet campaigns against the catastrophic conditions within psychosocial services for (ex)users and survivors of psychiatry, for example, in countries like Romania[2] that are not in the centre of European and Anglo-American interests. Such campaigns suggest that

---

1 See www.peter-lehmann-publishing.com/articles/genf_2001.htm

2 See www.enusp.org/documents/poiana/overview.htm

the demands for unrestricted internet access and for basic liberties and quality of life are not in opposition or mismatched to each other, but are rather complementary elements in this worldwide struggle.

Informational Pages and Communication Lists

The amount of information offered by (ex-)users and survivors of psychiatry on the internet has become so vast that overview-pages have become an essential tool for getting oriented. As an example, www.enusp.org/links offers links to independent international and national organisations in all continents, as well as sources of information about psychiatric drugs (special topic *Coming off)*, electroshock and insulin coma, and much more. By now there are a multitude of e-lists in several languages addressing various themes[1], among others:

- *Abuse in Therapy* is an inclusive, international e-list for psychiatric consumers/survivors, and those practitioners and others who are combating physical, sexual, and psychological assaults by mental health professionals and struggling to uplift all caring systems.
- *Antipsychiatric Humour*: Humour against Psychiatry.
- *ENUSP Discussion List:* the electronic arm of the European Network of (ex-)Users and Survivors of Psychiatry, with the purpose to communicate, exchange opinions, views and experiences in order to support each other in the political and social struggle against exclusion, injustice and discrimination.
- *INTERVOICE:* International Network for Training, Education and Research into Hearing Voices; an online community for people hearing voices and others who are interested in this phenomenon from a personal or scientific perspective.
- *MindFreedom-Global:* Networking site about news and campaigns regarding international activities, especially outside of the USA. Here you can find out how you can help MindFreedom International Committee campaigns toward the United Nations and the World Health Organization.

---

1 For an overview see www.peter-lehmann-publishing.com/info/mailinglists.htm

- *MindFreedom-News*, a public occasional announcement list with news and alerts primarily about winning campaigns for human rights and alternatives for people affected by the mental health system (reaching more than 10,000 people)
- *MindFreedom-Zapback:* This list is dedicated to supporting MindFreedom's campaign to end the use of electroshock.
- *Coming off Psychiatric Drugs* for people who want to take themselves off all kinds of psychiatric drugs (neuroleptics, antidepressants, lithium, carbamazepine, psychostimulants and tranquilizers) on their own and want to end addiction, recover from withdrawal syndromes and avoid ending up in the doctor's office once again. Also, there are special lists for people who want to share information about risks and withdrawal possibilities connected with "antipsychotics", antidepressants and benzodiazepines.
- *WNUSP Mailing List:* the electronic arm of the World Network of Users and Survivors of Psychiatry, focuses on global topics.

It is obvious that the internet can only be a means towards achieving certain goals. It does not replace personal engagement and direct communication, especially not the constructive confrontation with oneself and with others when trying to recognize and work on the problems that have led to psychiatric intervention.

Internet communication can certainly become more personal through the use of microphones and cameras, and telephone- and video-conferencing or simply chatting on Skype can alleviate this problem a little bit, which will especially have a positive impact on international relations. But we must not forget that many e-lists turn out to be rather ephemeral: people write one mail after another and spend a major part of their life in front of the screen. Once they have unloaded their frustrations, the energy has dissipated into the ether without anyone drawing conclusions or moving into action mode, like trying to find money for projects, start working groups or initiate campaigns.

Conclusion

Considering the differences that have repeatedly led to disempowering misunderstandings and confrontations within the movement of (ex-)users and survivors of psychiatry, we should all be aware of the tensions that operate both openly and covertly and can always lead to further confrontations. These are on the one hand the individual needs of the (ex-)users and survivors of psychiatry, who have the right to define their own conflicts, needs and willingness to engage in risk. And on the other hand the danger that comes from the power exerted by biological as well as community psychiatry, irresponsible politicians and the profit-oriented drug industry.

This tension can only be reduced successfully if consumers of psychotropic drugs as well as those who are given these drugs forcibly are guaranteed the following: 1) human rights irrespective of diagnoses[1]; 2) easy access to financial compensation when necessary; 3) a right to help without psychotropic drugs; and, 4) appropriate alternative non-psychiatric help.

The internet can support these goals in at least the following ways:

1. to mobilize people for certain campaigns.

2. to enable psychiatric patients to obtain user/survivor oriented information much quicker than previously, for example about psychiatric drugs, electroshock, natural healing methods, and non-medical alternatives to the psychiatric system. The internet can also provide information about holistic and humanistic approaches that explain and help overcome emotional problems and demoralization. With these resources, the internet can be useful in challenging the primitive mechanistic biological (reductionistic) image of humanity and presenting alternative points of view that promote our self-help potential.

3. The internet can facilitate interactions between persons who have dealt with the same kinds of problems and—perhaps—solved them. This increases the possibility of getting helpful advice.

Therefore, correctly used, the internet can deliver meaningful support, no matter if the psychiatrized people are imprisoned in a chicken-coop in Ivory Coast, in a cage-bed in Austria, an isolation ward in USA or if they carry the imprisonment in the form of a neuroleptic depot injection within their own bodies.

---

1   It should not be possible to disregard a human (or civic) right because of a psychiatric diagnosis or of disability.

Thus we can identify three cornerstones of the use of the internet by and for (ex-)users and survivors of psychiatry in the modern age of self-help:
- better possibilities for spreading information,
- support in bringing hope and breaking isolation,
- and mutual support.

Translation by Peter Lehmann, Mary Murphy and Peter Stastny

Why We Need Alternatives to Psychiatry

Introduction

Psychiatry has been continuously developed and reformed right from its beginnings. The quality of psychiatric training is improving, better psychiatric drugs are being developed as well as better electroshock and more precise diagnostic systems; more modern facilities are being set up, the planning and coordination of services are being optimized, more money is being spent, more jobs created—and everything is going to be fine. You can see in contemporary psychiatry where the reforms of recent years have led.

In April 1999, I (P.L.) took part in the conference "Balancing Mental Health Promotion and Mental Health Care," in Brussels, an event organized by the WHO and the European Commission (the Executor of the decisions passed by the European Council of Ministers and the European Parliament). Along with an estimated 70 government officials, people active in psychiatry and other representatives from organizations of interested parties in the psychosocial sector, I was invited as a representative of the European (ex-)users and survivors of psychiatry and was asked to present a paper on our position. At the end of the conference, when a draft of a consensus paper was presented, not one single proposal of ours on the promotion of mental health or psychosocial care was included.

I had asked, among other things, for the support of self-help and non-medical approaches, the active involvement of (ex-)users and survivors of psychiatry in political decisions on psychiatry and—with a view to strengthening human rights—for the emphasis to be placed on the freedom of choice of treatment. Not one psychiatrist nor one representative from the relatives associations (sponsored by the pharmaceutical industry) supported this position. It was only after the intervention of the Chair of the conference and representative of the European Commission, Alexandre Berlin, who apparently did not find the proposals so strange, that they were included in the consensus paper (World Health Organization / European Commission 1999) which was later adopted by the Conference of Health Ministers together with a lot of other papers (albeit without any progress on the proposals so far).

In view of current power structures as the example demonstrates, would it not be more sensible to put our energy into the reform of psychiatry rather than trying against all the odds to develop an alternative to psychiatry under such difficult conditions? But is a qualitative reform at all possible without a switch of paradigms? Assuming this, what might an alternative psychosocial system look like?

Source

World Health Organization / European Commission (1999). *Balancing mental health pro-motion and mental health care: A joint World Health Organization / European Commission meeting.* Booklet MNH/NAM/99.2, Brussels: World Health Organization / European Commission [Consensus paper retrieved January 4, 2007, from www.enusp. org/consensus].

Translated from the German by Mary Murphy

Marc Rufer

Psychiatry: Its Diagnostic Methods, Its Therapies, Its Power

Neuromythology and Psychoeducation

The critics of psychiatry have been quieter for some time now, in fact almost completely silent. Psychiatry has succeeded in recent years in very much improving its image, an image that had been rather severely damaged in the 1970s and 1980s. Psychiatrists have been aided in this by a development in which they were not at all involved: the major advancement in neurobiology.

Neurobiology is booming, governments and industry are investing billions. The media have blown up the findings of brain research into a huge success—brain research, *the* "science of the century," is in the process of becoming the new social science. A new mythology has emerged—neuromythology (see Rufer, 2006). The prominent neurobiologist Antonio Damasio is convinced that we will soon understand "how we experience happiness, sadness, desire and pain, and even the mechanisms of consciousness will no longer be a mystery" (cited by Kraft, 2004, p. 21). No one is appalled when the psychiatrist Brigitte Woggon proposes her reductionist vision of humanity: "Everything that we feel is simply chemical: being moved by looking into the sunset, love, attraction, whatever—they are all biochemical processes, we have a laboratory in our heads" (cited by *Alles*, 2000, p. 54),

The zeitgeist supports the notion that only neurobiology will be able to provide definitive answers not only to questions of mental capacity, but also to the problem of mental disorders. There is hardly anyone who has not heard that the balance of neurotransmitters determines how we feel and whether we are healthy or "mentally ill." The fact that we are dealing with an unproven hypothesis is being ignored. Thus the "knowledge" that psychological problems, even mild impairments in mental wellbeing have to be treated with psychiatric drugs is commonly accepted. What has been forgotten is the fact that human beings are formed by their culture—right down to the roots of their cognitive capacities and emotionality. Needless to say, culture also determines the incidence, form and course of all disturbances in wellbeing.

For psychiatry today, social causes of mental disturbances have lost almost all significance. The life circumstances and the biography of the individual is only of interest to psychiatrists for tactical reasons: "The social background of patients has an effect on their willingness and ability to cooperate and on whether they take their medication regularly" (Finzen, 1998, p. 62).

At the center of the interaction between psychiatrists and their clients is the search for symptoms which determine the diagnosis and the type of psychiatric drugs to be prescribed. Under such conditions, no equitable relationship can develop between doctor and patient. In all of this, we forget that only the knowledge that stems from the relationship of trust between two people can create the kind of consciousness that is the goal of every reasonable psychotherapy (Erdheim, 1988, p. 128). What counts today is an improvement in compliance, the willingness of pliant and submissive patients to take their prescribed medication obediently and without fail. In such circumstances, psychotherapy is being degraded to psychoeducation and thereby loses its potentially liberating and healing effect. "The term psychoeducation means systematic, didactic-psychotherapeutic interventions intended to inform the patients and their relatives about the illness and its treatment" (Wienberg, 2001, p. 189).

Psychoeducation aims at turning the patients and those close to them into experts about their respective mental disturbance, illness or disability (ibid.). This results in the internalization of the biological models and hypotheses. This is what clinical psychiatrists mean today when they speak about psychotherapy: for instance, someone who has been diagnosed as schizophrenic should be taking neuroleptics for many years. They must participate in a psychoeducational program to make sure that they do not become noncompliant within one year (i.e., decide autonomously to stop taking the drugs), like 50 percent of their peers, or within two years, like 75 percent (see Marder, 1998, p. 21).

By turning patients into competent pill-takers something occurs in hospitals and medical offices which should in fact be avoided. After all, everyone knows that even "psychotic" symptoms can disappear without being treated. This applies both to "manic states"—it is part of the way the condition is defined—as well as to the "schizophrenias." The psychotherapeutic treatment of schizophrenia without the use of psychiatric drugs is superior to treatment with psychiatric drugs or has a better prognosis. This has been demonstrated repeatedly (Goldblatt, 1995; Karon, 1989; Mosher & Menn, 1985; Perry, 1980; see also the contribution by Theodor Itten in this book). The same applies for "unipolar depression" (Steinbrueck, *et al.*, 1983). Furthermore it should not be forgotten that states described by psychiatrists as "psychotic" are within the range of normal human experiences or reactions (see Bock, 1999, pp. 29/346; Dittrich & Scharfetter, 1987; Erdheim, 1982, pp. 418/431; Rufer, 1998, pp. 531-532; Kernberg, 1978, pp. 51-52/76; Simoes, 1996). They may be understood as unusual states of consciousness (USC) or as (psychotic) regressions. USC—clinically not different from "acute paranoid schizophrenia"—can be triggered in anybody, by, among other things, through sensory deprivation, fasting, sleep deprivation, hyperventilation or by taking hallucinogenic drugs (see Dittrich & Scharfetter, 1987; Simoes, 1996).

Traumatization in Psychiatry

The advance of neurobiology described here was loudly celebrated by the media and makes any criticism of psychiatry almost impossible. The taboo which has already obstructed a clear unprejudiced view of psychiatry has become even more immutable, as if written in stone. "When people no longer dare to question or no longer even think about it, then we are dealing with a taboo" (Mitscherlich & Mitscherlich, 1977, p. 111). The taboo regulates attitudes towards a subject like an authority that does not tolerate any objections. This inhibits thinking and interferes with further understanding. As a result the damages caused by forced psychiatric measures are rarely acknowledged publicly.

Compulsory treatment is *the* major problem in psychiatry. But nevertheless the social psychiatrist Asmus Finzen, basically a considerate man, speaks of the right of patients to be helped against their will:

> There are situations in which the mentally ill have the right to be helped against their will (1993a).
>
> If the formal and definitional prerequisites are given—if there is a severe mental illness which impairs or eliminates the capacity for judgment of the person in question, then it is not only the right of society to compel such treatment. In such situations, we believe that the mentally ill person has a right to receive this treatment. If we deprive them of this even in the name of freedom it is not only an attack on their dignity. It is pure barbarism (ibid.).

Elsewhere, Finzen judges the behavior of those unwilling to be subjected to compulsory treatment even more harshly: "And one has to confront the fact that many people will speak of crimes against humanity and of barbarism in such situations—myself included" (Finzen, 1991, p. 213).

In the final analysis, forced treatment is always triggered by a refusal to swallow the prescribed psychiatric drugs. But there are good reasons for such refusals: treatment with psychiatric drugs is controversial and their therapeutic effects unproven (see Rufer, 2001). The damaging, at times even fatal, effects of the neuroleptics, which are almost always used in compulsory treatments, are in fact well known. Those who "have insight into their illness" swallow the "medication," those who do not, thereby prove their lack of judgment and can be subjected to compulsory treatment. Finzen's statement mirrors precisely the situation in psychiatric hospitals: psychiatrists who— whether in the name of freedom, or in the name of patient or human rights— are not prepared to coerce patients into treatment cannot be tolerated in present-day clinical psychiatry.

When necessary, a "contingency plan" is employed for compulsory treatment: as many as eight aides willing to exercise physical violence face a single helpless patient. Involuntary commitments, often carried out by the police, are frequently a dramatic occurrence involving "take-downs" and physical restraint. In terms of their traumatic nature, these interventions can be compared to rape, torture and sexual abuse (more on this subject in: Rufer, 2005).

For psychiatric patients, this type of traumatization goes along with experiencing the massive gap between power and powerlessness. The traumatic situation results in an overwhelming infantilization of the victim, while reawakening elementary childhood fears. What is happening here has been described as forced regression.The borderline between reality and fantasy becomes blurred. The traumatized ego tries to hold on to the belief that the actual perception of reality is merely a bad dream from which they will awaken shortly (Ehlert & Lorke, 1988, p. 506). The danger is that in that moment the victim might descend into a state of total confusion.

The trauma provokes a feeling of existential helplessness. Once the last vestiges of the victim's resistance have been broken he or she turns into an object at the mercy of the perpetrator. In this situation, regression means that the victim can return to the protection of parental figures which is associated with a desire to merge and to be loved (ibid., p. 509). Out of this arises a desire to be consoled for the suffering by precisely the people who have exercised the violence. The victim tries to behave exactly as expected by the perpetrator, their self-image becomes the same as the image of them held by the perpetrator. In this situation, psychiatric patients begin to believe that they really are mentally ill. Only by accepting the role of a patient—in other words, having insight into their illness—are they able to gain some measure of attention and recognition from those at whose mercy they find themselves.[1]

Splitting and dissociation are the main defensive mechanism with which the ego attempts to deal with such traumatization. The splitting of the ego can later become manifest as a flashback: the victim suddenly sees himself transported back into the traumatic situation. What often remains is a feeling of guilt as well as the tendency towards suicide.

Psychiatric patients experience additional aggravating circumstances beyond just the psychological consequences of the traumatization. They are already burdened by conflicts with relatives, employers, teachers that predated their commitment. Furthermore, they are subjected to the effects of the neuroleptics that impair intellectual capacity, repress the perception of feelings, and promote the occurrence of delirious syndromes or toxic deliria (confusion, disorientation, hallucinations) as well as depression and suicidal tendencies. Thereby, the ability to deal with the consequences of these traumatizations is seriously impaired. This would require as clear an awareness as possible and intact feelings. In addition, the isolation of the patients after forced treatment is devastating. The associated loss of sensory stimuli leads to USC, which includes disturbances of perception and hallucinations. Receiving a diagnosis—especially for the first time—is very difficult to deal with. Psychiatric diagnoses, but in particular the label of "schizophrenia" suddenly transforms the self-concept and thereby challenge the whole identity of a person.

Precisely those symptoms that the psychiatrists claim to treat—confusion, hallucinations and suicidal thoughts as well as the helplessness of the patients—can be worsened, made chronic or actually be caused by their inter-

---

1   The psychodynamics described in this paragraph can explain the intensity of the attachment to their persecutors often experienced by the victims of traumatizing situations. Thus it becomes easier to understand why so many (ex-)users of psychiatry remain in close contact with psychiatry and accept their diagnoses and years of treatment with psychiatric drugs.

ventions. What is happening here is a typical psychiatric vicious circle: in the end, symptoms caused by coercive measures confirm the diagnosis for the psychiatrist and retrospectively justify the exercise of violence. With common sense it should be possible to distinguish between violence and therapy, but in psychiatry this is obviously not the case.

In order to understand this, we need to take a look at the role of psychiatry in society. What is the task of psychiatry? It clearly has a dual function. It is not only meant to help or possibly heal people who are suffering (something rarely achieved, even under the best circumstances); it also has a function in maintaining order and exercising social control. This is most evident in the fact that psychiatrists are authorized to apply coercion and force, a force commissioned by the state. This authority brings psychiatry close to the police and is an extension of their powers. Where state-sanctioned interventions are considered necessary lacking the commission of a crime, the controlling power of psychiatry springs into action: "The mentally ill are the only people in democracies who can have their freedoms curtailed without having committed a crime" (Finzen, 1993, p. 13).

The controlling function of psychiatry is barely noticed since the exercising of force can easily be disguised as help and the best possible treatment. The link to medicine refines these interventions. Sanctions are legitimized as helpful and humane measures.

Questionable Diagnoses Justify Interventions

The media have turned the neurobiological bent of psychiatry into a matter of course. Buzzwords such as schizophrenia, depression and mania are now part of our everyday vocabulary. The magical power of these buzzwords influences not only lay people but they are now embedded in the core of specialized research; even highly renowned scientists areenthralled by them. The meaning of such words can no longer be logically tested.

The psychiatrist thus makes the diagnosis—a procedure with ritual connotations—and so everything becomes clear to everyone:

> Rituals have a pleasantly simplifying and relieving effect. At the same time they block independent thinking and usually serve to diminish the awareness of problems and the opportunities for

change. Rituals are behavioral instructions that are carried out automatically and make the world more manageable; their meaning should not be questioned (Erdheim, 1998, p. 36).

Nowadays psychiatric diagnoses—recorded in the ICD-10, the classification system of the WHO, and in the DSM-IV, endorsed by the American Psychiatric Association—are the most important instruments for creating and maintaining social order and its control. They have gained this status not because they have been scientifically proven but due to a social, economic and political process. The characterization of certain states and forms of behavior as sick or abnormal is an arbitrary social and moral definition signaling a need for action and where necessary resulting in and legitimizing interventions against the will of the patient.

These two psychiatric classification systems form the basis for the practically unavoidable administration of psychiatric drugs. The diagnostic procedures of the two classification systems, which are focused on certain objectively identifiable symptoms, omit the subjective experience of the individual and his/her sense of needing help, which should be the central criteria for diagnosing an illness. The decision whether a mental state is "in need of being altered" is made without input of the patient.

Interestingly, the specialists are in agreement that there is actually no basis for speaking of diseases in psychiatry:

> One only speaks of a disease when the cause, symptoms, course, prognosis and treatment of a disorder are known and uniform or if an underlying concept about this can be formulated. It is for this reason that the term "disorder" was introduced in ICD-10 in distinction from the term "disease" (Paulitsch, 2004, p. 34).

This point is being made quite clearly even in the introduction to the ICD-10: "The term 'disorder' is used in the whole classification system in order to avoid the problematic use of expressions such as 'disease' or 'illness.'" (Dilling, *et al.*, 2005, p. 22) The term "disorder" is also used throughout the DSM-IV—which is called accordingly: *Diagnostic and Statistical Manual of Mental Disorders*. The psychiatric classification systems have eliminated the term disease. The authors of ICD-10 and DSM-IV are in agreement that the foundation of knowledge is weak, so weak in fact that in the area of psychiatry the term "disease" should not be used. This conclusion alone challenges the competence of medicine in the treatment of mental disorders.

Psychiatric diagnoses are described in the specialist literature as constructs. In the journal *Psychiatrische Praxis (Psychiatric Praxis)*, Tilman Steinert refers to schizophrenia, the best known and most important diagnosis in psychiatry as a "fictional, abstracted idea of a disease" (1998, p. 3). Psychiatric diagnoses are also called conventions, concepts, patterns of seeing things, designations or precepts. Finzen writes: "Schizophrenia is a mental disorder that is not understood" (1993b, p. 9). In his article "Is there such a thing as schizophrenia?", the psychiatrist Daniel Hell concludes "that a schizophrenic illness does not exist in this form" (1998).

Among the inner circle of the psychiatric elite, the dearth of well-founded knowledge is a widely accepted fact. But there have been no consequences. The collective psychiatric mindset and the resulting way of thinking have become so well established (for more on this, see Rufer, 2006) that liberating these disorders from their neurobiological-medical corset has become unimaginable. Every discovery is trimmed, switched around and turned inside out until it supports the immutable basic assumptions.

Whoever makes a diagnosis exercises power. A psychiatric diagnosis has far more dramatic effects than the level-headed naming of the actual problems that triggered a crisis, such as conflicts in a relationship or fearing the loss of employment. Diagnoses such as "schizophrenia" or "mania" imply social death. The unique person with its potential for further development is essentially lost. At the same time he or she emerges anew—with a sick identity.

The other side of this exercise of power is the distance created by the diagnosis, which protects the psychiatrists from the often threatening closeness to their patients. Whoever is unwilling to become engaged with the actual feelings of the patients, their history and their sense of being, cannot understand them: they appear strange or mad, they become the fear-inspiring cabinet of monsters of the rejected self (Erdheim, 1993, pp. 167-168). That which frightens must be fought. This is the basis for the coldness and brutality with which psychiatrists often treat those in their care. Psychiatric drugs provide added distance. They transform the hypothesis that the deviation displayed by the patient is biological into a truth: biology—neurotransmitters, molecules, genes—cannot be understood, empathy is impossible. It is nature in its unalterable, pitiless, fateful form.

Even though psychiatrists know next to nothing about the "riddle of schizophrenia"—the title of the book by Heinz Häfner (2000)—they make dramatic pronouncements about their favorite construct. In the words of the well known psychiatrist Nancy Andreasen: "Schizophrenia is probably the cruelest and most devastating of the various mental illnesses" (2001, p. 193). The hospital director Wulf Rössler says on Swiss television in the presence of a psychiatric patient: "It is a very severe, mental illness which has dramatic consequences for the sufferer which go far beyond the disease itself" (2001). Such statements mark the course of the "schizophrenias" as self-fulfilling prophecies.

A calamitous development is set in motion with the diagnosis. It has a decisive effect on the behavior and experience of the (ex-)users and survivors of psychiatry as well as on the expectations of professional and private contacts. Psychiatric diagnoses thus become social roles and identification with these roles turns suffering or disturbing people into "true schizophrenics" who in the end behave as expected of them.

The "cruelty" of "schizophrenia" and of its chronification must therefore be understood as an iatrogenic phenomenon, in other words, caused by the intervention of doctors. This applies just as much to the suicides of psychiatric patients, which have increased significantly due to the wider administration of neuroleptics and antidepressants (more on this in Rufer, 2004; 2001), as well as to the course and prognosis of mania, depression and other mental disorders. Psychiatry therefore remains the institution that, in the short and the long run, "...produces phenomena which in turn become part and parcel of medical science" (Foucault, 1975, p. 74).

Psychiatrists encourage the early detection of "dangerous, schizophrenic psychoses" through general medical practitioners. Thereby, those identified can be treated early with psychiatric drugs—even when they are only considered at-risk. For this purpose the Swiss Early Psychosis Project was formed among others as a branch of the International Early Psychosis Association (IEPA). In Germany, the association "Early Recognition and Early Intervention" of the schizophrenia-specialists network has the same purpose. And this in spite of the fact that the symptoms to be identified are admittedly unspecific (Simon, *et al.*, 2001). Even more questionable than the psychiatric diagnosis of schizophrenia is the identification of an unspecific prodromal phase. Nonetheless, psychoeducation is being used even in this early stage, "to inform patients, adequately, early and realistically about their condition, its prognosis and treatment options" (Bechdolf & Juckel, 2006, p. 18).

Beyond psychoeducation, neuroleptics are prescribed as a matter of course in the "prepsychotic phase." According to the recommendation of the IEPA this treatment can be prescribed for an additional six months or even up to two years if an improvement is observed after six weeks (ibid., p. 78).

All of this concerns patients who have not even been diagnosed as "schizophrenic," but who were careless enough to subject themselves to the critical gaze of psychiatrists and general practitioners—for example young people with difficulties at school, troubled relationships or conflict with parents.
In the child- and adolescent psychiatry clinic at the University of Berne, treatment is started even before there is any certainty regarding the diagnosis: "Since it is very difficult to establish a clear diagnosis sometimes it becomes clear that we were dealing with a psychotic event only after the administration of drugs and the observation of their effect" (Rusch, 2001, p. 21).

We have to understood that these statements refer to young people between the ages of 12 and 18, who may be going through puberty, a difficult stage of development. The deleterious myth about the specificity of psychiatric drugs remains clearly unbroken: if symptoms viewed by the psychiatrist as distressing have been dampened by neuroleptics, this is taken as proof that a "real psychosis" has been treated.

Increasingly younger children are becoming the focus of "psychosis" hunters": for example, children who get noticed in school due to their social withdrawal, lack of concentration and performance difficulties are scheduled for blood tests to identify susceptibility genes; i.e., gene combinations that are being correlated with a "risk for the disease." If there are any risk indicators, the children are prescribed neuroleptics to prevent a supposedly threatening psychosis (Kompetenznetz, 2000).

The Uncertain Benefits of Psychiatric Drugs

Depressed individuals "need" antidepressants, schizophrenics "need" neuroleptics. Barely anyone questions this today: ideally, the vast majority of psychiatric patients must be treated with psychiatric drugs. Those who are "treatment resistant" are often given huge doses in order to force an effect. Drug treatment is supposed to last a very long time, quite possibly for the rest of their lives. Increasingly, persons diagnosed as "schizophrenic," "manic," or "depressive" are being slated for long-term treatment. In some countries, compulsory outpatient treatment has been introduced, while other countries are considering it. Slow-release implants that provide haloperidol or other drugs for up to a year are being placed surgically under the skin (Siegel, *et al.*, 2002).

The most comprehensive and careful studies on the therapeutic effect of psychiatric drugs have been conducted with antidepressants. In view of the immense consumption of antidepressants and the billion dollar revenues, even skeptics who distrust the pharmaceutical industry and psychiatry are surprised about the fact that good quality work challenging the efficacy of antidepressants can easily be found in the professional literature. Therapeutic resistance is the major problem for those who prescribe antidepressants. According to Woggon the effectiveness of antidepressants prescribed for the first time for people who are either severely depressed or hospitalized for it, is 50 percent (Pöldinger & Reimer, 1993, p. 182; Woggon, 1998, p. 35). But 50 percent of patients hospitalized for depression who receive only placebo also showed a marked improvement within two to six weeks (Zehentbauer, 2006, p. 150). In a variety of other studies, antidepressants were shown to be no more effective than placebos (ibid.; Breggin, 1983, p. 178; Breggin & Breggin, 1994, p. 56; Möller, 1991, pp. 44-45). These findings are lent even more weight in view of the fact that psychiatrists have a bias toward favoring established psychiatric drugs rather than placebos (Fisher, 1993, p. 347). Such biases can distort the results of placebo-controlled studies due to the fact that noticeable side effects can make a true double-blind condition nearly impossible. The strong variation of placebo effects found among different studies show clearly how important the human factor, the atmosphere and in particular the doctor-patient relationship are in every treatment. Placebos incurred an improvement of depression in significantly more than half of the subjects. In some studies, almost 90 percent of the cases showed an improvement on placebo (Breggin, 1994, p. 37).

To this day, the therapeutic usefulness of antidepressants has not been proven (for more on this Rufer, 2001; 2004). This applies not only to antidepressants, but to all psychiatric drugs, especially for neuroleptics, tranquilizers and mood stabilizers such as lithium and carbamazepine (Fisher & Greenberg, 1993, p. 348; 1989, p. 29). On the other hand, the potential for harmful and even fatal effects of different psychiatric drugs has been proven and is widely accepted.

Quite clearly, this indicates that psychiatric drugs have no specific effects. At best they are capable of suppressing or dampening certain symptoms, but in no way are they able to get at the cause of the disorder in the manner of antibiotics, for example, that are generally capable of eradicating bacterial infections. Certain effects of neuroleptics, such as tiredness, impairment of intellectual capacity and memory, and a numbing of emotional perceptions are observed as much in healthy test subjects as they are in people diagnosed with "schizophrenia" (see Lehmann, 1996, pp. 127-138).

What about Electroshock?

Nothing much is heard these days about this psychiatric treatment method which many people associate with torture, cruelty and the electric chair.

But this silence is artificially induced, it is tactical, because according to its practitioners, the reputation of this treatment had become too negative. Since the beginning of the 1980s the professional literature praised electroshock as a good method of treatment, especially for depression, that had only fallen into disrepute due to a "perfidious" campaign in the mass media. Following a temporary reduction in its use, the number of people receiving electroshock treatment has been on the upswing ever since.

Depression is still the most common indication for the application of electroshock treatment; but those diagnosed with "schizophrenia," "bipolar disorder" ("manic-depressive illness"), especially if they are considered suicidal, are also given electroshock. Over the years electroshock has been used for almost all existing psychiatric diagnoses. It is noticeable that women are being shocked far more frequently than men; depending on the source, the ratio is between 2:1 and 3:1. Nowadays, electroshock is usually the second choice of treatment and is used when the physician in charge is not happy with the results of drug treatment, when the patient is "therapy-resistant." And psychiatrists are often dissatisfied. Fritz Reimer, the former Chair of the German Society of Psychiatry and Neurology was speaking for his colleagues when he said: "I hope that soon all of us will be shocking" (cited by Förster, 1988, p. 22). Reimer's wish has largely been fulfilled. Many psychiatric hospitals that had stopped using shock during the 1970s, are employing it again on a regular basis.

Electroshock is always applied as a series of treatments; for "depression" it is generally six to 12, for "schizophrenia" and "bipolar disorders" 15 to 25 shocks. Today electroshock is occasionally used on an outpatient basis. Furthermore, there is the tendency following the completion of a series of electroshock to continue long-term or maintenance treatment for months or even years. In the past, fractures often occurred due to the strength of the convulsions, with the consequence that today the procedure is almost always given under anesthesia and drug-induced muscular paralysis. A current of 100 to 500 volts is run through the brain for 0.2 to 8 seconds. This triggers a grand-mal seizure lasting 30 to 60 seconds. Electroshock causes damage to nerve cells and blood vessels, associated with punctiform bleeding and increased permeability of the blood-brain barrier.

Depending on the number and intensity of the electric shocks, the patients suffer afterwards from a more or less pronounced acute organic brain syndrome characterized by: disorientation to time, space and person, memory disturbances, especially in relation to recent events. There is also a general disturbance of intellectual functions such as understanding, learning and abstract thinking as well as an impairment of judgment and critical ability and blunted or inappropriate emotional reactions alternating between euphoria to apathy, frequent severe headaches, nausea, physical exhaustion and feeling unwell as well as dizziness and unstable gait. The patients feel helpless and afraid. Gaps in memory lasting several weeks become irreversible.

The highly praised modifications have in fact increased the dangers associated with the electric shocks since the anesthetic and muscular paralysis represent an additional risk. This applies also to unilateral electric shocks since more intense or longer lasting currents must be used in order to achieve the results desired by the psychiatrists. Another variant of electroshock is short-pulse stimulation. While the pulses are shorter, the amount of energy per pulse is greater and, therefore, this is not an improvement. The American psychiatrist John Friedberg put it this way to Mark Smith of the *Houston Chronicle*, when he reported in 1995 on eight fatalities occurring in 1500 electric shocks in a 15-month period: "'To me it is just another big lie that the machines are safer,' Friedberg said" (Smith, 1995, p. 6A). There is nothing more to add to this.

Conclusion

Disturbing behavior as well as the suffering and desires of people should no longer be viewed as symptoms of illness. They must be separated from a diagnostic practice that justifies intervention. Every kind of sensible help for those in need, especially psychotherapy must be given without recourse to closed doors, coercion, violence, psychiatric drugs, electric shock and psychiatric diagnoses.

Through the omnipresent and undisputed claim to the truth of neurobiological thinking, psychiatric power and its effects are hardly noticed and tacitly accepted by most. Only those who have freed themselves from the deleterious neurobiological basis of psychiatry are in a position to offer real help to people in emotional difficulties. Because only then is it possible to approach the problems and needs of the patients in an open and unbiased manner.

Sources

Alles, was wir fühlen, ist Chemie. Glück, seelisches Leiden und Psychopillen: Die Pharmakotherapeutin Brigitte Woggon debattiert mit der Psychoanalytikerin Brigitte Bothe (2000, June 8). *Weltwoche,* p. 53-54.

Andreasen, N. C. (2001). *Brave new brain: Conquering mental illness in the era of the genome.* Oxford: Oxford University Press.

Bechdolf, A., & Juckel, G. (2006). *Psychoedukation bei Personen mit erhöhtem Psychoserisiko.* Stuttgart: Schattauer Verlag.

Bock, T. (1999). *Lichtjahre. Psychosen und Psychiatrie.* Bonn: Psychiatrie-Verlag.

Breggin, P. (1983). *Psychiatric drugs: Hazards to the brain.* New York: Springer Verlag.

Breggin, P., & Breggin, G. R. (1994). *Talking back to Prozac.* New York: St. Martin's Press.

Dilling, H., Mombour, W., Schmidt, M. H., & Schulte-Markwort, E. (Eds.) (2005). *Internationale Klassifikation psychischer Störungen.* 5., revised and completed edition. Berne / Göttingen: Huber Verlag.

Dittrich, A., & Scharfetter, C. (1987). Phänomenologie außergewöhnlicher Bewusstseinszustände. In A. Dittrich, & C. Scharfetter (Eds.), *Ethnopsychotherapie* (pp. 35-43). Stuttgart: Thieme Verlag.

Ehlert, M., & Lorke, B. (1988). Zur Psychodynamik der traumatischen Reaktion. *Psyche, 42,* 502-532.

Erdheim, M. (1982). *Die gesellschaftliche Produktion von Unbewusstheit.* Frankfurt/ Main: Suhrkamp Verlag.

Erdheim, M. (1988). *Die Psychoanalyse und das Unbewusste in der Kultur.* Frankfurt/ Main: Suhrkamp Verlag.

Erdheim, M. (1993). Das Eigene und das Fremde. Über ethnische Identität. In M. M. Jansen, & U. Prokop (Eds.), *Fremdenangst und Fremdenfeindlichkeit* (pp. 163-182). Basel / Frankfurt/Main: Nexus Verlag.

Erdheim, M. (1998). Wieviel Rituale braucht der Mensch? *Unimagazin. Die Zeitschrift der Universität Zürich,* (1), 36-38. Retrieved October 23, 2006, from www.unicom. unizh.ch/unimagazin/archiv/1-98/mensch.html.

Finzen, A. (1991). Sozialpsychiatrische Aspekte der Ethik. In W. Pöldinger / & W. Wagner (Eds.), *Ethik in der Psychiatrie* (pp. 206-215). Berlin / Heidelberg: Springer Verlag.

Finzen, A. (1993a, October 9). Hilfe wider Willen. Zwangsmedikation in der Psychiatrie. *Neue Zürcher Zeitung,* p. 13.

Finzen, A. (1993b). *Schizophrenie – die Krankheit verstehen.* Bonn: Psychiatrie-Verlag.

Finzen, A. (1998). *Das Pinelsche Pendel.* Bonn: Psychiatrie-Verlag.

Fisher, S., & Greenberg, R. P. (1989). Examining antidepressive effectiveness: Findings, ambiguities, and some vexing puzzles. In S. Fisher, & R. P. Greenberg (Eds.), *The limits of biological treatments for psychological distress* (pp. 1-37). Hillsdale / Hove / London: Lawrence Erlbaum.

Fisher, S., & Greenberg, R. P. (1993). How sound is the double-blind design for evaluating psychotropic drugs? *Journal of Nervous and Mental Disease, 181,* 345-350.

Förster, A. (1988). Skandal: E-Schock wieder im Aufwind. *Münchner Illustrierte,* (12), 21-22.

Foucault, M. (1975). Macht-Wissen. In F. Basaglia, & F. Basaglia-Ongaro (Eds.), *Befriedungsverbrechen* (pp. 63-80). Frankfurt/ Main: EVA.

Goldblatt, D. (1995). Die Psychose durcharbeiten. In T. Bock, D. Buck, J. Gross, E. Maß, E. Sorel, & E. Wolper (Eds.), *Abschied von Babylon: Verständigung über Grenzen in der Psychiatrie* (pp. 325-332). Bonn: Psychiatrie-Verlag.

Häfner, H. (2000). *Das Rätsel Schizophrenie.* Munich: Beck Verlag.

Hell, D. (1998). Gibt es die Schizophrenie? *Schweizer Archiv für Neurologie und Psychiatrie, 149*(1), 51-53.

Karon, B. P. (1989). Psychotherapy versus medication for schizophrenia: Empirical comparisons. In S. Fisher, & R. P. Greenberg (Eds.), *The limits of biological treatments for psychological distress* (pp. 105-150). Hillsdale / Hove / London: Lawrence Erlbaum.

Kernberg, O. F. (1978). *Borderline-Störungen und pathologischer Narzissmus.* Frankfurt/ Main: Suhrkamp Verlag.

Kompetenznetz Schizophrenie (2000). Ein Netz für den Menschen. Brochure. Düsseldorf: Kompetenznetz Schizophrenie. Retrieved July 5, 2007, from www.kompetenznetz-schizophrenie.de/rdkns/Dateien/netz-broschuere.pdf.

Kraft, U. (2004). Schöne neue Neuro-Welt. *Gehirn & Geist,* (6), 20-29.

Lehmann, P. (1996). *Schöne neue Psychiatrie, Vol. 1: Wie Chemie und Strom auf Geist und Psyche wirken.* Berlin: Antipsychiatrieverlag.

Mitscherlich, A., & Mitscherlich, M. (1977). *Die Unfähigkeit zu trauern.* Munich: Piper Verlag.

Möller, H.-J. (1991). Antidepressiva: gestern und heute. In H. Hippius, & W. Pöldinger (Eds.), *Phantasie und Wirklichkeit – Fluvoxamin* (pp. 34-55). Berlin / Heidelberg: Springer Verlag.

Mosher, L. R., Menn, A. Z. (1985). Wissenschaftliche Erkenntnisse und Systemveränderungen. Erfahrungen im Soteria-Projekt. In H. Stierlin, L. C. Wynne, & M. Wirsching (Eds.), *Psychotherapie und Sozialtherapie der Schizophrenie* (pp. 105-122). Berlin / Heidelberg / New York / Tokyo: Springer Verlag.

Marder, S. R. (1998). Facilitating compliance with antipsychotic medication. *Journal of Clinical Psychiatry, 59*(Supplement 3), 21-25.

Paulitsch, K. (2004). Praxis der ICD-10-Diagnostik. Vienna: Facultas Verlag.

Perry, J. W. (1980): Psychosis as a visionary state. In I. A. Becker (Ed.): *Methods of treatment in analytical psychology* (pp. 193-198). Fellbach: Bonz Verlag.

Pöldinger, W., & Reimer, C. (1993) (Eds.), *Depressionen.* Berlin / Heidelberg: Springer Verlag.

Reimer, F. (1992, August 3). Statement. In J. Webers, & P. Nuvoloni, *Elektroschocks,* editorial department "Monitor," First German Television (ARD).

Rössler, W. (2001, December 2). Statement. In *Gesundheitssprechstunde.* SF2 (Swizz Television, 2nd channel).

Rufer, M. (1998). Schizophrenie. In S. Grubitzsch, & K. Weber (Eds.), *Psychologische Grundbegriffe* (pp. 530-533). Reinbek: Rowohlt Verlag.

Rufer, M. (2001). Psychopharmaka – fragwürdige Mittel zur Behandlung von fiktiven Störungen. In: M. Wollschläger (Ed.), *Sozialpsychiatrie. Entwicklungen, Kontroversen, Perspektiven* (pp. 225-258). Tübingen: dgvt-Verlag.

Rufer, M. (2004). Ordnungsmacht Psychiatrie. *Widerspruch, 24*(46), 109-124.

Rufer, M. (2005). Traumatisierung in der Psychiatrie. *Rundbrief des Bundesverbands Psychiatrie-Erfahrener,* (4), 11-16. Retrieved October 10, 2006, from www.bpe-online.de/verband/rundbrief/2005/4/rufer.htm.

Rufer, M. (2006). Neuromythologie und die Macht der Psychiatrie. *Widerspruch, 26*(50), 145-156.

Rusch, M. (2001). Stationäre Behandlung von Psychosen bei Jugendlichen. *Pro mente sana aktuell,* (1), 21-22.

Siegel, S. J., Winey, K. I., Gur, R.E., Lenox, R. H., Bilker, W. B., Ikeda, D., Gandhi, N., & Zhang, W.-X. (2002). Surgically implantable long-term antipsychotic delivery systems for the treatment of schizophrenia. *Neuropsychopharmacology, 26,* 817-823. Retrieved July 8, 2007, from www.acnp.org/citations/Npp112801212/.

Simoes, M. (1994). Das akute paranoide Syndrom und veränderte Wachbewusstseinszustände (VBW). In A. Dittrich, A. Hofmann, & H. Leuner (Eds.), *Welten des Bewusstseins.* Vol. 3 (pp. 103-115). Berlin: VWB.

Simon, A., Berger, G., & Merlo, M. (2001). Diagnose und Behandlung der Frühphase schizophrener Erkrankungen. *Schweizer Ärztezeitung,* (9).

Smith, M. (1995, March 7). Eight in Texas die after shock therapy in 15-month period. *Houston Chronicle,* p. 1A and 6A.

Steinbrueck, S. M., Maxwell, S. E., & Howard, G. S. (1983). A meta-analysis of psychotherapy and drug therapy in the treatment of unipolar depression. *Journal of Consulting and Clinical Psychology, 51*(6), 856–863.

Steinert, T. (1998). Das Krankheits"bild" der Schizophrenie. *Psychiatrische Praxis, 25,* 3-8.

Wienberg, G. (1997). Gewaltfreie Psychiatrie – eine Fiktion. In: M. Eink (Ed.): *Gewalttätige Psychiatrie* (pp. 14-28). Bonn: Psychiatrie-Verlag.

Wienberg, G. (2001). Vom Objekt zum Subjekt – aus Sicht eines psychiatrischen Professionellen. In Aktion Psychisch Kranke (Ed.), *25 Jahre Psychiatrie-Enquete.* Vol. 1 (pp. 185-203). Bonn: Psychiatrie-Verlag.

Woggon, B. (Ed.) (1998). *Behandlung mit Psychopharmaka.* Göttingen: Huber Verlag.

Zehentbauer, J. (2006). *Chemie für die Seele. Psychopharmaka und alternative Heilmethoden.* 10. edition. Berlin: Antipsychiatrieverlag.

Translated from the German by Mary Murphy

Pat Bracken

Beyond Models, Beyond Paradigms
The Radical Interpretation of Recovery

The word "recovery" was first used to signal an alternative agenda in mental health in a number of prominent survivor narratives. In recent years, the word has been increasingly used in different contexts. Sometimes it is argued that what is needed is a shift from a "medical model" to a "recovery model." The word "paradigm" is also used. In the U.K., the move to a recovery agenda has been presented as a "paradigm shift" in our understanding of mental health problems. In this article, I will argue for a more radical interpretation and suggest the recovery movement is not about shifting from one paradigm to another (or one model to another) but about moving beyond paradigm thinking and models altogether.

First, it is important to be clear about what it is we are seeking an alternative to. Usually, this is presented simply as the "medical model." The problem is understood to be that the medical framing of experiences of madness and distress is wrong and destructive. This medical framing leads to the unnecessary and harmful use of drugs and ECT in a misguided attempt to treat "symptoms." While this is obviously a major problem, I believe that the medical model is only one manifestation of a more fundamental problem: the tendency to see human problems as technical difficulties of one sort or another. I call this the "technological paradigm." This paradigm shapes our most fundamental assumptions about ourselves and the nature of health and healing. It frames the way in which problems show up for us and works to orient our thinking on many different levels. Essentially it promotes a "model-based" way of looking at human difficulties. Through this, it underscores not just the medical model but also most psychological and managerial approaches to mental health. Alongside biological models of "symptom" production, we have cognitive-behavioural models, psychoanalytic models, even social models of different sorts.

The technological paradigm puts issues to do with the development of models, classification systems, comparisons of different interventions, etc., at the centre of the mental health discourse. That this is currently dominant is evidenced by a quick look through the pages of most psychiatric and psychological journals. In this technological paradigm, issues to do with values, meanings, relationships and power are not ignored but they are always secondary to the more important technical aspects of mental health. In this paradigm, the technical aspects are primary. Furthermore, this paradigm underscores the centrality of "experts": professionals, academics, researchers, codes of practice, training courses and university departments. Service users might be consulted and invited to comment on the models and the interventions and the research, but they are always recipients of expertise generated elsewhere.

For me, the recovery agenda and the emergence of a mental health discourse that is user/survivor led presents a radical challenge, not just to the medical model, but to the underlying technological paradigm. This user/survivor discourse is not about a new paradigm or a new model, but reorients our thinking about mental health completely. It foregrounds issues to do with power and relationships, contexts and meanings, values and priorities. In the non-psychiatric literature about recovery, these become primary. As I read it, this literature does not reject or deny the role of therapy, services, research and even drugs but it does work to render them all secondary. For example, when it come to drugs and their use, the literature emerging from independent users and survivors of psychiatry seeks to prioritise access to information about the mode of action, the unwanted effects and debates about efficacy. It also works to ensure that psychiatric drugs are only administered with consent and has exposed the profits made by Big Pharma in the area of psychotropics. It has challenged the ways in which corporate interests have shaped the agendas of university departments of psychiatry and examined how this alliance between academic psychiatry and Big Pharma has worked to shape the very models and classification systems that are used in psychiatry.

In my opinion, we should judge how much the recovery agenda is being accepted by looking at how much prominence is afforded this user/survivor discourse in the training of professionals and academics. The most radical implication of the recovery agenda, with its reversal of what is of primary and secondary significance, is the fact that when it comes to issues to do with values, meanings and relationships, it is users/survivors themselves who are the most knowledgeable and informed. When it comes to the recovery agenda, they are the real experts.

Peter Lehmann and Peter Stastny

Reforms or Alternatives?
A Better Psychiatry or Better Alternatives?

Modern Psychiatry

In line with the biological-medical paradigm, psychiatry presents itself as a pharmacological discipline, rooted in the practice of prescribing psychiatric drugs over the long term. This, in turn, is enhanced by laws that ensure, if necessary through coercion, the administration of these drugs either during hospitalization or in an outpatient setting. The laws also provide for the appropriate methods of surveillance as well as for any additional interventions deemed necessary such as electroshock or psychosurgery. Information regarding risk and side effects is generally withheld—with good reason.

Psychiatry underwent reforms everywhere after World War II. In particular, community psychiatry, also known as "social" or "democratic psychiatry", was developed and further advanced. In several countries, including Germany, many of the large old asylums were replaced by smaller new ones. Inmates were transferred to residential facilities close to their communities. The psychiatrist Harald Neumann longed for some of these community-based satellite facilities as early as 1961 and remarked,

... in the future, the main task of follow-up care provided by state psychiatric hospitals will be to monitor the provision of maintenance medication for discharged schizophrenics in order to keep as many psychiatric patients as possible in the community (1961, pp. 328-329).

Depot neuroleptic drugs played, and still play, a major role in this endeavor:

"... a reliable depot neuroleptic treatment is the absolute prerequisite for therapy outside the walls of the asylum" (Linde, 1976, p. 21).

"With the introduction of the depot neuroleptics, the reliability of the medication can be increased to nearly 100%" (Schindler, 1976, p. 350).

The damages caused by psychiatric drugs that have so far come to light occur even at low doses and after short periods of administration. Adverse effects can be expected, especially in the case of neuroleptics, even after a relatively short period of exposure and even with low doses of low potency substances. Klaus Dörner, one of the most "progressive" psychiatrists in Germany and a prototypical leader of reform psychiatry, explained the modern treatment principle of trying to make "psychological illnesses" disappear:

We temporarily turn the mentally suffering patient into a person with an organic brain disease, with ECT *(electroconvulsive "therapy")* it happens in a more global way, but for a substantially shorter period of time than with pharmacological therapy (Dörner & Plog, 1992, p. 545).

In the meantime, second and third generations of neuroleptics have become available. These so-called atypical neuroleptics, (the first of which, clozapine was developed in the early 1960s) are widely preferred since they appear to cause fewer neuromuscular problems. At first glance, they seem to be subjectively better tolerated. However, the "atypical" neuroleptics are widely suspected of causing increased circulatory problems, abnormal blood cell counts, obesity, diabetes and receptor changes that can lead to chronic psychoses. As early as 2003, Gerhard Ebner, President of the Swiss Association of Psychiatric Medical Directors (who served on Janssen Pharmeceuticals' advisory board regarding the introduction of Risperdal Consta, the first "atypical" depot neuroleptic), had to admit that there were "risks and injuries caused by the so-called atypical neuroleptics":

> It is not a case of fewer side-effects, but of different ones which can be just as debilitating even if the patient isn't immediately aware of them. Therefore, patients can be more easily motivated to take these drugs because they no longer suffer instantly and as much from the excruciating dyskinesias/extrapyramidal side-effects (Ebner, 2003, p. 30).

A critical view is also called for when it comes to the modern antidepressants—because of their sometimes massive adverse physical, mental and psychological effects and associated symptoms of dependency (see Healy, 2001, 2005). Psychiatrists have noted a tendency towards the chronification of depressions since the introduction of the classic antidepressants. This phenomenon is not likely to disappear due to the "down regulation" of serotonin and noradrenalin receptors. Down-regulation results in a degeneration of the receptors as a reaction to artificially raised transmitter levels at the synapses. Marc Rufer expressed the following warning regarding serotonin re-uptake inhibitors (SSRIs): "In the long run, they diminish the effect of serotonin. If the serotonin deficit hypothesis of depression were correct, SSRIs would have to cause rather severe depressions" (Rufer, 1995, p. 144).

No wonder then, that modern psychiatrists rely on clinical recommendations to combine antidepressants with electroshock or to administer weekly "maintenance ECT" on a long-term basis. They claim that modern electroshock has a better response rate than antidepressants. Furthermore, in its current revised form, ECT is supposed to be "only just as strong" as it takes to trigger an epileptic seizure (see e.g., Greve, *et al.*, 2006, pp. 41-42).

Since it is possible to avoid the administration of depot drugs by escaping or hiding and because involuntary hospitalization or outpatient commitment cannot always be implemented, psychiatrists and pharmacologists are working tirelessly on new forms of administration. A vision of the future was presented by the American psychiatrist Frank J. Ayd, "an honored world expert in psychopharmacology" (Kaplan, 2005), as early as 1973:

> I believe that in the near future there will be other new routes of drug administration. It may be possible to impregnate silicone with some of the neuroleptics. If an intrauterine device or a pessary

could be impregnated with a neuroleptic, it may be that a mini dose would be efficacious. We know from experience with the prosta-glandins that absorption from the vagina and uterus is very good. We also are beginning to appreciate more that the administration of medications through the eye, the nasal mucosa, the buccal mucosa, and the rectum bypasses certain metabolic pathways...Thus, in the next few years we may see injectable or implantable psychophar-maceuticals that may have a duration of action from 6 months to a year, as well as the administration of high doses through these routes for those patients who may need them (1973, pp. 9-10).

More than 30 years later Ayd looked once more into the future of his biologi-cal psychiatry: "The odds are high that we are going to develop new drugs that will be better, because that is where the emphasis is right now" (cited by Kaplan, 2005).

In the meantime, we have arrived in Ayd's future. It is already possible to implant a haloperidol depot with a one-year release into the back muscles of rats; molar teeth are also under consideration as depots. Over and above this, T-shirts with microchips sewn into them are already capable of monitoring body functions and transmitting the data to a doctor. Chips implanted in the brain are considered to be the state-of-the-art treatment for people diagnosed with "obsessive-compulsive disorder" who have "unfavorable" responses to psychiatric drugs (Klosterkötter, *et al.*, 2005).

The almost limitless development of synthetic substances goes hand-in-hand with a reform of diagnostics. Psychiatrists are not neglecting the part of the population who, up to now, has not had the benefit of being prescribed psychiatric drugs. The German psychiatrist Hanfried Helmchen and his col-league Bruno Müller-Oerlinghausen pointed in this direction almost 30 years ago:

If we generally search for drugs to treat known illnesses, in this case we are seeking indications for interesting substances...As-suming that our world is becoming ever more artificial and "man-made," and the demands by our modern performance-oriented so-ciety on our mental stability are constantly on the rise, wouldn't it make sense to investigate every possible chemical influence on mental functions with respect to its potential social usefulness? (Helmchen & Müller-Oerlinghausen, 1978, pp. 16-17)

If we were to define contemporary psychiatry in a nutshell, we could isolate its basic elements as follows:

- the administration of multiply combined synthetic drugs
- the additional application of electroshock or other (once again) popular methods of treatment
- the pressure to perfect the diagnostic system
- the desire to expand the pool of potential patients
- the attempt to win over psychotherapists and the associations of relatives.

A practice-oriented rethinking within psychiatry is simply not discernible.

A World That Offers Holistic Help without Relying on Force

Can we imagine a world which no longer espouses the currently standard psychiatric methods? A world in which a human being in dire straits need not fear to seek help, where someone looking for treatment does not risk being unexpectedly locked up, restrained, forcibly injected and only able to regain control of their life after an indeterminate period of time?

If people ask us whether a non-medical alternative to psychiatry is possible, either within the psychiatric system or outside, the answer is yes. However, the hope that the psychosocial system will change of its own accord is basically nil.[1] Reform of psychiatry towards appropriate, effective and low-risk treatment methods with patients being afforded the same legal rights as other "normal" patients is simply not taking place. The psychosocial system does not support in any substantial way the organizations of (ex-)users and survivors of psychiatry or the cooperation with other human rights or self-help groups, nor does it promote forms of living with madness outside of in-

---

1   Successful endeavors include the Santa Clara County Clustered Apartment Project (described in a book published by the American Psychiatric Association), which consisted of a large community of former psychiatric patients in California. These projects are not striving for so-called psychiatric rehabilitation, but for mutual support in a subculture basically viewed as positive. Unfortunately, projects like this are the exception (Mandiberg, 1995).

stitutional settings. It certainly cannot be claimed that the psychosocial system respects or values diversity in life at all levels. Concerning a paradigm shift by honoring human rights and offering real choices and non-medical alternatives, the opinions remain irreconcilably divided. Psychiatry still turns a cold shoulder to the movement of (ex-)users and survivors of psychiatry and its supporters, scorning its proposals for reform along with all the important knowledge it has generated; without political pressure, we can only find the occasional application of protective paternalism.

This is despite the fact that the myriad of potential fundamental reforms and practical alternatives could actually result in a system of support that would live up to its name. In such an alternative culture, people who have been diagnosed as mentally ill could actually regain their dignity. Perennial isolation would be replaced by environments where emotional distress can be overcome together and where the fantastic visions of dangerously talented minds are considered collectively, be they voices, images or unusual beliefs:

> We listen to one another, speak, and then listen again. We tell our truth, convinced of its existence, and we actually consider these perspectives to be truthful. And in this way we open the gateway to personal and encounter the warmth of others. This is the most normal thing that I expect from life.

—so Zoran Solomun (p. 66 of this book)

In an adequately equipped self-help domain, people with emotional difficulties exchange their ideas. Beyond diagnoses, they define their strengths and weaknesses and support each other in efforts to find hope and to break out of isolation. Alone or together, they work through crises via reflection in the group, in therapy or by writing. They confront their past diagnoses, become involved in the politics of psychiatry or view themselves and their surroundings from an holistic and critical perspective. They are able to prevent or minimize recurring crises by staying aware of the risks and leading a balanced lifestyle with diet, exercise, and sleep. They select members of their support system to serve in emergencies and consciously avoid dangerous locations. At times, they can mentally rehearse potentially problematic situations and further defuse crises through the preparation of an advance directive. Relatives, friends and other community members can be included in these kinds of self-care activities if they have learned to be tolerant, creative, and optimistic in painful and confusing experiences and alternate realities, and if they can help create an environment which promotes recovery. The availability of more than adequate mental health budgets and in most countries, substantial insurance coverage as well, can be used to finance a non-medical system of psychosocial help and support structures instead of paying for the management of so-called mental illnesses, as well as for the production and treatment of medical conditions resulting from the use of psychiatric drugs.

If outpatient services, self-help interventions or humanist psychotherapy are not sufficient to deal with the emotional difficulties and to maintain the communication with the individuals affected, crisis intervention is called upon without any duplicitous or isolating measures, and certainly without the exertion of force. Instead of an armamentarium of diagnostic manuals, injections and drugs, the spectrum of help consists of empathy, interest, openness, profound understanding and respect, a safe environment, long-term relationships based on dialogue and psychotherapy and an integrated approach to body, mind and spirit. In collaboration with the individuals affected, according to their wishes (in other words, without any coercion) and with their contacts of choice, supporters try to find solutions to a situation that has gotten out of hand, either in the person's home or at low-threshold crisis centers or recovery-oriented facilities à la Soteria or Windhorse. The insights of people who have been through crises are integrated as a valuable resource. Considering the vast range of choices in such a world, psychiatric facilities (should they still exist) have to compete for clients by sponsoring crisis centers, hotels and meeting places run by alternative associations that offer meaningful activity, work and, if necessary, accommodation.

The staff of psychiatry-free centers support children and young adults with emotional problems within their own environments, take them seriously, approach them with respect and interest, and respect their need for power and dignity. They avoid stigmatizing diagnoses and personality-changing psychiatric drugs. Everyone understands the need to search for sensible psychological and social solutions, as well as the importance of understanding one's own story and the meanings contained in the "symptoms." It is possible to understand a psychological crisis as a turning point and see it as an opportunity to develop and strengthen one's personality. Members of ethnic minorities who have gone through severe crises and their relatives are certainly not excluded from this knowledge. Neither are emotionally suffering people with different sexual orientations, or women in emotional crises or men who cannot fit into their presumed roles in a still-patriarchal world and who are in serious danger of becoming demoralized.

Groups of people with emotional distress are supported by enabling them to set up safe environments in a world which is not always peaceful. Relying on such places makes it possible to find understanding and support for their fears, weaknesses and secrets and to share them safely with others. People in the latter parts of their lives are no longer dismissed as annoying, rather they experience positive attention and we become engaged with them without ulterior motives and by permitting sensual feelings; all the while knowing that they are merely holding up the mirror of our own rapidly approaching future, and that the separation in "us" and "them" does justice to neither side.

Since there are currently no widely encompassing alternatives available that offer humane help, psychiatric ex-users and survivors must learn to make the best of the existing services. This means they need to protect themselves from arbitrary and callous treatment, especially physical harm, influence the quality of the services that are being offered, or advocate for alternatives that have the potential to transform the system.

They get organized, cooperate, conduct research, train themselves and others, practice user control and insist that they be given a share of the responsibility by effectively taking part in decision-making on all levels. Thereby, a modicum of quality can develop within existing services. Ombudsmen and -women and dedicated advocacy organizations can help to turn defenseless psychiatric patients into self-confident clients who assert their civil and human rights and their entitlement to appropriate supports.

Our panoply of choices among current alternative services should serve as an impetus and guidepost for everyone who wants to extract him- or herself from being dependent on psychiatry. At the same time, it is also a wake-up call. Listen up colleagues and friends, all you thousands who have followed the lure of power, money and theoretical or scientific acquiescence, other choices are definitely possible! Alternatives to psychiatry are essential and can be successful with enough dedication and a reasonable degree of financial stability! Humane ways of helping people with emotional problems of a social nature do exist and there is no need to pump them full of chemicals! Why do people experiencing emotional problems in our society not have the option to choose whether they should see a doctor and pick up some pills, or seek help from people who are willing to listen and to jointly seek lasting solutions to their difficulties?

Obviously, the project to build alternatives and to implement humane treatment conditions concerns everyone who is dedicated to healing, recovery, the strengthening of vital energies, and to communities that truly rely on tolerance and equality. This includes nurses, technicians, aides, psychologists, lawyers, social scientists, doctors, social workers, and relatives. Above all, it includes those (ex-)users and survivors of psychiatry who have joined the ranks of the helping professions, whether in spite of, or precisely because of, their experiences. Examples like Loren Mosher or Edward Podvoll show that even psychiatrists can make important contributions, and that neither professional titles nor the underlying training fully determine who people are. It is rather their fundamental humanist values (by which we mean the respect they bear even for their incomprehensible fellow human beings) mutual support, community, and the pursuit of justice, that account for their attitudes and actions. Ultimately these are the elements which make up a system of effective help for people in emotional distress. In particular, the knowledge of (ex-)users and survivors of psychiatry themselves can play a major role, since they are, in the final analysis, along with their families, the only group who have earned their status through their life situations or the impact of the diagnoses given to them. Exchanges of experiences, training in all possible types of self-help skills, and in publicity work are needed just as much as self-critical reflection about social life and behavior and the collective manner of dealing with each other—for in the end, a psychiatric diagnosis does not turn anyone into a better person.

Groups that are critical or independent of psychiatry are usually excluded from public funding. Therefore it is vital for such groups to receive active support or donations. What is stopping you from becoming actively involved in supporting and spreading alternatives beyond psychiatry and in advocating for humane treatment conditions?

Sources

Ayd, F. J. (Ed.) (1973). *The future of pharmacotherapy new drug delivery system.* Baltimore: International Drug Therapy Newsletter.

Dörner, K., & Plog, U. (1992). *Irren ist menschlich.* 7th edition. Bonn: Psychiatrie-Verlag.

Ebner, G. (2003). Aktuelles aus der Psychopharmakologie. Das Wichtigste vom ECNP-Kongress in Barcelona 05.-09.10.2002. *Psychiatrie*, (1), 29-32.

Greve, N., Osterfeld, M., & Diekmann, B. (2006). *Umgang mit Psychopharmaka. Ein Patienten-Ratgeber.* Bonn: Psychiatrie-Verlag.

Healy, D. (2001). The SSRI suicides. In C. Newnes, G. Holmes, & C. Dunn (Eds.), This is madness: Critical perspectives on mental health services (pp.58-69). Ross on Wye: PCCS Books.

Healy, D. (2005). Psychiatric drugs explained. Edinburgh: Churchill Livingstone

Helmchen, H., & Müller-Oerlinghausen, B. (1978). Klinische Prüfung neuer Psychopharmaka. In H. Helmchen & B. Müller-Oerlinghausen (Eds.), Psychiatrische *Therapie-Forschung – Ethische und juristische Probleme* (pp. 7-26). Berlin / Heidelberg / New York: Springer Verlag.

Kaplan, A. (2005). Through the times with Frank J. Ayd jr., M.D. *Psychiatric Times, 22*(1). Retrieved July 12, 2007, from www.psychiatrictimes.com/showArticle.jhtml? articleId= 60400126.

Klosterkötter, J., Lee, S. H., & Schormann, M. (2005, January 1). *Stereotaktische Tiefenhirnstimulation bei therapieresistenten Zwangsstörungen. Eine Information für unsere Patienten.* Letter for psychiatric patients. Retrieved July 12, 2007, from www.zwaenge. de/aktuelles/media/Tiefenhirnstimulation.pdf.

Linde, O. K. (1976). Zum Stand der Psychopharmakologie. Offprint from *Pharmazeutische Zeitung, 121*(43), 1695-1704.

Neumann, H. (1961). Bemerkungen eines Krankenhauspsychiaters zur Dauermedikation schizophrener Kranker. *Medicina experimentalis, 5,* 328-334.

Rufer, M. (1995). *Glückspillen – Ecstasy, Prozac und das Comeback der Psychopharmaka.* Munich: Knaur Verlag.

Schindler, R. (1976). Rezidivverhütung im Zeitalter von Depotneuroleptika und sozialer Psychiatrie. *Nervenarzt, 47*(5), 347-350.

Translated from the German by Mary Murphy

Index

About the Authors

Volkmar Aderhold, born in 1954. M.D. Doctor of psychiatry, psychotherapy and psychotherapeutic medicine, has worked since 1982 in psychiatry, 1996-2006 as a senior physician in the area of psychosis at the Clinic for Psychiatry and Psychotherapy in the University Clinic of Hamburg-Eppendorf. Since 2006, he has been active in the Institute for Social Psychiatry at the University of Greifswald, Germany. Publications include *Psychotherapie der Psychosen – Integrative Behandlungsansätze aus Skandinavien (Psychotherapy of Psychosis: Integrative Treatment Approaches from Scandinavia)*, in collaboration with Yrjö Alanen, *et al.*, 2003.

Laurie Ahern. Psychiatric Survivor, living in USA. Associate Director of Mental Disability Rights International (MDRI). Co-founder and co-director of the National Empowerment Center, Inc., a federally-funded recovery and technical assistance center. Former vice president of the National Association of Rights, Protection and Advocacy (NARPA). Recipient of the National Mental Health Association's Clifford Beers Award and the Bazelon Center for Mental Health Law's Advocacy Award. Co-author/investigator of the both MDRI-reports: *Hidden Suffering: Romania's Segregation and Abuse*

of Infants and Children with Disabilities (2006) and *Behind Closed Doors: Human Rights Abuses in Psychiatric Facilities, Orphanages and Rehabilitation Centers of Turkey* (2005).

Birgitta Alakare. Psychiatrist, psychotherapist (advance specialist level) and family therapy trainer, living in Finland. Working in Western Lapland District both in outpatient clinic and Keropudas Hospital since 1982. Involved in developing practices with people suffering from psychosis or showing its first signs.

Karyn Baker has worked in mental health since 1983 and has had her own family experience. Since 1996, she has been the Director of the Family Outreach and Response Program in Toronto, Canada. Karyn has developed education and support programs for families using a critical psychiatric perspective. Presently, she has been given the lead role in Toronto to develop programs for families with a relative recovering from first time label of psychosis. For more information, please go to www.familymentalhealthrecovery.org

Ulrich Bartmann, born in 1948 in Westfalen, Germany. Qualified psychologist and psychotherapist. While studying, worked in substance abuse services and as a teacher in technical colleges and specialized secondary schools for social pedagogy. From 1976 until 1996, he worked as a behavioral therapist in psychiatry. 1989 Doctorate work on the therapeutic effect of slow jogging on the psyche. Since 1996, he has been a professor of Social Work Methods at the University for Applied Sciences at Würzburg – Schweinfurt, and faculty leader for the track "Social work with individuals who experience substance-related and mental health problems." Supervisor for behavioral therapy. Published works: *Joggen und Laufen für die Psyche. Ein Weg zur seelischen Ausgeglichenheit (Jogging and Running for the Mind: A Path to Spiritual Balance),* 4ᵗʰ edition 2005, as well as publications about addiction disorders, clinical social work and quality assurance in social work.

Agnes Beier, born 1961. Art exhibits of paintings and written texts, public readings of her own poetry, and publications in anthologies. More information at www.pbase.com/agnesbeier

Regina Bellion, born 1941, in the Federal Republic of Germany, cleaning-woman, factory-worker, haute-couture sales-woman, teacher, waitress etc. Today living in early retirement in a rural intentional community near Bremen.

Wilma Boevink, born 1963, social scientist, an active member of the Dutch user-movement in psychiatry and board member of the European Network of (ex-)Users and Survivors of Psychiatry (ENUSP). Working in Utrecht at the Trimbos-Institute (the Dutch Institute of Mental Health and Addiction). She is the leader of a user-led training and consulting company in the area of recovery, empowerment and experiential expertise of persons with psychiatric disabilities. Since 2006, Chair of Stichting Weerklank, the Dutch organisation of people who hear voices and have psychotic experiences. Publications include *Samen werken aan herste. Van ervaringen delen naar kennis overdragen (Working Together on Recovery: From Sharing Experiences to Implementing Knowledge),* co-author, 2002; *Stories of Recovery: Working Together towards Experiential Knowledge in Mental Health Care,* editor, 2006.

Pat Bracken works half time at the University of Central Lancashire (in the U.K.) where he holds a chair in the new Institute for Philosophy, Diversity and Mental Health. The other half of his working life is spent as a clinician with the West Cork Mental Health Service (in Ireland) where he is a Consultant Psychiatrist and Clinical Director. He co-edited the book *Rethinking the trauma of war* with Celia Petty, published in 1998. His own book *Trauma: Culture, meaning and philosophy* was published in 2002. With his colleague, Philip Thomas, he published the book *Postpsychiatry: A new direction for mental health* in 2005.

Stefan Bräunling, born in 1967, staff worker at the Berlin Runaway House (www.weglaufhaus.de) since 1997. Qualified Psychologist, Master of Public Health. Also works with the Berlin Crisis Services. Father of two children.

Ludger Bruckmann. Born 1947, bicycle mechanic. Since 1980, active in antipsychiatric self-help organisations. Co-founder of the Verein zum Schutz vor psychiatrischer Gewalt *(Organisation for the Protection from Psychiatric Violence)*. Participated at the development and founding of the Berlin Runaway House, working there since the beginning in 1996. Board member of Für alle Fälle *(In Any Case)*.

Giuseppe Bucalo was born in Sydney (Australia) in 1962. Now living in Sicily, Italy. In 1986, co-founder of the *Comitato d'Iniziativa Antipsichiatrica* (Committee of Antipsychiatric Initiatives) and, in 1994, of *Telefono Viola* (www.ecn.org/telviola, Purple Telephone) and *La Sindrome Associativa* (The Associative Syndrome) in Sicily. Since 1996, member of Associazione Penelope in Taormina. Book publications among others: *Dietro ogni scemo c'è un villaggio (Behind Every Fool There Is a Village)*, 1993; *Malati di Niente (Sick of Nothing)*, 1996; *La malattia mentale non esiste (Mental Illness Does Not Exist)*, 1996; *Dizionario Antipsichiatrico (The Antipsychiatric Dictionary)*, 1997; *Sentire le voci (Hearing Voices)*, 1998.

Dorothea S. Buck-Zerchin, born 1917, sculptor. Victim of forced sterilization during the Nazi era. After free artistic activity, taught art and handicraft at the Technical College for Social Pedagogy in Hamburg from 1969-1982. Since 1970, active in the self-help movement. 1992, co-founder of

the *Bundesverband Psychiatrie-Erfahrener (BPE)* (German Federal Association of [ex-]Users and Survivors of Psychiatry), now Honorary Chair. 1989, co-founder of the "Psychosis-Seminars." Countless lectures in Germany and abroad and contributions in specialised journals and anthologies. 1997, awarded with the *Bundesverdienstkreuz erster Klasse* (decoration of the Federal Republic of Germany for service to the community). Publications include *Auf der Spur des Morgensterns – Psychose als Selbstfindung (On the Trail of the Morning Star: Psychosis as Self-Discovery)*, edited by Hans Krieger, 1990; *Lasst euch nicht entmutigen. Texte 1968 – 2001 (Don't Give Up: Texts 1968-2001)*, 2002; *70 Jahre Zwang in deutschen Psychiatrien – erlebt und miterlebt (u. a.) (Seventy Years of Coercion in German Psychiatric Hospitals, Experienced and Witnessed [etc.])*, 2006. Find more at www.bpe-online.de/english/ dorotheabuck.htm

Sarah Carr. Born 1971 in England. Sarah has had lifelong experiences of mental distress, with several diagnoses and treatments along the way. She studied Theology to Master's level. She now works as a research analyst for a social care organisation in London, specialising in service user/survivor participation in research and service development. But her real love is writing and film making, through which one day she hopes to speak the unspeakable.

Tina Coldham has been a user of mental health services since 1990. She has used this experience to promote user/ survivor perspectives in all her work when she became self-employed as a Trainer/Lecturer, Researcher and Consultant. She became active through setting up self-help groups, and also being part of a local campaigning user group. This led to national and international involvement. In 2003, Tina was elected to the National Advisory Panel for MindLink—the user/survivor arm of national Mind, the leading mental health charity in England and Wales, and is a member of the Partners Council at the Social Care Institute for Excellence (SCIE) advising their work. However, Tina still finds time to actively campaign at grass roots level for better mental health services which respect human rights.

Bhargavi Davar finished her Ph.D. in 1993 on the subject of the philosophical foundations of psychiatry and related sciences. She studied existential philosophy and psychotherapy, psychoanalysis, critical theory, anti-psychiatry, the history of psychiatry, philosophies of self, mind and freedom. She also contributed to a critique of psychiatry from women's point of view. In 1999, she created the Bapu Trust (www.baputrust.org), a national organisation advocating for change in the Indian mental health system. She has received several fellowships, grants and awards, including the prestigious Ashoka Fellowship. 2006 she finished a comprehensive study of traditional healing in India situating it in the context of inner life. She has a pas-

sion for research and writing, lives alone with her 1999 born daughter in Pune, India, and is an avid gardener.

Anne Marie DiGiacomo has been working in human services since 1977 in non-profit and community mental health arenas, receiving her Masters of Social Work in 1986. During the first 18 years of her career, she worked with children, adolescents and families in both residential and day treatment settings and private practice. Since 1996, she has worked at Windhorse Associates and Windhorse Community Services in the position of Clinical Director, Co-Executive Director, Admissions Manager and Senior Clinician. Anne Marie is a practicing Buddhist and brings a contemplative perspective to her therapeutic work as a psychotherapist and Sandplay therapist.

Constance Dollwet, born in 1964, grew up in Saarland, admitted to a psychiatric facility in 1986, then started anew in an intentional community of individuals experienced with psychosis in Wederath/Hunsrück. Involved in self-help activities of (ex-)users and survivors of psychiatry with readings, writing seminars, and cabaret acts as "Schizzobaby" together with Bianca Schmid. Book publications: *Schreiben – Mein Weg aus der Sprachlosigkeit (Writing: My Way Out of Speechlessness),* 2000.

Jeanne Dumont, Ph.D. is a researcher and psychiatric survivor living in New York State. She was the principal investigator of the US National Research Demonstration "Crisis Hostel Project."

She has considerable experience conducting concept mappings for theory development, program planning and evaluation. She has also served on numerous mental health related boards, committees and advisory groups. She served as a co-principal investigator for the project "Recovery: What helps and what hinders? A national research project for the development of recovery facilitating system performance indicators."

Merinda Epstein, living in Australia. Active in mad politics since 1991. Winner of the 2004 Australian Human Rights Award for her work with people diagnosed with mental illness. Working for the Victorian Mental Health Legal Centre, a NGO established to defend the legal rights of people with psychiatric diagnoses caught up with forced detainment and treatment, at risk of losing their children under Family Law statutes or embroiled within the criminal justice system. Publications and lectures about human rights issues for women diagnosed with "Borderline Personality Disorder" and the relationship between such labels, childhood abuse and neglect and real or perceived shortfalls of articulated mad politics.

Sandra Escher, PhD, working as researcher at the University of Maastricht, The Netherlands. Honorary Researcher at UCE (University of Central England) in Birmingham. Publications (together with Marius Romme) include *Accepting Voices* (1993; *Stimmenhö-*

ren akzeptieren, 2003); *Making Sense of Voices* (2000).

James B. (Jim) Gottstein. Born in Washington State in the USA in 1953. Juris Doctor from Harvard Law School in 1978. Subject to brief psychiatric hospitalizations in 1982 and 1985. Attorney advocate for people diagnosed with serious mental illness, including the successful billion dollar litigation reconstituting Alaska's one million acre Alaska Mental Health Land Trust and in 2006 the landmark Alaska Supreme Court decision on forced drugging in *Myers vs. Alaska Psychiatric Institute*. He has served and continues to serve on numerous boards and currently devotes most of his time to the Law Project for Psychiatric Rights (PsychRights), whose mission is to organize a serious, strategic, coordinated legal effort against forced psychiatric drugging. More information at www.psychrights.org

Chris Hansen. Born in New Zealand, Chris worked in mental health management until committed to a psychiatric ward. As a result, she became involved in user/survivor politics, including lead roles in the "Like Minds Like Mine" anti-discrimination campaign (NZ) and research from a user perspective on service development and policies. Since 2004, board member of the World Network of Users and Survivors of Psychiatry leading to work as a part of the NZ delegation to the United Nations working on the Convention for Rights of Persons With Disabilities. Currently developing work within USA and internationally, extending her activism to writing, teaching and developing trauma-informed peer support services, particularly alternatives to acute inpatient care. Please find more information at www.mentalhealthpeers.com

Geoff Hardy has been a gay activist since the early 1970s. A trained massage therapist and counsellor (College of Holistic Medicine), he is a Partner at The Natural Health Centre in Shrewsbury.

Petra Hartmann, born in 1969 in Baden-Württemberg, lives in Berlin since 1991. Graduate degree in Education. Two children. Worked in the self-help organization *Wildwasser Berlin*, a drop-in center and consultation service for women who have experienced sexual violence in childhood. Since 2002 she has been working at the Runaway House *Villa Stöckle*.

Alfred Hausotter. Born in 1954. Married with one son. Ph.D. in clinical psychology and health psychology. Between 1974 and 1983 survived several schizoaffective psychotic episodes. Active since 1997 in assisted living. Book publication: *Der GottTeufel – Innenansicht einer Psychose (The God-Devil: An Inner Look at Psychosis)*, 2006.

Michael Herrick was born in 1955. In 1976, became a student of Tibetan Buddhism under Chogyam Trungpa Rinpoche. Master's degree in Contemplative Psychotherapy at Naropa University in Boulder, Colorado, in 1984.

Experience in the mental health field since 1980: worked with the original Windhorse (Maitri Psychological Services) as a Housemate and a Team Therapist under Edward Podvoll. Concurrently worked in psychiatric hospitals for eight years. Five years as a home-based family counselor. Two years in emergency service and partial hospitalization work. Since the early 80s an avid student of the Integral Approach as presented by American philosopher Ken Wilber. 2001 return to Windhorse Associates, Inc. in Northampton, Massachusetts, as Team Leader. Executive Director of Windhorse since 2003.

Guy Holmes is a clinical psychologist living and working in Shropshire, U.K. He specialises in alternatives to psychiatry and challenging stigma through groupwork, and has published in the areas of male victims of childhood sexual abuse and the medicalisation of men's problems. Books include *This is Madness: A Critical Look at Psychiatry and the Future Mental Health Services* (1999) and *This is Madness Too: Critical Perspectives on Mental Health* (2001), both edited with Craig Newnes and Cailzie Dunn. More information can be found on www.shropsych.org

Andrew Hughes was born in 1953 in Rochdale, England. He has been married twice and has four children. He first received mental health services at the age of 17, followed by many periods of madness and several stays in hospitals with compulsory treatment. From the mid-1980s he had involvement in the self-advocacy movement, providing occasional "patient perspectives" and critiques of mental health service provision at conferences and training events. In 1988, he co-founded, together with Anne Plumb and Tony Riley, Distress Awareness Training Agency (DATA), the U.K.'s longest established survivor training group. Since March 2000 he has been self-employed as a trainer, researcher and consultancy worker in mental health and the wider health, social care and disability fields as Mental Health Training.

Theodor Itten. Born in 1952 in Langenthal, Switzerland. From 1971 to 1981 studied psychology at Middlesex and City University, psychotherapy and ethnology in London with Ronald D. Laing and Francis Huxley. Member of the United Kingdom Council of Psychotherapy. Since 1981, has practiced psychotherapy in St. Gallen; since 2003, committee member of the *Schweizer Psychotherapeutinnen und Psychotherapeuten Verband* (Swiss psychotherapists' association). Active for 12 years as council member of the Swiss Foundation *Pro Mente Sana*. In 2002, founded his own publishing company (www.ittenbooks.ch). Book publication: *Jähzorn – Psychotherapeutische Antworten auf ein unkontrollierbares Gefühl (Rage: Psychotherapeutic Responses to an Uncontrollable Emotion)*, 2007. For more information, see www. ittentheodor.ch

Maths Jesperson. Born 1954. From 1980 to 1981, inmate of an old mental hospital. From 1982 to 1988, producer at the theatre company, Mercuriusteatern, as well as local politician of the Green Party in Lund, Sweden. Converted 1984 to Catholicism. Since 1988, regional secretary of *Riksförbundet för Social och Mental Hælsa (RSMH)* (Swedish national organization of [ex-]users and survivors of psychiatry). Founding member of the European Network of (ex-)Users and Survivors of Psychiatry 1991. From 1991 to 2000, editor of the *European Newsletter of (ex-)Users and Survivors of Psychiatry*. Since 1999, writer of cultural articles in a daily newspaper. Parallel research at the University of Lund (faculty of theatre). Since 2000, actor in the *Stumpen-Ensemble*, a theatre group with psychiatric survivors, drug addicts and homeless people as actors. Married in 2004. Lives with wife and daughter in Malmö, Sweden.

Kristine Jones. Ph.D. is an economist working as a research scientist for the Statistics and Services Research Division, Nathan Kline Institute in Orangeburg, NY. Her research has included studies on the impact of having a trauma history on treatment costs associated with persons using mental health services and on the impact of managed care compared to fee for service delivery systems on social cost. She has conducted various cost-effectiveness analyses of specialty mental health services in operation in the U.S. Kristine has also done research on methods of designing payment mechanisms to providers of mental health services.

Hannelore Klafki, inspired by Marius Romme, Sandra Escher and Ron Coleman; was the main founding member of the German Netzwerk Stimmenhören *(Hearing Voices Network)* and was its chairperson for seven years. Since 2003, she was a board-member of the German *Bundesverband Psychiatrie-Erfahrener* (Federal Association of [ex-]Users and Survivors of Psychiatry) and she was a trainer for (ex-) users and survivors of psychiatry, their friends and supportive relatives, as well as sympathetic workers within the psychiatric system; she offered training on such topics as how to deal with hearing voices, empowerment, alternatives to psychiatry, self-help. Book publication: *Meine Stimmen – Quälgeister und Schutzengel. Texte einer engagierten Stimmenhörerin (My Voices—Tormenters and Guardian Angels: Texts of a Committed Voicehearer)*, 2006. When Hannelore died on Sept. 4, 2005, she was only 53 years old. More see at www.bpe-online.de/hannelore/klafki.htm

Miriam Krücke, born in 1979, education as a rehab-pedagogist and systemic consultant, experiences in the mental health system since 1998 and, since 2002, involved in anti-psychiatric activities. Works as the first contact and consultant in the German federal organisation of (ex-)users and survivors of psychiatry (BPE). For her master's thesis on the subject of "Rehab-Pedagogic," she occupied herself with the connections between prevention and independent coping strategies in a psychiatric context. In-training as a systemic psychotherapist.

Peter Lehmann. Born in Calw, Black Forest (Germany). Education as a social-pedagogist. Living in Berlin. Author and editor since 1986, then foundation of Peter Lehmann Publishing and Mail-Order Bookstore. 1989 co-founder of the Association for Protection against Psychiatric Violence (running the Runaway House Berlin). From 1994 to 2000, board member of the German organization of (ex-) Users and Survivors of Psychiatry. From 1997 to 1999, Chair of the European Network of (ex-)Users and Survivors of Psychiatry (ENUSP), since 2003, board member for the North East European region. 2002, co-founder of *Für alle Fälle* (In Any Case) and board member in this organisation. Since 2004, member of INTAR (International Network Toward Alternatives and Recovery). Publications include *Der chemische Knebel – Warum Psychiater Neuroleptika verabreichen (The Chemical Gag: Why Psychiatrists Administer Neuroleptics)*, 1986; *Statt Psychiatrie (Instead of Psychiatry)*, 1993 edited together with Kerstin Kempker); *Schöne neue Psychiatrie (Brave New Psychiatry)*, 1996; *Psychopharmaka absetzen. Erfolgreiches Absetzen von Neuroleptika, Antidepressiva, Lithium, Carbamazepin und Tranquilizern* (1998; *Coming off Psychiatric Drugs: Successful Withdrawal from Neuroleptics, Antidepressants, Lithium, Carbamazepine and*

Tranquilizers, 2004; *Liberarsi dagli psicofarmaci: Riuscire con pieno successo a liberarsi da neurolettici, antidepressivi, stabilizzante dell'umore, Ritalin e tranquillanti*, and Greek edition, 2008, both in preparation). More at www.peter-lehmann.de/inter

Bruce E. Levine, Ph.D., living in Cincinnati, USA. Clinical psychologist in private practice since 1985. Many lectures and workshops throughout North America. Member of the advisory council of the International Center for the Study of Psychiatry and Psychology and the editorial advisory board of *Ethical Human Psychology and Psychiatry*. Regular contributor to *Z Magazine*. Articles and interviews in numerous magazines. Book publications: *Commonsense Rebellion: Taking Back Your Life from Drugs, Shrinks, Corporations, and a World Gone Crazy* (2003); *Surviving America's Depression Epidemic: How to Find Morale, Energy, and Community in a World Gone Crazy* (2007). More information at www.brucelevine.net

Harold A. Maio. I live in Ft Myers Florida, I am husband, father, son, teacher, ceramicist, artist, retired editor. Although I from time to time deal with deep depression, that depression has not stopped my successes, or diminished my goals. One of those goals is to make certain that society acknowledges that the psychiatric industry has mistreated people terribly, and that this mistreatment must stop—in my lifetime.

Rufus May. Living in England. Rufus works as a clinical psychologist working in Bradford mental health services. He is one of the organisers of Evolving Minds a series of monthly public meetings that explore alternative approaches to mental health (see www.evolving-minds.co.uk). He has some writings available at www.brad.ac.uk/acad/health/research/cccmh/index.php

Shery Mead. Born 1953 in USA. Hospitalized in 1970 and several times in the early 90s. In response to the devastation of these hospitalizations, she developed some peer support programs including a peer run crisis alternative. Since that time she has helped develop many more such programs throughout the US. She is the author of a number of academic articles and co-author of two books with Mary Ellen Copeland: *WRAP and Peer Support* (2004) and *Community Links* (2006).

Kate Millett. Born 1934. Lived from 1961 to 1963 in Japan. Ph.D. from Columbia University, 1979. Lives in New York City and on her farm in Poughkeepsie, NY, where she runs an Art Colony for Women. Book publications include: *Sexual Politics* (1970); *Flying* (1974); *Sita* (1976); *The Basement* (1979); *The Loony-bin Trip* (1990); *The Politics of Cruelty* (1994); *A. D.: A Memoir* (1995); *Mother Millett* (2002). More see at www.katemillett.com

Maryse Mitchell-Brody (1984-): Maryse is a(n): organizer, proud tía, revolutionary, day-dreamer, tortured artist, badass facilitator, dancer, loud new yorker, good friend, and mad one. Along with her work with the Icarus Project, Maryse is an advocate for sex workers' rights and a member of the Rock Dove Collective, a radical community health exchange. Born and raised in New York City, she facilitates workshops that examine the links between sexual shame, trauma and emotional well-being, and explore the potential for sex as a healing modality.

David W. Oaks is a leader in the international psychiatric survivors movement also known as the "Mad Movement." He has been a human rights activist to transform mental health care since 1976. He experienced five lockups in psychiatric institutions, typical diagnoses, forced injections, etc. After joining the Mad Movement, he graduated with honors in 1977 and became free of the mental health system using non-drug alternatives. He is now director of MindFreedom International. He lectures in many countries all over the world. He now lives with his wife Debra in Eugene, Oregon, USA. More at www.MindFreedom.org

Peter Rippmann, Ph.D., born in 1925 in Switzerland in Stein am Rhein, began with Germanic studies, has worked over 40 years as a senior editor of the critical biweekly *Der Schweizerische Beobachter (The Swiss Observer)*. Among other topics, he was instrumental in uncovering and publishing articles about the responsibility of the Swiss authorities' in the discriminatory politics of the Nazi-regime vis-à-vis

Jewish refugees. He served as well for many years as board member of the Swizz psychiatry-critical non-profit organisation *PSYCHEX*.

Marius Romme was Professor for Social Psychiatry at the University of Maastricht, The Netherlands, from 1974 to 1999, and afterwards Visiting Professor at the University of Central England in Birmingham. Since 1987 in collaboration with Sandra Escher, he has studied the phenomenon of hearing voices, focusing on the experience of the voice hearers. Together they laid the foundation for the international hearing voices movement and published articles and books, including *Accepting Voices* (1993; *Stimmenhören akzeptieren*, 2003); *Making Sense of Voices* (2000).

Marc Rufer, M.D. Long-standing critic of psychiatric diagnostic systems, psychopharmacology and the use of force in psychiatry. Good contacts and exchange with independent (ex-) users and survivors of psychiatry. Book publications: *Irrsinn Psychiatrie (Insane Psychiatry)*, 1988, 3rd, revised edition 1997; *Wer ist irr? (Who's Crazy?)*, 1991; *Glückspillen. Ecstasy, Prozac und das Comeback der Psychopharmaka (Happy Pills: Ecstasy, Prozac and the Comeback of Psychotropic Drugs)*, 1995.

Gisela Sartori. Born 1952 in Endingen, southern Germany. MA in community psychology from Free University of Berlin. Emigrated to Canada in 1985, and has lived and worked in Canada's far north for the last 20 years. Founder and long-time co-ordinator of Yukon's

Second Opinion Society, a grassroots community organization offering alternatives to psychiatry. Developed an integrative non-medical approach to working with aboriginal and non-aboriginal people in emotional and social distress, and has facilitated workshops all across Canada. Has been involved with the anti-psychiatry movement since 1980, and is a member of the National Association for Rights Protection and Advocacy (NARPA) since 1992, as well as MindFreedom International and International Center for the Study of Psychiatry and Psychology (ICSPP). Former board member of World Network of Users and Survivors of Psychiatry (WNUSP), and since 2004 member of the International Network Toward Alternatives and Recovery (INTAR). Currently training in integrative body psychotherapy and transformational group process. Author of *Towards empathy* (1995), a training resource to help womens' shelters provide equal access for psychiatrized women.

Erich Schützendorf, born in 1949, married with three children. Studied education, psychology and sociology. Adult education program faculty leader on the subject of aging, lecturer for social gerontology at the college of Niederrhein. Over 30 years of interest in people with dementia. More recently, dealing with his own aging process and the development of ideas for life as an an old man, who might one day become dependent on others. Publications include *Das Recht der Alten auf*

Eigensinn (The Right of the Elderly to Obstinacy), 3rd edition 2004; *In Ruhe verrückt werden dürfen (Getting Crazy in Peace)*, in collaboration with Helmut Wallrafen-Dreisow, 12th edition 2004; *Wer pflegt, muss sich pflegen (To Work as a Carer, You Have to Care for Yourself)*, 2006; *In Ruhe alt werden können (Getting Old in Peace)*, 2nd edition 2006.

Jaakko Seikkula, Ph.D., Professor of psychotherapy at the Department of Psychology University of Jyväskylä, in Finland. Clinical psychologist, psychotherapist (advance specialist level) and family therapy trainer. Vice chair of the Finnish Family Therapy Association. He has been mainly involved in developing family and social network based practices in psychiatry for patients with psychoses.

Andy Smith lives on South coast of England with two goldfish and beautiful dawn skies.

Zoran Solomun. Film director, born in 1953 in Pola, Istria. 1973-1977 studied at the Belgrade Academy for Theater, Film, Radio and Television. From 1985 until 1990, leader of the independent film group *Pokret* (Movement) in Belgrade. Collaboration with various people and groups involved in anti-psychiatry. Since 1990, has lived in Berlin. In 1997, founded the film production company *Ohne Gepäck* (Without Luggage) together with Dagmar Fromme. Films include *Ah, jedan podanik!* (Oh! A Subject!), 1989, a documentary about the central psychiatric establishment in Belgrade; *Jedna zardjala ludnica* (A rusty mental institution), 1990, a documentary about alternatives to psychiatry; *Müde Weggefährten* (Tired Companions), 1996, a feature film, awarded the *Max-Ophüls-Prize* in 1997; *Der Chinesische Markt* (The Chinese Market), 2000, a documentary, awarded the *ARTE Documentary Film Prize* in 2001. More information please see at www.ohnegepaeck.de

Peter Stastny was born in Vienna, Austria, where he graduated from medical school in 1976. Since 1978, he has been working and residing in New York City. He is Associate Professor of Psychiatry at the Albert Einstein College of Medicine in the Bronx and has conducted several publically funded research projects in the area of vocational rehabilitation, social support and self-help, in collaboration with individuals who had survived personal crises and psychiatric interventions. Currently, he is working on the development of alternative services that obviate psychiatric intervention and offer autonomous paths towards recovery and full integration. These activities have engendered a close collaboration with the user-survivor movement, as manifested by joint research projects, publications, service demonstrations, and community work. He is a founding member of the International Network Toward Alternatives and Recovery (INTAR)

Chris Stevenson, Professor of Mental Health Nursing in Dublin City University, has 25 years working in the U.K.

as a nurse within psychiatry and on its margins, offering family meetings to people experiencing psychosis and eating distress. Chris is a founding member of the Institute for Mental Health Recovery, Ireland. Over a 100 publications, books and articles. Currently, heading a programme of suicidology research. Altschul award for psychiatric nursing scholarship in 2000. Book publications: *Good Practice Guide* (2005) for working in strategic partnership with people experienced in mental health services; *Care of the Suicidal Person* (co-authored with John Cutcliffe, 2007).

Dan Taylor. Born in 1963, grew up and is still living in Accra, Ghana. Diploma in Journalism and Marketing. In 2004, co-founder of MindFreedom Ghana to fight for human rights and better living- and treatment-conditions for (ex-)users and survivors of psychiatry. He is secretary of MindFreedom Ghana, has published articles in Ghanaian newspapers and abroad, organized symposia on prevention and rehabilitation in the mental health field, is engaged in radio and TV shows, and has organized a protest march against human rights abuses and stigma in psychiatry in July 2006 in Accra with 350 people. Dan calls for support and assistance to accentuate and strengthen the work of MindFreedom Ghana in a developing country like Ghana.

Philip Thomas. Professor of Philosophy, Diversity and Mental Health at the University of Central Lancashire, England. Chair of *Sharing Voices Bradford*, a community development project working with Bradford's Black and Minority Ethnic communities. Co-author of the column *Postpsychiatry* in *Open Mind* magazine. Founder member and co-chair of the Critical Psychiatry Network in Britain. Book publications: *Dialectics of schizophrenia* (1997), *Voices of Reason, Voices of Insanity* (2000, co-authored with Ivan Leudar), *Postpsychiatry* (2005, co-authored with Pat Bracken).

Jan Wallcraft, living in England. PhD in 2002. Manager of the Service User Research Group for England (SURGE) and freelance mental health consultant and researcher. From 1987 to 1992, co-ordinator of MIND's user network, Mindlink. In 1992, co-founder the U.K. Advocacy Network. From 1987 to 1990, member of Survivors' Speak Out's national committee. 1997 to 1999, lead researcher on the user-led Strategies for Living project at the Mental Health Foundation. Author of *Healing Minds* (1998); co-author of *On Our Own Terms: Users and Survivors of Mental Health Services Working Together for Support and Change* (2003); *Being There in a Crisis* (1997); contributions in: *Social Perspectives in Mental Health* (2005); *Mental Health at the Crossroads* (2005).

David Webb, born in 1955, has completed a PhD on suicide as a crisis of the self at Victoria University in 2005 in Melbourne, Australia. This research, motivated by David's personal history of suicide attempts, shows that first-person knowledge of suicidality is necessary to understand suicide, but that the first-person voice is systematically excluded from current suicide research. During his research, he has embraced Mad Culture as a liberating community of people fighting for greater depth, sensitivity, compassion and justice for those struggling for mental, emotional, social and spiritual wellbeing. Prior to his years of madness, David worked in the computer software industry as a programmer, designer and analyst, and as a university lecturer. He has lived in New York, Delhi and London and now lives among the gum trees and parrots on the edge of Melbourne.

Uta Wehde, born in 1963, psychologist. Since 1994, executive director of the *Ambulante Dienste* (Ambulatory Services) association in Berlin. Conceptualization and implementation of the Berlin Runaway House, founding member of the *Verein zum Schutz vor psychiatrischer Gewalt* (Organisation for the Protection from Psychiatric Violence) and long activity on the board. Publications critical of psychiatry, and various contributions. Author of *Das Weglaufhaus – Zufluchtsort für Psychiatriebetroffene (The Runaway House: Asylum for (ex-) Users and Survivors of Psychiatry)*, 1991).

Scott Welsch was born in New York State in 1969. He studied documentary filmmaking at Harvard College and developed manic-depressive symptoms during his senior year in 1990. Among other things, Scott likes music, trees, games, film, chocolate, ultimate Frisbee, and Indian food. Scott especially enjoys the spontaneity of children and is considering a career as a play therapist.

Salma Yasmeen. Living in U.K. Counselling and communication studies. Background as a psychiatric nurse, has worked in both the statutory mental health sector and the voluntary sector. Previously involved in setting up and leading Sharing Voices Bradford, which has pioneered the use of Community development approaches in mental health. 2006, leading and managing a project that is part of a national programme to tackle inequalities in mental health services for black and minority ethnic communities.

Laura Ziegler. Living in USA. In 1976, at age 17 she was locked up, diagnosed, and forcibly drugged until a court ordered it stopped. Active in the mad movement since 1983, she has been a paralegal at a mental disability law clinic, monitored mental health legal proceedings, participated in a half-year homeless protest encampment outside New York City Hall, and expressed her opposition to psychiatric oppression through testimony, whistleblowing, poetry, civil disobedience and street theater. Granddaughter of a victim of T-4. Past president of NARPA (National Association for Rights Protection and Advocacy). Since 1996, she has lobbied for disability rights and prisoners rights at the Vermont Statehouse.

Ursula Zingler, born 1939, married, mother and grandmother. 1975-2004, editor and proofreader at a scientific publishing house. In 1981, workplace harassment caused her depression. Since 1982, involved in the psychiatric reform movement. Committee work beginning in 1983, including as representative of the German federal organisation of (ex-) users and survivors of psychiatry (BPE) in the workshop for further development of psychiatric care at the Ministry of Health. 1991-1993 instrumental in the merger of (ex-)users and survivors of psychiatry on all levels. Board member of the BPE since its founding in 1992. In this role, she took a critical position on various topics. Find more information at www.bpe-online.de/zingler.htm

By Peter Lehmann Publishing

Coming off Psychiatric Drugs
Successful Withdrawal from Neuroleptics, Antidepressants, Lithium, Carbamazepine and Tranquilizers

Edited by Peter Lehmann

Prefaces by Judi Chamberlin, Pirkko Lahti and Loren R. Mosher

Soft cover · 352 pages · 2004
ISBN 978-0-9545428-0-1 (U.K. edition)
ISBN 978-0-9788399-0-1 (US edition)

€ 21.90 · £ 14.99 · CAD 33.60 · CHF 38.-
US-$ 24.95 · AUD 38.20 · JPY 2940

The book has a provocative message, life-experiences sometimes differ from scientific agreements. It is based on the personal experiences of (ex-) users and survivors of psychiatry and the few professionals helping people to come off psychiatric drugs. So it is a good place to begin the discussion. The book should be available in each medical practice, in each therapeutic ward, in each patients' library. *Pirkko Lahti, President of the World Federation for Mental Health, 2001-2003*

This book is a must read for anyone who might consider taking or no longer taking these mind altering legal drugs and perhaps even more so for those able to prescribe them. *Loren R. Mosher* †

Available in every good bookshop. In U.K. through Mind's publications service, publications@mind.org.uk, Tel. 0844 448 4448. In New Zealand from Patients Rights Advocacy, 65 Tawa St, Hamilton, http://prawi.sartorelli.gen.nz. In Canada & USA from MindFreedom Book Sales, 454 Willamette, Suite 216, Eugene, OR 97401, Tel. (541) 345-9106, Fax (541) 345-3737, www.madmarket.org

And direct from Peter Lehmann Publishing, Zabel-Krueger-Damm 183, 13469 Berlin, Germany, info@peter-lehmann-publishing.com, Tel. +1 30 85963706, Fax +1 30 40398752. To order, please see www.peter-lehmann-publishing.com/ withdraw.htm. And the convenience of payment via our bank-accounts in Austria, Belgium, Germany, Italy, Netherlands, Spain, Switzerland, USA and United Kingdom, or pay securely with any major credit card via www.paypal.com